GACE Program Admission Assessment

Test I Reading - 210
Test II Math - 211
Test III Writing - 212
Combined - 710

How to pass the GACE by using a comprehensive test prep study guide, proven strategies, relevant practice test questions, and relevant examples.

By: Kathleen Jasper, Ed.D.

Kathleen Jasper LLC
Estero, FL 33928
www.kathleenjasper.com | info@KathleenJasper.com

GACE Program Admission Assessment: How to pass the GACE by using a comprehensive test prep study guide, proven strategies, relevant practice test questions, and relevant examples.

Printed in the United States of America
ISBN: 9798409359355

Thank you for taking the time to purchase this book. I really appreciate it.

Would you mind leaving a review?

Did you purchase this book on Amazon? If so, I would be thrilled if you would leave an unbiased review at your convenience. Did you purchase this book from KathleenJasper.com? If so, you can leave a review on Facebook, Google, or directly on our website on the product page. Thank you for using my products.

Visit my Facebook Page.

I post videos, practice test questions, upcoming events, and other resources daily on my Facebook Page. Join us every Tuesday at 5 P.M. ET for our Facebook live math help session. https://www.facebook.com/KathleenJasperEdD.

Check out my other products.

I have built several comprehensive, self-paced online courses for many teacher certification exams. I also have other books, webinars and more. Go to https://kathleenjasper.com and use offer code **GACE20** for 20% off any of my products.

Join my private Facebook group.

Are you trying to become a teacher and are you looking for a community? Share insights, strategies and connect with other prospective teachers.

Go to: www.facebook.com/groups/certificationprep/ to request access.

Subscribe to my YouTube channel

Check out my enormous video library with tons of interesting and insightful content for teacher certification exams and more.

Subscribe here https://www.youtube.com/kathleenjasperedd.

If you have any questions, don't hesitate to reach out. It will be my pleasure to help.
Good luck on your exam.

–Kathleen Jasper, Ed.D.

This page intentionally left blank.

Table of Contents

III. Writing **342**

How to Use this Book

We work diligently to build the most comprehensive, most effective study guides. We ensure our books are aligned to the exam and that they cover everything you need to be successful on test day. We recommend a few practices when using this book. Following these suggestions will help you pass your exam.

Suggested Study Plan

This book was developed using the information provided in the GACE Program Admission Assessment blueprint and test specifications.

We have also laid out how to study for each section of the exam. We have found using the methods outlined below is the very best way to prepare for the exam.

Prepare for Reading

1. **Take a diagnostic test.** Use practice test 1 in the reading section to measure your current abilities.

2. **Review your pretest and analyze your correct and incorrect answers.** It is not enough to simply grade your test. Use the answer explanations to analyze why you chose certain answers and what you can do to improve.

3. **Read through the reading section of the study guide.** Read through all the information in the reading section and review important information about all the skills needed for the reading test.

4. **Take a posttest.** Use practice test 2 as a posttest. If you score 75% or higher, you are ready to take the exam. Remember to analyze your answers by using the answer explanations. If you do not score at least a 75%, review the content and information in the book again.

Prepare for Math

1. **Take a diagnostic math test.** Use practice test 1 as a diagnostic test. Measure your current math skills. Analyze your answers by using the answer explanations.

2. **Work through each section of the math skills section.** Read through every section and work through the skills.

3. **Complete the practice questions at the end of each section.** Measure your skills.

4. **Take a posttest.** Use practice test 2 as a posttest. See how much you have gone up. Analyze your answers by using the answer explanations.

5. **Review areas of need.** Decide what sections you need to refine and revisit those sections in the book.

6. **Take a final posttest.** Use practice test 3 as a final posttest. Analyze your answers by using the answer explanations. If you score a 75% or higher, you are ready to take your exam.

Prepare for Writing – Essay

1. **Read through the essay section.** Before trying any of the prompts, look over the writing strategy and sample essays.

2. **Review the rubric.** Be sure you read over the scoring rubric provided so you understand the expectations for the writing section.

3. **Practice using the prompts in the guide.** We've provided several practice prompts for the argumentative and source-based essays. Use them to practice. Remember, you can write to them more than once.

4. **Read your essays back to yourself.** When you practice your essays, use the rubric. Then analyze your writing and grade yourself based on the rubric. This is the most important thing you can do to prepare. If the essay doesn't make sense to you, it will not make sense to the graders. Keep practicing.

Prepare for Writing – Grammar

1. **Take a diagnostic grammar test.** Use practice test 1 in the grammar section to measure your current abilities.

2. **Review your pretest and analyze your correct and incorrect answers.** It is not enough to simply grade your test. Use the answer explanations to analyze why you chose certain answers and what you can do to improve.

3. **Read through the grammar part of the guide.** Read through all the information in the grammar section and review important information about all the skills needed for the reading test.

4. **Complete the practice problems at the end of each section.** After each section of the grammar portion of the book are practice problems. Use them to measure and reinforce your skills in each individual section.

5. **Take a posttest.** Use practice test 2 as a posttest. If you score 75% or higher, you are ready to take the exam. If you do not score at least a 75%, review the sections. Remember to analyze your answers by using the answer explanations.

We use callout boxes throughout the book to bring your attention to important information. Below are the icons we use to organize this information.

 QUICK TIPS: These tips are represented with a megaphone and include tips and vocabulary you need to know or strategies for answering questions for a particular skill or content category.

 TEST TIPS: Test tips are represented with a light bulb and are specific test taking strategies that can be, and should be, used while taking the exam.

 THINK ABOUT IT: These tips are not necessarily tested concepts, but they provide background information to help make sense of concepts and give necessary information to help answer questions on the exam.

 CAUTION: Caution tips explain what to avoid when selecting your answer choices on the exam. Test writers are very good at creating distracting answer choices that seem like good options. We teach you what to watch for when it comes to distractors, so you avoid these pitfalls.

Book organization

The sections of the book are arranged by subtest in this order: reading, writing, math. In addition, each content category is broken down by skill. The book mirrors the skills outlined in the GACE blueprint and test specifications. Within each of the skill sections are examples and explanations of what you need to know to be successful on the exam.

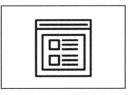

Extra practice

At the end of each content category, we include additional practice problems. These are problems on top of the full practice tests at the end of each subtest. Use these extra practice problems to determine if you have a firm grasp on each of the content category.

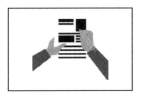

Practice tests

There are practice tests at the end of each subtest of the book. Questions and answer explanations are organized by content category, so you can see where you have strengths and where you have weaknesses. Remember to analyze your correct and incorrect answers using the answer explanations. There is a ton of information in the answer explanations, so be sure to read them even if you get the questions correct.

Quick Tip

Simply taking and scoring the practice tests is not enough. If you want to really get the most out of the practice tests, be sure to look over the answer explanations and analyze why you go something correct or incorrect. That is how you become a better test taker.

210 Reading

About the GACE Reading Test

You will have 85 minutes to complete 56 selected response (multiple-choice) questions based on a variety of readings and stimuli (charts, graphs, pictures).

The GACE reading subtest has four types of reading passages: short passages, long passages, double passages, and charts/graphs. These readings cover a variety of academic subjects and are simple enough that you won't need a great deal of prior knowledge of the subject matter to understand the readings. The questions are based directly on the readings.

There are two basic categories of questions on the GACE reading subtest exam:

1. **Content questions** require you to understand the explicit information presented in the readings. These are what many teachers call 'right there' questions—you can point to them directly in the text.

2. **Analysis questions** require you to analyze the readings for deeper understanding. In these questions, the answers are NOT explicitly stated in the passage and require the reader to use inference to answer the questions.

All questions in the GACE reading subtest are selected response questions. Some questions will require you to choose multiple answers by clicking multiple boxes or *all that apply*.

Quick Tip

Inference is when the reader comes to a logical conclusion based on the information in the passage. While inference questions are not explicitly stated in the text, the reader must use information in the text to answer inference questions correctly.

Test at a Glance	
Test Name	GACE Program Admission: Reading
Test Code	210
Time	85 minutes
Number of Questions	56 selected-response questions
Format	Selected response questions based on reading passages
Test Delivery	Computer delivered

Content Category	Approx. Number of Questions	Approx. Percentage of Exam
I. Key Ideas and Details	17-22	35%
II. Craft, Structure and Language Skills	14-19	30%
III. Integration of Knowledge and Ideas	17-22	35%

How to Study For the GACE Reading Exam

We are often asked, "How do I study fort the reading test?" The short answer is **read more every day**. We recommend 15-20 min of reading every day. You can do this using online sites like the Atlantic, New York Time, Washington Post, etc. Try not to scroll; read the entire article. This will strengthen your automaticity, speed, accuracy and vocabulary.

Here is what we recommend when studying using this book:

1. Take the first practice test as a pre-test. Document your score and determine in which categories you are low.

2. Study the reading section of the book.

3. Take practice test 2. Calculate your score and see if you are in rage of passing. If you score a 75% or more on practice test 2, you are ready to take your exam.

Types of Reading Passage

You will see several types of reading passages on the GACE reading subtest exam. Understanding how to navigate the different passages will help you succeed on the test. We have outlined the different passaged and some suggested strategies for tackling these passages.

Short passages

Short passages are single paragraphs and are followed by one to two selected response questions. These passages will be written on a variety of subjects—both informational and narrative. The questions will be focused on author's opinion, tone, purpose, vocabulary in context, etc. The questions may ask you to make inferences or to analyze a particular aspect of the text. We suggest reading the question(s) or question stem(s) first before reading the passage. This sets the purpose for reading. Do not read the answer choices because they contain incorrect answers, and you do not want to fill your brain with useless information. However, quickly looking over the questions first can help you be more efficient as you read. Then read the passage completely. It is important to read each passage completely because failing to do so will make it difficult to answer contextual and main idea questions.

Strategy for Short Passages

1. Set the purpose for reading. **Read the question(s) or question stem(s) first**. Do **NOT** read the answer choices. Just read the questions or question stems.

2. Read the passage in its entirety.

3. As you read, think about these things.

   • What is the tone of this passage?

   • Why would the author write this?

   • Is this an opinion piece or is it informational?

4. Answer the question(s) using the process of elimination (exclude wrong answers), and your understanding of the passage.

The following is an example of what a short passage will look like on the GACE reading subtest.

Heart of Darkness

by: Joseph Conrad

The sea-reach of the Thames stretched before us like the beginning of an interminable waterway. In the offing, the sea and the sky were welded together without a joint, and in the luminous space the tanned sails of the barges drifting up with the tide seemed to stand still in red clusters of canvas sharply peaked, with gleams of varnished sprits. A haze rested on the low shores that ran out to sea in vanishing flatness. The air was dark above Gravesend, and farther back still seemed condensed into a mournful gloom, brooding motionless over the biggest, and the greatest, town on earth.

The tone of the above passage can be described as:

    A. Optimistic as the author gazes at the greatest town on earth.

    B. Restless as the author is anticipating an upcoming voyage.

    C. Oblivious as the author is unaffected by the scenery.

    D. Ominous as the author is cautious about the surrounding area.

    E. Terminal as the author is sure he will die.

Explanation: If we read the question stem first, we understand that as we read, we should be paying attention to the tone or overall feeling of the passage. From the title—*Heart of Darkness*—and the descriptions in the text—*vanishing flatness, air is dark, a mournful gloom*—we can infer that this passage is probably not optimistic or relentless because those words do not fit here. Oblivious means unaware, but the author seems very aware of his surroundings. Terminal is too strong of a word here, and we cannot infer that the author is *sure he will die*. That is what we call strong language, and choices containing strong language are typically not the correct answers. Therefore, answer choice **D** is the best answer. Ominous can mean gloomy, and the word gloom is used in the last sentence.

Long passages

The long passages contain multiple paragraphs that are either fiction or non-fiction. These passages will be written on a variety of subjects from a variety of perspectives. These longer passages will be followed by 3-6 multiple-choice questions that relate directly to the piece. Apply the same strategy discussed earlier. Read the question(s) or question stem(s) first—do NOT read the answer choices. Then read the passage, keeping in mind the overall feeling of the passage, the purpose of the passage, and anything specific that stands out in the passage.

Strategy for Long Passages

1. Set the purpose for reading. **Read the questions first**. Do **NOT** read the answer choices. Just read the questions or question stems.

2. Read the passage in its entirety.

3. If you need to, take notes on your scratch paper as you read. We recommend taking a quick note after each paragraph that summarizes the paragraph. This is called active reading and can help you remember important information and help you stay focused on the passage.

4. As you read, think about these things.

    • What is the tone of this passage?

    • Why would the author write this?

    • Is this an opinion piece or is it informational?

5. Answer the questions using your notes, process of elimination (exclude wrong answers), and your understanding of the passage.

The following is an example of a long passage like the ones you will see on the GACE reading subtest.

The Art of Cross-Examination

By Francis L. Wellman

An amusing incident, leading to the exposure of a manifest fraud, occurred recently in another of the many damage suits brought against the Metropolitan Street Railway and growing out of a collision between two of the company's electric cars.

The plaintiff, a laboring man, had been thrown to the street pavement from the platform of the car by the force of the collision, and had dislocated his shoulder. He had testified in his own behalf that he had been permanently injured in so far as he had not been able to follow his usual employment for the reason that he could not raise his arm above a point parallel with his shoulder. Upon cross-examination the attorney for the railroad asked the witness a few sympathetic questions about his sufferings, and upon getting on a friendly basis with him asked him "to be good enough to show the jury the extreme limit to which he could raise his arm since the accident." The plaintiff slowly and with considerable difficulty raised his arm to the parallel of his shoulder. "Now, using the same arm, show the jury how high you could get it up before the accident," quietly continued the attorney; whereupon the witness extended his arm to its full height above his head, amid peals of laughter from the court and jury.

In a case of murder, to which the defense of insanity was set up, a medical witness called on behalf of the accused swore that in his opinion the accused, at the time he killed the deceased, was affected with a homicidal mania, and urged to the act by an *irresistible* impulse. The judge, not satisfied with this, first put the witness some questions on other subjects, and then asked, "Do you think the accused would have acted as he did if a policeman had been present?" to which the witness at once answered in the negative. Thereupon the judge remarked, "Your definition of an irresistible impulse must then be an impulse irresistible at all times except when a policeman is present."

Which of the following statements would the author of the passage agree? Choose all that apply.

❑ It is not easy to trick a plaintiff during a cross examination, especially when the judge becomes unfriendly with the plaintiff.

❑ To trick a witness in a cross examination, it helps to ask preliminary questions before asking the questions that will prove your case in court.

❑ A case of fraud and a case of murder are two different situations and require different approaches in cross examination.

❑ Cross examinations can be very amusing, especially when the plaintiffs or witnesses don't catch on to the tactics of the cross-examining attorney or judge.

❑ Fraud and insanity are hard to prove, and attorneys can easily discredit witnesses who rely on those defenses.

Explanation: The best answers are boxes **2 and 4**. In both instances, the author mentions the cross-examining attorney preparing the plaintiffs or witnesses with preliminary questions to trick them into saying what the attorney needs to win the case. In the first instance, preliminary questions were, "to be good enough to show the jury the extreme limit to which he could raise his arm since the accident." In the second case, preliminary questions were, "The judge, not satisfied with this, first put the witness some questions on other subjects, and then asked, 'Do you think the accused would have acted as he did if a policeman had been present?'" In both cases, the stories are humorous. Therefore, the 4th choice can also be correct. The 1st answer choice has elements of the passage but for only one part of the passage, the dislocated shoulder case. Answers 1, 3 and 5 are not applicable to the passage.

For what type of publication would the passage be best suited?

    A. A textbook for a criminal law course.

    B. The classified section of a local newspaper.

    C. A newspaper op-ed piece.

    D. A biography about a famous attorney.

    E. A non-fiction book about famous criminal trials.

Explanation: The best answer is choice **E**. The witness examination outlined in the piece is meant to show the reader the sometimes-humorous side of very tense criminal cases. You are much more likely to find anecdotes such as these in a non-fiction book than you would find in a textbook or academic piece of writing. Op-eds are opinion pieces; therefore, choice C is incorrect because the author is not discussing his opinion—he is simply telling stories. Choice B does not work because classified sections of newspapers are for advertisements and announcements. Choice D sounds good, but the author is discussing cases not an individual who tried the cases.

Double passages

During the GACE reading subtest, you will be presented with two passages covering the same topic in different ways. Remember, read the question(s) and question stem(s) first. That will set the purpose for reading.

Strategy for Double Passages

If you read all of passage 1 and all of passage 2 and then go through the questions in order, you will probably forget a lot of what you read in passage 1. In the double passages, we recommend breaking up the questions into only passage 1 questions, only passage 2 questions, and finally, passage 1 and 2 questions. Reading the questions for passage 1 first, then reading passage 1, and answering passage 1's questions will limit the number of times you have to go back and reread the passage. You are essentially breaking the passages up into two distinct passages with their own questions.

1. Set the purpose for reading for each passage. **Read only the questions for passage 1 first.** Do **NOT** read the answer choices. Just the questions or question stems.

2. Read passage 1.

3. Answer passage 1 questions.

4. **Read the questions for passage 2 next.** Do **NOT** read the answer choices. Just the questions or question stems.

5. Read passage 2.

6. Answer passage 2 questions.

7. Now answer the questions that have to do with both passages.

8. As you read, think about these things.

    • What is the tone of this passage?

    • Why would the author write this?

    • Is this an opinion piece or is it informational?

9. Answer the questions using your notes, process of elimination (exclude wrong answers), and your understanding of the passage.

Test Tip

You have scratch paper during the exam for a reason. Use it to jot down important information as you read. This may help you answer questions without having to go back and reread the passage.

The following is an example of a double passage like the ones you will see on the GACE reading subtest exam. Use the double passage strategy previously discussed.

Passage 1

The Tennessee Valley Authority (TVA) was tasked by President Franklin D. Roosevelt to build the Pickwick Dam, which would be a significant producer of hydroelectric power for the region. During the Great Depression, the towns of Waterloo and Riverton were sacrificed as a result of the construction of the dam. More than a loss of property, it was a sacrifice of community for the greater good. The people were happy to sacrifice their property in order to see their region prosper. This act resulted in a better region allowing for the creation of jobs, economic security, recreational facilities and a better quality of life for the residents of the Tennessee Valley. As in other lost towns throughout the region, these communities and the families living in them dedicated their properties, homes and histories to the creation of a vastly improved region and a stronger nation for their children and grandchildren.

Passage 2

When people talk about the great success of the Tennessee Valley Authority (TVA)—it helped ease some of the economic hardship not only in the state of Tennessee but also in parts of Kentucky, Alabama, Georgia, North Carolina, and Virginia— they often fail to consider those who lost everything to the government. These people are often billed as land and business owners who sacrificed their homes and livelihood for the future of the nation. The place where my grandparents raised my mother is now underwater, and the result of their sacrifice: they lost everything and nearly starved to death during the depression.

1. The main purpose of both passages 1 and 2 is to do which of the following?

   A. To determine the amount of work put in to building the Pickwick Dam.

   B. To celebrate the Tennessee Valley Authority.

   C. To show the reader the importance of sacrifice for one's community.

   D. To show that sacrifices were made to forward the progress of a region.

   E. Explain the massive success of the Pickwick Dam.

Explanation: The answer is **D**. Each of the passages show local landowners had to sacrifice their land and livelihood for the good of the region. Passage 2 has a negative view of the history of the TVA. Choices A and B are not discussed. Choice C is aligned with passage 1 only.

2. In passage 2, the term *billed* means which of the following?

   A. asked for payment

   B. offered a settlement

   C. are charged

   D. described as

   E. are beaked

Explanation: The correct choice is **D** because *billed*, in this instance, means to describe someone or something. Choices A, C and E are referring to different uses of the word billed that do not work in this context. Choice B doesn't work because a settlement is the opposite of what is being discussed.

READING

3. In passage 1, the author's position on the topic is which of the following?

    A. The landowners did not deserve to be treated the way they were.

    B. The landowners made a great fortune from their sacrifice.

    C. The Tennessee Valley Authority failed in their endeavors.

    D. The farms around the river were not very valuable.

    E. The landowners understood that their sacrifice was for the good of the region.

Explanation: The correct answer is **E**. In the passage the author states that, "The people were happy to sacrifice their property in order to see their region prosper." Choice A shows the opposite opinion. Answer choice B is incorrect because the landowners made a sacrifice without mention of financial restitution. Choice C is incorrect because the TVA is mentioned as being quite successful in the region. Finally, answer D is unknown.

Quick Tip

Notice how the question for passage 1 only is the 3rd question in the set. That is a tactic test makers use to make answering these questions difficult. If you read the passages in order and answer the questions in order, you will probably forget important information in the first passage and have to reread it to get #3 correct. That's why we recommend finding passage 1's questions, reading passage 1 and answering those questions first. It saves time and helps you beat the test makers at their own game.

4. Which of the following statement summarizes the overall tone and structure of both passages?

    A. Passage 1 generalizes favorably at the TVA, while passage 2 expresses a cynical personal experience of the TVA.

    B. Passage 1 draws from enjoyable personal experience of the TVA, while passage 2 expresses a generalized anger toward the project.

    C. Passage 1 extends is a cautious warning of the TVA, while the passage 2 expresses doubt of the TVA's success.

    D. Passage 1 is pessimistic about the TVA and other projects, while passage 2 is cautiously optimistic about the results of the TVA.

    E. Passage 1 praises the sacrifice of the government during the TVA, while passage 2 blames the government for people's suffering during the TVA.

Explanation: The answer is choice **A.** Passage one is favorable, so you can eliminate any answer choices that indicate passage 1 is negative; therefore, eliminate choices C and D. Only passage 2 draws on a personal experience; therefore, choice B is out. Choice E is close; however, passage 1 does not talk about the government's sacrifice, but rather the community members' sacrifices; therefore, E is out. This leaves you with choice A as the best answer.

READING

Graphs and Charts

On the GACE reading subtest, you will be required to evaluate data and information from a chart, graph, picture, infographic and more. These are referred to as *visual-information* questions. These visuals will contain a variety of information: business trends, changes in the weather, survey results, daily timetables, monthly calendars, etc. Each piece of visual information is followed by one or more questions.

Strategy for visual information (charts & graphs) questions

1. Look at the question stem(s) first. Knowing what you should be looking for in the graph will focus your approach.

2. Look over all the elements of the graph or chart—the title, legend, and information.

3. Pay attention to the *x*- and *y*-axes. There will be important information there, including the increments the data is presented. For example, the *x*-axis may display increments by months, quarters, or years. Information on the *y*-axis may be presented in thousands, millions, billions, etc. The x-axis and y-axis are labeled in the graph below: the x-axis displays quarters, and the y-axis displays numbers in the thousands.

4. Identify trends in the data and any patterns.

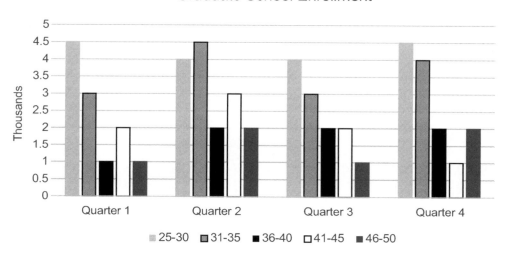

Graduate School Enrollment

1. The university above has a limited budget for marketing, and only has enough money to market for one quarter and towards one age group. If the university wanted to spend dollars on people most likely to enroll, where should marketing dollars be spent?

   A. School officials should use the marketing budget for the 25-30 age group.

   B. School officials should use the marketing budget for the 31-35 age group.

   C. School officials should use the marketing budget for the 36-40 age group.

   D. School officials should use the marketing budget for the 41-35 age group.

   E. School officials should use the marketing budget for the 46-50 age group.

Explanation: The correct answer is choice is A. Because the university wants to spend dollars on those who are most likely to enroll, first eliminate the age groups with the lowest enrollment. Just by looking at the chart, you can determine that age groups 36-40, 41-45 and 46-50 (answer choices C, D and E) are out. The remaining age groups are close; however, the group 25-30 beats out the age group 31-35.

2. According to the graph, the age group with the most consistent enrollment is:

   A. age 25-30

   B. age 31-35

   C. age 35-40

   D. age 41-45

   E. age 45-50

Explanation: Answer choice **A** is the best choice here. Look at the trends in the data and you will see that the age group 25-30 enrollment stays relatively the same over all 4 quarters compared to the other age groups.

This page intentionally left blank.

I – Key Idea and Details

A. Main Idea and Primary Purpose

Identify accurate summaries or paraphrases of the main idea or primary purpose of a reading selection.

B. Supporting ideas

Identify accurate summaries or paraphrases of the supporting ideas and specific details in a reading selection.

C. Inferences

Identify inferences and implications that can reasonably be drawn from the directly stated content of a reading selection.

A. Main Idea and Primary Purpose

Questions on the reading subtest will often ask about the central or main idea of a passage or specific paragraph. The main idea is more than just a topic or single, specific detail from the text. The main idea is not specific details in the text. Instead, the collection of details in the text lead you to and support the main idea.

Example Passage: Identify the Main Idea

The movie *Titanic* was a blockbuster hit and the highest-grossing movie of the 1990s. With its great success at the box office, no one would have guessed all the controversial behind-the-scenes filming and questionable spending that occurred during its making. So much work and detail went into making *Titanic* that it was the most expensive movie produced during its time, costing the studio $200 million. This amount was so high that its writer/producer/director, James Cameron, forfeited his salary to help with the costs. But it was all worth it, from the making of the ship to the long hours of filming during its sinking, the details, acting, and storyline won the hearts of movie-goers. Although many thought Cameron forfeiting his $8 million salary was risky, the $2 billion earned at the box office was well worth the risk.

The movie received high ratings and positive reviews from every aspect, including scholars, critics, and patrons. *Titanic* won awards from several organizations, including the Golden Globes, Grammy Awards, Academy Awards, and the People's Choice Awards. The movie dominated the *Academy Awards*, taking home a total of 11 awards, including the award for best picture. Awards spanned every aspect of film making from Best Motion Picture and Best Actress/Actor to Best Original Score and Best Original Visual Effects.

Identify the most accurate statement of the main idea of the passage.

    A. The movie *Titanic* was the most expensive movie of its time to film.

    B. Despite the overwhelming cost, *Titanic* was a hugely successful movie and worth the risk.

    C. The director of *Titanic* forfeited his salary to help with costs.

    D. The movie *Titanic* swept the awards scene, winning 11 Academy awards.

    E. The movie *Titanic* was a blockbuster hit and the highest-grossing movie of the 1990s.

I – Key Idea and Details | 21

SOLUTION

We can eliminate answer choices A, C, D, and E because they refer to specific details from the passage that support the main idea. The only answer that is about the main idea is answer choice B. All the supporting details in the passage (blockbuster hit, high-grossing movie, positive ratings and reviews, and award winning) connect to the idea that *Titanic* was a hugely successful movie.

Correct Answer: B

Caution

Avoid answer choices that are too specific when answering main idea questions. Test makers will try to trick you with main idea answer choices that happened in the text but are too specific to be the main idea. Remember, just because it occurred in the passage does not make it the main idea. The main idea is the central theme and must be an overarching, general statement or phrase.

B. Supporting Details

Supporting ideas and details are words or phrases that help answer questions about the text. Key ideas and details within the text can give clues about the meaning of words in a passage, help make sense of a passage, and convey information like *who, what, where, when*, and *why*. Think of the main idea as an umbrella with the supporting details from the text under that umbrella.

Questions on the reading subtest that relate to key ideas and supporting details may be asked a number of ways:

- According to the passage…
- According to the author…
- Based on the selection…

For all questions relating to this skill, you will find the answer in the text. Be careful; sometimes answer choices will NOT be worded exactly as they appear in the text. Sometimes you will need to look for an answer choice that is a re-wording of a detail.

Example Passage: Identifying Supporting Details

DNA, which stands for deoxyribonucleic acid, is a micro molecule that is vital for all living beings, and it determines how cells in our bodies develop, reproduce, and die. It is shaped like a twisted double helix and is made up of two strands. The replication of DNA is important because newly developed cells need instructions on how to function. In addition, the replication of DNA ensures the preservation of traits. To start the replication process, the DNA double helix separates, which is performed by an enzyme called helicase. Once apart, the two separated DNA strands then act as templates for the new DNA that will be created. Following this step, two other enzymes work to create new DNA bases.

All of the following ideas relate to DNA replication EXCEPT:

A. The double helix needs to separate before the replication process begins.

B. Only one enzyme is involved in the replication of DNA.

C. The helicase enzyme begins the separation of the double helix.

D. The two separated DNA strands act as templates for the new DNA strands.

E. DNA replication of is important because newly developed cells need instructions on how to function.

SOLUTION

Key details give information by asking questions like who, what, where, when, and why. This question is asking for the exception. This means that four of the five answer choices will be key ideas and details you can find in the text. Only one answer choice will not be supported by the text. The one that isn't in the text is the correct answer choice. By process of elimination, we can see that the correct answer is B because it is a false statement that is not supported by the text. Three different enzymes are involved in DNA replication, not one.

Caution

Choices that contain strong language, such as, **never, only, solely, always, unequivocally**, etc., are typically incorrect. Therefore, be careful when you encounter answers with those words in them.

Correct Answer: B

Specific Events

In literary and informational text, the individuals, events, and ideas all influence each other. By analyzing these relationships, readers can have a better understanding of the central idea. Often, there will be a turning point in the narrative which indicates the development of the character, event, or idea. You will need to be able to recognize a major event in the story from the key ideas and details in the passage.

Example Passage: Identify Specific Events

Helen Keller was an American author and an activist who lost her ability to see and hear at a young age due to an illness. She communicated with her mother using signs she made up and was able to recognize people by the vibrations of their footsteps. However, Helen was frustrated and unruly because she could not communicate with others. She was smart, but she did not have the skills to interact and communicate socially. At age six, Helen's family searched for an instructor who would work closely with Helen to provide her with a formal education. Anne Sullivan, who was also visually impaired, was hired as Helen's instructor and was by her side for the next five decades. Anne was instrumental in helping Helen learn how to communicate. Helen learned how to read braille and was able to read sign language with her hands. She was accepted to Radcliffe College, now Harvard University, at the age of 20. Her education was paid for by the famous Henry Rogers of Standard Oil, who was introduced to Helen by author Mark Twain. Helen was the first deaf-blind person to earn a bachelor's degree from Radcliffe College. She moved on to become a famous author, political activist, and lecturer. She was honored on many occasions for her lifetime of accomplishments. She was most known for her advocacy for people with disabilities.

Which of the following events was instrumental in shaping the success of Helen Keller?

A. Her loss of sight and sound at a young age

B. Working with Anne Sullivan to improve her communication

C. Meeting Henry Rogers of Standard Oil

D. Graduating from Radcliffe College at the age of 24

E. Being accepted to Harvard University at age 20.

SOLUTION

All of the answer choices are mentioned in the paragraph. The key here is to understand that the question is asking for an event that was *instrumental* in shaping her success. Without Helen's ability to communicate, the success she had would most likely not have happened. It was because of her ability to communicate that she went to college and ultimately achieved the success that she did. The only answer choice that supports this is answer choice B.

Correct Answer: B

Test Tip

Remember to read the questions first. Reading the questions first sets the purpose for reading and will make choosing the correct answer easier than if you read the passage first and then answer the questions.

C. Inferences

An **inference** is an idea based on evidence and reasoning. Inferences are not explicitly stated in the text. Instead, the reader has to draw a logical conclusion based on the information provided in the passage. On the reading subtest, inference questions tend to have a high cognitive complexity, meaning they require a deeper understanding of the text and the question. Questions that require you to make an inference, or draw a conclusion that is not explicitly stated, include phrases or question stems such as:

- What can be inferred about...?
- Why does the main character feel angry about...?
- Which statement tells us that the character thinks...?
- Which example from the text shows that the character was happy about...?

For each of the examples above, you have to draw a logical conclusion from the text based on a connection to words or phrases within the text. For example, if you have to show the character was happy, you may choose a statement from the text that is an example of how someone might behave when they are happy or a statement that includes a synonym for being happy. *Misha jumped for joy after finding a $50 bill on the ground* is an example of a statement that implies Misha was happy.

Example Passage: Making Inferences from a Text

Margot stood in the driveway with her arms crossed and her foot tapping the ground. Occasionally, she glanced down at her watch and then returned her stern gaze to the stop sign at the end of the street. She briefly paced the width of her driveway from the mailbox, to the shrubs, and back. Her gait was stiff, and she planted her boots into the ground with each unyielding step. Finally, Todd's black coupe came swiftly around the corner, barely breaking for the stop sign.

What can be inferred about Margot and Todd? Choose all that apply.

- A. Margot is excited to see Todd.
- B. Margot is sad because Todd is late.
- C. Margot is impatiently waiting for Todd.
- D. Margot doesn't know Todd is coming.
- E. Todd is late and Margot is frustrated.

SOLUTION

The passage does not explicitly state the overall relationship between Margot and Todd, but it does provide enough clues for the reader to draw a conclusion about what is happening. The passage describes Margot's body language as someone who is annoyed. Her arms are crossed, and her foot is tapping the ground. She is almost stomping her feet as she paces, and she has a stern look on her face. This is not describing an excited or sad person, so answer choices A and B can be eliminated. Margot is standing outside and looking down the street at the stop sign. The passage doesn't explicitly state what she is looking for, but the reader can assume she is looking for Todd. Therefore, we can eliminate answer choice D. Todd speeds through the stop sign, most likely because he knows he is late, and Margot is impatiently waiting for him. Thus, answer choice C and E are he best answer choices.

Correct Answer: C and E

Discriminate Among Inferences, Conclusions, and Assumptions Based on Textual Evidence

▶ **Inference**

An assumed fact based on evidence in a passage or piece of text. As stated previously, inferences are not explicitly stated in the text but are implied based on the author's choice of words.

Example:

Text: *Everyone who eats green leafy vegetables is healthy. Maria eats green leafy vegetables.*

Inference: It can be inferred that Maria is healthy because she eats green leafy vegetables. The inference is the logical fact based on the given fact that everyone, which includes Maria, who eats green leafy vegetables is healthy.

▶ **Conclusion**

An assumed next logical step based on the given information, but one that cannot be inferred from the given information.

Example:

Text: *Everyone who eats green leafy vegetables is healthy. Maria eats green leafy vegetables.*

Conclusion: It can be concluded that Maria is healthy because she eats green leafy vegetables.

▶ **Assumption**

An unstated fact assumed to be true, even though there is no evidence in the text to support it. Assumptions are made based on what the reader assumes to be a conclusion drawn from a statement in the text.

Example:

Text: *Everyone who eats green leafy vegetables is healthy. Maria is very healthy.*

Assumption: We can assume that because Maria is very healthy, she eats green leafy vegetables. This assumption is based on the fact that everyone who eats green leafy vegetables is healthy and the assumed conclusion that Maria is very healthy.

The reader must look for clues in the text to answer questions about inferences, conclusions, and assumptions. They are all very similar with subtle differences that define them. For inferences, think based on facts. For conclusions, think next step in a series of facts. For assumption, think filling in a missing fact given a conclusion.

Sam is coming from Ms. Smith's office with her head down. You notice she has tears in her eyes, and she is holding her research paper in her hand. It is widely known throughout the entire student body to avoid Ms. Smith's Advanced Composition 1 class because she rarely gives a passing grade on the research assignment.

From the above paragraph, it can be inferred that:

    A. Sam had an argument with Mrs. Smith.

    B. Sam received a bad grade on the research paper.

    C. Sam is feeling ill.

    D. Sam received an A on her research paper.

    E. Sam has avoided Ms. Smith.

SOLUTION

Recall that an inference is not explicitly stated in the text but is derived from facts and can be supported by evidence from the text. Therefore, the answer to this question will not be stated directly in the text, but information in the passage will lead you to a logical conclusion. It is evident that after leaving Ms. Smith's office Sam was upset. It is also evident that she has a research paper from Ms. Smith's class in her hand. We can eliminate answer choices A and C because the text does not provide evidence that an argument occurred or that Sam was sick. We can also eliminate answer choice D because there is no evidence to support Sam receiving an A on her research paper (people are typically happy, not sad, when receiving an A as a grade). The last sentence of the paragraph provides evidence that Ms. Smith has a reputation for rarely giving passing grades on the research paper. So, we can reasonably infer based on Sam's body language and Ms. Smith's reputation that Sam received a poor grade on her paper.

Correct Answer: B

Example Passage: Making Assumptions

Mark looked around panicked when he noticed all the other students brought protractors to physics class. Mark thought there was a quiz coming up soon, but he had not read the syllabus to know the exact date. Beads of sweat started pouring down his forehead as he realized he couldn't pass the quiz without a protractor. Mark scrambled to find a protractor to use in hopes of passing the quiz. Mark's classmates sat calmly at their desks, with their protractors in hand.

Which of the following statements can be assumed about Mark's classmates?

    A. They read the syllabus.

    B. They didn't have an extra protractor for Mark.

    C. They always brought protractors to class.

    D. They are proud of themselves for being prepared.

    E. They studied harder than Mark.

SOLUTION

An assumption is an unstated premise, or a fact derived from what we assume to be the conclusion or outcome. In this case, the stated outcome is that Mark's classmates came prepared for class with protractors. We don't know for sure if the classmates read the syllabus, but we are given a set of facts. The classmates brought protractors to class; Mark did not. The classmates looked confident and prepared; Mark was not. Therefore, the reader can assume the classmates read the syllabus which provided them information to arrive to class on that day with a protractor.

Correct Answer: A

II – Craft, Structure, and Language Skills

A. Attitude and Tone

Identify accurate descriptions of the author's tone or attitude toward material discussed in a reading selection.

B. Organization and Structure

1. Identify key transition words and phrases in a reading selection and how they are used.

2. Identify accurate descriptions of how a reading selection is organized in terms of cause/effect, compare/contrast, problem/solution, etc.

3. Identify the role that an idea, reference, or piece of information plays in an author's discussion or argument.

C. Meanings of Words

Identify the meanings of words as they are used in the context of a reading selection.

D. Fact or Opinion

Determine whether information presented in a reading selection is presented as fact or opinion.

A. Attitude and Tone

On the reading subtest you will be required to analyze how specific word choices shape attitude and tone. The **tone** of a piece of literature is the way the author conveys feelings or attitude through writing. A tone can be happy, sad, angry, peaceful, funny, sincere, etc.

Authors use word choice to affect the tone, attitude, imagery, and voice of their writing so that they can communicate a feeling they want readers to experience when reading the passage. A single key word or phrase can make a difference in the way a person feels or imagines a scenario. In this way, the author's word choice shapes the meaning and the tone of the work. The examples that follow show how different synonyms for happy can communicate different feelings or bring to mind different images.

Alternate Word Choice for Happy	Possible Imagery or Attitude the Word Elicits
I am at peace with his choice.	I'm accepting a poor decision.
I am content with his choice.	I'm satisfied with his choice.
I am pleased with his choice.	I'm feeling a little smug about the choice I knew was a good one.
I am over the moon with his choice.	I'm running around the room happy about his decision!

When presented with a question on the reading subtest that asks about the tone of a passage, understand the question is asking about the author's attitude toward the subject, a person in the text, or the reader. For questions about tone, analyze how the word choices the author uses in the work characterizes what the author wants to convey.

Example Passage: Word Choices that Identify Tone

Kristy's brother, James, was a troublemaker. He was in and out of jail constantly. I used to see them argue all the time about him being away so much, but he couldn't help it. He had to look after Kristy, and the only way to do that and support the family was by taking "side jobs" that usually got him into trouble. I felt bad for them. Their parents passed at a young age, and they only had each other. James felt it was his responsibility to provide for the family. I would occasionally give them some money, but it was never enough.

The tone of the author can be best described as:

A. neutral

B. biased

C. angry

D. concerned

E. judgmental

SOLUTION

Remember, the tone of a passage is the overall feeling or attitude of the passage. In this case, the tone cannot be categorized as neutral because the author provides opinions about the situation. Therefore, we can eliminate answer choice A. There is also nothing to indicate that the author is angry, so we can eliminate answer choice C as well. Answer choice B and E are viable distractors because even though James is characterized as a "bad guy," the author excuses James' poor decisions because of James' circumstance. However, because biased means favoring one thing over another, it is not the best fit because the author isn't favoring James over someone or something else. Answer choice D is the most appropriate answer choice because several word choices and phrases can be characterized as concerned, including, he *couldn't help it, I would…give them some money.*

Correct Answer: D

Test Tip

When reading any passage try to determine the overall feeling conveyed. This will help you answer questions about tone.

B. Organization and Structure

On the reading subtest you will be required to analyze how the author uses organization and text structure(s) to convey meaning.

Text structure refers to how the information is organized in the text. Understanding structural elements of text can help you interpret the author's intent. If you can identify the clues that indicate the structure of the passage, you can make sense of the information presented. The following table provides descriptions and clue words for different types of text structures.

Text Structure	Description	Clue Words/Phrases
Cause/Effect	Authors use this structure when they want to establish a causal relationship between an event and the events that come after.	because of, as a result of, due to, for this reason, in order to, since, the cause, as a result, therefore, then/so, this led to, thus, so, consequently
Chronological/ Sequential	Events in this structure are organized in chronological order or reverse chronological order.	after, at, before, during, finally, first, second, third, last, next, then, until
Compare/ Contrast	Authors use this structure to communicate the similarities and differences between a set of events, concepts, ideas, or people.	more/less, in contrast to, in spite of, instead of, nevertheless, on the other hand, rather than, similarly, still, though, unlike, as, as opposed to, however, despite, likewise, either/or
Descriptive	Authors use descriptive language and imagery to paint a picture for the reader.	for example, for instance, looks like, sounds like, feels like, any descriptive adjectives
Problem/ Solution	Authors present an issue or set of issues and possible solutions, then examine the effects of the solutions presented.	one part of, consequently, if/then, remedy, solution, problem, issue
Question/ Answer	Authors pose a question at the beginning and answers the question in the course of the text.	answer, it could be that, one may conclude, perhaps, problem, question, solution, the best estimate, how, what, when, who, why

Not all text structure questions relate to a "formal" text structure given in the previous table. For example, a piece of text may give an anecdote at the beginning and then wrap up with a connection to the anecdote at the end. Be prepared to answer text structure questions that describe specifically how the paragraph or passage is structured or that can be described using one of the more formal terms given in the table.

Think about it!

An **anecdote** is a short, amusing or interesting story about a real incident or person. For example, while giving a presentation, a teacher conveys a funny story about students; the story supports the presentation and provides context. You may see the term anecdote in an answer choice on the reading subtest.

Example Passage: Identifying Text Structure

In 1965, we moved to Alabama. I was only 10 years old. My mom got a job as a nurse at some big hospital, so she left my dad and never looked back. During that time, we were happy; my mom was happy. But after a while, she started getting into trouble at work and things went downhill from there. We spent a few years in Alabama before moving to New York City. I remember it took us five days to drive up the east coast from Alabama to New York. Finally, we arrived in the city. I had never seen such an exciting place in my life. Shortly after arriving, we settled in a 500 square foot apartment where we spent the next seven years. I made so many friends and will never forget how much moving to New York City changed my life.

How is the above paragraph organized?

    A. Chronological order

    B. Order of importance

    C. Comparison and contrast

    D. Problem and solution

    E. Question and answer

SOLUTION

This paragraph is organized chronologically. The author reveals events according to time in which each event occurred. Key words here are *during that time, after a while, a few years, shortly after,* and *finally.* The author also provides dates, duration of time, and her age. The information is organized in the order in which it occurred in time. We can eliminate answer choice B, order of importance, because the author does not list events from most important to least important or vice versa. The author also does not compare and contrast anything, so we can eliminate answer choice C. Although it is mentioned that the mom gets into trouble and moves, this is only one detail of the piece and does not address the organization, so we can also eliminate answer choice D, problem and solution. Finally eliminate answer E because questions are neither being asked nor answered. Thus, answer choice A is the best answer because the author presents her story from the beginning, middle, and end.

Correct Answer: A

Determine Cause and Effect Relationships

A cause and effect relationship is often indicated by a change or event where one action is the result of the other. In other words, the effect happens because of the cause. It is important to understand cause and effect relationships in text. Being able to identify such relationships helps increase reading comprehension.

It is important to note that one cause is not limited to producing only one effect. A single cause can create several effects. Consider the following example:

Because Nick forgot to set his alarm clock, he missed the bus, was late for school, and missed a math quiz.

Three different effects occurred as a result of Nick forgetting to set the alarm clock. There is no set rule; the event (cause) determines the number of outcomes (effects).

The individuals and ideas in the passage help provide the textual evidence needed to determine the cause and effect relationship. In the previous example, the individual, Nick, was the catalyst for the event, which created a cause and effect relationship.

Signal words or keywords and phrases that writers use in text to inform the reader of the cause and effect relationship include the following:

- As a result of
- Because
- Because of this
- Consequently
- Due to
- If
- Reason
- Since
- So that
- Then
- This has led to
- Thus
- Unless
- When

The Moon has long been linked to the changes in people's moods and behaviors. Science has shown that people tend to be more social during a full moon due to exposure to moonlight, and when the Moon disappears, people are likely to be more reserved. It has been found that many people get much less sleep during a full moon than they do during any other phase of the lunar cycle. Researchers have suggested that as a result of the full moon, deep sleep reduces by about 30%. Another way the Moon subtly affects our behavior is through its gravitational pull and the effect on the Earth's magnetic field. Studies have linked the Moon's effect on the magnetic field to schizophrenia and suicide. Many erroneously believe that the Moon affects mood and behavior because of its colossal size; however, no current research supports that claim.

Which of the following is NOT identified as a reason the moon can affect mood and behavior?

A. Exposure to moonlight tends to affect people's level of sociability.

B. Deep sleep is reduced a the full moon, and therefore, the mood and behavior are affected.

C. The Moon's effect on the magnetic field has been linked to various health issues and personality disorders.

D. The Moon has a gravitational pull on the Earth.

E. The size of the Moon affects the neurotransmitters in the brain, causing people to change their behavior.

SOLUTION

The first hint that this is a cause-and-effect question is the question itself, which asks for the reason the moon affects mood and behavior. Additional hints are provided throughout the paragraph with the use of cause-and-effect signal words such as *when, as a result of,* and *because.* Be careful when choosing the answer because the question asks which answer choice is *NOT* a reason. Remember, it is easiest to eliminate the answer choices that are reasons the moon affects mood, and then pick the answer choice that does not affect mood. Answer choice E is the only option that is not supported by the information in the passage. The last sentence says that people erroneously believe the size of the moon affects mood, and research does not support that claim.

Correct Answer: E

C. Meanings of Words

It is important to understand how to interpret words in context to determine the author's intent. On the reading subtest, you will have to read passages that may contain words or phrases that are part of figurative language, connotative language, or technical language, which may need to be interpreted in the context of the text. Because writers use various styles of writing and language to create meaning for their work, it is important to understand various types of language and how to interpret the meaning of words when their literal meaning is not the intent. You also may come across a question that asks you to define a word that you have never heard before. Knowing how to interpret different language styles can help guide you to the correct answer without actually having prior knowledge of the word.

Figurative Language

Figurative language is language that uses figures of speech, and figures of speech include the use of words in a way other than their intended literal meaning. Figures of speech are either designed to make a comparison, like metaphors, similes, and personification, or they are used to give a more dramatic effect, like alliterations, onomatopoeias, and hyperboles. Understanding the difference between figurative language and figures of speech is not important for the reading subtest. What is important is being able to identify when figurative language or figures of speech are being used and what the intended meaning is in the context of the passage.

Because figurative language adds a certain flair or emphasis to a story, it is often found in descriptive writing and narrative writing. The table that follows includes figures of speech that are most commonly used in figurative language.

Device	Definition	Examples
Simile	Using like or as	She was as thin as a rail.
Metaphor	Used to make a comparison between two things that are not alike but may have a characteristic in common	He was a lion filled with rage.
Personification	Attributing human characteristics to something not human	The cat judged me from across the room.
Onomatopoeia	The formation of a word from a sound associated with it	sizzle, kerplunk, pow, bam
Hyperbole	Exaggerated statements or claims not meant to be taken literally	The cake must have weighed 500 pounds!

Denotative and Connotative Language

Denotative language is the dictionary definition of a word. In other words, it is the literal meaning of a word.

Connotative language refers to a meaning that is implied by a word and is often associated with the emotion surrounding the word.

Denotative Language

Example:

The rain drops were beating against the side of the house during the storm.

In this example, beating is being used in accordance with the dictionary definition: to strike (an object) repeatedly so as to make a noise.

Connotative Language

Example:

Her confidence took a beating after she read the harsh article about her leadership.

In this example, beating is being used with the emotional association of feeling overwhelmed or defeated.

Technical Language

While reading informational text, you will often come across technical language, which is different than general academic language. **Technical language** includes words that are related to a specific process. Technical texts provide an in-depth discussion of a particular subject and lack figurative language. Examples of technical texts might include user manuals or textbooks designed to provide specific details about a skill or topic.

Dr. Pipping graduated at the top of his class at the University of Texas. He majored in engineering and was the valedictorian of his class. At the time of his graduation, he had many job offers from multinational companies. Five years after graduating, Dr. Pipping is still in demand; his work experience makes him an invaluable asset to any company.

As used in the paragraph, *demand* most nearly means:

    A. An act of asking with authority

    B. Willingness and ability to purchase a service

    C. Something claimed as due or owed

    D. Someone who is overbearing

    E. A state of being sought after

SOLUTION

All of the answer choices are acceptable and literal definitions of the word, *demand*. You must go back into the paragraph and look at the context in which the word is used in order to choose the correct answer. In the paragraph, the word *demand* is used in the following way: Dr. Pipping is still in demand. Prior to this sentence, the paragraph states that many companies offered Dr. Pipping a job. Thus, in the context of this paragraph, *demand* means sought after. We can eliminate answer choices B, C and D because the text has nothing to do with purchasing, taking something that is owed, or being overbearing. We can also eliminate answer choice A because no one is stating anything in an authoritative tone. Answer choice E is the most appropriate choice given the context.

Correct Answer: E

D. Fact or Opinion

In some passages on the reading subtest, you will be required to determine whether something is a fact or an opinion. There is a simple way to do this. Ask yourself, could I or someone else argue with this statement. If the answer is yes, it is an opinion. Now, sometimes opinions are embedded in passages with lots of facts. For example, a passage may contain dates and statistics, but it may also contain claims or opinions made by the author, so be careful when determining fact from opinion.

John Smith was the oldest son of an oil refinery worker in a family of 14 children. Growing up on the outskirts of Chicago, college was economically unattainable for many people in his neighborhood. However, he received a scholarship to Harvard in 1922. He worked at a restaurant at nights to save the money he needed for books and other expenses. He's an inspirational figure because while all of the other students came from rich families, he struggled and worked. He did all this while graduating magna cum lade.

Which of the following statements is most clearly stated as opinion rather than fact?

    A. Growing up on the outskirts of Chicago, college was economically unattainable for many people in his neighborhood.

    B. However, he received a scholarship to Harvard in 1922.

    C. He worked at a restaurant at nights to save the money he needed for books and other expenses.

    D. He did all this while graduating magna cum lade.

    E. He's an inspirational figure because while all of the other students came from rich families, he struggled and worked

SOLUTION

Finding something inspirational is subjective or an opinion. People find different thing inspirational. Answers A, B, C, and D are all statements that can be verified. The only statement that cannot be verified is answer E.

Correct Answer E

Contrast the Point of View of Two or More Authors

The **point of view** of a piece of literature is the perspective from which a story or passage is told. Often, in testing situations, when two or more passages are presented about a common topic, they are written from differing points of view. It is your task to determine from what point of view each passage is told and then analyze how these differing points of view affect the tone and meaning of each.

There are five basic points of view from which a story can be told. The table that follows outlines each of these points of view. It is not important that you know the formal definition or vocabulary associated with these points of view, but it is important to be able to identify if a passage is told in first person, second person, or various forms of the third person.

Point of View	Description
First Person	A narrator in the story recounts his or her own perspective, experience, or impressions. The pronouns I, we, me, us, are used in the text.
Second Person	The narrator tells the story to another character or the audience. The pronouns you and your are used in the text.
Third Person Objective	The narrator remains a detached observer, telling only the story's action and dialogue. The pronouns he, she, they, and them are used in the text.
Third Person Limited Omniscient	The narrator tells the story from the viewpoint of one character in the story. The pronouns he, she, they, and them are used in the text.
Third Person Omniscient	The narrator has unlimited knowledge and can describe every character's thoughts and interpret their behaviors. The pronouns he, she, they, and them are used in the text.

Quick Tip

In academic/informational/expository writing, a third person perspective is used to give an objective, unbiased point of view. For example, "Congress voted to give itself a raise in salary for the third consecutive year," is written in 3rd person.

Claims an author makes are the main idea or point the writer is trying to get across. **Evidence** is the supporting detail the author gives to reinforce that the claim is valid. **Reasoning** is the justification provided by the author for why the evidence or claims are valid. When reading multiple passages for questions on the reading subtest, make note of the point of view, the claims the author makes, and the evidence provided to support such claims.

Example Passage: Identifying points of view

Passage A

Over 18 months ago, Hurricane Mario made landfall in Emerald Beach City, Florida as a category 4 storm. The impacts were devastating; 18 people lost their lives, 2000 homes were completely destroyed, and 75 businesses have closed indefinitely. Officials estimate over $1 billion in damage to homes, businesses, and public infrastructure. Since then, government agencies have been excruciatingly slow to provide assistance. Piles of debris lined the streets for months with putrid waste from old appliances and failed sewer systems prompting public health and safety concerns. Over a year after the incident, many parts of the city remain on a boil water notice. Whole communities of homes are reduced to cement slabs with no sign of rebuilding in the near future. Several schools near the coast still have not reopened causing overcrowding in other parts of the district. Local, state, and federal officials are blaming a paperwork backlog that is delaying critical aid to survivors. There are clearly communication issues at all levels of government regarding the disaster response and recovery. Without a more coordinated effort from government agencies, parts of the community might not ever recover from Hurricane Mario.

Passage B

It was the longest night of my life when Hurricane Mario barreled down on our city. I saw the evacuation notices and warnings the days before the storm, but I knew we were safe. Our home was built after Hurricane Andrew, and we were three miles from the coast. There was no reason to evacuate. When the storm hit, it sounded like a freight train screaming through our home. The power was out, and the flood waters started to breech our front door. There was nowhere to go. The entire neighborhood was flooded, and the water was rising. In what seemed like a matter of minutes, I was forced to move my family upstairs. The water kept coming, and finally, we had to move to the roof through the attic. There I sat on the roof in the wind and rain with my wife and two kids, panicking because we were out of options. And then, I heard the faint rhythm of chopper blades in the distance. It was the U.S. Coast Guard; they were coming to rescue us. I don't know how they knew where we were. Cell phone service had not worked in hours. They saved our lives. And when we landed, a bus took us to a shelter where we were given hot food, warm blankets, and clean clothes. We had nothing. Everything in our home was destroyed. The staff at the shelter helped us contact our extended family, file paperwork with our insurance company, and register for disaster assistance. Every government employee we encountered was kind and knowledgeable. They helped my family and me get our lives back together after the scariest event we had ever experienced.

Which of the following describes the point of view of both passages?

A. Passage A is a personal recount of a positive experience with government agencies, and Passage B is a negative third-person review of government agencies.

B. Passage A is a neutral, third-party recount of the events of a disaster, and Passage B is personal experience praising government agencies.

C. Passage A is a negative third-person review of government disaster response, and Passage B is personal experience praising government disaster response.

D. Both Passage A and Passage B are objective recounts of the events of a disaster.

E. Both Passage A and Passage B are opinion pieces.

SOLUTION

Passage A is written in third person and provides a scathing review of the government's response to Hurricane Mario. It is not a personal experience, and it is not neutral, so you can eliminate answer choice A and answer choice B. Keep in mind, texts can be written in third person and still be negative or positive. The author of Passage A negatively describes the government with examples such as "excruciatingly slow," and there are "clearly communication issues." These word choices are not neutral. Passage B is written in first-person and recounts the author's positive experience with government agencies during Hurricane Mario. Answers D and E are incorrect because both passages are different. Answer choice C is the best option.

Test Tip

Sometimes you don't have to read both passages to answer questions about both passages. Notice in this example, by reading just the first few words of each answer choice you can eliminate A, B, D, and E.

Correct Answer: C

Analyze Point of View and Purpose

It is crucial to understand why an author has written a particular passage. The **purpose** is the reason for communicating with someone. Analyzing the author's purpose and point of view can provide insight into how to answer questions about the text. Several purposes for writing are outlined in the table below.

Purpose	Description
Describe	• employs imagery by "painting a picture" for the reader • explains ideas in great detail • often uses metaphors and symbols
Inform	• aims to inform the reader about a topic • is objective and free of bias • most commonly found in textbooks
Persuade	• aims to convince the reader to adopt the author's opinion • one side of an issue is supported and maintained throughout the essay • often uses emotional language
Entertain	• aims to amuse the reader • usually in the form of stories, novels, or poems
Explain	• aims to tell the reader how to do something • explains how something works

READING

The Pearl Harbor attack on December 7, 1941 was a day to remember. The naval base in Hawaii was attacked by the Japanese Navy in the early morning. Japanese aircraft carriers carried out attacks on U.S. ships and planes. Over 2,000 American men and women were killed as a result of this attack, and the U.S. subsequently entered World War II.

The author's primary purpose is to:

A. Articulate his annoyance with what happened during the attack.

B. Inform the reader about the events that took place during the attack.

C. Persuade the reader to take action in support of what happened.

D. Describe the events so the reader can visualize what happened.

E. Reinforce the importance of supporting U.S. troops.

SOLUTION

Carefully analyze questions about the author's purpose. You need to make an inference regarding why the author chooses a certain word, phrase, sentence, paragraph, or determine the structure of the whole passage. This paragraph is strictly informational. The author is not trying to persuade the reader to take action nor is the author expressing annoyance with what happened, so answer choices A, C and E can be eliminated. The tone is objective. Choice D is incorrect because the author does not employ imagery to paint a picture for the reader; the paragraph lacks detail and does not include metaphors or symbols.

Correct Answer: B

READING

This page intentionally left blank.

III – Integration of Knowledge and Ideas

A. **Diverse Media and Formats**

Identify accurate interpretations of texts that include visual representations.

B. **Evaluation of Arguments**

1. Identify the relationships among ideas presented in a reading selection.

2. Determine whether evidence strengthens, weakens, or is relevant to the arguments in a reading selection.

3. Determine the assumptions on which an argument or conclusion is based.

4. Draw conclusions from material presented in a reading selection.

C. **Analysis and Comparison of Texts**

1. Recognize ideas or situations that are similar to what has been presented in a reading selection.

2. Apply ideas presented in a reading selection to other situations.

3. Recognize points of agreement and disagreement between two texts.

A. Diverse Media and Formats

On the reading subtest, you will be asked to evaluate and compare content presented in different formats. You may have to evaluate a photograph of an ancient relic and relate how the relic can provide information to the reader. You could also be asked to analyze a chart and use the information you gather, along with information in a given passage, to answer corresponding questions. Finally, you may have to identify important data displayed in an infographic.

Evaluating Sources

It is important to evaluate source information for relevancy, validity, and reliability, but this is especially important with internet sources. Credibility, which relates to the ability of the source to honestly provide information that is authoritative and objective, is important when you are choosing to share information you've found about a topic with your students. The lists that follow describe various sources of information and common primary and secondary sources.

▶ Primary vs Secondary Sources

A **primary source** is one that is a first-hand account of a topic. A **secondary source** is one step removed from a primary source and often references a primary source. It is not necessary to memorize these terms or different types of each source, but it is important to understand their differences when evaluating sources for their validity.

Source	Humanities	Sciences
Primary Sources	• Diaries, journals, and letters • Interviews with people who lived during a particular time (e.g., survivors of the Holocaust) • Songs, plays, novels, stories • Paintings, drawings, and sculptures • Autobiographies	• Published results of research studies, scientific experiments, and clinical trials • Proceedings of conferences and meetings
Secondary Sources	• Biographies • Literary criticism • Book, art, and theater reviews • Newspaper articles that interpret	• Publications about the significance of research or experiments • Analysis of a clinical trial • Review of the results of several experiments or trials

▶ Peer-Reviewed Journals/Articles

These academic sources of materials are found on a database and can be considered credible. These are effective when you need very specific research information on a topic but are not very helpful for general background information.

▶ Charts and Graphs

You will see charts and graphs on the reading subtest, and you will be required to derive meaning from these representations of information.

The following are the most common types of charts and graphs you will see on the exam.

Line Graph

A line graph is a type of chart used to show information that changes over time. You would use a line graph to show investments trending up or down, students' scores over time, and even population growth.

Data		Graph

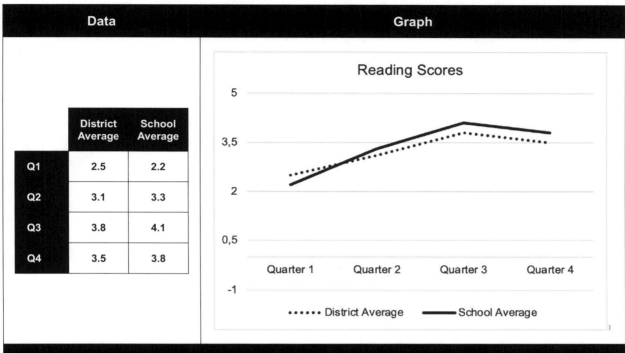

	District Average	School Average
Q1	2.5	2.2
Q2	3.1	3.3
Q3	3.8	4.1
Q4	3.5	3.8

Sample Question

Which of the following statements is true based on the data? Choose all that apply.

   A.   In quarter 3 the district and school average reading scores were the same.

   B.   In quarter 1 the district had higher average reading scores than the school.

   C.   The school surpassed the district in reading score averages in quarter 2.

   D.   The school was able to maintain a lead over district averages from quarter 2 on.

   E.   Quarter 4 was the lowest for reading scores of all the other times of the school year.

Correct Answers: B, C, and D

The dotted line is the district, and you can see that in quarter 3 the school had higher averages than the district, making answer A incorrect.

Quarter 1 was the only time the district had higher reading scores than the school, making answer B and D correct.

In quarter 2, the school surpassed the district in average reading scores and stayed ahead of the district through quarter 4, making answers C and D correct.

The lowest time of the year for reading scores was quarter 1 not quarter 4 making answer E incorrect.

Bar Graphs

Bar graphs are used to represent categorical data. For example, a bar graph would be appropriate to use to represent how many discipline referrals students received each month. You could also break up the data between boys and girls or other categories.

Data	Graph

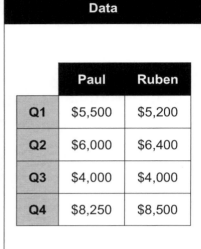

	Paul	Ruben
Q1	$5,500	$5,200
Q2	$6,000	$6,400
Q3	$4,000	$4,000
Q4	$8,250	$8,500

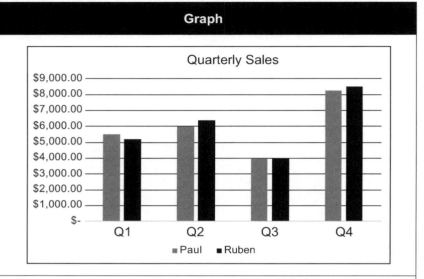

To graph, draw a bar to the height of each of the data points for Paul. Repeat for Ruben, keeping bars in the same category grouped together.

Sample question:

What is the range in Paul's quarterly sales?

  A. $500

  B. $2,750

  C. $3,750

  D. $4,250

  E. $4,550

Correct answer: D

To find the range, subtract the smallest value, $4,000, from the largest value, $8,250.

$8,250 - 4,000 = 4,250$

Be careful not to subtract Q1 from Q4.

Line Plots / Dot Plots

A line plot is a linear graph that shows data frequencies along a number line.

Data	Graph
Number of Hours Spent Studying 1, 3, 7, 2, 2, 1, 1, 1, 3, 10, 5, 2, 7, 1, 3, 4, 7, 5, 1, 4, 3, 3, 1, 1 *To graph, place an x or dot above the number each time it appears.*	 x x x x x x x x x x x x x x x x x x x x x x x x ← 0 1 2 3 4 5 6 7 8 9 10 →

Sample question:

The line plot shows the number of hours students spent studying over a two-week period for the exam. Find the median number of hours studied.

Correct answer: D

  A.   10

  B.   9

  C.   5

  D.   3

  E.   1

The values are already in order on the graph. Cross off numbers on both ends until the middle number is reached. Be careful not to count the blank spaces.

Pictographs

A pictograph uses picture symbols to convey the meaning of statistical information

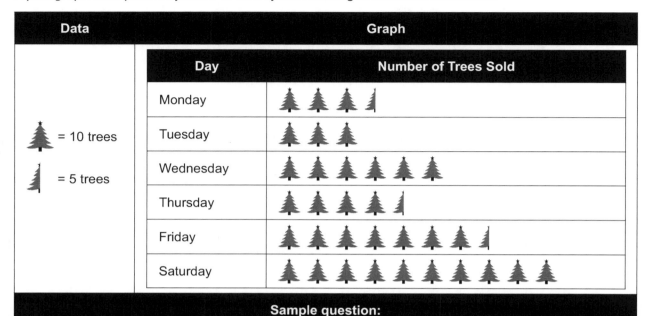

Day	Number of Trees Sold
Monday	🌲🌲🌲🌲
Tuesday	🌲🌲🌲
Wednesday	🌲🌲🌲🌲🌲🌲
Thursday	🌲🌲🌲🌲🌲
Friday	🌲🌲🌲🌲🌲🌲🌲
Saturday	🌲🌲🌲🌲🌲🌲🌲🌲🌲

🌲 = 10 trees

🌲 = 5 trees

Sample question:

How many more people bought a tree on Friday than on Tuesday?

   A. 5.5

   B. 8.5

   C. 45

   D. 55

   E. 60

Correct answer: C

If each whole tree represents 10 trees sold and each half tree represents 5 trees sold, 75 trees were sold on Friday and 30 trees were sold on Tuesday. Thus, 45 more trees were sold on Friday than Tuesday.

Frequency Tables

Frequency tables can be useful for describing the number of occurrences of a particular type of datum within a dataset.

Example

SAT Math Score Range	Frequency
200-299	1
300-399	0
400-499	1
500-599	8
600-699	7
700-799	2

Histograms

Histograms provide visual representation of data distribution. Histograms can display a large amount of data and the frequency.

Data	Graph
Class test grades	

Class test grades

91, 88, 100, 82, 73, 88, 52, 76, 95, 55, 85, 65, 99

87, 90, 65, 93, 75, 92, 66, 78, 80, 68, 84, 85, 91, 98

Grade Range	Frequency
51-60	2
61-70	4
71-80	5
81-90	8
91-100	7

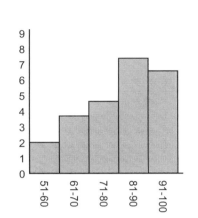

Determine equally created ranges. Determine the number of data points that fall within each range. Create a bar chart, making sure that bars touch, to show the frequency within each range.

Sample question:

Which of the following can be found using only a histogram?

Correct answer: E

   A. mean

   B. median

   C. mode

   D. range

   E. none of the above

A histogram does not display values, only a range of values, so a single value cannot be found from the display.

Circle Graphs / Pie Charts

A pie chart is best used when trying to work out the composition of something.

Data	Graph
200 female students at a college were surveyed about their favorite type of shoe. The results of the survey are listed in the table.	To make a circle graph, find the percent of that each shoe type is and draw an angle that size from the center of the circle.

Favorite Shoe Type	
sandals	32%
boots	8%
loafers	16%
sneakers	25%
slides	9%
heels	10%

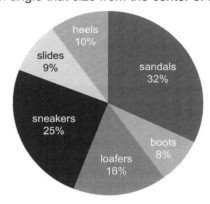

Sample question:

How many students responded that either heels or loafers were their favorite type of shoe?

Correct answer: E

   A. 10

   B. 16

   C. 26

   D. 35

   E. 52

Add the two categories together, $16 + 10 = 26$. Find 26% of 200 students, $200 \cdot 0.26 = 52$ students.

▶ **Infographics**

An infographic is a collection of images, charts, and text that gives an easy-to-understand overview of a topic.

As in the following example, infographics use striking, engaging visuals to communicate information quickly and clearly. Notice there is a lot of information in this infographic, but it is presented din a way to make the information digestible and

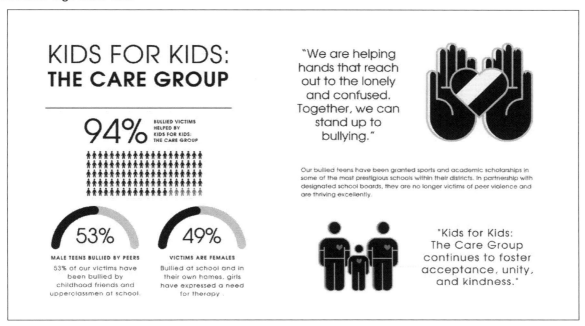

B. Evaluation of Arguments

Arguments or claims in a reading passage are opinions. Sometimes these claims are supported with evidence, which is crucial when presenting claims, but these are still opinions. One of the things you will be required to do on the GACE Reading test is to distinguish between fact and opinion and distinguish between and among different authors' claims or opinions. This usually comes in the form of a double passage where one author is claiming one thing and the other has contrasting claims. Another way this may be presented is in questions where you are asked, "Which of the following statements discredits the author's claims in the passage?"

Evaluate Specific Claims

An author's **claims**, or assertions, should always be supported by evidence in order for the claim to be convincing. The evidence that the author presents can be supported by facts or other examples. As the reader on the Reading subtest, you should be able to analyze the relevancy, sufficiency, and validity of an author's evidence and reasoning for both the question-and-answer choices.

For evidence to be **relevant**, ask yourself, *is the evidence important or connected to the claim?*

For evidence to be **sufficient**, ask yourself, *is there enough evidence to support the claim?*

For evidence to be **valid**, ask yourself, *is the evidence logical?*

When answering questions about the author's claim, remember that there should be evidence provided to sufficiently support the claim.

Many education leaders believe teacher training programs are invaluable. Teachers can earn certification credentials, improve general skills, and gain technical skills by attending various training programs. Recently, Bokea University implemented a new training program designed to help teachers apply assessment requirements in the classroom. However, this new program has shown to be ineffective. Because of the rigorous implementation requirements, teacher satisfaction is down, and the completion rate of the training is significantly reduced. Over 50% of the enrolled teachers have failed to fully implement the assessment pro- gram. The program needs to be reevaluated, and changes need to be made to provide more useful results.

The author's claim that the new program is ineffective is:

    A. Valid because the claim is made in an objective tone.

    B. Valid because specific details supporting the claim are presented.

    C. Invalid because most programs are 'invaluable.'

    D. Invalid because specific details are missing to support the claim.

    E. Valid because many teachers were interviewed about the program.

SOLUTION

Once the claim is made that the program is ineffective, the author goes on to provide specific evidence as to why it is not effective. Therefore, the claim is valid. In these types of questions, you need to find evidence that supports the claim. If there is no evidence, then the claim is not valid.

Correct Answer: B

Synthesize Information from a Range Of Texts

Synthesizing refers to being able to combine elements or ideas of multiple sources of information to develop a deeper understanding of content or to create a new perspective. On the reading subtest, you will be required to make connections among various excerpts on common topics in order to show that you can connect them to one another or to the main idea of the texts.

Synthesize information

Sentence, 1: Electric cars have many long-term benefits when compared to gas-powered cars, and one notable benefit is the lower cost in fuel.

Sentence 2: Lower fuel cost is one of many benefits of electric cars compared to the gas-powered cars.

What is the relationship between these two sentences?

    A. Sentence 1 contradicts the claim made in sentence 2.

    B. Sentence 1 describes a solution to the problem in sentence 2.

    C. Sentence 2 provides an explanation for the information in sentence 1.

    D. Sentence 2 restates the claim made in sentence 1.

    E. Sentences 1 and 2 discredit each other.

SOLUTION

Sentences 1 and 2 discuss the same topic, and they support each other; therefore, we can eliminate choice A and E, which states that the two sentences contradict each other. Eliminate B because the sentences do not discuss a problem related to electric cars or gas-powered cars. They simply provide information on the benefits of electric cars. Choice C is incorrect because sentence 2 does not explain anything; it simply restates what was already mentioned in sentence 1.

Correct Answer: D

C. Analysis and Comparison of Texts

When analyzing multiple texts, you will be asked to compare or contrast the mode, points of view, genre, and craft of multiple authors. For these types of questions on the reading subtest, there will be two passages to read in order to answer the questions. Recall from the previous section, we discussed the approach to writing from differing points of view (first, second, third person). Additional approaches to writing, e.g., the mode, author's craft, and genre, all help to shape the main idea and are important to understand when analyzing text.

Mode

Mode refers to the basic type of writing. The most common modes of writing are narrative, persuasive, and expository.

- **Narrative** – writing that tells a story.
- **Persuasive** – writing to convince the reader of a claim or argument.
- **Expository** – writing that describes or explains a concept.

Author's craft

Author's craft refers to the tools or techniques used by the author to engage the reader. Examples include:

- **Characterization** – author takes time to describe a character in detail and refers to details throughout the text, e.g., the behavior of the character.
- **Plot** – events that make up the main part of a passage
- **Setting** – the time and place a piece of literature takes place
- **Literary devices** – words or style of writing used to enhance a piece of literature

Genre

A genre is a category of artistic composition, as in music or literature, characterized by similarities in form, style, or subject matter. The main genres recognized in English language arts instruction include:

- fiction
- nonfiction
- poetry
- dramas

Sample Passage: Analyzing Multiple Texts

Passage A

In my family, we celebrate Hanukkah which is the Jewish holiday also known as the Festival of Lights. Hanukkah is celebrated for eight days to commemorate rededication of the Temple in Jerusalem. Each night during Hanukkah, we light a candle on the menorah, and we have a huge family dinner with an array of traditional Jewish foods and desserts. We eat a lot of potato pancakes and doughnuts that are fried in oil, but my favorite traditional food is the challah bread. We also play games and give gifts during Hanukkah. It's a wonderful celebration with family and friends.

Passage B

Many colleges and universities are offering more online courses than ever before. Students can register for online courses using the same system as in-person courses. Online courses offer flexibility for the student and the institution. Students can create a schedule of both in-person courses and online courses to meet their needs. Instructors have an array of tools to facilitate online courses including web conferencing, learning management systems, and discussion boards. Online courses are a great way to reach a broad audience of students.

The main purpose of both passages is to:

- A. Convince the reader of a claim.
- B. Tell a story about a topic.
- C. Argue for the reader to take a stance on the issue.
- D. Appeal to the senses of the reader.
- E. Explain a concept to the reader.

SOLUTION

At first glance, these two passages do not seem similar. Passage A is written in first person and describes traditional Hanukkah celebrations. Passage B is written in third person and discusses online courses. However, both passages are expository and provide details of a concept to the reader. Passage A describes the background of Hanukkah and lists the activities the author does to celebrate the holiday. Passage B describes the process and features of online courses. Even though the passages are written in different points of view and on completely different topics, they are similar in that they explain a concept to the reader.

Correct Answer: E

At Home Reading Practice Plan

The best way to improve your reading skills is to read as much as you can. You should set-aside 10-20 minutes each day to read. Find websites, books, and magazines that offer light academic reading. The GACE reading subtest offers passages on a variety of academic subjects; however, none of the passages require more than a superficial knowledge of the subject.

While you're reading, begin to identify main ideas, details, specific examples, and organization. You should also practice identifying vocabulary based on the context of the piece—if you don't understand a word, try and figure out the meaning based on the piece as whole and the words surrounding it before you look it up. It is important that you understand what the test will be asking you to do and incorporating that information into your practice. The best way to improve your timing and accuracy is to practice with the test structure in mind.

Quick Tip

While this book has many great passages to practice from, you may need more support. We recommend using released ACT or SAT reading passages to practice. The questions are similar to the ones you will see on the GACE. Released tests can be found on ACT and The College Board websites, and they are FREE. Just Google, "released ACT tests" or "released SAT tests," and you should have no problem finding them.

How to Study for the GACE Reading

1. Take the first practice test as a pre-test. Document your score and determine in which categories you are low.

2. Study the reading section of the book.

3. Take practice test 2. Calculate your score and see if you are in rage of passing. We recommend at least a 75% correct to pass.

If you are studying for the reading, the following is a study plan to help you focus your approach. Just like anything else, getting better at reading for a standardized test takes practice. Reading 20-45 min a day can improve your reading skills exponentially.

Weekly Practice Plan for Reading

Day	Total Time	Practice
Monday	20-30 min	1 ACT Passage (unlimited time) – Analyze your answers; your goals should be accuracy.
Tuesday	45 min	2 SAT Passages (unlimited time) – Identify the main idea questions and key details questions.
Wednesday	20-30 min	1 ACT Passage for time – 10 min. Shoot for >70% accuracy. Analyze your answers. Evaluate why certain answers are correct and incorrect.
Thursday	45 min	2 ACT Passages for time – 20 min. Shoot for >70% accuracy. Analyze your answers. Evaluate why certain answers are correct and incorrect.
Friday	20-30 min	1 SAT Passage for time – 10 min. Shoot for >80% accuracy. Analyze your answers. Evaluate why certain answers are correct and incorrect.
Saturday	20-30 min	Read anything you want: news article, reading passage, book, etc.
Sunday	0 min	Take the day off. Get back to it in 24 hours.

Reading
Practice Tests

Questions 1 – 2 refer to the following passage.

Adapted from *Heart of Darkness* by Joseph Conrad

It was in 1868, when nine years old or thereabouts, that while looking at a map of Africa of the time and putting my finger on the blank space then representing the unsolved mystery of that continent, I said to myself, with absolute assurance and an amazing audacity, which are no longer in my character now: "When I grow up I shall go there."

1. Which of the following statements would the narrator most likely agree?

   A. Regret is unproductive; one must look to the future.

   B. Young people are full of adventure and conviction, something desperately needed later in life.

   C. To live life fully, one must travel often.

   D. Exploring blank spaces is something people should do when they're young.

   E. Examining one's past and present character can be heartbreaking.

2. The narrator of this passage can be described as a(n):

   A. 17th century explorer looking back on his life with regret over not having gone to Africa.

   B. Young adult explaining his travel plans for when he grows up.

   C. Grown man looking back at his younger self with admiration.

   D. Old man explaining his biggest regret to his grandson.

   E. Child who is curious about the world.

Questions 3 – 4 refer to the following passage.

Hunter Thompson carved out his niche early. He was born in 1937, in Louisville, Kentucky, where his fiction and poetry earned him induction into the local Athenaeum Literary Association while he was still in high school. Thompson continued his literary pursuits in the United States Air Force, writing a weekly column for the base newspaper. After two years of service, Thompson endured a series of newspaper jobs—all of which ended in disaster—before he took to freelancing in Puerto Rico and South America for a variety of publications. The vocation quickly evolved into a compulsion.

3. The main purpose of this passage is to:

   A. Celebrate the accomplishments of a great American writer.

   B. Chronical a brief history of a great American writer.

   C. Explain what makes writers leave the U.S. for other countries.

   D. Show how military service can lead to exciting opportunities abroad.

   E. Describe a great American writer and his niche.

4. Which of the following can be assumed of Hunter Thompson?

   A. He enjoyed the adventure the United States Airforce brought him and used that in his weekly column.

   B. He spent years trying to figure out his purpose.

   C. While in high school, he developed a love for poetry.

   D. When he tired of his newspaper jobs, he left the U.S. and moved to Puerto Rico.

   E. While he was not fond of his newspaper jobs, he became obsessed with writing as a freelancer.

Questions 5 – 6 refer to the following chart of data.

Ms. Rodriquez is collecting data to see how her students scored on a state test. The test has multiple sections—math, English, reading, and essay. A score of 200 is the passing score for each section.

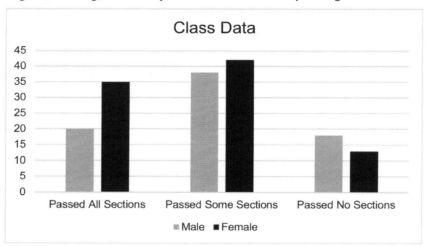

5. What can Ms. Rodriguez affirm based on the data above?

   A. Female students, as a whole, had a harder time passing some sections of the exams than male students.

   B. Fewer males than females passed no sections on the exam.

   C. There was a bigger gap between student performance for those who passed all sections than between those who passed some sections.

   D. Male students outperformed female students 1:3 in passing all sections of the exam.

   E. Female students outperformed male students 2:1 in passing all sections.

6. Which of the following statements below is supported by the data.

   A. Even though females passed all sections of the exam at higher rates than males, more males than females passed some sections of the exam.

   B. More males than females scored a 200 on some sections of the exam.

   C. More females than males scored below a 200 on all sections of the exam.

   D. While more females than males passed all sections and some sections of the exam, more females than males took the exam.

   E. While more females than males passed all sections and some sections of the exam, more males than females took the exam.

Questions 7 – 9 refer to the following passages.

As any good high school student should know, the beaks of Galápagos "finches" (in fact the islands' mockingbirds) helped Darwin to develop his ideas about evolution. But few people realize that the polar bear, too, informed his grand theory.

Letting his fancy run wild in *On the Origin of Species*, the man accustomed to thinking in eons hypothesized "a race of bears being rendered, by natural selection, more and more aquatic in their structure and habits, with larger and larger mouths, till a creature was produced as monstrous as a whale." Darwin based this speculation on a black bear the fur trader-explorer Samuel Hearne had observed swimming for hours, its mouth wide open, catching insects in the water. If the supply of insects were constant, Darwin thought, and no better-adapted competitors present, such a species could well take shape over time.

7. What is the main idea of the passage?

   A. Finches were not the only species to inform Darwin's theory of evolution.

   B. Galápagos finches were the best evidence of natural selection.

   C. Land animals can evolve to become aquatic in nature.

   D. When food supplies are sparse, natural predators will take over.

   E. Whales have large mouths because of evolution.

8. Why does the author use quotations and parenthesis in the first line (reproduced below) of the passage?

   As any good high school student should know, the beaks of Galápagos "finches" (in fact the islands' mockingbirds) helped Darwin to develop his ideas about evolution.

   A. To emphasize an important aspect of Darwin's research.

   B. To provide an anecdote about Galápagos finches.

   C. To provide an image of what the Galápagos looks like.

   D. To clarify a previously stated phrase.

   E. To support a claim made by Darwin.

9. The tone of the passage can best be described as:

   A. cautionary

   B. skeptical

   C. curious

   D. indignant

   E. endearing

Questions 10 – 11 refer to the following chart of data.

A local coffee company, Kind Koffee, sells regular coffee and fair-trade coffee for distribution within the US. Below is the data collected for the 3rd and 4th quarter of the year.

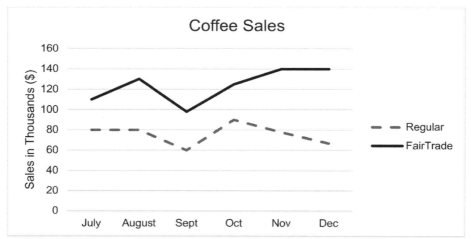

10. The biggest difference in the sales between fair-trade coffee and regular coffee happened in the month of:

    A. August

    B. September

    C. October

    D. November

    E. December

11. What can be inferred about the coffee business based on the data in the graph?

    A. Kind Koffee's best month for regular coffee was November.

    B. Kind Koffee's worst month for fair-trade coffee was July.

    C. Kind Koffee sold the least amount of regular coffee and fair-trade coffee in September.

    D. Kind Koffee sold the most fair-trade coffee and the least regular coffee in July.

    E. Kind Koffee's fair-trade coffee sales steadily declined in the months of July through September.

Question 12 refers to the following passage.

In the seventeenth century, Europeans began to drink coffee, hot chocolate, and tea for the very first time. For this brand-new clientele, the brews of foreign beans and leaves carried within them the wonder and danger of far-away lands. They were classified at first not as food, but as drugs—pleasant-tasting, with recommended dosages prescribed by pharmacists and physicians, and dangerous when self-administered. As they warmed to the use and abuse of hot beverages, Europeans frequently experienced moral and physical confusion brought on by frothy pungency, unpredictable effects, and even (rumor had it) fatality.

12. Based on the information in the passage, how would the early Europeans most likely react to today's energy drinks?

    A. They would prohibit the consumption of energy drinks.

    B. They would over-indulge in the use of energy drinks.

    C. They would test the effects of energy drinks extensively before drinking.

    D. They would accept the energy drinks as a miracle potion.

    E. They would regulate energy drinks at first until the drinks became mainstream.

Questions 13 – 16 refer to the following passage.

The harp was the favorite musical instrument, not only of the Irish, but of the Britons and other northern nations, during the middle ages, as is evident from their laws, and from every passage in their history in which there is the least allusion to music. By the laws of Wales, the possession of a harp was one of the three things that were necessary to constitute a gentleman, that is, a freeman; and no person could pretend to that title, unless he had one of those favorite instruments, and could play upon it.

In the same laws, to prevent peasants from pretending to be gentlemen, it was expressly forbidden to teach or to permit them to play upon the harp; none but the king, the king's musicians, and gentlemen, were allowed to have harps in their possession. A gentleman's harp was not liable to be seized for debt because the want of it would have degraded him from his rank and reduced him to a peasant.

The harp was in no less estimation and universal use among the Saxons and Danes; those who played upon this instrument were declared gentlemen by law; their persons were esteemed inviolable and secured from injuries by very severe penalties; they were readily admitted into the highest company and treated with distinguished marks of respect wherever they appeared.

13. Which of the following statements best summarizes the main idea of the passage?

    A. Peasants of the time period wanted to learn to play the harp but were forbidden as the instrument was reserved for the authentic gentlemen.

    B. The harp, or music produced by the harp, was always mentioned in historical passages from the Middle Ages proving its importance at the time.

    C. The harp could not be taken by law from the owner as it would degrade the owner of his station in life.

    D. During the Middle Ages, in many European countries, owning and knowing how to play a harp was a status symbol separating the upper-class gentlemen from the lower-class peasants.

    E. The reputation of the harp spread to other countries and continued to represent a distinction between classes.

14. During the Middle Ages, why were peasants prohibited from playing the harp?

    A. The king considered the peasants not capable of learning or appreciating the harp which represented the music of the upper-class.

    B. The lawmakers feared that peasants may learn to play the harp in order to gain status and pretend to be a gentleman.

    C. Only the king's men and the gentlemen were permitted the leisure time to enjoy the harp.

    D. The harp was reserved for upper-class functions only, making the talent of playing one useless for peasants.

    E. Peasants did not have time to play the harp because of their duties and obligations throughout the day.

15. The passage suggests members of nobility during the Middle Ages would agree with which of the following statements? Select all that apply.

    ❑ Peasants should be seen and not heard.

    ❑ Peasants are a nuisance to society.

    ❑ The harp is a symbol of socio-economic status and is reserved for upper-class members.

    ❑ The harp and music produced by the harp should be respected by all members of society.

    ❑ The harp is a complicated instrument that could not possibly be mastered by the peasants.

16. What does the term inviolable (reproduced below) mean?

*Their persons were esteemed **inviolable** and secured from injuries by very severe penalties.*

    A. reprehensible

    B. unbreakable

    C. disgraceful

    D. scrupulous

    E. intelligent

Questions 17 – 20 refer to the following passage.

Born in 1893 in the Georgian village of Baghdadi (later renamed Mayakovsky), Vladimir Mayakovsky was the son of a forestry officer. By the time of the 1905 revolution, Mayakovsky was already working with the local social democrats, and when his family moved to Moscow a couple of years later, he joined the Bolsheviks. He wrote propaganda for the party until his arrest in 1908, which resulted in an imprisonment of eleven months.

The imprisonment was crucial to his artistic and political development, as he spent the time reading the classics of world literature. Nevertheless, upon leaving prison, he became a key figure of the artistic avant-garde in Moscow, becoming a Futurist, an artistic movement resolutely opposed to all that was old and bucolic, and which praised the city, speed and modernity. As their manifesto said: "We alone are the face of our time. Time's trumpet blares in our art of words. The past is stifling... Throw Pushkin, Dostoevsky, Tolstoy, etc., overboard."

From this time until the revolutions of 1917, Mayakovsky was one of the most visible members of the Russian artistic scene. He wrote rough, declamatory poetry and cultivated the image of a hooligan. *A Cloud in Trousers* and *I* were among the most important works of the time.

17. The author of this passage would most likely agree that:

    A. Mayakovsky was a radical artist creating works that were innovative and impressionable in his time.

    B. Mayakovsky, while talented as an artist, did not let politics infiltrate his work.

    C. Pushkin, Dostoevsky, and Tolstoy are too bucolic and should not be considered great authors.

    D. The imprisonment of Mayakovsky stifled his writing ability and interest in politics.

    E. Being the son of a forester impacted Mayakovsky art and political positions.

18. The word *bucolic* (reproduced in the excerpt below) most likely means:

    Nevertheless, upon leaving prison he became a key figure of the artistic avant-garde in Moscow, becoming a Futurist, an artistic movement resolutely opposed to all that was old and bucolic, and which praised the city, speed and modernity.

    A. modern

    B. artistic

    C. rural

    D. innovative

    E. dreary

19. It can be inferred the author wrote this article to:

    A. Exploit the works of a little-known poet to show how socialism ruined a country.

    B. Explain how the poetry skills of a socialist author helped to bring down a regime.

    C. Persuade people to focus on modern, urban poetry rather than old-fashioned prose.

    D. Outline the tumultuous life of a radical poet who helped shape a movement.

    E. Present a cautionary tale of what can happen when one decides to go against the status quo.

20. Based on what is presented in the article, the poem *A Cloud in Trousers* mentioned in the passage most probably depicts:

    A. subjects of love, revolution, religion and art.

    B. a life in prison and lessons learned.

    C. a focus on the old-world order.

    D. images of the Russian countryside.

    E. style that is indicative of the time before the revolution of 1905.

Questions 21 – 23 refer to the following passage.

The past 18 months shook up state education communities preparing students to earn a high school equivalency certificate. With some states dropping the old test for new ones, states choosing to have multiple options, and the implementation of College and Career Ready (CCR) standards, the landscape drastically changed in a short period of time.

Here is what educators and those looking to achieve this educational milestone should know about the past year and a half:

- Twenty states administered alternative tests after choosing to either drop the GED test within their state or offer multiple tests for students to choose from. The HiSET exam developed by Educational Testing Service and the TASC Test Assessing Secondary Completion by CTB/McGraw Hill allow those who have not completed high school the opportunity to earn their high school equivalencies. Introducing numerous branded tests broke conventional terms and understanding of how people actually go about earning a high school credential.

- People are learning you don't "get a GED." Employers, education administrations, and institutions of higher education incorrectly ask whether an applicant has his or her "GED." Having proof of a high school credential is essential for many careers and postsecondary education opportunities. However, the GED is a test, not something earned. HiSET, GED, and TASC scores are mobile, meaning they can be used for employment and college applications throughout the United States. Test takers now have a choice as to what test they choose to take based on various categories such as price or whether the test is available in paper and/or computer-delivered formats.

- The results are the same. All three tests measure high school equivalency skills, and each has implemented CCR standards. Whether one takes the HiSET, GED, or TASC test, the end result when passing these tests is the individual earning a state-issued credential. For example, in California, a student can take either test and earn the California High School Equivalency Certificate when passing each test's subject areas.

The trend toward alternative testing shows no signs of slowing as more states consider new test options and vendors in the near future. Options in how one earns a high school credential have changed, but the outcomes are the same—increasing one's ability to achieve a more secure future by reaching this education milestone.

21. According to the passage, what common misconception surrounds the GED?

A. Employers do not recognize it.

B. It is earned through a program.

C. It is being phased out.

D. There are many test options.

E. Most people do not pass this exam.

22. According to the passage, the HiSET, GED and TASC:

A. Require courses to demonstrate test-readiness.

B. Are tailored to specific state standards.

C. Follow the guidelines of the CCR standards.

D. Measure completely different outcomes.

E. Are administered in 20 states.

23. What assertion does the author make in the concluding paragraph?

    A. Options for alternative vendors for these exams is important to state officials.

    B. Assessment companies can expect to earn record-breaking profits as more people choose to test.

    C. Credentials for earning a high school diploma will remain relatively unchanged in the near future.

    D. It has become increasingly difficult for students to demonstrate mastery of the new CCR standards.

    E. Options for a successful future hinge upon earning a high school diploma or its equivalent.

Questions 24 – 26 refer to the following passage

Exquisitely green mountains overlook a charming New England landscape as families gaze upon their graduates sitting along mahogany benches. One cannot help but think this scene is from an IVY League graduation day.

"We're the HiSET jail; we get inmates an education," said correctional educator Kenn Stransky.

For Stransky, to have a real impact, it's about creating an education-focused culture.

"A student is a student," says Stransky. One of the prison's most successful programs is the alumni tutoring program, in which inmates who've earned their high school equivalency certificate help current inmates who are preparing to take the tests.

"I'm here only once a week, so that's a limited opportunity, but their inmate peers are here all the time and can provide continuous support," Stransky said.

Support for education is everyone's job in this prison. Down to each correctional officer, everyone shares the responsibility to motivate inmates to enroll voluntarily and earn their high school equivalency.

"Confidence and a sense of achievement are feelings that make a difference on whether we'll see them again," says one of the correctional officers. In fact, research shows inmates who participated in education programs have a 43% lower chance of recidivating than those who did not, according to a recent RAND Corporation study funded by the U.S. Departments of Education and Justice.

The facility's honor graduate during this recent graduation is 45-year-old Mary Howard. Howard said that coming from a broken home, hanging around with the wrong crowd, and illegal substance use led her to drop out of school early. However, the support and encouragement she received from fellow inmates and the facility's staff kept her focused and driven.

"I have a completely different outlook on my future because there are more opportunities for me when I get out," Howard said.

24. As used in the passage, what does "recidivating" most closely mean?

    A. Rehabilitating

    B. Regressing

    C. Relapsing

    D. Reentering

    E. Recovering

25. According to the passage, what makes the Grafton County Department of Corrections high school equivalency program successful?

    A. The setting of the correctional facility.

    B. The support and encouragement of fellow inmates and staff.

    C. The implementation of a strict study schedule.

    D. The conventional educational environment.

    E. The promise of a shorter sentence if inmates complete the program.

26. Which technique does the author employ for the first paragraph and the sentence that follows in the passage?

    A. Engage in storytelling to entertain the reader.

    B. Use surprising statistics to shock the reader.

    C. Report background information to inform the reader.

    D. Use metaphor to distract the reader.

    E. Provide a detailed description to hook the reader.

Questions 27 – 32 refer to the following passage.

Academic performance for American students has not increased for several years, and China is consistently outperforming the U.S. in multiple subjects. According to the most recent Program for International Student Assessment (PISA), China outperformed the U.S. in reading, science, and math. Experts say the scores on the PISA can be directly linked to a country's economic performance, so U.S. officials are concerned. However, officials cannot pinpoint where U.S. students are specifically lacking, which makes fixing this problem difficult.

Experts say, one of the reasons it's difficult to tell why American students are falling behind is because, unlike China which has a centralized education system, U.S. schools are run by individual states with their own standards and accountability systems. This makes tracking methods and progress difficult.

Other experts say the population China serves in its education system is much different than the population the U.S. serves in its education system—many students in the U.S. come from low socioeconomic backgrounds. Still others say the U.S. emphasizes test scores over learning, which could account for the deficit.

The teacher shortage in the U.S. has resulted in fewer highly qualified instructors in American classrooms, which can also be attributed to the stagnant and declining scores. While some cite low wages for the shortage, recent studies suggest something else—a lack of interest in the profession. While China promotes the teaching profession like it does the medical profession and jobs in technology, the U.S. has a difficult time retaining effective teachers.

As China continues to take first place on the world's stage for education, U.S. lawmakers scramble to implement policy to fix the deficits in American public schools. However, this problem doesn't seem to be going away. Just this year, reading scores in the U.S. declined by an average of 2% nationwide.

27. What organizational structure does the author use in this passage?

    A. The author describes a problem and presents possible solutions.

    B. The author describes a phenomenon and its possible causes.

    C. The author lists events in a chronological pattern.

    D. The author presents an opinion and provides support for that opinion.

    E. The author compares and contrasts two different teaching styles.

READING

28. The term *centralized* in paragraph 2 means:

    A. middle

    B. incorporated

    C. collected

    D. national

    E. circumvented

29. Where would this piece of writing be most appropriately displayed if the author wanted to show the reader the most important parts of the study while also making it appear visually stimulating?

    A. Education blog

    B. Academic journal

    C. Parenting magazine

    D. High school newspaper

    E. Infographic

30. Which of the following is the main idea of the passage?

    A. The latest PISA scores show China has outperformed the U.S. in reading, science, and math.

    B. Researchers are looking into reasons why China is consistently outperforming the U.S. academically.

    C. China has a centralized education system, and the U.S. does not.

    D. The U.S. has many students from low socioeconomic backgrounds.

    E. A lack of interest may be causing American students to score low on the PISA.

31. Which of the following is NOT mentioned as a possible cause for the low academic scores in the U.S.?

    A. A decentralized education system

    B. Students from low socioeconomic backgrounds

    C. Officials cannot pinpoint the issue.

    D. The teacher shortage in the U.S.

    E. An emphasis on test scores and not learning

32. The passage states that having fewer highly qualified teachers in classrooms is a result of (choose all that apply):

    A. A teacher shortage

    B. Low wages

    C. An emphasis on test scores

    D. A centralized education system

    E. A lack of interested in the profession

Questions 33 – 35 refer to the following information.

Technology's Impact on Child Development

33. According to the infographic, what percentage of parents associated their children's strong comprehension of literacy with tablet use?

   A. 14%

   B. 15%

   C. 28%

   D. 72%

   E. 86%

34. According to the information, experts say screen time should not replace:

   A. child development

   B. human interaction

   C. consciousness

   D. literacy

   E. educational content

35. Why would an organization distribute and infographic like this to the public?

   A. To show the difference between fact and opinion.

   B. To reduce the amount of screen time kids are using.

   C. To show parents that screen time can lead to high literacy rates.

   D. To increase exposure to facts about screen time and child development.

   E. To display data in a format that most people can read.

Questions 36 – 45 refer to the following passages.

Passage A

When Pablo Escobar, a narcoterrorist, Columbian drug lord was shot in 1993, the Columbian government seized his property and took control of his luxury estate. Included in the estate was a luxury zoo filled with exotic animals. Most of the animals were taken to other zoos or shipped to other places. There was no practical way to remove the hippos; the four hippos were left in the Columbian town 4 hours east of Medellin. Now there are more than 80 of these semi-aquatic, vegetarian giants.

The Columbian government has been trying to curb the increasing population of the hippos for 25 years. The tropical climate of Columbia agrees with the hippos, though, and they have been able to thrive and reproduce at an exponential rate. Another challenge is that the hippos are not in one pack; they have fanned out, formed other families, and reproduced rather rapidly.

The hippos present quite a problem for the government. David Echeverri, a researcher with the Colombian government's environmental agency Cornare, which is overseeing management of the animals, says the hippos are an invasive species that could displace endemic animals like otters and manatees. Because hippos can be extremely aggressive, they also pose a danger to local residents, though there are no reports of serious injuries or deaths caused by the hippos.

In 2009, one of the hippos was shot, and a public outcry ensued; this squelched any plans to cull the hippos. However, the animals are foreigners having a dramatic impact on the landscape. Because they feed on land but excrete their waste in water, they funnel nutrients from terrestrial to aquatic environments. And when they alter water chemistry, they can make fish more vulnerable to predators. Just by moving their enormous bodies through muddy areas, they can create channels for water flow that alter the structure of wetlands. That is why hippos are considered "ecosystem engineers." This makes them key members of their native African communities, but it also means they could have strong effects on their new habitat.

For now, scientists continue to monitor and study the animals. The story of the hippos adds to the allure of the Pablo Escobar saga. In fact, the hippos draw many tourists each year.

Passage B

Hippopotamuses, once owned by drug lord Pablo Escobar before he was killed and his estate seized have mostly remained on the Escobar property. However, some hippos have found their way into the Magdalena River and have increased in population. These massive, sometimes aggressive animals are changing the ecosystem, which may not be a bad thing according to some scientists.

Jens-Christian Svenning, a biologist with Aarhus University in Denmark, argues that Escobar's hippos are one of several species introduced to South America that might contribute "ecosystem services" provided by large herbivores that are now gone. More research is needed, but so far, scientists think the hippos may be funneling nutrients from land to water, altering the structure of wetlands, and keeping grassy plants in check by eating them.

John Shurin, an ecologist with University of California San Diego who studies the animals, says the hippos may be providing a valuable service for native plants that once relied on large, now-extinct mammals to disperse their seeds. "We're planning to look at their poop and see what's in there," he says.

To Arian Wallach, an ecologist with the University of Technology, Sydney in Australia, whether they can perfectly fill a lost niche or not isn't really the point. She stresses that hippos are considered vulnerable to extinction and thinks having a refuge population outside of Africa to be a benefit. "The fact that there are wild hippopotamuses in South America is a wonderful story of survival, of agency, of pioneering," she says

36. In Passage A, all of the following are listed as reasons the hippos are a problem for the community except:

   A. The hippos are ecosystem engineers.

   B. The hippos can impact endemic species.

   C. The hippos have injured several locals.

   D. The hippos alter the water chemistry.

   E. The population of hippos was increasing rapidly.

37. The word *endemic* in Passage A means:

   A. Common

   B. Shared

   C. Parasitic

   D. Invasive

   E. Contained

38. According to Passage B, which statement would contradict the assertion by Jens-Christian Svenning that hippos contribute to ecosystems services?

   A. Grassy plants have invaded several parts of the river where the hippos live.

   B. Scientists have observed an increase in hippo waste in the river over the last 25 years.

   C. River soil contains important nutrients necessary for the survival of grassy plants.

   D. Funneling nutrients from land to the water causes dysregulation in pH levels.

   E. Hippos are considered vulnerable to extinction and need refuge outside of Africa.

39. Which of the following explains the main difference in Passage A and Passage B?

   A. The tone in Passage A is optimistic while the tone in Passage B is cautionary.

   B. The tone of Passage A is inquisitive while the tone in Passage B is humorous.

   C. Passage A relies on scientific evidence while Passage B offers anecdotes about the hippos.

   D. Passage A offers anecdotes about the hippos while Passage B focuses on scientific evidence.

   E. Passages A focuses on extinction while passage B focuses mostly on conservation.

40. Which of the following can be inferred about the term *ecosystems engineer* in Passage A and the term *ecosystem services* in Passage B?

   A. The term *ecosystems engineer* is used in a humorous manner in Passage A while the term *ecosystem services* is used in an monotonous manner in Passage B.

   B. The term *ecosystems engineer* is used in an optimistic manner in Passage A while the term *ecosystem services* is used in a cautionary manner in Passage B.

   C. The term *ecosystems engineer* is used in a humorous manner in Passage A while the term *ecosystem services* is used in a confident manner in Passage B.

   D. The term *ecosystems engineer* is used in a confident manner in Passage A while the term *ecosystem services* is used in a humorous manner in Passage B.

   E. The term *ecosystems engineer* is used in a cautionary manner in Passage A while the term *ecosystem services* is used in an optimistic manner in Passage B.

41. Which of the following is the main idea of Passage B?

   A. The hippos left behind by Pablo Escobar are funneling nutrients from land to water, altering the structure of wetlands, and keeping grassy plants in check by eating them.

   B. Hippos are considered vulnerable to extinction and having a refuge population outside of Africa is beneficial to Columbia.

   C. Hippos may be providing a valuable service for native plants that once relied on large, now extinct mammals to disperse their seeds.

   D. Several species introduced to South America that might contribute "ecosystem services" provided by large herbivores that are now gone.

   E. Scientists are optimistic about an increase in hippo population originating by hippos once owned by Pablo Escobar.

42. According to Passage A, what can be assumed about the local residents where the hippos have been living?

   A. The residents see the hippos as an invasive nuisance and want Columbian officials to remove the hippos.

   B. The residents see the hippos as residents themselves and want Columbian officials to leave the hippos alone.

   C. The residents are happy the hippos are reengineering the ecosystem in Columbia.

   D. The residents are concerned the hippos are reengineering the ecosystem in Columbia.

   E. The residents want to hunt the hippos during hunting season.

43. Which of the following is NOT true about hippos according to Passage A and Passage B?

   A. Hippos thrive in tropical environments.

   B. Hippos funnel nutrients from water to land, impacting terrestrial ecosystems.

   C. When hippos move through water, they create channels for water flow.

   D. Hippos feed on land and excrete their waste in water.

   E. The hippos are an invasive species that could displace endemic animals.

44. What type of publication would both Passage A and Passage B best suited?

   A. Academic Journal

   B. A science textbook

   C. Classroom blog

   D. Online science magazine

   E. Infographic

45. Which of the following describes the point of view used by the author of Passage A and the author of Passage B?

    A. The author in passage A uses first-person narrative; the author in passage B uses third person narrative.

    B. The author in passage A uses third-person narrative; the author in passage B uses first-person narrative.

    C. Both passages use third person narrative, and both passages are objective.

    D. Both passages use first-person narrative, and both passages are subjective.

    E. Both authors use second person narrative, and both passages are objective.

Questions 46 – 47 refer to the following passage.

Playwright Gertrude Stein (1874-1946) stands as a major avant-garde influence primarily for her experimentation with language. Stein moved to Paris is in 1903 and would eventually become closely associated with several modernist painters such as Picasso, Matisse, George Braque, and Cezanne, sharing with them an interest in abstraction. In particular, Picasso's Cubism and Cezanne's ideas about movement in painting influenced Stein, who subsequently developed a theory of landscape theater based on ideas she had loosely adapted from the visual arts.

46. Which of the following assumptions is most likely made by the author of the passage?

    A. Gertrude Stein understood the artistic styling of many of the modernist and abstract painters.

    B. Gertrude Stein was fortunate to live near some of the famous painters of the time.

    C. Gertrude Stein copied the artistic styling of many famous painters in her work.

    D. Gertrude Stein was criticized for her work that was influenced by the painters.

    E. Gertrude Stein bought several of Picasso's paintings to use for inspiration.

47. What does the term *loosely* (reproduced below) mean?

She had subsequently developed a theory of landscape theater based on ideas she had loosely adapted from the visual arts.

    A. ill-fitting, not tight

    B. falling apart

    C. unsuccessful, but accepted

    D. close, but not exactly

    E. barely noticeable

Questions 48 – 51 refer to the following passage

My father once warned me that I should never ask a man what he does for a living upon meeting him. Eventually, I came to understand that what he meant by that was that I should never ask a question that would give me reason to judge people without knowing them. To ask a stranger what he does for a living is tantamount to asking: *How much money do you have? How educated are you? How do you compare to me?*

I thought about this and my father as I crossed Third Avenue heading west on 27th street. My barber, Boris, opened the shop three years ago. The shop was no bigger than a small studio apartment with three barber chairs—the old school kind with big chrome peddles and chrome handle that the barbers would work back and forth to adjust each patron to the desired height. Several TV's graced the wall, usually showing a variety of international soccer games, the teams and pronunciation of the players' names mysterious to me having been raised on American football, being broadcast on some esoteric satellite network. In the corner he had a small college-boy refrigerator—the type that tempted me as a small child in high-end hotel rooms—that they kept stocked with European beer and a strange homemade whiskey that had been made by Boris' father back in Kazakhstan.

Boris' shop is an ethnic, religious, and socioeconomic, melting pot. The conversation is the conversation of men, as women did not often, I'd imagine not ever, frequent the shop. Which means the conversation typically revolved around, of course, *women*. Conversations left unfinished from the last haircut continued as if there were no two-week interruption. Men smoked cigars and made prop bets on whatever game was on at the time. They talked about guns, the pros and cons of Israeli vs. American pistols. No one discussed money, or socio-economic status, and if anyone in the shop had an abundance of either one, I didn't know about it.

48. What is the overall structure of the passage?

    A. A claim is made in the beginning that asking someone how much they make can be intrusive, and that claim is refuted by the end of the passage.

    B. An institution is described in the beginning of the passage, and examples of that institution are listed in the following paragraphs of the passage.

    C. An anecdote is mentioned in the beginning of the passages, and eventually a connection is made from what is said at the beginning to what is experienced in the barbershop.

    D. The passage is a chronological account of a young boy's experience with his father growing up going to the barbershop.

    E. The passage uses cause and effect to demonstrate the pitfalls of asking someone personal questions about money.

49. Based on the description of interaction within the barbershop, which of the following would most likely not be a topic of discussion on a typical day?

    A. The new shorter style of dresses worn by women in the neighborhood.

    B. The predicted outcome of an upcoming sports game.

    C. The best gun to use for protection.

    D. The unequal pay among ethnic groups in the community.

    E. The latest cigars on the market.

50. Which of the following, if true, would weaken the argument that the barbershop was free of discussion of tension-filled topics?

   A. Men of diverse ethnic groups favored the barbershop.

   B. Occasionally, a fistfight would erupt in the barbershop as one man insulted another's heritage.

   C. A sign on the wall stated that "all men are created equal."

   D. A famous Italian movie star patronized the barbershop.

   E. Music from all over the world was shared periodically on the shop's record player.

51. The author's attitude toward the interactions in the barbershop can be described as which of the following?

   A. disapproving

   B. confused

   C. concerned

   D. tormented

   E. intrigued

Questions 52 – 56 refer to the following passage

The story of Rudy is about an undersized legend with a fierce desire to play football for Notre Dame, which made him one of the school's most famous graduates in history. Rudy has the kind of tenacity you can't help but admire.

You may have seen the 1993 movie "Rudy" from Tristar Productions, but the Daniel "Rudy" Ruettiger's autobiography "Rudy: My Story" shows the story behind the man—Ruettiger's childhood and his motivations, failures, and successes.

He was the oldest son of an oil refinery worker in a strapped family of 14 children. It wasn't the kind of childhood that encouraged ambitious goals, but Rudy's dreams rose out of his modest home on the outskirts of Chicago.

Although Ruettiger is an inspirational hero who showed us how pure integrity and perseverance always triumph, his autobiography goes behind the scenes to reveal a regular guy. Ruettiger now uses the mistakes he made and the lessons he learned to motivate audiences across the country as an inspirational speaker.

But anyone who reads "Rudy" the book will learn more than that. They'll learn of a little boy's growing love for the Fighting Irish as he watched them at night on TV.

"Growing up in the Midwest, you start hearing about this place called Notre Dame before you can talk. You weren't even sure what college really meant, but the idea of it, the myth of it, the legend loomed large: It was like you automatically had this dream of Notre Dame planted in your head. And if you went to Notre Dame, you were somebody."

52. As used in paragraph 1, "tenacity" most nearly means:

   A. aggressiveness

   B. perseverance

   C. obstinacy

   D. vehemence

   E. indifference

53. Which of the following statements most accurately sums up the passage?

    A. It is possible to overcome obstacles in order to realize a challenging goal.

    B. Failures are just as important as successes in escaping a dire situation.

    C. Sports provide a pathway for lower middle-class students to attend college.

    D. Success in life is dependent on meeting societal expectations and ideals.

    E. People who live in the Midwest all want to go to Notre Dame.

54. It can be reasonably inferred that Rudy's motivation in penning an autobiography is to:

    A. Reignite public excitement about his phenomenal success at Notre Dame

    B. Reflect on his journey from the dire conditions of his childhood to infamy

    C. Clear up the misconceptions that the movie "Rudy" perpetuates

    D. Relate that it is not just his triumphs that define him, but also his failures

    E. Show others that they do not really know the true Rudy.

55. The tone of the passage suggests that the author:

    A. Admires the real Daniel "Rudy" Ruttger

    B. Prefers the movie over the autobiography

    C. Is disinterested in the story behind the real Rudy

    D. Has a stake in the success of the autobiography

    E. Feels the story of Rudy is missing fundamental elements

56. The purpose of this passage is most likely to:

    A. Promote the sale of "Rudy: My Story."

    B. Provide a synopsis of "Rudy: My Story."

    C. Compare the movie, "Rudy" to "Rudy: My Story."

    D. Introduce a new generation to the movie "Rudy."

    E. Help people understand how he was able to make the team at Notre Dame.

This page intentionally left blank.

GACE Reading Practice Test 1 Answer Explanations

Number	Answer	Category	Explanation
1	B	I	This question requires you to understand the implied main idea of the passage. In this case, the author is looking back at a time when he believed he could go anywhere in the world. He stated that he had "amazing audacity and assurance, which are no longer in my character now." This leads to the idea that he misses this in his present adulthood age.
2	C	I	This is an inference question that asks you to conclude information about the author from stated facts within the passage. In this case, the author states that, "when nine years old" at the beginning of the passage. Toward the end he states that this is "no longer my character now," which alerts the reader time has passed and the narrator has changed. He also uses the terms assurance and audacity favorably as he looks back at himself.
3	B	II	This question is asking you to determine the main purpose of the passage, which includes how the passage is structured. The passage details, in order (chronological), the milestones throughout Hunter Thompson's life, making B the best answer. Choice A is incorrect because the passage does not celebrate the author's accomplishments. Choice E is incorrect because the passage does not describe the author's characteristics or his niche. Choices C and D have nothing to do with the passage.
4	E	III	This question is asking you to assume information that is not specifically stated within the passage. We can gather clues about Thompson's feelings toward working at the newspapers. Phrases such as "ended in disaster" and "he endured" alert the reader that Thompson did not enjoy his early work. The last sentence, however, states that his freelancing work "quickly evolved into a compulsion," suggesting he could not resist this type of writing.
5	C	III	Answer choice C is the only answer that is supported by the data. Answer E is tempting because females did outperform males. However, for the females to outperform the males, the female bar would have to hit 40—40:20, or 4:2, or reduced to 2:1. However, according to the data, females did not outperform males by that much.
6	D	III	By using the numbers on the y axis, you can determine the number of boys and girls who took the exam. For females, approximately 35 passed all sections, 42 passed some sections, and 12 passed no sections—approximately 89 females took the exam. For males, approximately 20 passed all sections, 39 passed some sections, 16 passed no sections—approximately 75 males took the exam. This makes answer choice D the correct answer. Choice E is the opposite of D, which is incorrect. Choices A-C are also incorrect based on the chart.

Number	Answer	Category	Explanation
7	A	I	Choice A restates the main idea. While finches are the most common animal associated with Darwin's theory, he also looked at other animals like polar bears. This is the main point of the entire passage. Choices B-E are supporting ideas of the passage and too specific to be the main idea or central theme.
8	B	II	Sometimes an author will use quotes to set something off from the rest of the passage because the phrase in quotes is interesting or anecdotal. In this case, the author wants you to know that these "finches" were more like mockingbirds than they were finches. Therefore, B is the best answer choice here. Choice A focuses on Darwin's research rather than the word finches. Choice C connects the quotes to the Galapagos Islands rather than the finches. Choices D and E do not happen in the text.
9	C	I	The curious tone of this passage is captured in the author's description of the polar bear observation which showcases Darwin's own curiosity in the animal.
10	E	III	The difference in sales between free-trade and regular coffee can easily be determined by looking for the largest gap between the two lines and calculating the differences between the two. In this case, August and December have the biggest gaps among all the other months. However, if you look closely, you will see December's gap is bigger than August's gap, leaving choice E as the best answer.
11	C	III	By viewing the yearly sales chart, we can see that both types of coffee were at lowest amount sold in September. The other choices are incorrect based on the data.
12	E	I	This question is asking you to predict what would most likely occur in another situation not mentioned in the passage. In this passage, we learn that early European enjoyed new foreign drinks, but they also had some reservations. Thus, if they were introduced to a modern-day energy drink, they would most likely consume it with some concerns in mind.
13	D	I	This question asks you to determine the main idea of the entire passage. Choice A, B, C, and E are mentioned in the passage but are specific details.
14	B	I	This question asks you to review a specific supporting idea. Choice B restates the supporting idea that the king did not want peasants pretending to be gentlemen by playing the harp. The other choices are not stated or implied in the passage.

Number	Answer	Category	Explanation
15	Box 1, 3 & 4	III	Members of nobility would most likely agree that peasants should not be heard in that they did not want them playing the harp, making box 1 correct. Also, throughout the entire passage, the harp is regarded as a status symbol and that the harp should be respected as a status symbol, making box 3 and 4 correct. The other two statements, choices 2 and 5, are most likely not true as we know that peasants, although not respected, were useful to society and the king for labor purposes. Likewise, peasants were not considered too unintelligent to play the harp, as the king clearly feared they could play it and pretend to be noblemen.
16	B	II	*Inviolable* means unchallengeable or unbreakable. The words that follow *inviolable* are *secured from injuries by very severe penalties*, which reinforces they were unbreakable, choice B. Reprehensible and disgraceful are negative words and do not fit here. Scrupulous means meticulous or thorough, which also does not fit here. Intelligent is a favorable word, but unbreakable is better here.
17	A	I	This question asks you to decide which statement the author would agree with based on the information in the passage. Choices B-E are specific facts that we cannot determine based on information given. However, choice A offers a general observation that is supported throughout the passage.
18	C	II	Bucolic means rural. The artistic movement discussed was opposed to anything old and bucolic (rural); whereas the movement praised anything from modern times and city life.
19	D	I	This question asks you to determine the author's purpose for writing this article. Although the author does not specifically state this, it can be inferred based on the tone of writing and information provided within the text—Mayakosovsky was imprisoned, and he was one of the most visible members of the movement. Also, the first word on each answer choice—exploit, explain, persuade, outline, present—offers additional clues for determining the correct answer. In this case the author is outlining or presenting, so choices A, B, and C are not the best answers. This is not a cautionary tale of going against the status quo, leaving E out. Therefore, choice D is the best answer here.
20	A	III	Because we have learned from the passage that Mayakosky was a *Futurist*, we can conclude that his works would embrace this model as well. Thus, choices B-E represent choices that include old-fashioned and/or past events.

Number	Answer	Category	Explanation
21	B	I	The answer is embedded in the second bullet in this passage. "However, the GED is a test—not something earned." This indicates that the misconception people have is that the GED is something they get or earn, making answer B the correct answer. Information in bullet 2 also eliminates choice A. Information in the last paragraph contradicts answer choice C. Also, while there are several test options, choice D does not answer the question. Avoid this trap. Finally, answer E was never addressed in the passage.
22	C	I	The answer is embedded in the third bullet. Answer choice A can be eliminated because no programs are *required* before taking these tests. Because the standards are College and Career Readiness standards, they are not specific to the states, making choice B incorrect. Answer choice D is contradicted by information in the text (see bullet 3). Finally, answer E is incorrect because it says that states phased out the GED, and since GED is in the question stem, it makes answer E incorrect.
23	E	I	Only choice E is supported by information in the passage. The last line says, "increasing one's ability to achieve a more secure future by reaching this education milestone." Information in the paragraph contradicts answer choice C. Answer choices A, B, and D are not supported by anything in the last paragraph or the passage in general.
24	C	II	Recidivating means *relapsing*, making this the best choice. *Rehabilitating* is the goal; therefore, it would not be desirable to reduce it, making answer choices A and E incorrect. The same can be applied to answer choice B, *remorsefulness*. *Reentering* is close, but if you swap it for *recidivating* in the passage, it doesn't make sense. *Relapsing* is the best answer.
25	B	I	Answer choice B is reiterated throughout the text, making it the best choice. While the picturesque setting is nice, it has no bearing on the success of the program, eliminating choice A. A strict study schedule is not mentioned, making choice C incorrect. Eliminate choice D because this program is unconventional, not conventional. Finally, answer choice E is never mentioned in the passage.
26	E	II	The imagery used in paragraph 1 provides a detailed description of the picturesque grounds of what may seem like a college. Then the author flips this assumption with the following sentence and the reader learns this is a prison, not a traditional university.
27	B	II	This article presents a phenomenon—China is outperforming the U.S. academically. It also discusses the causes—a decentralized education system and students from low socioeconomic backgrounds. You can eliminate the other answer choices because the passage is not chronological, does not offer solutions to this problem, does not offer an opinion or claim, and does not compare or contrast other two education styles.

Number	Answer	Category	Explanation
28	D	II	The word *centralized* in the context of the passage means that the education system in China is a national system. China's national government has one system while the U.S. has many.
29	E	III	This piece is academic and has a lot of information. If the author wanted to shorten this and make it visually appealing while also conveying important information, an infographic would be the best format.
30	B	I	Be careful. Answer A is very tempting. However, the passage is about *why* China outperforms the U.S. China outperforming the U.S. in reading, math and science is only a detail. The only answer choice that is general enough to be the main idea is answer B. All the other choices are too specific to be the main idea.
31	C	I	Answer choice C is mentioned in the passage but is not listed as a cause. It is an additional issue in reporting and figuring out the issue. All the other answer choices are listed as possible reasons for the lack of performance on the PISA by American students. .
32	A, B, & E.	I	Answer choices C and D are the only 2 answer choices not directly connected to a lack of qualified people in the classroom. The teacher shortage is one reason why there are not enough qualified people in the classroom, and that shortage is linked to low wages and lack of interest in the profession. Therefore, answers A, B, and E are correct.
33	E	I	According to the graphic, 86% are satisfied with their children's screen time and link it to strong literacy.
34	B	II	Reference the middle of the graphic for this question. The importance of consciousness is mentioned. However, it specifically says, according to experts, screen time should not replace human interaction.
35	E	III	The reason to use an infographic is to take a lot of data and turn it into an easy-to-read representation. This helps to get more people to engage with the information. If this information is in a lengthy study, most people will not read it. However, when the data is represented in a way that is engaging and visual, people will tend to read it. In this case, the infographic is simply a medium to present data and information, not to take a position or push an agenda.
36	C	I	Answer choice C was never mentioned in the passage. It was mentioned that hippos are aggressive and government officials were concerned. However, no local community members have been injured.
37	A	I	According to the passage, hippos are the invasive species, and they may be pushing out species, such as manatees and otters, common to the area. The best answer in this context is *common*. Parasitic does not fit with manatees or otters. Finally, shared does not make sense in this context.

Number	Answer	Category	Explanation
38	D	III	Because the scientist Jens-Christian Svenning asserts that when hippos funnel nutrients from land to water it is a positive circumstance, answer choice D directly contradicts that. By saying the funneling of nutrients actually dysregulates (a negative circumstance) water pH, the scientist's claim is contradicted. All the other answer choices either are not related or support the scientist's assertions.
39	D	II	Answer D is correct because passage A uses anecdotes, or small stories about the hippos. Passage A starts off with the story of Pablo Escobar. In the middle, the passage describes how there was a public outcry after a hippo was shot. Finally, at the end, the author describes how tourists come every year to see the hippos. Passage B relies on scientific evidence to describe what is happening with the hippos. In fact, Passage B sites 3 different scientists. This is the opposite of Answer choice C; therefore, choice C can be eliminated. You can eliminate answer choice A because Passage A is not optimistic; in fact, it is the opposite—it talks about all the problems the hippos are causing. Passage B is not cautionary because it talks about all the good things happening to the environment because of the hippos. Finally, answer B is incorrect because Passage A is not inquisitive, and Passage B is not humorous. Answer E can be eliminated because it does not accurately describe either passage A or passage B.
40	E	III	Passage A outlines the downside of the hippos being ecosystem engineers while Passage B highlights the positive. Therefore, answer choice E is the best answer.
41	E	I	Answers A, B, C and D are all specific details that happened in the passage and can be eliminated because they are details and not the main idea. Answer choice E is general and outlines the main idea of the passage.
42	B	I	Because there was a public outcry when one of the hippos was shot, as indicated in paragraph 4, we can assume the locals like the hippos and consider the Columbian town their home.
43	B	II	Answer B is not true because hippos do not funnel nutrients from water to land. According to the fourth paragraph in passage A and the second paragraph in passage B, hippos transfer nutrients from land to water, the opposite of what is stated in answer choice B.
44	D	II	These two passages, while informational and reference some scientific examples, are not academic studies and would not be best suited for an academic journal. That eliminates answer A as an option. The articles are entertaining and intriguing and would be most appropriately published in an online science magazine. An Infographic is not the appropriate representation for this information.

Number	Answer	Category	Explanation
45	C	III	Both passages use third person, and both are objective. Neither of the passages uses first person narrative (I, me, or we), eliminating answer choices A, B, and D. Remember, objective means unbiased. Subjective means to express an opinion or argument. Neither passage is subjective; both are objective.
46	A	I	For assumption questions, you are asked to determine unstated ideas or facts that the author accepts as true. The author, in this case, assumes that Gertrude Stein was able to understand the meanings behind the famous paintings as she continued the ideas in her own work. Choice C may seem like a good answer, but the author states that she was influenced by the painters, not that she directly copied them.
47	D	II	The term loosely in this context means closely. Stein was able to closely mimic ideas she learned though visual arts.
48	C	II	This question asks you to look at the overall structure of the paragraphs. In this case, the author mentions the advice his dad gave him about not asking another person something that would give the author reason to judge another person—money, socioeconomic status, etc. That is an anecdote. Then at the end of the passage, the author observes how these men in the barbershop never brought up such topics.
49	D	II	For this question, you are asked to predict something about the characters or events that is *not* mentioned in the passage. Choices A, B, C, & E are all topics that were mentioned through examples. Choice D is the best choice because it is implied that the men in the barbershop avoid the subject of money amongst ethnic groups.
50	B	III	This question requires you to understand the main idea of the passage, and then determine which statement would weaken the main point. In this case, a fistfight in the barbershop would discredit the main idea that it was a place free of tension. The other choices would all strengthen the argument.
51	E	II	The author writes about interactions in a neutral tone, but it is obvious he is curious about the unusual occurrences for the time at the barbershop. Choices A-D lean toward a negative attitude, which is not evident based on the passage.
52	B	II	*Tenacity* means *persistence* and *determination*, and it is the best answer out of the four. *Aggressiveness* aligns with the word *hostile*. *Obstinacy* means *stubborn*. *Vehemence* is *a feeling of passion*. *Indifference* means not caring or having any feelings about something.

READING

Number	Answer	Category	Explanation
53	A	I	This is the only answer that is about the main idea. Answer choice B contains specific details only, making it incorrect. Answer choices C and D are not supported in the passage. Finally, E is a specific detail and is not the main idea.
54	D	I	The reader can infer this because of this line in the passage, "Ruettiger now uses the mistakes he made and the lessons he learned to motivate audiences across the country as an inspirational speaker."
55	A	II	The passage is about an autobiography, not the movie. Therefore, the reader can assume the author is interested in the real-life person. The other answer choices do not fit.
56	B	II	Overall, this is a quick summary or synopsis of the autobiography. There is no promotion of anything in the passage, just an explanation of the autobiography.

Questions 1 – 5 refer to the following passage.

In the early 1970s, coal workers' pneumoconiosis, or black lung disease, affected around one-third of long-term underground miners. After new dust regulations took effect, rates of black lung plunged. Today, however, black lung rates are rising dramatically.

Scientists first noticed a troubling trend in 2005, when national surveillance conducted by the National Institute for Occupational Safety and Health (NIOSH) identified regional clusters of rapidly progressing severe black lung cases, especially in Appalachia. These concerns were confirmed in follow-up studies using a mobile medical unit providing outreach to coal mining areas, with later research showing that West Virginia was hit particularly hard. Between 2000 and 2012, the prevalence of the most severe form of black lung rose to levels not seen since the 1970s, when modern dust laws were enacted.

Scarier still, the new generation of black lung patients have the disease, and in many cases, progresses far more rapidly than in previous generations. Today, advanced black lung can be acquired within as little as 7.5–10 years of beginning work, says Edward Petsonk, a pulmonologist at West Virginia University. But not all cases progress so quickly; thus, occupational health researchers fear that what they are seeing now is only the tip of the iceberg.

1. According to the passage, why do health researchers fear there are more black lung cases that have yet to be discovered?

   A. Miners are not seeking medical care.

   B. Black lung advances within 7.5-10 years.

   C. Some cases will progress more slowly.

   D. The average age for onset cases is decreasing.

   E. Between 2000 and 2012 cases of black lung rose

2. It can be reasonably assumed that laws enacted in the 1970s

   A. Helped scientists identify new cases of black lung.

   B. Increased the cases of the most severe form of black lung temporarily.

   C. Had no effect on the number of cases of the most severe form of black lung.

   D. Permanently eradicated the most severe form of black lung.

   E. Reduced the cases of the most severe form of black lung.

3. According to the passage, clusters of quick-progressing black lung cases:

   A. Were first noticed by the National Institute for Occupational Safety and Health (NIOSH) in West Virginia, with later studies pinpointing Appalachia as a hard-hit area.

   B. Went unnoticed for years by the National Institute for Occupational Safety and Health (NIOSH) in Appalachia and West Virginia.

   C. Were quickly brought under control through government-mandated programs offered by the National Institute for Occupational Safety and Health (NIOSH).

   D. Were first noticed by the National Institute for Occupational Safety and Health (NIOSH) in Appalachia, with later studies pinpointing West Virginia as a hard-hit area.

   E. Began to slow after new dust regulations took effect in places like Appalachia and West Virginia.

4. With which statement would the author most likely agree?

    A. The increase in black lung cases is a national health crisis.

    B. Black lung cases are worse among those who smoke.

    C. It is concerning that many new cases of black lung advance rapidly.

    D. Stricter dust laws need to be adopted to decrease new cases of black lung.

    E. More mobile medical units are needed for Appalachia.

5. Which of the following statements would not be considered fact?

    A. Scarier still, the new generation of black lung patients have the disease, and in many cases, progresses far more rapidly than in previous generations.

    B. These concerns were confirmed in follow-up studies using a mobile medical unit providing outreach to coal mining areas.

    C. In the early 1970s, coal workers' pneumoconiosis, or black lung disease, affected around one-third of long-term underground miners.

    D. Between 2000 and 2012, the prevalence of the most severe form of black lung rose to levels not seen since the 1970s.

    E. After new dust regulations took effect, rates of black lung plunged. Today, however, black lung rates are rising dramatically.

Questions 6 – 7 refer to the following graph.

The following graph outlines the sales for a local construction company. Quarter 1 includes months January-March. Quarter 2 is April through June. Quarter 3 is July through September. Finally, quarter 4 is October through December.

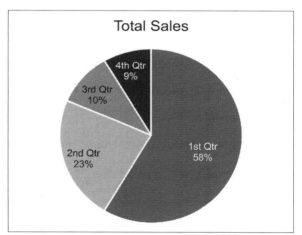

6. According to the pie graph, which of the following statements are true? Choose all that apply.

    A. The dip in quarter 4 sales was due to the holidays.

    B. More than half of the sales for the year happened in quarter 1.

    C. Quarter 3 was the worst quarter for sales.

    D. Quarter 1 sales were more than quarters 2, 3, and 4 combined.

    E. Quarter 2 sales were more than quarter 3 and 4 combined.

7. Which of the following statements cannot be determined according to the graph? Choose all that apply.

    A. Sales in Jan-March were the highest of the year.

    B. Sales in December were the lowest of the year.

    C. Sales in April through December did not beat sales in quarter1.

    D. Sales in September were 10%.

    E. The second highest sales happened in April-June.

Questions 8 – 10 refer to the following passage.

A local humane society is an organization that fights for the welfare of animals. These organizations take in animals of all kinds for various reasons and care for them until they are adopted. Many local humane societies are stand-alone, non-profit organizations that are not county, state, or federally funded. They also do not receive any funding from large national organizations such as the ASPCA. Instead, these local organizations rely solely on donations, grants, and fundraising events in order to provide for the animals. Volunteers are an asset to local humane societies that are non-profit organizations. Not only are volunteers needed for a number of jobs on site, but volunteers also play an important part of the humane society attaining grant funding. In order to receive grant funding, the humane society must show that they receive support in a variety of ways, which includes help from volunteers.

Local humane societies work tirelessly to provide medical attention, training, compassion, and a clean and healthy environment for animals, but they cannot do it without the support of the community. Fundraisers and community events help to support adoptions, secure donations, and increase awareness of the organization. No donation of money, supplies, or time is too small. From community outreach to grounds maintenance to cuddling puppies, there are numerous ways to volunteer or support your local humane society in its efforts to care for rescued and surrendered animals.

8. Which of the following best supports the main idea of this passage?

    A. Local humane societies are often non-profit organizations.

    B. Grant funding requires the applicant to show various means of support.

    C. The survival of local humane societies relies on donations and volunteers.

    D. A volunteer can cuddle puppies at the humane society to help provide support.

    E. Local humane societies work tirelessly to provide medical attention, training and compassion.

9. Which of the following statements would the author most likely agree? Choose all that apply.

    ❑ Humane societies should try to find funding in other places rather than just relying on volunteers and donations.

    ❑ Without volunteers, local humane societies would not be able to support the welfare of animals.

    ❑ People should not support the ASPCA because they receive large grant funding and do not need the funds as much as local organizations.

    ❑ The only way local humane societies will survive in the future is to secure grant funding and other funding sources.

    ❑ If you are looking for a place to get volunteer hours, you should consider your local humane society.

10. Which of the following would be an appropriate title for this passage?

    A. Why You Should Give Money to Your Local Humane Society

    B. Love Animals? Donate to or Volunteer with your Local Humane Society

    C. Local Humane Society is Looking for Donations

    D. On the Brink of Bankruptcy: How Humane Societies are Running out of Money.

    E. How the ASPCA is Undermining Local Humane Society Efforts

Questions 11 – 20 Refer to the following passage.

Noise and Body Fat: Uncovering New Connections | Wendee Nicole

Studies on environmental noise and human health have uncovered associations with cardiovascular disease and diabetes. New research is delving further into possible metabolic effects of noise—specifically a possible link to weight gain. Investigators report that exposure to traffic noise at home was associated with body composition outcomes, such as larger waist circumference and higher body mass index (BMI).

The cross-sectional study used data from the Danish Diet, Cancer, and Health Cohort, assessing 52,456 Danes between the ages of 50 and 64. The study tracked each participant's residential address history for the previous 5 years. The authors used noise-mapping software to estimate exposures from road traffic, railways, and air traffic for each address based on the most noise-exposed façade of the home. Four measures of body composition were recorded for each participant—BMI, waist circumference, body fat mass index (BFMI), and lean body mass index (LBMI).

Residential exposure to traffic noise has been associated with measures of weight gain. The body's response to both stress and lack of sleep may help explain why.

After adjusting for potential confounding factors (socioeconomic status, age, sex, and exposure to railway and aircraft noise), the researchers found that all measures of adiposity were significantly associated with road traffic noise. Each 10-dB increase in average road traffic noise exposure over 5 years was associated with an average increase in waist circumference of 0.35 cm and an average increase in BMI of 0.18 points. BFMI and LBMI also showed small but statistically significant increases in association with greater road traffic noise exposure. Co-exposure to railway noise louder than 60 decibels appeared to heighten the associations with BMI, waist circumference, and BFMI.

"The linear association we observed was consistent throughout the exposure range," says lead author Jeppe Christensen, a PhD candidate in epidemiology with the Danish Cancer Society Research Center. This is in line with other studies of similar health effects.

The authors propose that noise may activate the hypothalamus–pituitary–adrenal axis and the sympathetic nervous system—the body's "fight or flight" response. Evidence for this mode of action from other studies includes increased levels of cortisol associated with exposure to louder road noise. Noise may also disturb sleep, which is associated with increased food intake possibly due to dysregulation of hunger-related hormones, including leptin and ghrelin. Epidemiological studies have also reported that lack of sleep in children and young adults is associated with a higher percentage of body fat and increased waist circumference. A major strength of the study was its sheer size, and according to Bente Oftedal, an epidemiologist at the Norwegian Institute of Public Health, the results and conclusions matched the rigor of the performed analyses. "The main weakness is the lack of data on noise-related individual characteristics, such as noise annoyance and noise sensitivity," she says. "Both characteristics may modify associations between traffic noise and health outcomes, representing vulnerable subpopulations to noise exposure." Oftedal was not involved with the study.

"This is one of only a handful of studies investigating the association between exposure to noise in the environment and metabolic effects," says Charlotta Eriksson, a researcher at the Karolinska Institute's Institute of Environmental Medicine in Stockholm, who led one of the first studies to link aircraft noise with obesity. "The study by Christensen therefore adds valuable knowledge into this field of research."

The estimated effects of noise are small, Eriksson adds, but she says this is to be expected because other risk factors, such as heredity and lifestyle factors, are much stronger predictors of obesity for the individual. "Nevertheless," she says, "since a large proportion of the population is exposed to road traffic noise, the public health impact may be substantial."

11. According to the passage, exposure to road traffic noise:

    A. Is the strongest predictor of obesity in individuals.

    B. Has not been associated with weight gain.

    C. May substantially impact public health.

    D. Has been unequivocally linked to obesity.

    E. Has been linked to diabetes.

12. The title suggests that:

    A. The association between obesity and noise is widely accepted.

    B. The scientific study of obesity and noise is a relatively novel concept.

    C. The author disagrees with the idea that noise can cause increased weight.

    D. The link between increased weight and noise is a long-standing concept.

    E. Noise and obesity are a problem in this country.

13. According to the article, what is one issue with the study?

    A. The abundance of data on noise annoyance and sensitivity

    B. The small number of studies conducted in the field

    C. The lack of linear association throughout the exposure range

    D. The number of subjects involved in the study

    E. The absence of data on noise annoyance and sensitivity.

14. Which is NOT identified as a possible reason that noise exposure can affect weight?

    A. Activation of "fight or flight" response

    B. Disruption of hunger-related hormones

    C. Increased levels of cortisol

    D. Heightened risk for diabetes

    E. Sleep disturbance

15. Which title would be an appropriate substitute?

    A. Noise and Obesity: A Link Unveiled

    B. Lack of Sleep and Larger Waist Size

    C. Noise Exposure and Weight-Related Diseases

    D. Sleep with your windows closed or you'll get fat!

    E. Study Uncovers Link between Adiposity and Noise Exposure

16. Which is NOT a measure of adiposity in this study?

    A. Waist circumference

    B. Body fat mass index

    C. Fat density

    D. Lean body max index

    E. None of the above

17. As used in context, *dysregulation* most nearly means:

    A. impaired response

    B. normal development

    C. genetic transmission

    D. congenital defect

    E. weight gain

18. What is the main idea of the first paragraph?

    A. Decreased exposure to environmental noise will result in better overall health.

    B. There is a definitive link between environmental noise and increased weight.

    C. Exposure to environmental noise is being explored as a possible cause of weight gain.

    D. Cardiovascular disease and diabetes risks increase with exposure to environmental noise.

    E. Environmental noise is linked to diabetes.

19. As used in context, the phrase *metabolic effects* are

    A. Repercussions of environmental factors that affect cardiovascular health.

    B. Outcomes of exposure to environmental factors that affect the regulation of weight.

    C. Results of increased exposure to environmental factors that affect overall health.

    D. Consequences of increased exposure to environmental factors that affect mental health.

    E. A measure of overall health including cardiovascular disease, diabetes, and weight gain.

20. Which statement contradicts information presented in the passage?

    A. Heredity and lifestyle factors have a minor impact on obesity.

    B. Exposure to traffic noise may increase the risk for obesity.

    C. Noise exposure is just one risk factor for obesity.

    D. Noise pollution is not the only possible factor in weight gain.

    E. Noise pollution affects a large part of the population.

Passage A

Diwali, or the Festival of Lights, is India's most significant holiday. It's a five-day celebration in autumn that includes food, fireworks, and lights—candles and lamps. Diwali honors the victory of the forces of light over the forces of darkness. In India, light is a metaphor for knowledge and consciousness.

Diwali is one of the major festivals where rural Indians spend a significant portion of their annual income. Before Diwali celebrations, Indians prepare their homes and workplaces for celebratory events; people decorate their homes with diyas—oil lamps. During Diwali, Indians dress in fine clothes and share foods and gifts.

Passage B

Diwali celebrations have increased air pollution in India. The celebratory fireworks used during Diwali have reduced our already declining air quality. Thankfully, our Supreme Court is taking action with a ban on the sale of these fireworks. Some believe the ruling was judicial overreach and bias against Hindu culture. However, isn't public health more important than a silly celebration? Afterall, if people are getting sick because of India's air quality, what good is this Festival of Lights?

21. Which of the following would the author of Passage B most likely agree?

 A. People should be able to shoot off fireworks on their own property.

 B. If a national holiday becomes a public health crisis, it should be canceled.

 C. It is up to people to decide how they celebrate, not the courts.

 D. India's air quality should be secondary to carrying on traditions.

 E. The festival of lights is a tradition that is celebrated responsibly by many Indian people.

22. Which of the following compares the tone in Passage A to the tone in Passage B?

 A. The tone in Passage A is concerned while the tone in Passage B is jovial.

 B. The tone in Passage A is celebratory and the tone in Passage B is cheerful.

 C. The tone in Passage A is approving while the tone in Passage B is concerned.

 D. The tone in Passage A is unfavorable while the tone in Passage B is favorable.

 E. The tone in passage A is cautionary while the tone in passage B is indifferent.

23. With which of the following details in Passage A would the author of Passage B most likely find disappointing?

 A. Diwali is one of the major festivals where rural Indians spend a significant portion of their annual income.

 B. Before Diwali celebrations, Indians prepare their homes and workplaces for celebratory events.

 C. Diwali honors the victory of the forces of light over the forces of darkness.

 D. During Diwali, Indians dress in fine clothes and share foods and gifts.

 E. Before Diwali celebrations, Indians prepare their homes and workplaces for celebratory events.

24. What is the main idea of Passage A?

 A. Diwali is a time for Indians to share food with family and dress in extravagant clothing.

 B. People decorate their homes in lights for Diwali.

 C. Diwali is a 5-day celebration in India that celebrates the forces of light over the forces of darkness.

 D. Before Diwali celebrations, Indians prepare their homes and workplaces for celebratory events.

 E. Rural Indians spend a significant portion of their annual income on Diwali celebrations.

READING

Questions 25 – 34 refer to the following passage.

Americans are living longer and working past retirement age, and it is not uncommon to see up to five different generations in the public sector workforce. These employees have vastly different skillsets and motivators. It is imperative for public administrators to recognize these differences and create a work environment that maximizes each employee's potential for success.

Each of the five generations has a different set of unique characteristics that can make managing the group collectively very challenging. The Silent Generation is the group of employees born before 1945. These folks were shaped by the Great Depression and World War II. They tend to be highly loyal to the organization and tightfisted with resources. Baby Boomers (also called Boomers) were born between 1946 and 1965. Many were affected by the Vietnam War. These employees value years of service to the organization over skill level and education. Many were negatively impacted by the 2008 financial crisis, resulting in Boomers staying in the workforce longer than expected. People from Generation X (also called Gen X) were born between 1966 and 1980. These employees were shaped by the Cold War and an unstable market, making Gen Xers skeptical of government institutions but adaptive and independent. Generation Y (or Millennials) were born between 1981 and 1995. These employees are highly educated and have been shaped by rapid advancements in technology. They are global-centric employees and value lifestyle over promotion or status. Generation Z are employees born between 1995 and today. Their worldview has been shaped by the September 11th terrorist attacks and mass shootings. These employees value tolerance and equity but they have a low regard for interpersonal communication.

Often, Baby Boomers disregard Millennials because of their lack of experience in the workforce. Generation X employees like to work independently rather than in groups. Generation Z employees can get frustrated with Boomers and Gen Xers for their lack of understanding of technology. These dynamics can create an antagonistic and dysfunctional work environment. Finding ways to bridge the generation gaps can help synergize the team to accomplish the organization's goals.

There are several techniques managers can use to foster a productive, multigenerational work environment. Establishing a mentorship program can help generations work effectively together. Managers can select the mentorship pairings to avoid employees from choosing mentors that are similar to themselves. Managers can also set tasks so that each participant in the program has an opportunity to mentor their partner on their strengths. For example, Baby Boomers can mentor their partner on their institutional knowledge gained over their years of experience, and Millennials can mentor their partners on new technology programs to increase connections. Another technique managers can use to increase collaboration across generations is to implement diversity in project management opportunities. Managers can select project leaders based on areas of expertise rather than years of experience or job title. Instead of selecting the most senior staff member, a manager can choose the person with the most interest in the outcome.

When it comes to managing a multigenerational workforce, the differences among employees can seem overwhelming. Employees are influenced by vastly different experiences and value almost completely opposite work factors. While their dissimilarities may seem polarizing, there are ways managers can increase employee collaboration that leads to a synchronous and successful organization. Creating opportunities for all employees to showcase their skillsets and impact organizational change will allow managers to effectively lead their diverse staff.

25. Which of the following is the main idea of the passage?

   A. It is not unusual to have five different generations working together on one job.

   B. As the work force becomes more age diverse, managers must use effective tactics to motivate workers.

   C. When it comes to managing a multigenerational workforce, the differences among employees can seem overwhelming.

   D. Because there are so many different generations in the workforce, sometimes working relationships are contentious.

   E. Americans are working past retirement age and managers must use collaboration techniques with workers to ensure success.

26. All of the following details relate to the idea in the passage that employees sometimes struggle to get along in the workplace EXCEPT:

   A. Often, Baby Boomers disregard Millennials because of their lack of experience in the workforce.

   B. Finding harmony among the generations within the workforce can be problematic.

   C. Managers can select the mentorship pairings to avoid employees from choosing mentors that are similar to themselves.

   D. These dynamics can create a contentious and dysfunctional work environment.

   E. Generation X employees like to work independently rather than in groups.

27. Based on the details in the passage, what might be a typical interaction between some of the generations mentioned in the passage? Choose all that apply.

   A. Baby Boomers get annoyed with Millennials because Millennials hoard resources and don't want to spend money.

   B. Generation X get annoyed with Baby Boomers because Baby Boomers are quiet and keep to themselves.

   C. Baby Boomers get frustrated with Generation Z because of the lack of communication Gen Z shows Boomers.

   D. Generation X sees Generation Z as out of touch with new realities in the work force.

   E. Millennials get frustrated with Baby Boomers lack of tech knowledge and ability.

28. According to the passage, which generation prefers to work independently rather than in groups?

   A. Baby Boomers

   B. Generation X

   C. Generation Y

   D. Generation Z

   E. None of the above.

29. According to the passage, what event has shaped Generation Z's world view?

   A. World War II

   B. The Vietnam War

   C. The Cold War

   D. September 11

   E. The financial crisis

30. The word *antagonistic* in the 3rd paragraph most likely means

   A. Incompatible

   B. Indifferent

   C. Average

   D. Harmonious

   E. Congruent

31. What type of structural pattern does the passage follow?

    A. Chronological

    B. Narrative

    C. Cause and effect

    D. Problem and solution

    E. Question and answer

32. Which of the following statements would align with the point of view of the author?

    A. Organizations should hire managers who have an understanding of different generations.

    B. Rapid advancements in technology is harming worker relationships.

    C. Workers should do their best to get along, regardless of generational divide.

    D. Managers should strive to increase diversity in the workforce.

    E. Baby Boomers are working too long, which is causing discord in the workplace.

33. Which 2 statements discredit the author's claim that choosing project leaders based on experience rather than on seniority leads to better collaboration?

    A. Millennials feel that quality of work is more important than years in the workforce.

    B. Employees are influenced by vastly different experiences and value almost completely opposite work factors.

    C. Baby Boomers disregard Millennials because Millennials lack experience in the workforce.

    D. Finding harmony among the generations within the workforce can be problematic when managing day-to-day operations.

    E. Even though millennials say they value experience over tenure, they tend to get angry when new people get promotions.

34. The information in this passage would be most effective if presented in the format of a:

    A. Textbook for a business management class

    B. Brochure outlining management information

    C. Presentation during a management training

    D. Letter to supervisors and managers

    E. In an academic journal for labor force researchers

READING

Questions 35 – 38 refer to the following graph.

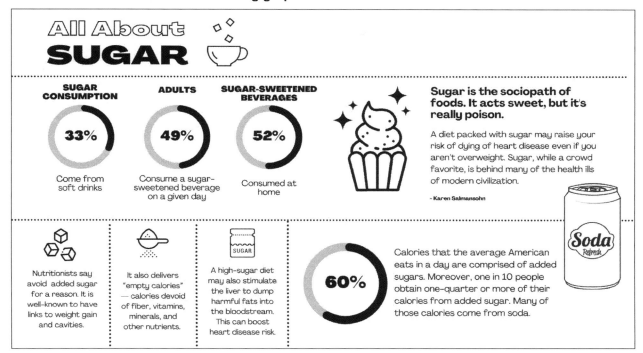

35. What statement aligns with the information given in the infographic?

    A. Most people consume sugar sweetened beverages in fast food restaurants.

    B. Approximately 40% of sugar consumed comes from soft drinks.

    C. Less than half of average Americans' diet comes from sugar.

    D. Approximately 1 in 2 people consume at least one sugary beverage every day.

    E. A high-sugar diet stimulates the kidneys to dump harmful fats in the bloodstream.

36. According to the infographic, what could Americans do that would cut down on harm caused by sugar?

    A. Eat leafy green vegetables

    B. Get their livers checked for harmful chemicals.

    C. Stop eating at restaraunts.

    D. Stop eating foods like cupcakes and candy.

    E. Cut out soft drinks from their diets.

37. Who is the most appropriate intended audience of this infographic?

    A. Teachers

    B. Parents

    C. Nutritionists

    D. Children

    E. Doctors

38. What can you infer about the purpose and placement of the cupcake and the word *sociopath* in the infographic?

   A. To hook the reader with an engaging graphic so they read further.

   B. To highlight the dangers of sugar are disguised in pretty foods.

   C. To balance out the other images in the infographic.

   D. To make children want to read the infographic too.

   E. To make the language and information less scientific and easy to read.

Questions 39 – 41 refer to the following passage.

Passage 1

You—the writer, director, actor—enter the building from the back alley where a solid steel door materializes out of a canyon of brick. The patrons—the paying customer—are corralled under a brightly lit façade advertising the name of this *thing* you've toiled over for months and they will, probably, forget about before the end of their subway ride home. However, you understand it's the journey, not the destination, where your reward lies in the *doing*. Because once you walk through that ominous steel door, through dark hallways, tiny dressing rooms, past trays of inedible food, cold coffee and warm beer, you and your feelings no longer matter: the ticket holder must be entertained, or you have failed.

Passage 2

What is a theatre production's responsibility to the audience? In short, it has none. In the theatre the artistic integrity of a written, directed, and rehearsed piece must not be affected by the emotional, critical, or political response of the mass audience. The optimal result of a theatre going experience is to leave the theatre ravaged: by fear, guilt, joy, shock, love, or some combination. For good or ill, that result is subjective and should be of no concern to the artists.

39. The main purpose of both Passage 1 and 2 is to which of the following?

   A. To determine amount of work that is needed to create a successful theatre production?

   B. To argue that the effect the production has on the audience determines the success of the show.

   C. To determine the best results for a theater production.

   D. To debate the artist's responsibility to entertain the audience.

   E. To argue that the success of a theater production is based on artwork and not the audience reaction.

40. Which of the following best describes the organization of both passages?

   A. An observation is made, and both paragraphs uses evidence to support that observation.

   B. Each paragraph compares the same topic with each reaching a different conclusion.

   C. A generalization is made followed by specific examples.

   D. A specific example is made followed by generalized conclusions.

   E. The passage offers and idea and then refutes it.

41. In Passage 1, the author's position on the topic is which of the following?

   A. Both the artist and the audience will feel many of the same emotions during the production.

   B. The producer's work is done once the curtain goes up.

   C. The audience's reaction to the production should not reflect onto the artist.

   D. If the audience is not entertained, then the artist has not created a successful production.

   E. The audience does not truly appreciate the time and work needed to create a theatre production.

Questions 42 – 46 refer to the following passage.

This Side of Paradise
F. Scott Fitzgerald
CODE OF THE YOUNG EGOTIST

Before he was summoned back to Lake Geneva, he had appeared, shy but inwardly glowing, in his first long trousers, set off by a purple accordion tie and a "Belmont" collar with the edges unassailably meeting, purple socks, and handkerchief with a purple border peeping from his breast pocket. But more than that, he had formulated his first philosophy, a code to live by, which, as near as it can be named, was a sort of aristocratic egotism.

He had realized that his best interests were bound up with those of a certain variant, changing person, whose label, in order that his past might always be identified with him, was Amory Blaine. Amory marked himself a fortunate youth, capable of infinite expansion for good or evil. He did not consider himself a "strong character," but relied on his facility (learn things sorta quick) and his superior mentality (read a lotta deep books). He was proud of the fact that he could never become a mechanical or scientific genius. From no other heights was he debarred.

Physically—Amory thought that he was exceedingly handsome. He was. He fancied himself an athlete of possibilities and a supple dancer.

Socially—here his condition was, perhaps, most dangerous. He granted himself personality, charm, magnetism, poise, the power of dominating all contemporary males, the gift of fascinating all women.

Mentally—complete, unquestioned superiority.

Now a confession will have to be made. Amory had rather a Puritan conscience. Not that he yielded to it— later in life he almost completely slew it—but at fifteen it made him consider himself a great deal worse than other boys... unscrupulousness... the desire to influence people in almost every way, even for evil... a certain coldness and lack of affection, amounting sometimes to cruelty... a shifting sense of honor... an unholy selfishness... a puzzled, furtive interest in everything concerning sex.

There was, also, a curious strain of weakness running crosswise through his make-up... a harsh phrase from the lips of an older boy (older boys usually detested him) was liable to sweep him off his poise into surly sensitiveness, or timid stupidity... he was a slave to his own moods and he felt that though he was capable of recklessness and audacity, he possessed neither courage, perseverance, nor self-respect.

Vanity, tempered with self-suspicion if not self-knowledge, a sense of people as automatons to his will, a desire to "pass" as many boys as possible and get to a vague top of the world... with this background did Amory drift into adolescence.

42. It can be inferred from the passage that the author most likely believes Amory Blaine is generally

   A. shy

   B. conceited

   C. trustworthy

   D. sad

   E. charming

43. Which of the following would strengthen the author's assessment of Amory Blaine's personality?

   A. Amory Blaine believed he could easily win the heart of the most beautiful woman in his town.

   B. Amory Blaine lived life as a hermit away from society.

   C. Amory Blaine did not attend school

   D. Amory Blaine hid his physique under heavy coats.

   E. Amory Blaine became extremely nervous when he socialized with his superiors.

44. According to the author, the only time that Amory Blaine displayed self-doubt was during which of the following social interactions?

   A. with family

   B. with females

   C. with older boys

   D. with church clergy

   E. with teachers

45. The passage suggests that Amory Blaine would have agreed with which of the following statements.

   A. Some of the brightest people today are found within the Science Department of the local state university.

   B. Puritan beliefs are far more accurate than the non-secular beliefs among many young people in modern days.

   C. All humans are created equal.

   D. Success is achieved through the survival of the fittest.

   E. Intelligence is acquired through learned skills and trades.

46. Which of the following conclusions is best supported by the passage?

   A. Amory Blaine's adopted code to live by earned him many admirers.

   B. Amory Blaine's overall intelligence and physical appearance was something that most young men continue to strive for even to this day.

   C. Amory Blaine's transition from childhood was marked by uncomfortable situations.

   D. Amory Blaine was, above all, egotistical in his opinion of himself.

   E. Amory Blaine remained stuck in his childhood fantasies for many years into his young adult life

Questions 47 – 48 refer to the following passage.

You find a time machine and travel to 1920. A young Austrian artist and war veteran named Adolf Hitler is staying in the hotel room next to yours. The doors aren't locked, so you could easily stroll next door and smother him. World War II would never happen.

But Hitler hasn't done anything wrong yet. Is it acceptable to kill him to prevent World War II?

This is one moral dilemma researchers often use to analyze how people make difficult decisions. Most recently, one group analyzed answers from more than 6,000 subjects to compare men's and women's responses. They found men and women both calculate consequences such as lives lost. However, women are more likely to feel conflicted over what to do; having to commit murder is more likely to push them toward letting Hitler live.

"Women seem to be likely to have this negative, emotional, gut-level reaction to causing harm to people in the dilemmas, to the one person, whereas men were less likely to express this strong emotional reaction to harm," Rebecca Friesdorf, the lead author of the study, tells *Shots*. A master's student in social psychology at Wilfrid Laurier University in Waterloo, Ontario, Friesdorf analyzed 40 data sets from previous studies. The study was published Friday in the *Personality and Social Psychology Bulletin*.

47. Which of the following best summarizes the findings of the study mentioned in the passage?

A. Both men and women think it's acceptable to kill Hitler to prevent World War II.

B. Women are less capable than men to make hypothetical decisions.

C. Women and men differ in their approaches to making moral decisions.

D. Men are more likely to calculate consequences of the decision.

E. Women will make decisions based on the easiest answer possible.

48. How is this passage organized?

A. Second person narrative is used to convey a hypothetical situation, and the passage goes on to outline research related to that situation.

B. First person narrative is used to convey a hypothetical situation, and the passage goes on to outline research related to that situation.

C. A chronological account of a story is used in the first part of the passage, and the passage goes on to support that chronological account.

D. Cause and effect are used to outline an issue in world history, and the passage goes on to describe that time in world history.

E. A research study is introduced, and the passage goes on to outline important researcher's and their work in the study.

Questions 49 – 50 refer to the following passage.

At the conclusion of the Civil War, long-standing dreams of a bridge across the Mississippi River at St. Louis were revived. Such a bridge was a necessity by the late 1860s. The width of the river at St. Louis had created a problem with commercial transportation after the advent of the railroads. Without a bridge, freight could not be transferred in bulk across river but instead had to be off-loaded from trains to ferry boats, a procedure which raised costs tremendously. The construction of the St. Louis Bridge was necessary for the area to thrive in the 19th and 20th century.

James B. Eads presented a daring plan to build the bridge. The plan was approved in 1867. Although a rival, Lucius Boomer, still had the rights to build the bridge, he took no legal action against the Eads project. Boomer had already delayed construction long enough for four new bridges, built further upstream, to serve Chicago's railroads.

49. What can be inferred regarding why Boomer's company did not take legal action against Eads' company?

    A. Eads' plan was more daring than Boomer's plan and would have costed Boomer too much money.

    B. Boomer was afraid to take legal action against Eads because Eads was radical in his thinking.

    C. Eads would have counter-sued Boomer's company for stalling the construction.

    D. At the conclusion of the Civil War, people wanted the bridge, and Boomer did not want to disappoint them.

    E. Boomer's company was already too busy with work from other delayed projects and seeking legal action would put them farther behind.

50. What can be inferred by the passage?

    A. Two tycoons fought over the rights to build the St. Louis Bridge.

    B. People in the Mississippi and St. Louis area wanted to build the bridge before the Civil War.

    C. The St. Louis Bridge was going to be too expensive to build before the Civil War.

    D. Production on the bridge was halted because funds needed to go towards the war effort.

    E. Once the Civil War started, people were not interested in building the bridge.

Question 51 refers to the following passage.

The New York University computer-science department sits inside Warren Weaver Hall, a fortress-like building located two blocks east of Washington Square Park. Industrial-strength air-conditioning vents create a surrounding moat of hot air, discouraging loiterers and solicitors alike. Visitors who breach the moat encounter another formidable barrier, a security check-in counter, immediately inside the building's single entryway.

51. By using the phrase "breach the moat," the author is trying to convey what effect? Choose all that apply.

    ❑ Anger at the fact that the computer science building is so difficult to get into

    ❑ Sarcasm in explaining that getting into the computer science building is like breaking through an almost impossible barrier.

    ❑ Humor in describing the image of industrial-strength air-conditioning blowing solicitors away from the doors.

    ❑ Persuasion in getting people to see the importance of the barriers to the computer science building.

    ❑ Cause and effect in showing how a moat and security check-in can cause restrict entrance to the building.

Questions 52 – 56 refer to the following passage

More than 1 million insects have been discovered and named, but many millions have yet to be described. It's undeniable that Earth is becoming increasingly inhospitable to some insects–but nightmarish conditions for one may be heaven to another.

Put another way, there is no perfect environment for all insects. And human impacts on the environment, like climate change and land development, very well may hurt beneficial insects and help harmful ones. Several studies have been devoted to examining the insect decline.

The first study to set off alarms was published in 2017 by entomologists in Germany, who reported that over 27 years the biomass of flying insects in their traps had declined by 75%. Another study from the Luquillo Long Term Ecological Research program site in the Puerto Rican rainforest reproduced an insect survey from the 1970s. It found that the biomass of arthropods–a large group of organisms that includes insects–had declined 10- to 60-fold in that time, and that lizards, frogs and birds that ate arthropods had also declined.

Underscoring this theme, in April 2019 two scholars published a review that synthesized over 70 reports of insect decline from around the world and predicted mass insect extinctions within a human lifetime. They took an alarmist tone and have been widely criticized for exaggerating their conclusions and selecting studies to review with the word "decline." Other studies have found that many insects have yet to be discovered or described, making it difficult to predict extinction.

These discussions are important, but they don't mean an insect apocalypse is under way.

To predict an apocalypse, entomologists worldwide will need to conduct careful large-scale studies that involve collecting, identifying and counting many different insects. There are very few insects for which scientists have enough data now to reliably predict how many individuals there will be from year to year, let alone confidently chart a decline in each species. Most of the insects for which this information exists are species that are important for agricultural or human health, such as managed honeybees or mosquitoes.

And human actions are shifting balances between insect species. As an example, the mosquitoes that are best at spreading pathogens that cause disease have evolved to thrive near us. Entomologists call them anthropophilic, which means they love people.

That love extends to human impacts on the land. Insects that flutter from flower to flower won't be happy when developers bulldoze a meadow and scatter tires around, but human-biting mosquitoes will be buzzing with excitement.

52. As used in the passage, the term *pathogen* means

    A. Disease

    B. Bacteria

    C. Insect

    D. Poison

    E. Toxins

53. Why does the author mention the 2 studies in paragraph 6?

    A. To emphasize the point that there has been a 75% decline in insect populations

    B. To discredit these scientists as not showing that some insect populations have increased

    C. To show that taking an alarmist tone in research is biased

    D. To show the reader the author is an authority in the area of insects.

    E. To show examples of studies where the research supports large declines in insect populations.

54. Which of the following statements would the author most likely agree?

A. Because so many insects have yet to be discovered, and even those that have been discovered have yet to be described, insect extinction predications may be skewed.

B. All of the studies about insect extinction are wrong and do not take into account the factors that say insects are thriving.

C. If people continue to bulldoze and build, they will have to deal with a huge mosquito problem.

D. Insect extinction is very serious, and it deserves attention because without insects, ecosystems will die.

E. Because mosquitos are spreading pathogens, they should be eradicated entirely.

55. Which of the following would discredit the claim the author makes in the 4th paragraph?

A. Recent studies have found that mosquitoes thrive where other insects might die.

B. Many of the insects that have not been described yet have shown resistance to pesticides and climate change.

C. Even the insects that have not been described yet have shown possible extinction within the next few years.

D. Several studies have shown that most insects have been discovered and described.

E. Because so many insects have yet to be discovered and described, we cannot predict extinction.

56. The tone of the passage is:

A. Annoyed

B. Optimistic

C. Skeptical

D. Exasperated

E. Overwhelmed

GACE Reading Practice Test 2 Answer Explanations

Number	Answer	Category	Explanation
1	C	I	This answer can be found in the last line of the last paragraph: *But not all cases progress so quickly; thus, occupational health researchers fear that what they are seeing now is only the tip of the iceberg.*
2	E	I	This *inference question* will not be stated directly in the text, but information in passage will lead you to a logical conclusion. In paragraph 2, it says "After new dust regulations took effect rates of black lung plunged. Today, however, they are once again rising dramatically." Paragraph 5 also states that "Between 2000 and 2012, the prevalence of the most severe form of black lung rose to levels not seen since the 1970s when modern dust laws were enacted." These two pieces of information tell you that the cases were reduced, but not eliminated altogether, as evidenced by the resurgence of cases, making answer choice E the correct choice. The other answer choices contradict this information. Notice that answer choice D uses the phrase, permanently eradicated, which is strong language and is incorrect here.
3	D	I	This answer to this *detail question* can be found in paragraph 5. The NIOSH identified cases in Appalachia with later research pinpointing West Virginia as a hard-hit area. Answer choice A states the opposite. Answer choices B, C and E are not supported by the text.
4	C	II	The trick answer here is choice D. While it seems like a reasonable statement, the author does not assert that stricter dust laws should be enacted. Answer choice A is not correct because the disease is not a national crisis; it seems to be a regional crisis in Appalachia. There is no evidence to support the connection between smoking and black lung, eliminating choice B. Answer E is not supported by the text. The author would agree with answer choice C because this is the focus of the passage; she is bringing attention to the issue as a concern that needs to be acknowledged. The correct answer is answer choice C.
5	A	II	The word *scarier* is what sets this statement off as an opinion and not fact. What is scary to one may not be scary to another. All the other statements can be verified.
6	B, D, & E	III	Because sales in quarter 1 were 58%, that means answers B and D are correct. Answer E is correct because the total sales for quarter 3 and 4 is 19%, and quarter 2 sales were 23%. Answer C is incorrect because quarter 4 was the worst for sales, not quarter 3. Finally, answer A cannot be determined by the information in the graph.

Number	Answer	Category	Explanation
7	B & D	III	Use the information above the graph to help you with this question. Because the chart shows quarterly sales, we cannot determine specific sales for individual months. Therefore, answers B and D are correct.
8	C	I	The main idea of the passage is about the ways local humane societies are funded and how important volunteers are to the organization. We can eliminate answer choice D because it does not relate at all to funding. Answer choices A and B can also be eliminated because they are single supporting details about the main idea of the passage. Answer choice C is correct because it includes the supporting details without being too specific.
9	Box 2 & 5	III	The passage is largely about how the humane society needs volunteers and donations. Therefore, boxes 2 and 5 are correct. The passage does not discourage people from giving to other organizations like the ASPCA, so box 3 can be eliminated. The passage also does not focus on areas where local human societies should find additional funding, eliminating boxes 1 and 4.
10	B	I	Most of the passage is about funding and volunteering. Therefore, answer B is the best title for this passage.
11	C	I	The correct choice is supported in the last paragraph: *Because so many people are exposed to traffic noise, the link between traffic noise and obesity can affect a significant part of the population.* The information in answer choice A contradicts information in the last paragraph: *heredity and lifestyle factors are stronger predictors of obesity for the individual.* Answer choice B contradicts the main point of the entire passage. Answer choice D uses strong language (*unequivocally*) that eliminates it as the correct choice. Finally, answer choice E is not supported by the text.
12	B	I	Answer choices A, C, and D can be eliminated because they all contradict the wording of the title. Answer choice E is not related to the title at all. Answer choice B is the only choice that captures the idea that noise exposure is a newly studied concept.
13	E	I	The quote from Bente Oftedal in paragraph 6, "The main weakness is the lack of data on noise-related individual characteristics, such as noise annoyance and noise sensitivity," reveals that answer choice E is the correct choice. The other choices contradict information in the passage.
14	D	I	Although diabetes is mentioned in paragraph 1, it is a separate issue that has already been studied along with cardiovascular disease. Because it is often associated with obesity, background knowledge might lead you to choose the wrong answer. Remember to only use the information in the passage for these types of questions.

Number	Answer	Category	Explanation
15	E	I	Choice A uses language (*definitive*) that does not match the tone of the passage. The author uses terms such as *possible* and *may*. Definitive means *conclusive,* and the author definitely does not present the link between noise and weight gain as conclusive. Answer choice B only addresses one point made in the passage; therefore, it would not make a good title. Answer choice C is intended to throw you off with the term *weight-related diseases.* The article does not talk about the diseases associated with weight gain, just the link between noise exposure and increased obesity risk. Answer choice D is a bit absurd and does not fit the scientific article. Answer choice E is the only choice that rewords the title but still keeps the original meaning and intent.
16	C	I	In paragraph 2, BMI, BFMI, waist circumference, and lean body mass index are all mentioned. Fat density is not mentioned.
17	A	II	Using knowledge of prefixes will help you here. The prefix *dys* means *abnormal* or *impaired*. Think of other words you know that begin with this prefix (*dysfunctional*, for example). Knowing this will eliminate choice B. Answer choices C and D both relate to something you are born with and can therefore be eliminated as well. Answer E, weight gain, is not part of dysregulation.
18	C	I	The first paragraph sets the stage for a research study on noise exposure and weight gain, making answer choice C the correct choice. Choice A seems like a reasonable statement but is not even a consideration because it has nothing to do with the first paragraph. Choice B uses that word definitive again, and we know the link the study made is not that strong. Answer choice D is inaccurate. While diabetes is mentioned in the first paragraph, it is not the main topic or main idea, so eliminate answer E.
19	B	II	The first word of each choice is a synonym for *effect*. However, the qualifying information in the rest of the answer choices for A, C, D and E is inaccurate. The passage refers to weight gain, not cardiovascular health, overall health, or mental health, making choice B correct.
20	A	II	This is a *key ideas and details question;* therefore, the answer can be located within the text. Choice A contradicts information presented in the passage: *because other risk factors, such as heredity and lifestyle factors, are much stronger predictors of obesity for the individual.* The rest of the answer choices mirror information presented in the passage.
21	B	I	The author of Passage B is outraged and believes people's public health is more important than traditions like fireworks. Therefore, this author most likely believes that if holidays are bad for people, they should be canceled. All the other answer choices go against what the author in Passage B is saying.

READING

Number	Answer	Category	Explanation
22	C	II	The tone in Passage A is positive toward Diwali and therefore approving. The tone in Passage B is concerned for the public health implications caused by Diwali fireworks.
23	A	III	Because the author of Passage B believes public health is more important than celebrations, the author of Passage B would most likely find the fact that Indians spend most of their annual salary on Diwali disappointing.
24	C	I	All of the statements in the answer choices are mentioned in Passage A. However, only one encompasses the main idea, which is Diwali is a 5-day celebration in India that celebrates the forces of light over the forces of darkness.
25	B	I	The central idea of this passage is that the workforce is diverse, and managers must use different approaches to make the workforce productive. Answers A, C, D and E are too specific to be a main idea.
26	C	I	The only answer choice that does not support the discord or disharmony in the workforce is answer choice C. Managers pairing others with proper mentors helps to avoid discord. All the other answer choices relate to the discord.
27	C & E	1	Based on the passage, Generation Z does not emphasize interpersonal communication, where Baby Boomers do, making C a correct answer choice. Millennials are technologically savvy and may get annoyed with those who are not, making E a correct answer. All the other answer choices do not align with how the passage describes the generations.
28	B	I	This answer can be found directly in paragraph 3.
29	D	I	The second paragraph explains the historical influences on different generations. According to paragraph 2, Generation Z is influenced by the September 11th terrorist attacks.
30	A	II	The vocab word antagonistic is followed by a simile, dysfunction. This makes answer A, incompatible, the best choice.
31	D	II	This passage presents a problem or a challenge—generational diversity in the workforce that may cause contention—and a solution—creating opportunities and programs for all employees to feel appreciated and connected.
32	A	III	The author in the passage is advocating for managers to use techniques to bring different generations in the workforce together. Therefore, answer A is the best choice here.

Number	Answer	Category	Explanation
33	C & E	III	Both of the statements in answer choices C and E contradict the notion that merit is more important to people than years on the job. All of the other answer choices would reinforce the author's claim, not discredit it.
34	C	III	This information would be best used as a presentation for a manager training. The other answer choices are ok, but a training would be the most effective format because the strategies in the piece lend themselves to professional development for supervisors.
35	D	III	Because 49% (almost half) of people surveyed said they drink a sugary beverage in a day, we can approximate 1 in 2 or ½ of people have at least one sugary beverage in a day. Answer A is incorrect because it says 52% of people consume their sugar beverages at home. Answer B is incorrect because 33% of sugar consumed comes from soft drinks. Answer C is incorrect because 60% of the average American's diet comes from added sugars. Finally, answer E is incorrect because it is the liver not kidneys that dumps harmful fats in the bloodstream when someone eats too much sugar.
36	E	III	Most of the infographic focuses on the consumption of sugary drinks and why that is a problem. Therefore, E is the correct answer.
37	B	III	Doctors and nutritionists most likely know this information. Because of the stats and text, children are probably not the intended audience. Teachers might be a good fit for this, but the best audience is parents. Parents are in charge of what food is in the home, and the infographic says that 52% of sugary drinks are consumed at home.
38	A	III	While all of the answer choices could be a reason for the cupcake and the word *sociopath*, the most effective use of these two elements is to get the reader to read on.
39	D	III	Be careful; the question asks you to draw from **both** passages. Both passages are debating the role the artist holds in entertaining the audience. Choice A and C talk about the amount of work in and results of a production, and those are not applicable here. Choice B may seem like a good choice; however, it matches the argument proposed only in Passage 1. Likewise, choice E is stating only the issue for Passage 2. Choice D, on the other hand, encompasses the main idea for both passages.
40	B	II	For this question, you are asked to determine the organization of the entire passage. Choices A and E are incorrect because neither try to disprove or refute a statement previously mentioned in the passage. Choices C and D are wrong because both passages are written as generalizations. Choice B is the best answer because both passages are talking about the same thing but coming to different conclusions—that the artist *is responsible* for the audience's reaction, and that the artist *is not responsible* for the audience's reaction.

READING

Number	Answer	Category	Explanation
41	D	I	This question asks you to determine the main argument from Passage 1. The last line says: *the ticket holder must be entertained, or you have failed.* This makes answer choice D correct.
42	B	I	Based on the author's description of Amory Blaine, we can infer that the author felt the character was conceited. He states that Blaine thought himself "exceedingly handsome," "fancied himself and athlete," "granted himself charm and magnetism, "and thought himself to have "complete, superiority" in mental capabilities.
43	A	III	Because we know that Blaine was conceited, he would most likely feel he could win the heart of most women. Choices B-E suggest characteristics that are of someone with low self-esteem.
44	C	I	A supporting idea of the passage is that the only time Blaine felt any insecurities was when the older boys made comments about him. We can infer then that he remained confident in other social situations mentioned in choices A, B, D, and E.
45	D	III	This question asks you to determine the results of a hypothetical event based on information gleamed from the passage. Choices A, B, and E can be refuted by analyzing the personality descriptions listed in the writing. Choice C can be inferred as the wrong choice because we know that Amory felt he was superior to other humans, so they could not all be created equal. He would most likely agree with the survival of the fittest notion as he felt he could excel amongst his peers as he believed he was the most fit in mental, social, and physical capacities.
46	D	I	Based on the reading, we can conclude that Blaine was quite egotistical—it's even in the title of the piece. Choice A and B suggest that people admired his conceited behavior. Choices C and E are not mentioned or implied in the passage, making D the best choice.
47	C	I	This question asks you to determine the overall point or main idea of the passage. Choices A and D are supporting ideas. Choice B and E are never stated or implied in the passage. Choice C is the main idea of the entire passage.
48	A	I	The first word in the passage is **You**; therefore, second person narrative is used. Also, the beginning of the passage is hypothetical because it talks about a fake situation where you can kill Hitler and prevent WWII. Finally, the passage goes on to introduce a study that pertains to the hypothetical solution of whether or not to kill Hitler.
49	E	I	This sentence from the passage explains why answer choice A is the answer: "Although a rival Lucius Boomer still had the rights to build the bridge, he took no legal action against the Eads project. Boomer had already delayed construction long enough for four new bridges, built further upstream, to serve Chicago's railroads."

Number	Answer	Category	Explanation
50	B	I	The first link in the passage alludes to the fact that there were dreams to build the bridge, but they were not realized probably because the Civil War happened. Then after the Civil, those dreams were *revived*. The term *revived* indicates there were plans for the bridge before the war.
51	Box 2 & 3	II	The author is using the word moat both sarcastically and humorously to describe how difficult it is do enter the building. It does not seem that the writer is angered; anger is too strong of a word here, so box 1 is out. Persuasion and cause and effect are not relevant here, so boxes 4 and 5 are out.
52	B	I	As used in the article, pathogens spread diseases. Bacteria also spread diseases. Therefore, B is the best answer choice. Pathogens spread diseases and are therefore not diseases, eliminating answer A. Pathogens are not insects or poison eliminating answers C and D. Toxins are the same as poison, eliminating E.
53	E	II	The author is trying to emphasize that many studies have been devoted to showing large declines in insect populations. Showcasing 2 studies helps to legitimize that claim.
54	A	III	The author is careful not to side with the alarmists about insect population decline. Therefore, A is the best answer here. Answer choices B, C, and D are too extreme for what the author has presented in this piece. Answer E uses strong language and is not appropriate.
55	C	III	Choices A, B and E support the author's claim and can be eliminated. Only answer choices C and D go against what the author is saying. Answer C is better than answer D because the author is not just asserting that insects haven't been discovered, he is also asserting that because millions of insects haven't been discovered, researchers really do not know if they are experiencing mass extinction.
56	C	II	Throughout the essay, the author is skeptical about current research claiming insect populations are rapidly declining. The tone is not angry or negative. Therefore, choices A and D can be eliminated. Also, annoyed and exasperated mean the same thing. Because you cannot choose two answers they should be eliminated. While the tone is friendly and scholarly, it is not optimistic.

READING

This page intentionally left blank.

References – Works Used for Reading Passages

Some of our passages are Original works. Others are from the public domain or adaptations of original works. Below is a list of all non-originals in the order they appear in the practice tests.

Conrad, Joseph, 1857-1924. (1996). *Heart of darkness. Charlottesville,* Va.: Boulder, Colo.: University of Virginia Library; NetLibrary. Retrieved from the Public Domain.

Brinkley, D. & *McDonell*, T. (2000). Hunter S. Thompson, The Art of Journalism No. 1. *The Paris Review (156).* Retrieved from https://www.theparisreview.org/interviews/619/the-art-of-journalism-no-1-hunter-s-thompson

Artist Unknown *(1879s). Polar Bear. Retrieved from the* Public Domain.

Jones, C.A. (2015). *Hot chocolate has been prescribed to cure everything from infertility to bad teeth.* Retrieved from https://qz.com/353056/the-caffeine-cure-why-chocolate-was-once-prescribed-as-medicine/

ETS (n.d.). *What we've learned from high school equivalency.* Retrieved from https://news.ets.org/stories/what-weve-learned-about-high-school-equivalency/

Vibbert, J. (n.d.). *The Barbershop.* Reproduced with permission from the author.

Staff Report (2015). *Value of education brings success among unique student population.* Retrieved from http://www.sfltimes.com/education/value-of-education-brings-success-among-unique-student-population

Goldstein, D (2019). 'It Just Isn't Working': PISA test scores cast doubt on U.S. education efforts. *The New York Times.* Retrieved from https://www.nytimes.com/2019/12/03/us/us-students-international-test-scores.html

Post Bulletin (2012). *Rudy: Autobiography Reveals Real Story Behind the Legend.* Retrieved from https://www.postbulletin.com/incoming/online_features/book_review/sports-icon-rudy-bares-all-in-autobiography/article_32e4f084-59ff-501b-a2ad-e140f8b354ac.html

Arnold, C. (2016). *A Scourge Returns: Black Lung in Appalachia.* Reproduced with permission from Environmental Health Perspectives. Retrieved from https://www.ncbi.nlm.nih.gov/pmc/articles/PMC4710586/

Nicole, W. (2016). *Noise and body fat: Uncovering new connections.* Reproduced with permission from Environmental Health Perspectives. Retrieved from https://ehp.niehs.nih.gov/doi/10.1289/ehp.124-a57.

Selph, C. (2012). *Managing Five Generations in the Workforce,* Derived from *Implementation Challenges with Mentor Relationships Across Generation* for the University of Central Florida

Adapted from *Barbershop*, Justin Vibbert (Practice Test 3)

Fitzgerald, F.S (1920). This side of paradise. Code of rhe Young Egoist. Available on the Public Domain.

Rutsch, P. (2015). *Men and women use different scales to weigh moral dilemmas.* Retrieved from https://www.npr.org/sections/health-shots/2015/04/03/397280759/men-and-women-use-different-scales-to-weigh-moral-dilemmas

Williams, S. (2002). Free as in Freedom: Richard Stallman's Crusade for Free Software. Retrieved from https://www.oreilly.com/openbook/freedom/ch02.html

Lovette, B. (n.d.) *Is an 'insect apocalypse' happening? How would we know?* Reproduced with permission. Original work is from *The Conversation.* Retrieved from https://theconversation.com/is-an-insect-apocalypse-happening-how-would-we-know-113170

211 Math

About the Test

The GACE Mathematics Subtest is comprised of a variety of math skills over a broad range of math categories. The following guide is designed to highlight specific skills and strategies needed to maximize time and efficiency when taking the GACE mathematics subtest.

Test at a Glance	
Test Name	GACE Program Admission: Mathematics
Test Code	211
Time	90 minutes
Number of Questions	56
Format	Selected response questions – select one answer choice
	Selected response questions – select one or more answer choices
	Numeric entry questions
	On-screen calculator available
Test Delivery	Computer delivered

Content Category	Approx. Number of Questions	Approx. Percentage of Exam
I. Number and Quantity	20	36%
II. Data Interpretation and Representation, Statistics, and Probability	18	32%
III. Algebra and Geometry	18	32%

This page intentionally left blank.

Formulas Sheet

IMPORTANT: You will not have access to a formulas sheet on the exam. So please familiarize yourself with these formulas.

Area

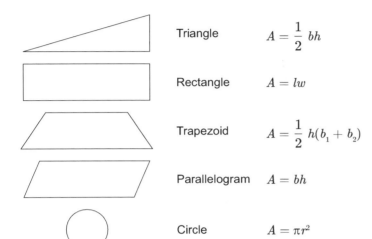

Triangle	$A = \dfrac{1}{2}\,bh$	
Rectangle	$A = lw$	
Trapezoid	$A = \dfrac{1}{2}\,h(b_1 + b_2)$	
Parallelogram	$A = bh$	
Circle	$A = \pi r^2$	

KEY	
b = base	d = diameter
h = height	r = radius
l = length	A = area
w = width	C = circumference
$S.A.$ = surface area	V = volume
	B = area of base

Use 3.14 or $\dfrac{22}{2}$ for π

Circumference
$$C = \pi d = 2\pi r$$

Surface Area

1. Surface area of a prism or pyramid equals the sum of the areas of all faces.

2. Surface area of a cylinder equals the sum of the areas of the bases and the area of its rectangular wrap.

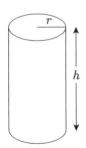

$$S.A. = 2(\pi r^2) + 2(\pi r)h$$

3. Surface area of a sphere: $S.A. = 4\pi r^2$

Volume

1. Volume of a prism or cylinder equals the Area of the Base (B) times the height (h).

$$V = Bh$$

2. Volume of a pyramid or cone equals $\dfrac{1}{3}$ times the Area of the Base (B) times the height (h).

$$V = \dfrac{1}{3}Bh$$

3. Volume of a sphere: $V = \dfrac{4}{3}\pi r^3$

Pythagorean Theorem: $a^2 + b^2 = c^2$

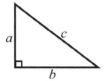

Simple interest formula: $I = prt$

I = simple interest, p = principal,

r = rate, t = time.

Distance formula: $d = rt$

d = distance, r = rate, t = time.

Given a line containing points (x_1, y_1) and (x_2, y_2)

• **Slope of line**

$$\frac{y_2 - y_1}{x_2 - x_1}$$

• **Distance between two points**

$$\sqrt{(x_2 - x_1)^2 + (y_2 - y_1)^2}$$

• **Midpoint between two points**

$$\left(\frac{x_1 + x_2}{2}, \frac{y_1 + y_2}{2} \right)$$

Conversions

1 yard = 3 feet = 36 inches

1 mile = 1,760 yards = 5,280 feet

1 acre = 43,560 square feet

1 hour = 60 minutes

1 minute = 60 seconds

1 cup = 8 fluid ounces

1 pint = 2 cups

1 quart = 2 pints

1 gallon = 4 quarts

1 pound = 16 ounces

1 ton = 2,000 pounds

1 liter = 1000 milliliters = 1000 cubic centimeters

1 meter = 100 centimeters = 1000 millimeters

1 kilometer = 1000 meters

1 gram = 1000 milligrams

1 kilogram = 1000 grams

Metric numbers with four digits are presented without a comma (e.g., 9960 kilometers).

For metric numbers greater than four digits, a space is used instead of a comma (e.g., 12 500 liters).

MATH

How to use the on screen calculator

The calculator provided is a basic 4-function calculator. A four-function calculator can only perform the operations of addition, subtraction, multiplication, and division.

Finding the square root of a number

To find the square root of a number, enter the number, then press the square root key ($\sqrt{}$).

You do NOT need to press the equal (=) key. The number that appears on the display will be the square root of the number you entered.

Practice finding the square root of a number before test day.

Example: Find the value of $\sqrt{2}$.

Press 2 then press the square root key. You should get 1.4142135...

(Because the square root of 2 is an irrational number, it continues forever without repeating, but the screen will only display the number of digits that can fit on the screen. Because calculators are all different, some display more numbers than others.)

Entering a negative number

To enter a negative number on the TI-108, you must first enter the number, then press the ± key. If you press the ± key first, the calculator will not register that you are entering a negative number. Look at the screen and check that the numbers you enter are correct when working with negative values.

Practice working with negative numbers before test day.

Example: Find the value of $-1- (-3)$.

- Press 1, then press ±
- Press the minus key
- Press 3, then press ±
- Press the = key to get a result of 2.

This page intentionally left blank.

I – Numbers and Quantity

A. Solve problems involving integers, decimals, and fractions

B. Solve problems involving ratios and proportions

C. Solve problems involving percent

D. Solve problems involving constant rates (e.g., miles per hour, gallons per mile, cubic feet per minute)

E. Demonstrate an understanding of place value, naming of decimal numbers, and ordering of numbers

F. Demonstrate an understanding of the properties of whole numbers (e.g., factors, multiples, even and odd numbers, prime numbers, divisibility)

G. Identify counterexamples to statements using basic arithmetic

H. Solve real-life problems by identifying relevant numbers, information, or operations (including rounding)

I. Solve problems involving units, including unit conversion and measurements

D. Solve problems involving integers, decimals, and fractions

Number sense goes beyond the surface of understanding how to count and perform basic mathematical operations. A strong background in number sense ensures that you can quickly perform operations, especially when using mental math, and compare numbers in a variety of scenarios. This includes being able to write a number in more than one way, being able to compare numbers written in a variety of forms, and being able to perform operations on numbers by converting between different forms.

On the GACE Mathematics Test, you will need to be familiar with converting numbers from the following forms to a decimal:

- Fraction

- Mixed number

- Square root

- With a positive exponent

- With a negative exponent

- Absolute value

- Scientific notation with a positive exponent on the power of 10.

- Scientific notation with a negative exponent on the power of 10.

All numbers can be written in decimal form, and decimal numbers are the easiest to compare, so we suggest **converting fractions to decimals when possible**. When doing so, it is important to include the first three digits after the decimal point. Often, when comparing numbers, the first digit or the first two digits of numbers written as a decimal are the same, and it is the third decimal number, the number in the thousandths place, that identifies a number as larger or smaller than another number.

Test Tip

You will have to convert different forms of numbers to decimals on the exam. Make sure you know how to convert all types of numbers to decimals.

Number Type	How to Convert	Example
Decimal 0.03	Because the number is already a decimal, add zeros at the end to bring the number out three decimal places.	$0.03 = 0.03\underline{0}$
Fraction $\dfrac{3}{4}$	Divide the numerator (top number) by the denominator (bottom number). Add additional zeros at the end or round if needed.	$\dfrac{3}{4} = 3 \div 4 = 0.75$ $0.75 = 0.75\underline{0}$
Mixed Number $4\dfrac{2}{3}$	Convert the fraction to a decimal by dividing the numerator (top number) by the denominator (bottom number). Add additional zeros at the end or round if needed.	$\dfrac{2}{3} = 2 \div 3 = 0.66666...$ $4\dfrac{2}{3} = 4.66666...$ $4.66666... = 4.66\mathbf{7}$
Square Root $\sqrt{24}$	To find the square root, use your calculator. First, type in the number. Next, press the square root key. Add additional zeros at the end or round if needed.	$\sqrt{24} = 4.89897...$ $4.89897... = 4.89\mathbf{9}$
Positive Exponent 2^3	Rewrite the expression as a product and solve. The exponent tells how many times the base is multiplied by itself. Add additional zeros at the end or round if needed.	$2^3 = 2 \cdot 2 \cdot 2 = 8$ $8 = 8.\underline{\mathbf{000}}$
Negative Exponent 3^{-2}	A negative exponent refers to a small number, not a negative number. Rewrite the expression as a fraction with one as the numerator (top number) and the expression with a positive exponent as the denominator (bottom number). Next, rewrite the expression as a product and simplify; then change the fraction to a decimal. Add additional zeros at the end or round if needed.	$3^{-2} = \dfrac{1}{3^2} = \dfrac{1}{3 \cdot 3} = \dfrac{1}{9}$ $\dfrac{1}{9} = 0.111... = 0.11\mathbf{1}$
Absolute Value $|4.2|$	Absolute value represents how many units from zero a number is on the number line. Thus, the value is **always** positive. Add additional zeros at the end or round if needed.	$|4.2| = 4.2$ $|4.2| = 4.2\underline{\mathbf{00}}$

MATH

Number Type	How to Convert	Example
Scientific Notation *Positive Exponent* 3×10^2	Move the decimal point to the right the number of spaces equal to the value of the exponent. The decimal point is at the end of the number if it is not visible. Add zeros as place holders if there are missing numbers between the original digit and the decimal. Add additional zeros at the end or round if needed.	$3 \times 10^2 = 3. \times 10^2$ $\downarrow$ $3. \times 10^2 = 3\underline{00}.$ $\downarrow$ $300 = 300.\underline{000}$
Scientific Notation *Negative Exponent* 3×10^{-2}	Move the decimal point to the left the number of spaces equal to the value of the exponent. The decimal point is at the end of the number if it is not visible. Add zeros as place holders if there are missing numbers between the original digit and the decimal. Add additional zeros at the end or round if needed.	$3 \times 10^{-2} = 3. \times 10^{-2}$ $3. \times 10^{-2} = 0.03$ $0.03 = 0.03\underline{0}$

Comparing Decimal Values

To compare numbers once they are all in the same form, it is helpful to align the numbers vertically so that you can compare the digits in the first place value, then the digits in the next place value, and so on until you've reached the last decimal place. When comparing numbers, remember:

- Positive numbers get smaller the **closer** they are to 0 on the number line. For example, 0.01 is closer to 0, or smaller than 2.

- Negative numbers get smaller the **farther** they are from 0 the number line. For example, −8 is farther from 0, or smaller than −2.

Example 1. Ordering Numbers

Order the following from least to greatest.

$\dfrac{1}{3}, 3^{-2}, -\dfrac{1}{4}, 0.33$

A. $\dfrac{1}{3}, 3^{-2}, -\dfrac{1}{4}, 0.33$

B. $3^{-2}, -\dfrac{1}{4}, 0.33, \dfrac{1}{3}$

C. $-\dfrac{1}{4}, 3^{-2}, 0.33, \dfrac{1}{3}$

D. $-\dfrac{1}{4}, \dfrac{1}{3}, 3^{-2}, 0.33$

Test Tip

When ordering numbers, use the process of elimination first to narrow down your answer choices. If the question is asking for least to greatest, you can eliminate non-negative numbers in the first position. If it is asking from greatest to least, you can eliminate negative numbers in the first position.

Correct answer: C

Before changing the numbers all to decimals, look at the answer choices to see if you can narrow down the options. Because we are ordering least to greatest, the negative number must be in the first position. Therefore, we can eliminate any answer choice that does not have the negative value listed as the first number. After eliminating choices A and B, notice that we only need to know if $\frac{1}{3}$ or 3^{-2} is the next smallest number based on answer choices C and D. Converting each to a decimal, we have:

$$\frac{1}{3} = 1 \div 3 = 0.333 \text{ (rounded)}$$

$$3^{-2} = \frac{1}{3^2} = \frac{1}{9} = 1 \div 9 = 0.111 \text{ (rounded)}$$

The 3^{-2} is smaller, so C is the correct answer choice.

Example 2. Comparing numbers

Which of the following symbols should be placed between the numbers to form a true statement?

$$-\frac{2}{7} \underline{\hspace{2cm}} -\frac{3}{11}$$

   A. $=$

   B. $<$

   C. $>$

   D. $\geq$

   E. $\leq$

Correct answer: B

Change each of the values to decimals to compare.

$$-\frac{2}{7} = -2 \div 7 \approx -0.286$$

$$-\frac{3}{11} = -3 \div 11 \approx -0.273$$

Remember that the larger the negative number, the smaller it is, so the correct answer choice would be B.

Test Tip

Memorize the decimal value of fractions commonly used on standardized math assessments. Commonly used fractions include:

$$\frac{1}{2} = 0.5 \qquad \frac{1}{4} = 0.25 \qquad \frac{1}{9} = 0.1\bar{1}$$

$$\frac{1}{3} = 0.3\bar{3} \qquad \frac{3}{4} = 0.75$$

$$\frac{2}{3} = 0.6\bar{6} \qquad \frac{1}{5} = 0.2$$

Quick Tip

A wavy equal sign means approximately equal to or that the final answer has been rounded.

E. Solve problems involving ratios and proportions

A **ratio** is a comparison of two numbers using a fraction, a colon, or the word *to*. **Rates** are ratios with different units. Rates are often expressed as unit rates and are read using the word *per* instead of *to*. It is common to reference a unit rate in everyday language.

Rates and Ratios	
Verbal statement	Four dogs for every three cats
Manipulatives/picture	
Fraction	$\dfrac{4}{3}$
Colon	4 dogs : 3 cats OR 4:3

A **unit rate** is a rate with a denominator of 1. Examples of unit rates include 60 miles per hour $\left(\dfrac{60 \text{ miles}}{1 \text{ hour}}\right)$, $3 per box $\left(\dfrac{\$3}{1 \text{ box}}\right)$, or 22 students per teacher $\left(\dfrac{22 \text{ students}}{1 \text{ teacher}}\right)$. Any rate can be converted to a unit rate by dividing the numerator of the fraction by the denominator.

When two ratios are equivalent, they can be set equal to one another to form a proportion.

Test items that contain proportional relationships may involve any of the following:

- A scale

- Equivalency statements

- Descriptions of similar figures

- Geometric shapes

- Real-world scenarios

All questions with proportional relationships are set up and solved the same way; it is up to the problem solver to recognize when a question requires a proportion. For some exam questions, two proportions may be needed in order to find the solution. In this case, there will be two ratios given in the problem. The following example highlights the "clues" in the problem that indicate a proportional relationship when it is not explicitly stated.

Quick Tip

Ratio: $\dfrac{2 \text{ feet}}{3 \text{ feet}}$ same units

Rate: 25 mph

Proportion: $\dfrac{3 \text{ inches}}{14 \text{ miles}} = \dfrac{x \text{ inches}}{84.5 \text{ miles}}$

Test Tip

Use the ***matchy-matchy*** strategy when setting up proportions. This means making sure the units in each numerator are the same, and the units in each denominator are the same.

Proportions: Given a scale

A scale is typically given using a colon and questions include a map or a model. The units may or may not be part of the scale, but they will be given in the problem or in an accompanying picture.

Example 1. Given a scale

A model of a new parking garage being built downtown has a height of 12.5 inches. If the scale of the model to the actual building is 2:15 and represents inches to feet, how tall is the actual parking garage?

    A. 1.67

    B. 24.0

    C. 93.75

    D. 187.5

    E. 200.5

Correct answer: C

Set up the first part of the proportion using the scale.

$$\frac{2 \text{ inches}}{15 \text{ feet}}$$

Quick Tip

How do you identify using a proportion?

✓ Contains a scale (2:15).

✓ Each of the numbers contains units.

✓ There are 3 numbers with units, and the problem asks for a 4th number with units.

Next, finish setting up the proportion by using what we call ***matchy-matchy***. The second fraction will contain an unknown variable and the remaining number in the problem. Match the units in the first fraction with the units in the second fraction; if inches are in the numerator in the first fraction, inches must also be in the numerator for the second fraction.

$$\frac{2 \text{ inches}}{15 \text{ feet}} = \frac{12.5 \text{ inches}}{x \text{ feet}}$$

Last, cross multiply and solve the equation to find the value of the variable.

$$\frac{2 \text{ inches}}{15 \text{ feet}} = \frac{12.5 \text{ inches}}{x \text{ feet}}$$

$2x = 12.5(15)$ Note: Once you cross-multiply, the fraction has been eliminated.

$2x = 187.5$

$$\frac{2x}{2} = \frac{187.5}{2}$$

$x = 93.75$

Proportions: Given an equivalency statement

An equivalency statement is a constant rate using words, such as a number of envelopes stuffed every 20 minutes or a number of chaperones for every 15 students. Proportions using equivalency statements will have 3 numbers, and you will be asked to find the 4th number.

Example 2. Given an equivalency statement

A pie crust making machine can press 15 pie crusts into pie tins in 20 minutes. How many pie crusts can be pressed into pie tins in 4 hours?

   A. 30

   B. 53

   C. 179

   D. 180

   E. 200

Correct answer: D

Set up the first part of the proportion using the equivalency statement.

$$\frac{15 \text{ crusts}}{20 \text{ minutes}}$$

> **Quick Tip**
>
> How do you identify using a proportion?
>
> ✓ Contains an equivalency statement that represents a constant rate
>
> ✓ Each of the numbers contains units
>
> ✓ There are 3 numbers with units, and the problem asks for a 4th number with units.

Next, finish setting up the proportion, remembering **matchy-matchy**. Be careful because the time for the second fraction is in hours. Convert hours to minutes so that the units are the same.

4 hours = 4 · 60 minutes = 240 minutes

$$\frac{15 \text{ crusts}}{20 \text{ minutes}} = \frac{x \text{ crusts}}{240 \text{ minutes}}$$

Last, cross-multiply and solve the equation to find the value of the variable.

$$20x = 240(15)$$

$$20x = 3,600$$

$$\frac{20x}{20} = \frac{3,600}{20}$$

$$x = 180 \text{ pie crusts}$$

Proportions: Given a description of similar figures

Some word problems describe a situation that is proportional without explicitly giving this information. In this case, the situation may represent similar figures. The side lengths of similar figures are proportional, which is why the problem does not have to state anything about proportionality. If all the units are alike, this may indicate similar figures.

Example 3. Given a description of similar figures

The height of a tree can be found using similar triangles. A 12-foot tall tree casts a 7-foot shadow. If a nearby tree casts a 5-foot shadow, how tall is the tree?

   A. $2\frac{11}{12}$

   B. $8\frac{4}{7}$

   C. $9\frac{3}{7}$

   D. $11\frac{2}{3}$

   E. $16\frac{4}{5}$

Correct answer: B

Draw a picture and label the lengths.

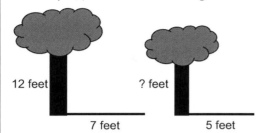

12 feet ? feet

7 feet 5 feet

Next, use the picture to set up the proportion. Notice that the labels on the picture are already in the right place for a proportion.

$\dfrac{12}{7} = \dfrac{x}{5}$ Note: The units are not included

here because they are all the same.

Last, cross-multiply and solve the proportion for the variable.

$7x = 12(5)$

$7x = 60$

$\dfrac{7x}{7} = \dfrac{60}{7}$

$x = 8\dfrac{4}{7}$ feet

Quick Tip

How do you identify using a proportion?

✓ Contains similar figures that can be drawn

✓ Each of the numbers contains units

✓ There are 3 numbers with units, and the problem asks for a 4th number with units.

Proportions: Given geometric shapes

Questions that contain a proportional relationship may also ask for the missing side of a figure or shape. In this instance, the shapes should be the same shape but a different size. If the relationship is proportional, the question will always state that the figures are similar.

Example 4. Given geometric shapes

The rectangles below are similar. What is the length of the missing side, x? Round to the nearest tenth.

5 cm 8 cm 5 cm x cm

A. 3.1 cm

B. 3.2 cm

C. 4.0 cm

D. 4.3 cm

E. 4.5 cm

Quick Tip

When figures are similar, always set up a proportion to find the missing side.

Correct answer: A

Be careful when setting up the proportion for this question because the second rectangle is rotated so that the shorter side is the length. When setting these up, think about matchy-matchy. If the first fraction in the proportion is set up as the shorter side over the longer side, make sure it is the same in the second fraction.

$$\frac{5}{8} = \frac{x}{5}$$

$$8x = 5(5)$$

$$8x = 25$$

$$\frac{8x}{8} = \frac{25}{8}$$

$$x = 3.125$$

Remember to round to the nearest tenth.

$$x = 3.1 \text{ cm}$$

Proportions: Given a real-world scenario

Most problems involving proportions are real-world scenarios, but some are more obvious than others. All examples in this section so far, with the exception of the geometric figures, have been real-world scenarios. Often, real-world scenarios that don't follow the patterns above contain a percent. The following example is a problem that is solved using a proportion.

Example 5. Given a real-world scenario

In a recent survey of 200 students at a university, 56% of the students responded that they wear earbuds when walking to class. If there are 14,800 students at the university, predict how many students of the total population wear earbuds while walking to class.

    A. 26,428

    B. 8,288

    C. 5,625

    D. 925

    E. 828

Correct answer: B

There are two ways to solve this problem. The first way is by finding 56% of the total population by multiplying 0.56 by 14,800.

The second way to solve this problem is using a proportion. The trick is to realize that you first need to find out how many students of the 200 students surveyed wear earbuds or find 56% of 200 students. To find the percent of a number, change the percent to a decimal and multiply the decimal by the number.

56% of 200

0.56 × 200 = 112

Next, use the information 112 students wear earbuds out of 200 total students for the first fraction in the proportion, and use a variable over 14,800 total students for the second fraction of the proportion. After the proportion is set up, cross-multiply to solve for the variable.

$$\frac{112 \text{ students}}{200 \text{ students}} = \frac{x \text{ students}}{14,800 \text{ students}}$$

$$200x = 112(14,800)$$

$$200x = 1,657,600$$

$$\frac{200x}{200} = \frac{1,657,600}{200}$$

$$x = 8,288 \text{ students}$$

MATH

Additional Example Problems: YOU TRY

57. Four students each set up the following problem as shown in the box below.

    5 insulated cups weigh 16 ounces. How much do 8 insulated cups weigh?

    $$\frac{5}{16} = \frac{x}{13} \qquad \frac{5}{8} = \frac{x}{16} \qquad \frac{5}{8} = \frac{16}{x} \qquad \frac{5}{13} = \frac{16}{x}$$

    Student A $\qquad$ Student B $\qquad$ Student C $\qquad$ Student D

    Which student set the problem up correctly?

    A. Student A

    B. Student B

    C. Student C

    D. Student D

    Correct answer: C

    There are two different ways a proportion can be set up to represent the question.

    $$\frac{5 \text{ cups}}{16 \text{ ounces}} = \frac{8 \text{ cups}}{x \text{ ounces}} \quad \text{or} \quad \frac{5 \text{ cups}}{8 \text{ cups}} = \frac{16 \text{ ounces}}{x \text{ ounces}}$$

    Either way is correct; after cross-multiplying, the proportions will result in the same equation. Student C used the second proportion, so C is the correct answer choice.

58. Sam has a job assembling motorcycles. On average, it takes him 36 hours of labor to assemble 2 motorcycles. How many days will it take him to assemble 15 motorcycles?

    A. 10

    B. 11

    C. 12

    D. 13

    E. 14

    Correct answer: C

    First set up a proportion.

    $$\frac{2 \text{ motorcycles}}{36 \text{ hours}} = \frac{15 \text{ motorcycles}}{x \text{ days}}$$

    Because the units are not the same in the denominator of the fractions, we need to convert hours to days.

    36 hours ÷ 24 hours = 1.5 days

    $$\frac{2 \text{ motorcycles}}{1.5 \text{ days}} = \frac{15 \text{ motorcycles}}{x \text{ days}}$$

    Cross-multiply and solve for x.

    $2x = 1.5(15)$

    $2x = 22.5$

    $x = 11.25$

    The correct answer choice is C, 12 days. Be careful. While you may be tempted to round down to 11 days, remember, 11.25 goes into the next day. He does NOT assemble 15 motorcycles in 11 days. He needs another day to finish. Therefore, the answer is 12 days.

59. A 22-foot tall flagpole casts a shadow that is 30 feet long. A sign next to the flagpole casts a shadow that is 8 feet long. How tall is the sign? Round to the nearest tenth of a foot.

A. 4.3 feet

B. 5.0 feet

C. 5.9 feet

D. 6.2 feet

Correct answer: C

To solve this problem, it may be helpful to draw a picture. Because the real-world objects create similar triangles, we can set up a proportion and solve for the missing height of the sign.

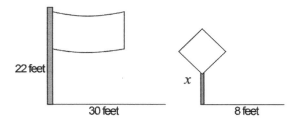

$$\frac{22}{30} = \frac{x}{8}$$

Cross-multiply and solve.

$30x = 22(8)$

$30x = 176$

$x = 5.86$ feet, rounded to the nearest tenth, $x = 5.9$ feet.

F. Solve problems involving percent

Realistic problems involving operations with real numbers often include fractions, decimals, and percents. The following are examples of problems with real numbers that may be on the GACE Mathematics subtest exam:

- Percent of increase/decrease

- What percent

- Percent of a number

- What fraction

- Sales tax, tip, commission

Percent of Increase/Decrease

Questions that require finding the percent of increase or decrease will either ask for percent of increase/decrease or the percent of change. To find the percent of change, first find the fraction that represents the change:

$$\frac{\text{new number} - \text{original number}}{\text{original number}}.$$

Quick Tip

The negative sign is not included in the answer of a percent decrease. It is instead denoted with the word, decrease.

Next, convert the fraction to a decimal and then to a percent. If the percent is positive, the change was an increase. If the percent is negative, the change is a decrease.

Example question

Last month the local gas station sold 18,590 gallons of gas. This month, the same gas station sold 20,230 gallons of gas. Find the percent of change to the nearest tenth and identify it as an increase or decrease.

    A. 8.1% increase

    B. 8.1% decrease

    C. 8.5% increase

    D. 8.8% increase

    E. 8.8% decrease

Correct answer: D

$$\frac{20{,}230 - 18{,}590}{18{,}590} = \frac{1640}{18{,}590} = 0.0882 = 8.8\% \text{ increase}$$

The result is an increase because the original number 18,590 increased to 20,230.

What Percent

When a question asks what percent a situation represents, this requires finding the fraction associated with the problem, converting the fraction to a decimal, and then converting the decimal to a percent.

Example question

At a local baseball tournament of 1,500 players, 476 of the players did not record a strikeout at the plate. What percent of the players, to the nearest whole percent, did record a strikeout during the tournament?

    A. 68%

    B. 69%

    C. 32%

    D. 46%

    E. 54%

Correct answer: A

First find the number of those striking out: $1500 - 476 = 1{,}024$

Next, write this number as a fraction out of the total number of players: $\frac{1024}{1500}$

Convert to a decimal and then a percent: $\frac{1024}{1500} = 0.6827 \approx 68\%$.

The correct answer choice is A, 68%.

Percent of a Number

When a problem is asking for the percent of a number, convert the percent to a decimal by moving the decimal point two places to the left, and then multiply this decimal by the number given. Percent of a number questions are often embedded in data questions, requiring you to extract information from a table or graph (often a pie chart) to solve the problem.

A pizza restaurant gets an average of 250 orders on a weekend night. Of those orders 24% are for pickup, and the rest are for delivery. How many orders, to the nearest whole number, does the restaurant get for delivery on a weekend night?

A. 60

B. 100

C. 180

D. 185

E. 190

Correct answer: E

If 24% of the orders are for pickup, therefore, 76% are for delivery (100% − 24% = 76%). To find 76% of 250, multiply the two values.

$0.76 \times 250 = 190$

The correct answer choice is E, orders are for delivery.

What Fraction

A question sometimes may want to know what fraction, usually in simplest form, represents a situation. Determine the two numbers for the fraction and reduce. If you are unable to reduce, change your answer and all the answer choices to decimals.

Example question

A married couple each make $40,000 per year salary. Any additional income they earn is from investments. At the end of the year, their gross earnings were $85,000. What fraction of their income was from investments?

A. $\dfrac{1}{16}$

B. $\dfrac{1}{17}$

C. $\dfrac{1}{2}$

D. $\dfrac{8}{17}$

E. $\dfrac{16}{17}$

Correct answer: B

Together the couple grossed $80,000. From investments they earned $85,000 − $80,000 = $5,000.

The fraction of investments for their total income is $\dfrac{5,000}{85,000}$. Reducing the fraction, $\dfrac{5,000}{85,000} = \dfrac{5}{85} = \dfrac{1}{17}$.

The correct answer choice is B, $\dfrac{1}{17}$.

MATH

Sales Tax, Tips, Commission

Sales tax, tips, and commission are all the same as finding the percent of a number. Often an additional step is required in these instances, for example, once the tip is found, the question may ask for the total amount paid.

Example question

Charlie makes $20 per hour plus 8% commission on all his sales. This week he worked 30 hours and sold $11,000 worth of product. How much did he gross this week?

    A. $9,400

    B. $5,440

    C. $1,480

    D. $880

    E. $600

Correct answer: C

To solve, determine how much Charlie made hourly, then find the amount of commission he earned. Last, add these two values together.

$20 × 30 = $600 hourly wage for the week; 11,000 × 0.08 = $880 commission

Total for the week: $600 + $880 = $1,480; The correct answer is answer choice C.

G. Solve problems involving constant rates (e.g., miles per hour, gallons per mile, cubic feet per minute)

Proportions: Given a Constant Rate

Recall that a rate is a ratio that includes units, such as a number of envelopes stuffed every 20 minutes or the number of chaperones needed for every 15 students. A constant rate is a rate that does not change. For example, the car gets 32 miles per gallon of fuel, is a statement with a constant rate. Because rates in real world examples are often constant, or do not change, expect to see them throughout the exam.

Additional Examples

A factory produces 10 pillows every 45 minutes. If the factory produces pillows 8 hours each day, how many pillows will it produce in a 5-day work week?

    A. 36

    B. 45

    C. 106

    D. 533

    E. 888

Correct answer: D

The final answer asks for the number of pillows over 5 days. Be sure to convert 8 hours to 480 min.

Quick Tip

How do you identify using a proportion?

✓ Contains an equivalency statement that represents a rate

✓ Each of the numbers contains units

✓ There are three numbers with units, and the problem asks for a fourth number with units.

$$\frac{10}{45} = \frac{x}{480}$$

$$45x = 4{,}800$$

$$x \approx 106.67$$

Don't forget, we have to multiply by 5 because it is a 5 day work week.

$$106.67 \times 5 \approx 533$$

Because the company cannot make a fraction of a pillow, 533, answer choice D, is the correct solution.

Example

In a pet shop, for every 3 cats there are 5 dogs. How many dogs are there if there are 12 cats total in the pet shop?

Solution:

$$\frac{3 \text{ cats}}{5 \text{ dogs}} = \frac{12 \text{ cats}}{x \text{ dogs}}$$

$$\frac{3}{5} = \frac{12}{x}$$

$$(3)(x) = (5)(12)$$

$$\frac{3x}{3} = \frac{60}{3}$$

$$x = 20$$

There are 20 dogs in the pet shop.

Example

On a farm, the ratio of pigs to cows is 1:3. If there are 100 animals on the farm, how many are pigs? How many are cows?

Solution:

First, notice the phrase "ratio of pigs to cows is 1:3." This means the pigs correspond with 1, and the cows correspond with 3. The pigs and the cows represent the subgroups. Therefore, for every 1 pig on the farm, there are 3 cows. If there are 2 pigs, then there are 6 cows, if there are 3 pigs, then there are 9 cows, and so on.

Next, let's look at the total. Since the ratio is the rule, the fewest number of animals on the farm is 4. For every 1 pig there are 3 cows which means $1 + 3 = 4$. This forms the third subgroup in the problem, which is total animals.

For this problem, there are three subgroups: pigs, cows, and total animals. Let's solve for pigs first, using the subgroups pigs and total animals.

$$\frac{\text{pigs}}{\text{total animals}} = \frac{1}{4}$$

The fraction $\frac{1}{4}$ represents a ratio we can use to solve for pigs. Next, set up the proportion using the total number of animals, 100.

$$\frac{\text{pigs}}{\text{total animals}} \quad \frac{1}{4} = \frac{x}{100}$$

MATH

$(1)(100) = (4)(x)$

$100 = 4x$

$\dfrac{100}{4} = \dfrac{4x}{4}$

$x = 25$

This means that on a 100-animal farm where the ratio of pigs to cows is 1:3, 25 of the animals are pigs.

To solve for cows, repeat the same procedure.

$\dfrac{\text{matchy}}{\text{matchy}} = \dfrac{\text{cows}}{\text{total animals}} \qquad \dfrac{3}{4} = \dfrac{x}{100}$

$(3)(100) = (4)(x)$

$300 = 4x$

$\dfrac{300}{4} = \dfrac{4x}{4}$

$x = 75$

This means that on a farm where the ratio of pigs to cows is 1:3 and there are 100 animals, 75 of them are cows. (You can also subtract 25 from 100 to get the number of cows.)

Ratios are not limited to two comparisons. In the event that there are multiple comparisons in a ratio, such as 1:2:5, treat this type of ratio just as above. Let's take the farm animal example and add another animal.

Example question

On a farm, the ratio of pigs to cows to chickens is 1:3:6. If there are 100 animals on the farm, how many are pigs? How many are cows? How many are chickens?

Solution:

The extra number represents the subgroup for chickens and changes the number of animals in each subgroup and also changes the total of the ratio from 4 to 10 ($1 + 3 + 6 = 10$).

pigs	cows	chickens
$\dfrac{\text{pigs}}{\text{animals}}$	$\dfrac{\text{cows}}{\text{animals}}$	$\dfrac{\text{chickens}}{\text{animals}}$
$\dfrac{1}{10} = \dfrac{x}{100}$	$\dfrac{3}{10} = \dfrac{x}{100}$	$\dfrac{6}{10} = \dfrac{x}{100}$
$(1)(100) = (10)(x)$	$(3)(100) = (10)(x)$	$(6)(100) = (10)(x)$
$100 = 10x$	$300 = 10x$	$600 = 10x$
$\dfrac{100}{10} = \dfrac{10x}{10}$	$\dfrac{300}{10} = \dfrac{10x}{10}$	$\dfrac{600}{10} = \dfrac{10x}{10}$
$x = 10$	$x = 30$	$x = 60$

This means that on a 100-animal farm where the ratio of pigs to cows to chickens is 1:3:6, 10 animals are pigs, 30 animals are cows, and 60 animals are chickens.

H. Demonstrate an understanding of place value, naming of decimal numbers, and ordering of numbers

The value of a certain digit is determined by the place it resides in a number. In our number system, each place has a value of ten times the place to its right. Take the following number as an example:

2,487,905.631

This number should read as two million, four hundred eighty-seven thousand, nine hundred five, and six hundred thirty-one thousandths.

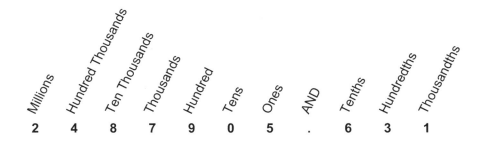

It is important to know how to manipulate a number using the base 10 system. Moving the decimal point to the left (to create a smaller number), is the same as dividing by increments of 10 or multiplying by fractional increments of $\frac{1}{10}$. Conversely, moving the decimal point to the right (to create a larger number) is the same as multiplying by increments of 10. Increments of 10 include 10, 100, 1,000, 10,000…etc.

Examples

2,487,905.631 ÷ 10 =

248,790.5631

The decimal point moves one space to the left, reducing the original number.

2,487,905.631 × 100 =

248,790,563.1

The decimal point moves two spaces to the right, increasing the original number.

When comparing and ordering numbers in a variety of forms, convert all numbers to decimals. Take all decimal numbers out three places (to the thousandths place). Add zeros at the end of any decimal numbers that only extend to one or two decimal places (tenths or hundredths). The table that follows includes numbers in a variety of forms and explains how to convert them to decimals if ordering or comparing them.

Number	Conversion	Decimal Representation
$\sqrt{25}$	A square root means you are looking for a number when multiplied by itself is 25. For 25, the square root is ± 5 because $5 \times 5 = 25$ and $(-5) \times (-5) = 25$. When solving an equation, you will need both answers, but when the question asks for the square root of 25, you will only need the positive answer.	5
$\lvert -0.575 \rvert$	The absolute value of a number is how far away from zero on the number line the number in the absolute value bars is. Because this is referring to distance, the number will always be positive.	0.575
$\dfrac{3}{8}$	To convert a fraction to a decimal, divide from the top down. $$\frac{3}{8} = 3 \div 8 = 0.375.$$	0.375
$\dfrac{1}{9}$	Ninths are good to memorize in order to save time. Any fraction with 9 in the denominator is the number in the numerator repeating. $$\frac{1}{9} = 1 \div 9 = 0.1111...$$	$0.11\overline{1}$
$\dfrac{3}{4}$	To save time, memorize your quarters. You should be able to see $\dfrac{3}{4}$ and think 0.75 quickly. Standardized tests often use a variation of fourths and ninths throughout test questions. $$\frac{3}{4} = 3 \div 4 = 0.75.$$ When ordering or comparing numbers, it is good practice to add zeros at the end of a decimal like this to bring it out 3 places.	0.750
2.01	Already in decimal form, 2.01 may only need zeros at the end if comparing or ordering.	2.010
4.5%	Percents are numbers out of 100. Thus, to change a percent to a decimal, we are dividing by 100, which moves the decimal point 2 places to the left. $$4.5\% = 04.5 = 0.045$$	0.045

I. Demonstrate an understanding of the properties of whole numbers (e.g., factors, multiples, even and odd numbers, prime numbers, divisibility)

Numbers are classified into various groups based on their properties. Numbers used on the GACE Mathematics subtest exam are all part of the Real Number System. Numbers in the Real Number System are classified further into the groups shown in the table below.

Classification of Numbers	
Real Number System	
Counting Numbers	$1, 2, 3, 4, 5, 6, \ldots$
Whole Numbers	$0, 1, 2, 3, 4, 5, 6, \ldots$
Integers	$-5, -4, -3, -2, -1, 0, 1, 2, 3, 4, 5, \ldots$
Rational Numbers	Any number that can be written as a ratio or a fraction $\frac{a}{b}$, where a and b are any integer. Rational numbers include all terminating and repeating decimals. Example: $0.2, 4\frac{1}{2}, 7, \frac{1}{3}$
Irrational Numbers	Any number that cannot be written as a fraction. Ex: $\pi, \sqrt{3}$
Additional Classifications	
Prime	A positive integer that only has 1 and itself as factors. Example: $2, 3, 13, 29$ *Note: 1 is neither prime nor composite*
Composite	A positive integer that has factors other than 1 and itself. Example: $4, 12, 27, 44$
Even	A number that is divisible by 2
Odd	A number that is not divisible by 2

Terms used to classify real numbers may be sprinkled throughout the test. Know what type of number each of these terms represent in the event the term is used in a problem. For example, a question may ask to find the probability of a spinner landing on an even integer. In order to determine the solution, it is likely that test takers need to know the definitions of both even and integer.

Prime Factorization

Prime factorization refers to finding all the prime numbers multiplied together that result in a composite number. For example, the prime factorization of 24 is $2 \cdot 2 \cdot 2 \cdot 3$ or $2^3 \cdot 3$. A common method for finding the prime factorization of a number is using factor trees. Using a factor tree to find the prime factorization of 24 is shown below.

 ← Any two positive integers other than 1 and 24 that multiply to 24.

← Repeat the process for each of the above factors until all the ends of the branches contain a prime number.

Knowing the prime factorization of common numbers will make simplifying or solving problems requiring factors easier.

Numbers to know the prime factorization of include:

- $4 = 2 \cdot 2$
- $9 = 3 \cdot 3$
- $25 = 5 \cdot 5$
- $49 = 7 \cdot 7$
- $81 = 3 \cdot 3 \cdot 3 \cdot 3$
- $100 = 2 \cdot 2 \cdot 5 \cdot 5$
- $121 = 11 \cdot 11$
- $125 = 5 \cdot 5 \cdot 5$
- $169 = 13 \cdot 13$

While this list is not all inclusive, it does represent the numbers most often used in math problems where prime factorization is part of the solution process.

Example

Which of the following is the prime factorization of 28 × 42?

A. $2^4 \times 3^2 \times 7^2$

B. $2^3 \times 3^2 \times 7^2$

C. $2^3 \times 3 \times 7^3$

D. $2^3 \times 3^2 \times 7$

E. $2^3 \times 3 \times 7^2$

Correct answer: E

To find the prime factorization of numbers being multiplied, find the prime factorization of each individual number, then combine factors.

$28 = 2 \times 2 \times 7$

$42 = 2 \times 3 \times 7$

Prime factorization of $28 \times 42 = 2 \times 2 \times 2 \times 3 \times 7 \times 7 = 2^3 \times 3 \times 7^2$, which is answer choice E.

Least Common Multiple and Greatest Common Factor

For the GACE Mathematics Subtest exam, you will most likely be required to apply knowledge of least common multiple (LCM) and greatest common factor (GCF), not necessarily finding these values as a final answer. Knowing both divisibility rules and times tables through 12 is useful when finding both the LCM and the GCF.

Word problems that include these concepts include ideas such as 12 people per ride or every 50th person through the door winning a prize.

Using the least common multiple also allows fraction denominators to be as small as possible. This is useful when calculating, because it is always easier to compute with smaller numbers, and it also helps with being able to understand the relative size of fractions. Visualizing $\frac{3}{4}$ is easier than visualizing $\frac{24}{32}$, even though they are the same value. Being able to visualize or have an understanding of the size of the fraction helps to determine if the solution makes sense.

Knowing how to find the greatest common factor allows for reducing a fraction to simplest terms. Because answers will most likely be in simplest form, being able to simplify a fraction is a useful skill. The greatest common factor will be the largest number that divides into both the numerator and denominator of a fraction. While identifying the GCF when reducing fractions saves time, there is nothing wrong with taking an extra step or two when reducing. Converting the answer and all the answer choices to decimals is an acceptable strategy as well; this method will just take a little longer.

Divisibility Rules		
A Number is Divisible by…	**If…**	**Examples**
2	The last digit is an even number (ends in 0, 2, 4, 6, 8)	248 — ends in 8
		12,550 — ends in 0
3	The sum of the digits is divisible by 3	18 — $1 + 8 = 9$; 9 is divisible by 3
		312 — $3 + 1 + 2 = 6$; 6 is divisible by 3
4	The last two digits are divisible by 4	416 — 16 is divisible by 4
		1,912 — 12 is divisible by 4
5	The last digit is 0 or 5	435 — ends in 5
		2,220 — ends in 0
6	The sum of the digits is divisible by 2 and 3	204 — ends in even number and $2 + 0 + 4 = 6$; 6 is divisible by 3
		66 — ends in even number and $6 + 6 = 12$; 12 is divisible by 3
8	The last three digits are divisible by 8	1,088 — 088 is divisible by 8
		5,800 — 800 is divisible by 8

Divisibility Rules

9	The sum of the digits is divisible by 9	5,445	$5 + 4 + 4 + 5 = 18$; 18 is divisible by 9
		81	$8 + 1 = 9$; 9 is divisible by 9
10	The last digit is 0	400	ends in 0
		8,720	ends in 0

Example question

Select all of the following that are true about 12,033.

I. The number is divisible by 2.

II. The number is divisible by 3.

III. The number is divisible by 6.

IV. The number is divisible by 9.

    A. II only

    B. I and II

    C. II and IV

    D. II, III, and IV

    E. I, II, and III

Correct answer: C

12,033 does not end in an even number, so I does not work. The sum of the digits is 9, so II works. Option III is not possible because I does not work. The sum of the digits is 9, so IV also works. Therefore, the correct answer choice is C.

J. Identify counterexamples to statements using basic arithmetic

A **counterexample** is an example that proves that the original statement is incorrect. Only one counterexample is needed to prove a statement is wrong, although there may be more than one. These types of problems are testing your knowledge of number sense rather than if you understand the concept of a counterexample.

Examples of the types of statements that may ask for a counterexample may look similar to the following:

- The quotient of a decimal number divided by a decimal number will always be a decimal number.

- The sum of two odd numbers is also odd.

- The product of two fractions is always a number less than 1.

- The difference of two numbers is always smaller than the greatest number in the problem.

Because the skill is finding a counterexample using arithmetic, the statement will involve an operation between numbers.

Which of the following answer choices is a counterexample to the statement, *"Whenever you divide two numbers, the result is always less than both of the numbers?"*

A. 2 and 3

B. 4 and 5

C. −1 and 8

D. 10 and 3

E. −2 and −5

Correct answer: E

For this problem, dividing the numbers given in options A through D either way produces a smaller number than either of the numbers listed. For option E, a negative divided by a negative is a positive, so the solution will be greater than either of the numbers in the answer choice.

K. Solve real-life problems by identifying relevant numbers, information, or operations (including rounding)

Real-life problems often require the application of multiple skills, especially in the number and quantity content category because the category can include so many different concepts. Be prepared to apply the following skills when solving these types of problems:

- Identifying relevant information from a table

- Identifying relevant information from a graph or diagram, including line graphs, scatter plots, bar graphs, timelines, and circle graphs

- Converting between units

- Combining data to find a value needed as part of solving a problem.

This list gives you an idea of the skills needed to gather the necessary information to solve a problem. Questions on the exam may even ask what information is missing in order to solve the problem.

Example question

What additional information is needed in the scenario below to be able to answer the question?

Joanie drove at a constant rate for 6 hours to get to her mother's house. What was Joanie's rate of speed?

A. In what city Joanie's mother lives

B. What time Joanie left home

C. How many gallons of gas were in Joanie's car

D. How many miles Joanie drove

E. How many other cars were on the road

Correct answer: D

In order to determine Joanie's rate of speed, or miles per hour, the number of miles she drove are needed since the scenario already includes the amount of time it took her.

L. Solve problems involving units, including unit conversion and measurements

In addition to using formulas to solve problems, some problems may require you to convert between measurements. Questions may be structured as a math conversion problem or as a real-world problem. You will not be given a formula sheet for this exam. Therefore, you will need to remember basic standard conversions like the ones below.

Standard (U.S.) conversions

When converting measurements within the U.S. system, expect multiple conversions within the same problem. For example, you may be expected to convert from gallons to pints. Don't worry that there is no conversion from gallons to pints on the formula sheet. Instead, convert from gallons to what is given (quarts in this case), and then from quarts to pints. Exam items usually require multiple steps, so take your time, and start with what you can do and work from there.

1 yard = 3 feet = 36 inches	1 pint = 2 cups
1 mile = 1,760 yards = 5,280 feet	1 quart = 2 pints
1 acre = 43,560 square feet	1 gallon = 4 quarts
1 hour = 60 minutes 1 minute = 60 seconds	1 pound = 16 ounces
1 cup = 8 fluid ounces	1 ton = 2,000 pounds

1 liter = 1000 milliliters = 1000 cubic centimeters

1 meter = 100 centimeters = 1000 millimeters

1 kilometer = 1000 meters

1 gram = 1000 milligrams

1 kilogram = 1000 grams

Metric conversions

The metric conversions on the math subtest will most likely be part of a question that requires multiple steps to solve. For example, a proportion question may give one unit in centimeters and another in millimeters, which would require you to convert them to the same unit before solving the proportion.

Example 1. Single metric conversion

4.5 g = _____ kg

    A. 0.045

    B. 0.0045

    C. 45

    D. 450

Correct answer: B

This problem can be solved one of two ways. The easiest way is to move the decimal point. If you know that grams and kilograms are three place values apart, move the decimal point three places to the left.

If you do not have a good understanding of moving among different measures in the metric system, use a proportion to find the value needed.

$$\frac{1 \text{ kilogram}}{1000 \text{ grams}} = \frac{x \text{ kilograms}}{4.5 \text{ grams}}$$

Cross-multiply and solve for the variable.

$1000x = 4.5(1)$

$1000x = 4.5$

$\dfrac{1000x}{1000} = \dfrac{4.5}{1000}$

$x = 0.0045$

Example 2. Double metric conversion

4 km = _____ mm

    A. 4,000,000

    B. 40,000

    C. 400

    D. 40

Correct answer: A

The conversion is going from a larger unit to a smaller unit. Therefore, the decimal point moves to the right. Kilometers and millimeters are 6 place units apart, so the decimal point moves 6 places to the right. If you would rather solve using proportions, you will need to solve two different proportions.

$$\dfrac{4 \text{ kilometers}}{1} \times \dfrac{1000 \text{ meters}}{1 \text{ kilometer}} \times \dfrac{1000 \text{ millimeters}}{1 \text{ meter}}$$

Next, cancel out the terms kilometer and meter. Notice that the remaining term is millimeters, which is what the question specifies.

$$\dfrac{4 \text{ \cancel{kilometers}}}{1} \times \dfrac{1000 \text{ \cancel{meters}}}{1 \text{ \cancel{kilometer}}} \times \dfrac{1000 \text{ millimeters}}{1 \text{ \cancel{meter}}}$$

Finally, multiply the values.

$4 \times 1000 \times 1000 = 4,000,000$

M. Evaluate expressions involving order of operations

The acronym, PEMDAS, Please Excuse My Dear Aunt Sally, is often used to remember the order of operations.

Please, or parentheses, includes all grouping symbols, which may include brackets [ ], braces { }, and absolute value bars | |. If there is math that can be computed inside grouping symbols, do that FIRST, then the grouping symbols may be removed.

Excuse, or exponents, means anything raised to a power should be simplified after there are no more parentheses.

My **D**ear, or multiplication and division, are essentially the same "type" of operation and are therefore done in order from left to right, just as you would read a book. All multiplication and division should be completed BEFORE any addition or subtraction that is not inside parentheses.

Aunt **S**ally, or addition and subtraction, are also essentially the same "type" of operation and are also done in order from left to right. These operations should always come last, unless they were inside parentheses.

On the exam, you will be expected to perform the order of operations. When solving these types of problems, pay close attention to negative signs and the order in which you are solving.

IMPORTANT: Working with negative numbers.

$(-1)^2 = -1 \cdot -1 = 1$

$(-1)^3 = -1 \cdot -1 \cdot -1 = -1$

$-(-1)^2 = -(-1 \cdot -1) = -(1) = -1$

$-(-1)^3 = -(-1 \cdot -1 \cdot -1) = -(-1) = 1$

P	**Parentheses**
E	**Exponents**
M D	**Multiplication & Division**
A S	**Addition & Subtraction**

Example 1. Order of Operations

Simplify:

$(16 - 4) \div (5 - 2) \times (10 - 8)$

    A. 1

    B. 2

    C. 4

    D. 6

    E. 8

Correct Answer: D

$\underline{(16 - 4)} \div \underline{(5 - 2)} \times \underline{(10 - 8)}$ Problems in different parantheses can be solved at the same time.

$= \underline{12 \div 3} \cdot 2$ Parentheses are not necessary once all operations are completed.

$= 4 \cdot 2$

$= 8$

Caution

Remember multiplication and division are "on the same level" in order of operations, so do whichever comes first when reading from left to right.

MATH

Example 2. Order of operations with negative numbers

Simplify the expression.

$(-2)^3 - (-4) - (-1)^2$

    A. -5

    B. -3

    C. 11

    D. 13

    E. 15

Correct Answer: A

Be very careful with the minus and negative signs in this expression. When simplifying an expression like this, don't try to rush or do too many steps at one time.

$\underline{(-2)^3} - (-4) - \underline{(-1)^2}$

$= \underline{-8 - (-4)} - 1$

$= -4 - 1$

$= -5$

Example 3. Order of operations with variables

Simplify: $4(2 \times 3b + b) \div (4 \times 2b)$

    A. 3.5

    B. $3.5b$

    C. 4

    D. $2 + 2b$

    E. 2

Correct Answer: A

Variables in an order of operations problem are tricky because we tend to revert to collecting like terms instead of following order of operations when we see them. Good number sense is being able to apply order of operations even when variables exist in the expression.

$4(\underline{2 \times 3b} + b) \div (\underline{4 \times 2b})$

$= 4(\underline{6b + b}) \div 8b$

$= \underline{4(7b)} \div 8b$

$= 28b \div 8b$

$= 3.5$

This page intentionally left blank.

I – Numbers and Quantity Practice Problems

1. Choose the symbol that correctly completes the statement.

   $\dfrac{4}{5}$ _____ 7.8×10^{-1}

   A. $<$

   B. $\geq$

   C. $=$

   D. $\leq$

   E. $>$

2. Between which two integers is $-\sqrt{140}$?

   A. -141 and -140

   B. -139 and -140

   C. -11 and -12

   D. -13 and -12

   E. -13 and -14

3. Milton spends $\dfrac{12}{25}$ of his sales job driving from one location to another. What percent of his job is NOT spent driving?

   A. 48%

   B. 52%

   C. 5%

   D. 12%

   E. 75%

4. Which of the following is an equivalent expression to $12 - 6x \div 3x - 4 \cdot 2x$?

   A. $7\dfrac{4}{5}x$

   B. $12 - 6x$

   C. $10 - 8x$

   D. $\dfrac{1}{2}x$

   E. $2x - 4$

MATH

5. Of the 24,400 students graduating with a 4-year degree at a university, 6,422 will apply for entrance into a higher education degree program. To the nearest tenth of a percent, what percent of students will leave the university after receiving their 4-year degree?

   A. 25.1%

   B. 26.3%

   C. 73.7%

   D. 73.2%

   E. 75.3%

6. A hotel offers reward points based on the number of nights per booking. A booking of three or more nights receives 40 reward points, a booking of two nights receives 30 reward points, and a one-night booking receives 20 reward points. How many reward points per booking is a person averaging if they have stayed a total of 28 nights at the hotel, 12 of which were 3-night bookings, 10 of which were 2-night bookings, and the rest were 1-night bookings? Round to the nearest tenth.

   A. 15.4

   B. 28.7

   C. 32.1

   D. 60.0

   E. 72.3

7. Simplify the expression: $1 + 2(18 \div 9 \times 2) - (-3)^2$

   A. 12

   B. 3

   C. 0

   D. −4

   E. −8

8. A toy company is shipping out 16 boxes of dolls. Ten of the boxes each contain 24 dolls. The remaining boxes are split evenly between 12-20 dolls and 16-24 dolls. What is the minimum number of dolls the toy company shipped out?

   A. 192

   B. 300

   C. 324

   D. 372

   E. 385

9. Which of the following is equivalent to $-3(24 - 4^2) \div (-6 \times -2) \div (-4)$?

A. $\dfrac{1}{2}$

B. 2

C. 8

D. -8

E. -10

10. Which of the following is the smallest number?

$$-\frac{1}{3} \qquad -0.33 \qquad -\frac{3}{10} \qquad 3 \times 10^{-3} \qquad 3 \times 10^{-6}$$

A. $-\dfrac{1}{3}$

B. -0.33

C. $-\dfrac{3}{10}$

D. 3×10^{-3}

E. 3×10^{-6}

This page intentionally left blank.

Practice Problems Answer Explanations

Number	Answer	Explanation
1.	E	Convert each number to a decimal. $\dfrac{4}{5} = 0.80$ and $7.810^{-1} = 0.78$. After converting, the correct answer is E, >.
2.	C	When looking at square roots, perfect squares should come to mind. $\sqrt{140}$ is close to $\sqrt{144}$, or 12. Use this knowledge to estimate: because $-\sqrt{140}$ is negative, it is between -11 and -12.
3.	B	To solve, find the fraction NOT driving by subtracting $\dfrac{12}{25}$ from 1, which is, $\dfrac{13}{25}$, convert to a decimal, and then to a percent $\dfrac{13}{25} - 13 \div 25 = 52\%$.
4.	C	To simplify, follow order of operations: $12 - 6x \div 3x - 4 \cdot 2x$ $12 - 2 - 4 \cdot 2x$ $12 - 2 - 8x$ $10 - 8x$
5.	C	Of the 24,400, if 6,422 are applying for a higher degree program then $24{,}400 - 6{,}422 = 17{,}978$ are not applying for a higher degree program. To find this number as a percent, first write it as a fraction over the total number of students, then convert to a decimal, and last convert to a percent. $\dfrac{17{,}978}{24{,}400} = 0.73680\ldots = 73.7\%$
6.	B	To solve this problem, you need to determine how many bookings there were for each of the reward levels. 12 nights of 3-night bookings is 4 bookings. 10 nights of 2-night bookings is 5 bookings. 6 nights remaining of 1-night bookings is 6 bookings. Next, multiply the number of bookings by the respective reward points. 3-night: 4 40 160 reward points 2-night: 5 30 150 reward points 1-night: 6 20 120 reward points To find the average reward points per booking, add all the rewards points together and divide by the number of stays; be careful not to divide by the number of nights – reward points are given per stay. Total number of stays: $4 + 5 + 6 = 15$ Total number of reward points: $160 + 150 + 120 = 430$ Average per booking: $430 \div 15 \approx 28.7$

MATH

Number	Answer	Explanation
7.	C	This problem looks pretty straight forward but contains three different arrangements that are commonly miscalculated. The first common miscalculation occurs with the leading $1 + 2$. Test takers often do this first because it is the first thing you see, and it is easy to do. The next common miscalculation occurs with the division before multiplication in the parentheses; people often think multiplication comes before division because of the acronym PEMDAS. The third common miscalculation occurs with the minus next to a negative with an even exponent; people tend to see the two negatives in a row and make it addition. If you made one of these errors, know you are not alone! Remember to take your time when solving. If you got the answer correct, pat yourself on the back for not falling for any of these testing pitfalls. Following order of operations, you get the following: $1 + 2(\underline{18 \div 9} \times 2) - (-3)^2$ $= 1 + 2(\underline{2 \times 2}) - (-3)^2$ $= 1 + 2(4) - (\underline{-3})^2$ $= 1 + \underline{2(4)} - 9$ $= \underline{1 + 8} - 9$ $= 9 - 9$ $= 0$
8.	C	To solve, we have to find the minimum number of dolls that are in each box. In the first 10 boxes, there is a fixed amount of 24 dolls, which is a total of 240 dolls. The remaining 6 boxes are evenly split between 12-20 dolls and 16-24 dolls, meaning 3 boxes have 12-20 dolls and 3 boxes have 16-24 dolls. The minimum number of dolls in the first 3 is 12 for a total of 36 dolls, and the minimum number of dolls in the second set of 3 is 16 for a total of 48 dolls. Therefore, the minimum number of dolls the toy company could have shipped out is $240 + 36 + 48 = 324$ dolls.
9.	A	Following order of operations, you get the following: $-3(24 - \underline{4^2}) \div (\underline{-6 \times -2}) \div (-4)$ $= -3(\underline{24 - 16}) \div 12 \div (-4)$ $= \underline{-3(8)} \div 12 \div (-4)$ $= \underline{-24 \div 12} \div (-4)$ $= -2 \div (-4)$ $= \dfrac{1}{2}$

MATH

Number	Answer	Explanation
10.	A	To solve, convert all numbers to decimals. Remember for easy comparison, write each decimal out three places. $-\dfrac{1}{3} = -0.333$ $-0.33 = -0.330$ $-\dfrac{3}{10} = -0.300$ $3 \times 10^{-3} = 0.003$ Because the number in scientific notation is not zero, it can be eliminated because negative numbers are smaller than all positive numbers. When comparing negative numbers, remember the larger negative values are smaller numbers because they are farther away from zero. Thus, $-\dfrac{1}{3}$ is the smallest number.

MATH

This page intentionally left blank.

II – Data Interpretation and Representation, Statistics, and Probability

A. Work with data and data representations to solve problems

B. Solve problems involving measures of central tendency (e.g., mean, median) and spread (e.g., range, standard deviation)

C. Use data from a random sample to draw inferences about characteristics of a population

D. Identify positive and negative linear relationships in scatterplots

E. Use a linear model for a data set to make predictions

F. Differentiate between correlation and causation

G. Compute simple probabilities, and use probabilities to solve problems

Statistics and probability questions on the GACE Mathematics Subtest exam include reading various types of graphs and diagrams, extracting and interpreting data from graphs and diagrams, and applying knowledge of number sense and algebra to arrive at a final answer. In addition, questions from this content category will include questions about simple probability and the counting theory. Expect many questions from this category to contain multiple steps.

A. Work with data and data representations to solve problems

Graphs that you should be familiar with for the GACE Mathematics Subtest include:

- Venn diagrams
- Bar graphs
- Histograms
- Stem-and-leaf plots
- Timelines
- Scatter plots
- Pictographs.

> **Test Tip**
>
> Because the exam is multiple choice, no question requires making a graph, but a question may ask for the graph that correctly displays a data set.
>
> A test question may ask for a specific statistical value, such as the range or median, from the graphical representation of a data set.

Venn Diagrams

Venn diagrams are useful for depicting the likelihood of an event occurring and for making comparisons. Data in a Venn diagram is **categorical data**, meaning that the data falls into specific categories. Venn diagrams are used to show relationships among sets, using overlapping circles to depict relationships. Any relationships that overlap are counted in the region where the circles of the diagram also overlap (Overlapping data is when data falls in more than one category).

In lower grades two categories of data is common. In upper grades, 3 or more categories are often present in Venn diagram questions, so be prepared for 3 sets of data as well as values that fall outside all the categories in the diagram. Sometimes data does not fall into the categories used to make the Venn diagram. In this case, a number is placed outside the circles, and the entire set is enclosed in a rectangle.

Data in Venn diagrams is often referred to using the terms union and intersection.

Union – represented by the symbol ∪, is all of the data in the sets put together.

Intersection – represented by the symbol ∩, is only where data sets overlap.

Data	Graph

Math only certification: 42

Science only certification: 28

Math & science certification: 8

To graph, create a circle for each category. Data that does not overlap stays outside the overlap. Data that includes both categories should be in the overlap section.

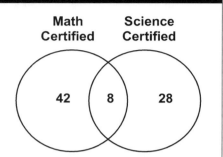

Sample question:

A survey of 100 families found that 34 of the families have a cat, 41 families have a dog, 26 families have fish, 10 have a dog and fish, 12 have a cat and fish, 8 have a dog and a cat, and 3 have all three animals. How many families surveyed have just one type of family pet – either a dog, cat, or fish?

Correct answer: D

A. 1

B. 11

C. 20

D. 32

E. 38

To solve, use the information from the word problem, draw three overlapping circles, and fill in all the categories that overlap.

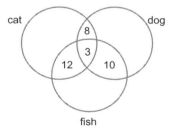

To find the number of families that have only one type of animal, subtract the families with overlaps from the totals given in the problem. See description below.

Fish: $26 - (12 + 3 + 10) = 26 - 25 = 1$

Cats: $34 - (12 + 3 + 8) = 34 - 23 = 11$

Dogs: $41 - (8 + 3 + 10) = 41 - 21 = 20$

Add these totals, and you get 32 families that have only one type of pet.

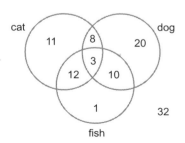

Bar Graphs

Data in a bar graph is also categorical data. A bar graph is typically used to track or compare change over time. Examples of when a bar graph might be used to display data include:

- Total electric bill for each high school in the county during the month of June

- Number of students enrolled in 7th grade advanced math over the last 6 years

- Students' grade in a course each quarter during the school year

A bar graph may be used to compare the same categorical data for more than one set of data on the same display. In the last bullet point, students' grade in a course each quarter during the school year, more than one student could be tracked on the same graph, providing both data that can be compared over time and data that compares one student to others.

	Data		Graph

	Paul	**Ruben**
Q1	$5,500	$5,200
Q2	$6,000	$6,400
Q3	$4,000	$4,000
Q4	$8,250	$8,500

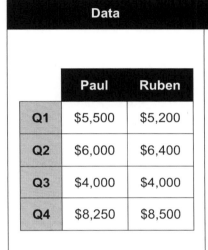

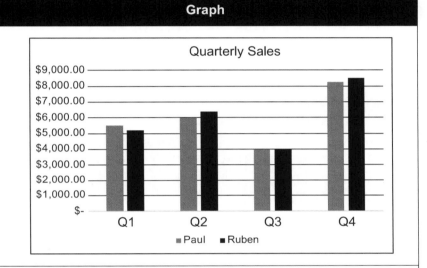

To graph, draw a bar to the height of each of the data points for Paul. Repeat for Ruben, keeping bars in the same category grouped together.

Sample question:

What is the range in Paul's quarterly sales?

- A. $500
- B. $2,750
- C. $3,750
- D. $4,250
- E. $4,550

Correct answer: D

To find the range, subtract the smallest value, $4,000, from the largest value, $8,250.

8,250 − 4,000 = 4,250

Be careful not to subtract Q1 from Q4.

MATH

Line Plots / Dot Plots

A line plot, sometimes called a dot plot, is a graph that uses numerical data and displays where all the values in a set lie in relation to one another. A line plot is often used to find the range, median, mode, and mean. The visual representation of data on a line plot allows for quick identification of the mode, range, and outliers.

Data	Graph
Number of Hours Spent Studying 1, 3, 7, 2, 2, 1, 1, 1, 3, 10, 5, 2, 7, 1, 3, 4, 7, 5, 1, 4, 3, 3, 1, 1 *To graph, place an x or dot above the number each time it appears.*	 x x x x x x x x x x x x x x x x x x x x x x x x x ← 0 1 2 3 4 5 6 7 8 9 10 →

Sample question:

The line plot shows the number of hours students spent studying over a two-week period for the exam. Find the median number of hours studied.

Correct answer: D

A. 10

B. 9

C. 5

D. 3

E. 1

The values are already in order on the graph. Cross off numbers on both ends until the middle number is reached. Be careful not to count the blank spaces.

Example question

A small business collected data on how customers are finding out about the business to determine where money for advertising should be focused. The number of contacts by method is listed in the table.

	June	July	August	September
Internet Search	42	50	78	63
Radio Advertisement	18	22	11	21
Friend Referral	10	15	25	32

Which of the following types of graphs would be best for displaying the data for comparison?

    A. Line plot

    B. Three individual bar graphs

    C. Triple bar graph

    D. Stem-and-leaf plot

    E. Frequency table

Correct answer: C

The data is categorical because the company is analyzing advertising methods. This eliminates a line plot and stem-and-leaf plot because they use numerical data. Because the data includes three methods of advertising, a triple bar graph would be best to compare the three methods.

Pictographs

A pictograph is a graph that uses pictures to represent numerical data. The visual representation of data on a pictograph allows for quick identification of the mode and distribution of the data set. A key is important for a pictograph so that the reader of the graph knows what each picture, or image, represents.

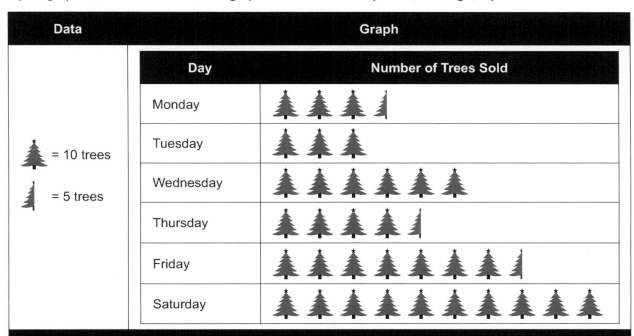

Sample question:

How many more people bought a tree on Friday than on Tuesday?

    A. 5.5

    B. 8.5

    C. 45

    D. 55

    E. 60

Correct answer: C

If each whole tree represents 10 trees sold and each half tree represents 5 trees sold, 75 trees were sold on Friday and 30 trees were sold on Tuesday. Thus, 45 more trees were sold on Friday than Tuesday.

Frequency Tables

A frequency table counts or tallies how many times a value falls within a defined range of values in a data set. Some frequency tables display the frequency of individual values while others display the frequency of a range of values occurring in a data set. An example of a range of values would be the number of students in a class scoring an A, scoring a B, scoring a C, or scoring a D on a quiz. Because an A may range from 91-100, the individual scores are unknown, but the number of scores falling within the A-range are known.

Example

SAT Math Score Range	Frequency
200-299	1
300-399	0
400-499	1
500-599	8
600-699	7
700-799	2

Histograms

Although a histogram looks similar to a bar graph, that is where their relationship ends. A histogram uses numerical data instead of categorical data and displays the frequency or distribution of data that falls within equally spaced ranges of values. In addition, the bars of a histogram touch each other.

Data	Graph
Class test grades 91, 88, 100, 82, 73, 88, 52, 76, 95, 55, 85, 65, 99 87, 90, 65, 93, 75, 92, 66, 78, 80, 68, 84, 85, 91, 98	

Grade Range	Frequency
51-60	2
61-70	4
71-80	5
81-90	8
91-100	7

Determine equally created ranges. Determine the number of data points that fall within each range. Create a bar chart, making sure that bars touch, to show the frequency within each range.

Sample question:

Which of the following can be found using only a histogram?

Correct answer: E

A. mean

B. median

C. mode

D. range

E. none of the above

A histogram does not display values, only a range of values, so a single value cannot be found from the display.

Example question

Which of the following graphs would best display the results of students' favorite elective?

A. Bar Graph

B. Histogram

C. Venn diagram

D. Table

E. Line Graph

Correct answer: A

A bar graph would best display the results because a bar graph compares data that is sorted by category, which is the favorite elective in this example. Option B would not be best because the survey was not looking for the frequency of a data range. Option C is not the best choice because the survey asked for one response (favorite elective), so there is no overlapping data. Option D is not best because the data could be written in a table, but the results of the data would not be as clear as with a bar graph.

Circle Graphs / Pie Charts

A circle graph, sometimes called a pie chart, visually shows how categories, or categorical data, is broken up into percentages. All the percentages for the categories should equal 100%.

Quick Tip

Circle graphs are used frequently in math test questions because they can test your knowledge at reading a graph, identifying missing information, and finding a percent of a number.

Data	Graph
200 female students at a college were surveyed about their favorite type of shoe. The results of the survey are listed in the table.	To make a circle graph, find the percent of that each shoe type is and draw an angle that size from the center of the circle.

Favorite Shoe Type	
sandals	32%
boots	8%
loafers	16%
sneakers	25%
slides	9%
heels	10%

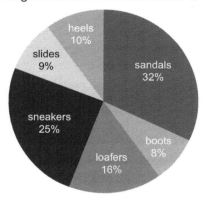

Sample question:

How many students responded that either heels or loafers were their favorite type of shoe?

Correct answer: E

A. 10

B. 16

C. 26

D. 35

E. 52

Add the two categories together, $16 + 10 = 26$. Find 26% of 200 students, $200 \cdot 0.26 = 52$ students.

In a recent survey of 120 people at a grocery store, 20% said they were there to buy snacks, 45% said they were there for their weekly shopping, 15% said they were there to buy lunch, and the remaining people were there to purchase nongrocery items. How many people surveyed are buying nongrocery items?

    A. 3

    B. 20

    C. 24

    D. 25

    E. 72

Correct answer: C

Subtract the percents given from 100 to get the percent of people shopping for nongrocery items, $100 - 45 - 15 - 20 = 20$. Next, find 20% of 120 people, $0.20 \cdot 120 = 24$

Stem-and-Leaf Plots

A stem-and-leaf plot organizes numerical data in a way that allows the reader to quickly calculate the mode and range of a data set. The mean and median can also be found from a stem-and-leaf plot, but it just may take more than a glance or quick calculation. A stem-and-leaf plot is best for data with stems that are no more than 10 numbers apart from one another. This is because the value of the stems must only increase by 1.

Data And Graph	How To Graph
Number of participants a in study group for the last 10 meetings: 20, 27, 22, 24, 28, 32, 35, 51, 22, 50 Stem Leaf 2 | 0 2 2 4 7 8 3 | 2 5 4 | 5 | 0 1 key 2 | 0 = 20	• Organize the data from least to greatest. • Create a table with two columns and label the first column stem and the second column leaf. • Each leaf can only contain a single digit. If all the numbers in a data set have two digits, the stem and leaf will both contain one digit. If the values contain three digits, like 341, then each stem will have two digits and each leaf will still only have one digit. • Identify the smallest and largest stems in the data set. In the table, list the first stem and continue listing stems, going up by increments of one until reaching the largest stem. Do NOT skip any values in the list of stems. • List each leaf with its corresponding stem, in order, with no commas or decimal points. • Include a key to show how to read each value in the table.

MATH

Find the mode of the data set from the stem-and-leaf plot.

  A. 22

  B. 10

  C. 20

  D. 28

  E. 2

Correct answer: A

The number 22 is repeated twice, which can be seen in the row starting with the stem of 2.

The following table summarizes the information that each type of graph displays.

Data Display	Purpose
Venn Diagram	Compares categories of data, including overlaps; likelihood of events
Bar Graph	Compares categories of data, sometimes over time
Pictograph	Uses visuals related to the data to compare categories
Table	Organizes a list of data
Line Graph	Best to show change over time; two categories of data, e.g., time and distance
Stem-and-Leaf Plot	Useful for organizing decimal values and larger sets of data that are somewhat close together
Histogram	Determine the range or frequency where most data falls
Frequency Table	Organize data in a table by how frequently it occurs
Circle Graph	Visual representation of proportional relationships; comparison of parts to a whole
Scatterplot	Shows the correlation between two sets of data

B. Solve problems involving measures of central tendency and spread

Measures of center, or **measures of central tendency**, include mean, median, and mode. These statistical values are referred to as measures of center because they are symbolic of the middle values in the data set. Test questions that ask for the value of the mean, median, or mode may have data sets presented in a table, in a graph, or in a list, which may be out of order.

Measures Of Center/Central Tendency	
Mean	Find the average; add all the numbers and divide by how many numbers were added. *We think of the mean as "mean" because it's mean to make you do so much work to get an answer.*
Median	Place numbers in order; find the middle number. If there are two middle numbers, add them and divide by 2. *Remember, median is in the middle, just like the median in the road.*
Mode	The number or numbers that occur the most. *Mode and most both start with MO...**MO**DE **MO**ST.*

Example question

On a quiz in Mrs. Fingal's class, 8 students scored a 70%, 12 students scored an 80%, and 4 students scored a 95%. What is the mean score for the quiz? Round to the nearest whole number.

   A. 79

   B. 82

   C. 80

   D. 85

   E. 86

Correct answer: A

To find the mean of a list that groups values in sets, it is not necessary to list out all the numbers. Instead, find the sum of each like group of values, then add the sums together and divide by the total number of values.

Partial Sums:	*Total sum:*	*Mean:*
$8 \times 70 = 560$	$560 + 960 + 380 = 1,900$	$1,900 \div 24 = 79$
$12 \times 80 = 960$		
$4 \times 95 = 380$		

Therefore, the correct answer choice is A.

Range

To find the range, arrange the numbers in the data set in order, then subtract the smallest value from the largest value.

Example question

Find the range of the data set. {6, 3, 1, 10, 12, 4, 9}

   A. 3

   B. 10

   C. 11

   D. 11.5

   E. 12

Correct answer: C

Place the values in order, {1, 3, 4, 6, 9, 10, 12}, then subtract the smallest from the largest, $12 - 1 = 11$. The correct answer is C.

Example question

Find the mode of the data: {3, 3, 5, 6, 4, 5, 6, 2, 4, 5, 1, 10}

   A. 7

   B. 5

   C. 4

   D. 3

   E. 2

Test Tip

When finding the median and mode, make sure the data is in order first.

Correct answer: B

To find the mode, first put the numbers in order, then find the number that is repeated the most.

{1, 2, 3, 3, 4, 4, 5, 5,5, 6, 6, 10}

The number repeated the most is 5, so the correct answer choice is B.

Example question

Find the median age given the table.

Age	Frequency
25	4
30	7
35	3
40	2

Test Tip

An **outlier that is much greater** than the other numbers will skew the value of the **mean** so that it **is higher**.

An **outlier that is much smaller** than the other numbers will skew the value of the **mean** so that it **is lower**.

A. 30

B. 32.5

C. 35

D. 37

E. 38

Correct answer: A

The frequency in the table refers to how many times the number repeats in the list. Age 30 appears 7 times, with 4 numbers to the left, and 5 numbers to the right. Without writing out the entire list, we can deduce that 30 is the middle number (if this is not apparent, write out the list if small enough).

Example question

The range for data set A is 8, and the range for data set B is 15. What do these range values indicate about the data sets?

A. The data sets contain similar values.

B. The data sets contain several values that are the same.

C. The values in set A are closer together than the values in set B.

D. The values in set A are all different than the values in set B.

E. No comparison can be made from the range values.

Correct answer: C

The range indicates how far apart the data is, so a smaller range indicates values that are closer together.

The graph of the data below shows the number of bagels a company buys for its employees each month.

If the outlier is removed, how does this effect the mean of the data set?

    A. The mean increases.

    B. The mean decreases.

    C. The mean stays the same.

    D. There is no longer a mean.

    E. There is no effect on the mean.

Correct answer: B

An outlier that is much higher than the rest of the data increases the mean, so removing the outlier decreases the value of the mean.

Example question

Five friends all go to a farm to pick blueberries. At the end of an hour, the number of berries picked was 78, 273, 312, 287, and 301. If the outlier is removed, which best describes the change in the data set?

    A. The mean and median both increase, with the mean having a greater increase.

    B. The mean and median both increase, with the median having a greater increase.

    C. The mean increases, and the median stays the same.

    D. The mean decreases, and the median stays the same.

    E. Nothing in the data set changes.

Correct answer: A

Both the mean and the median will increase. The mean will have a greater increase because the outlier was much lower than the other data points. The median will shift, but only slightly because the remaining data points are close together.

C. Use data from a random sample to draw inferences about characteristics of a population

Because a survey is a sampling of a population, questions may ask for a prediction to be made about the whole population based on survey results or data gathered from a sampling of people. To solve these types of problems, identify the information needed from the sampling, then use a proportion to predict for the entire population.

Example question

Of the 45,500 students who attend a university, 1,500 were surveyed about the number of credit hours of courses they take each semester. The results are in the table below.

Number of Credit Hours	Number of Students
8	180
9	300
12	600
15	420

Based on the information in the table, predict how many students at the college enroll in 15 credit hours each semester.

   A. 108

   B. 420

   C. 1,270

   D. 12,470

   E. 12,740

Correct answer: E

To predict the number of students who enroll in 15 credit hours each semester, set up a proportion and solve for x. The ratios in the proportion represent the partial number of students to total number of students.

$$\frac{420}{1,500} = \frac{x}{45,500}$$

Cross-multiply, then solve for x.

$1,500x = 420(45,500)$

$1,500x = 19,110,000$

$x = 12,740$

D. Identify positive and negative linear relationships in scatterplots

A scatter plot is a graph that contains bivariate data, or two data sets. An easy way to identify data as univariate or bivariate is if the information is graphed on a single number line or a coordinate plane, which contains two number lines (one vertical and one horizontal). Points graphed on a scatter plot create a visual representation of the correlation between the two sets of data. Data points on a scatter plot have a **positive correlation**, **negative correlation**, or **no correlation**.

A trendline is often drawn on a scatterplot to help visualize the relationship between the data and to make future predictions about the data.

Graphs

Positive correlation

A trendline with a positive slope can be drawn to model the direction of the data.

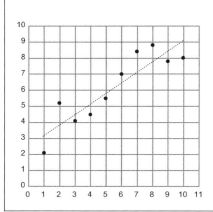

Negative correlation

A trendline with a negative slope can be drawn to model the direction of the data.

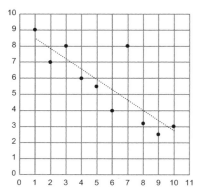

No correlation

No trendline can be drawn to model the direction of the data.

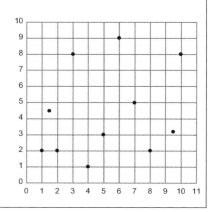

Example question

Naomi surveyed 11 teachers in her school about the number of pets and the number of televisions each of them has at home. The graph of the data is shown below. What kind of correlation between these two data sets is most likely?

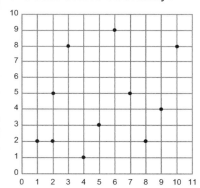

   A. Positive correlation

   B. Negative correlation

   C. No correlation

   D. Dual Correlation

   E. Not enough information

Correct answer: C

There is no correlation on the graph between the number of pets a person has and the number of televisions they have in their home.

How do you know when the data in a scatter plot has no correlation?

    A. When a trendline can be drawn to show the data is increasing

    B. When a trendline can be drawn to show the data is decreasing

    C. When two trendlines can be drawn

    D. When no trend in the data is apparent enough to say that it is increasing or decreasing

    E. When the trendline is curved

Correct answer: D

If there is no apparent overall trend of the data increasing or decreasing, there is no correlation between the data.

Example question

The scatter plot displays the relationship between a person's arm span and their height.

Based on the graph, what type of correlation exists between the two data sets?

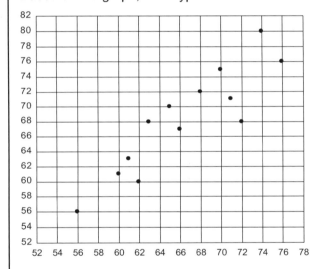

    A. High, positive correlation

    B. Weak, positive correlation

    C. Negative correlation

    D. No correlation

    E. Low, positive correlation

Correct answer: A

The data is close together and increasing, so there is a high positive correlation. If it appeared that the data was increasing but was spread out, or far from a trendline, the data would indicate a loose or weak positive correlation.

MATH

E. Use a linear model for a data set to make predictions

A linear model is the comparison of two data sets that are increasing or decreasing at a constant rate of change. Linear models are often given in a graph or as a scenario in a word problem. Real-life examples of linear models include scenarios such as:

- Total pay after working a number of hours
- Amount left after paying the same payment each month
- The number of items at one cost and the number of items at another cost
- Miles traveled after a number of hours
- Height after a number of months.

Linear models require that you understand the rate of change (slope), the x-intercept of the graph, the y-intercept of the graph, and how to predict or read the graph of the situation. Test questions may ask to identify the correct graph of a situation or to identify or interpret the x- or y-intercept or rate of change in relation to the scenario.

Example question

Once a seedling has sprouted 2 cm, Randy begins measuring its growth over several weeks and finds that the plant grows at a constant rate of 3 cm per week over 8 weeks. Which of the following graphs correctly represents this situation?

A.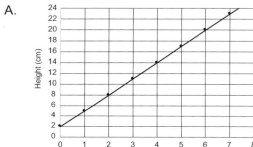

B.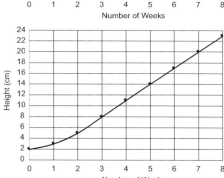

C.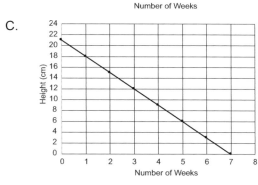

D.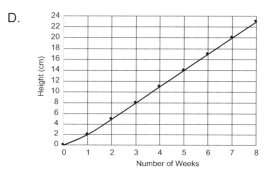

E.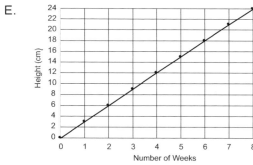

Correct answer: A

The plant height is increasing, which means the line should also be increasing from left to right, so option C can be eliminated. Randy begins measuring the plant when it is 2 cm. The height of the plant is on the x-axis, so the graph should start at 0 weeks and a height of 2 cm. This eliminates choices D and E because they both start at a height of 0 cm. Option B for week 1 has the height of the plant at 3 cm, but the plant grew 3 cm and should be at 5 cm. This leaves option A as the correct answer choice.

F. Differentiate between correlation and causation

Correlation and causation are two options of how two separate sets of data relate to one another. Questions dealing with correlation and causation are often accompanied by a scatterplot because scatterplots display two sets of data on one graph.

A **correlation** in a data set shows that there is some sort of pattern in the data such that as one set changes the other set changes as well. A correlation in the data does NOT mean that one set of data is the reason for the other set of data changing. While this may be the case, a correlation does not confirm it to be true. When reading scatterplots, be careful not to assume that because both sets of data are increasing that one was caused by the other. For example, test scores may appear to increase as the number of hours studied increases, but it may not be the cause. Although it is likely, there may be other factors that affected the test scores.

Quick Tip

Data in scatterplots show a correlation. Keep this in mind when test questions ask for a description in the data set.

A **causation** means that one set of data causes the other set of data to change. For example, if you work more hours at an hourly rate, you will earn more money. The amount you work changes the total you earn.

G. Compute simple probabilities, and use probabilities to solve problems

Probability is the likelihood that an event will occur. Regardless of the scenario, the method for finding probability is always the same. All probability must be put in its simplest form or as a percentage.

$$\text{Probability} = \frac{\text{Desired number of outcomes}}{\text{Total number of possible outcomes}}$$

When there are more than one opportunity or consecutive events, each probability is generated and then multiplied together. When there is more than one event, the probability is referred to as compound probability.

Sometimes when consecutive events occur the total number of possible outcomes changes with the occurrence of each event. An example of this would be drawing a name out of a hat and then NOT replacing the name and drawing another name. When this occurs, it is important to change the total number of possible outcomes in all the individual probabilities that occur after the first one.

Example question

What is the probability of selecting a queen from a standard deck of 52 playing cards?

Solution:

To calculate the probability of selecting a queen, recall that are 4 queens in every deck and a total of 52 cards from which you are choosing. Thus, the probability is the number of cards that have a queen on them over the total number of cards.

$$\frac{\text{number of queens}}{\text{total number of cards}} \quad \frac{4}{52} = \frac{1}{13} \text{ or } 8\%$$

MATH

Example question

What is the probability of rolling a 6 on a standard die for two consecutive rolls?

Solution:

To calculate the probability of rolling a 6 two times in a row, first determine the probability for each individual event.

$$\frac{\text{Rolling a 6}}{\text{Rolling 1, 2, 3, 4, 5, 6}} = \frac{1}{6}$$

Next, multiply each of the probabilities together for the probability of the two events together.

$$\frac{1}{6} \times \frac{1}{6} = \frac{1}{36} \text{ or } 3\%$$

Example question

The principal of a school is randomly choosing volunteers for a project. Out of a group of 5 freshman and 10 juniors, what is the probability of the principal choosing a junior in his first two picks?

Solution:

First determine the probability of selecting a junior for the principal's first pick. Because there are 10 juniors and 15 total students, the probability of the first selection is $\frac{10}{15}$.

Next, determine the probability of the second selection. After the first selection, there are only 9 juniors left and 14 total students. Thus, the probability of this event is $\frac{9}{14}$.

Last, now that the individual probabilities have been determined, multiply them to find the probability of the compound event.

$$\frac{\text{Juniors}}{\text{Freshman and Juniors}} \qquad \frac{10}{15} \times \frac{9}{14} = \frac{90}{210} = \frac{3}{7} \approx 43\%$$

Experimental probability is what happens when an experiment is performed.

Theoretical probability is what is expected to happen when the experiment occurs.

For example, when flipping a coin, we expect that it will land on heads 50% of the time. When a quarter is flipped 10 times, it may actually land heads up 6 times, or 60% of the time. What we expected, 50%, is the theoretical probability, and what actually happened, landing on heads 6 times, is the experimental probability.

When an experiment is conducted for a limited number of trials, the results can be used to predict what will happen if a much larger experiment were conducted. For example, if you flipped the coin 100,000 times, landing on heads will be close to 50%.

The same principle is true for theoretical probability. What is expected to happen in a small sampling can be used to predict what should happen in a much larger sample.

For either type of probability, proportions are used to make predictions.

Mel and Thomas spun a spinner that was divided evenly into 4 colors, blue, red, green, and yellow. Find the number of times the spinner will theoretically land on green after 80 spins.

    A. 4

    B. 12

    C. 16

    D. 20

    E. 25

Correct answer: D

To make a prediction using theoretical probability, determine the probability of the spinner landing on green. Because there is 1 green section out of 4 total sections, the probability is $\frac{1}{4}$. Next, set up and solve a proportion to predict how many times the spinner lands on green after 80 spins.

$$\frac{1}{4} = \frac{x}{80}$$

$$4x = 80$$

$$x = 20$$

Example question

After conducting the experiment in the previous problem, Mel and Thomas found the spinner landed on blue 18 times. Use this information to predict how many times the spinner will land on blue after 1,000 spins.

    A. 56

    B. 225

    C. 280

    D. 360

    E. 388

Correct answer: B

In the last problem, the spinner was spun 80 times. Set up and solve a proportion using the fact that the spinner landed on blue 18 out of 80 times.

$$\frac{18}{80} = \frac{x}{1,000}$$

$$80x = 18,000$$

$$x = 225$$

MATH

This page intentionally left blank.

II – Data Interpretation and Representation, Statistics, and Probability Practice Problems

1. The Smith's total monthly budget is $1,600. How much do they allocate to utilities and eating out?

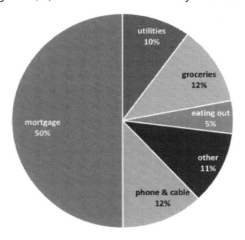

A. $120

B. $165

C. $220

D. $240

E. $300

2. Gloria is organizing her sock drawer. The table displays the colors of pairs of socks she has.

Blue	2
Red	10
Black	8
Green	6

Without looking, she selects a red pair of socks from the drawer. If she does not put the selected pair of red socks back in the drawer, what is the probability of Gloria selecting a blue pair of socks next?

A. $\dfrac{8}{13}$

B. $\dfrac{5}{13}$

C. $\dfrac{2}{25}$

D. $\dfrac{2}{26}$

E. $\dfrac{1}{26}$

3. Which trial has the lowest mean?

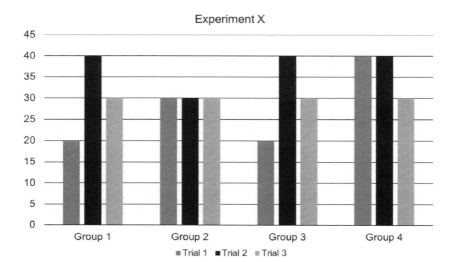

Experiment X

A. Trial 1

B. Trial 2

C. Trial 3

D. Trials 1 and 3

E. Trials 1 and 2

4. Find the mode of the following:

Stem	Leaf
94	2 3 6
95	1 2 6 7
96	2 2 2 5 8
97	3 4 4 6 6

Key 97 | 3 = 97.3

A. 94.2

B. 95.1

C. 96.2

D. 97.4

E. 97.6

5. Which of the following scenarios does the tree diagram represent?

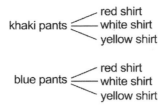

A. There are 6 different combinations of shirts and pants.

B. The probability of selecting a red shirt is $\frac{1}{2}$.

C. There are two outfits that can be made with blue pants.

D. There are 12 possible outfits because $2 \times 6 = 12$.

E. None of the above are true about the diagram.

6. The list below shows the number of different salads several local restaurants have.

$$\{6, 4, 3, 8, 7, 4, 5, 2\}$$

What is the median number of salads offered for these restaurants?

A. 4

B. 4.5

C. 5

D. 6

E. 7

7. The information below depicts the number of sales members of a sales team have for the month.

Team Member	Number of Sales
Henley	42
Callie	37
Tabatha	32
Jace	40
Bailey	82
Nida	35
Inaya	42

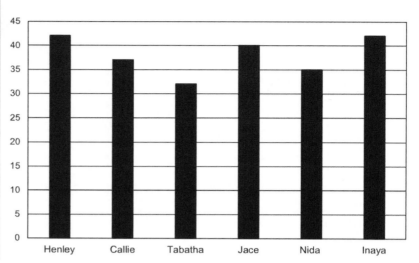

Which of the following could be misleading about the data in the graph?

A. The vertical scale should be more spread out.

B. The values should be in order.

C. Some of the data has been omitted.

D. There should be a smaller vertical scale.

E. The x and y axis should be switched.

8. The list below shows the sales price of used cars for a car lot for the first week of the month.

$24,400

$18,600

$25,500

$22,000

$21,000

$52,000

$18,600

$19,500

Which measure should the manager use to promote that their used car prices are better than other car dealers?

A. Mean

B. Median

C. Standard deviation

D. Range

E. Mode

9. The mean number of questions correct on a state teacher exam is 42, and the standard deviation is 4.2. The state has determined if a test taker is within one standard deviation, they can retake the test with a $20 discount, and if a test taker is within two standard deviations of the mean, they can retake the test with a $10 discount. If a person got 38 questions correct, which of the following is true?

   A. They will have to pay full price to retake the test.

   B. They are able to retake the test with a $20 discount.

   C. They are able to retake the test with a $10 discount.

   D. A graph is needed to determine a discount.

   E. None of the above are true.

10. In which of the following sets of data are the values for the mode and median the same?

   A. {2, 5, 9, 3, 8, 5, 5, 3}

   B. {1, 1, 3, 3, 7, 1, 2, 10}

   C. {5, 2, 1, 7, 9, 8, 9, 4}

   D. {3, 3, 3, 3, 4, 4, 4, 5}

   E. {1, 1, 4, 4, 10, 11, 12, 13}

MATH

This page intentionally left blank.

Practice Problems Answer Explanations

Number	Answer	Explanation
1.	D	Use the circle graph to identify the percents of the budget that are allotted for *utilities* and *eating out*. Add the percents for these two categories together to determine what percent of the total budget is spent on the combination of these categories. Eating out: 5% Utilities: 10% Combined percentage of budget: 15% Next, find 15% of the total budget to determine the amount spent on both. $0.15 \times 1{,}600 = \$240$
2.	C	Probability is the number of possible outcomes over the total number of outcomes. Initially, the total number of outcomes is 26. Once Gloria pulls out a pair of red socks, the number of pairs of socks in the drawer reduces to 25. With 2 blue pairs of socks in the drawer, the probability of selecting a blue pair of socks without looking is $\dfrac{2}{25}$.
3.	A	Find the data points for each trial and then find the mean of these points for each trial. Trial 1 data points: 20, 30, 20, 40 Trial 2 data points: 40, 30, 40, 40 Trial 3 data points: 30, 30, 30, 30 Finding the mean of the data points for each trial, we get the following: Mean for Trial 1 $= \dfrac{20 + 30 + 20 + 40}{4} = \dfrac{110}{4} = 27.5$ Mean for Trial 2 $= \dfrac{40 + 30 + 40 + 40}{4} = \dfrac{150}{4} = 37.5$ Mean for Trial 3 $= \dfrac{30 + 30 + 30 + 30}{4} = \dfrac{120}{4} = 30$ Trial 1 has the lowest mean. You can also eyeball it. When looking at the data, you can see that Trial 1 has the lowest numbers, so it will have the lowest mean. It is not always that easy, but when it is, grab the correct answer and move on.

Number	Answer	Explanation
4.	C	When looking for the mode in a stem and leaf plot, pay attention to the second column and find the row with the most frequent number. In this case, 2 occurs most frequently in the row beginning with 96. Therefore 96.2 happens the most frequently and is the mode. **Stem** | **Leaf** 94 | 2 3 6 95 | 1 2 6 7 96 | 2 2 2 5 8 97 | 3 4 4 6 6
5.	A	The tree diagram shows the total number of choices possible given two pairs of pants and three shirts. khaki pants — red shirt / white shirt / yellow shirt blue pants — red shirt / white shirt / yellow shirt To find the total number of choices possible, you can use a tree diagram or the fundamental counting principle, which states the total number of possible choices can be found by multiplying the number of choices in each category. The fundamental counting principle is quicker because you are simply multiplying, $2 \times 3 = 6$.
6.	B	To find the median, put the numbers in order. The median is the number in the middle once the numbers are in order. If there are two numbers in the middle, add them and divide by 2 to find the median. $\{6, 4, 3, 8, 7, 4, 5, 2\}$ $= 2, 3, 4, 4, 5, 6, 7, 8$ Both 4 and 5 are in the middle, so $(4 + 5) \div 2 = 4.5$.
7.	C	Notice that Bailey's sales are missing from the graph. Leaving out information is one way that graphs can be misleading. Answer choices A and D may help to clarify the graph, but the vertical scale is appropriate for the data, so answer choices A and D are not actually misleading. Answer choice C is also not misleading because although it may be helpful to put the data in order, it is not necessary or misleading not to do so.

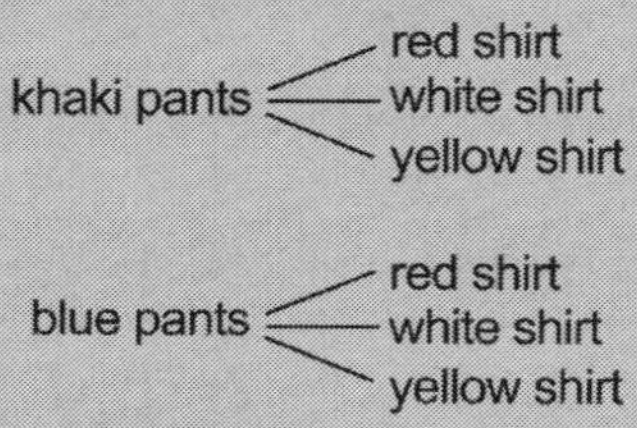

MATH

Number	Answer	Explanation
8.	E	Start by putting the car prices in order. Then find the median, mode, and range. Save the mean for last because it is the most time consuming to find. $18,600 $18,600 $19,500 $21,000 $22,000 $24,400 $25,500 $52,000 median: $(21,000 + 22\,000) \div 2 = 21,500$ mode: 18,600 range: $52,000 - 18,600 = 33,400$ The mode is the lowest value of the median, mode, and range. Without calculating the mean, we can see that it will be higher than $18,600 because this is the smallest sales price in the list. Therefore, the manager should use the mode to promote their used car prices.
9.	B	Find the range of values 1 standard deviation from the mean and 2 standard deviations from the mean by adding and subtracting the standard deviation value to/from the mean. 1 standard deviation: $42 + 4.2 = 46.2$ $42 - 4.2 = 37.8$ Range for 1 standard deviation: 37.8 to 46.2 2 standard deviations: $42 + 4.2 + 4.2 = 50.4$ $42 - 4.2 - 4.2 = 33.6$ Range for 2 standard deviations: 33.6 to 50.4 A score of 38 falls within the range for 1 standard deviation from the mean, so the test taker is able to retake the test with a $20 discount.
10.	A	Put each set in order to easily find the mode and median. A: {2, 3, 3, 5, 5, 5, 8, 9} mode: 5, median: 5 Because answer choice A has a mode and median that are equivalent, we do not need to do with any other answer choices because answer choice A is the correct answer.

MATH

This page intentionally left blank.

III – Algebra and Geometry

Algebra and geometry concepts are integrated throughout the math portion of the exam. For questions falling under this competency, you are expected to be able to write linear equations and inequalities from word problems, graphs, and tables. You should also be able to solve linear equations and simple quadratic equations. Geometry questions include concepts about angle pairs, angles formed by parallel and intersecting lines, properties of two-dimensional figures, and formulas for perimeter, area, and volume. Questions in this competency will be both math problems and word problems that include the application of multiple skills.

A. Algebra

1. Demonstrate an understanding of the properties (commutative, associative, and distributive) of the basic operations (addition, subtraction, multiplication, and division) without needing to know the names of the properties

2. Demonstrate the ability to follow an arithmetic or algebraic procedure (e.g., using a step-by-step procedure, using a simple flowchart, applying a simple recurrence sequence) by carrying it out or analyzing it

3. Use properties of operations to identify or generate equivalent algebraic expressions (e.g., multiplication of whole numbers gives the same result as repeated addition, multiplication by 0.1 gives the same result as division by 10)

4. Write an equation or expression that models a real-life or mathematical problem

5. Solve word problems, including problems involving linear relationships and problems that can be represented by Venn diagrams

6. Solve linear equations in one variable algebraically

7. Solve simple quadratic equations (e.g., $x^2 = 49$)

Seeing Structure in Expressions

Understanding how problems are structured helps when having to deconstruct a problem to answer a question. Math is versatile in that there are multiple ways to solve a problem. Knowing various properties that create structure will save time and increase the amount of correctly solved problems on the exam.

1. **Demonstrate an understanding of the properties of the basic operations without needing to know the names of the properties**

Several properties exist that allow for simplifying algebraic expressions and equations. Knowing the names of the properties is not required; you only need to know how to apply the properties and identify mistakes made when solving based on these properties. The properties of operations are described in the following table.

Property of Operations	Rule	Description
Commutative Property of Addition	$a + b = b + a$	Changing the order of two numbers being added does not change the sum.
Commutative Property of Multiplication	$a \cdot b = b \cdot a$	Changing the order of two numbers being multiplied does not change the product.
Associative Property of Addition	$(a + b) + c = a + (b + c)$	Changing the grouping of the addends does not change the sum.
Associative Property of Multiplication	$a \cdot (b \cdot c) = (a \cdot b) \cdot c$	Changing the grouping of the factors does not change the product.
Additive Identity Property of 0	$a + 0 = 0 + a = a$	Adding 0 to a number does not change the value of that number.
Multiplicative Identity Property of 1	$a \cdot 1 = 1 \cdot a = a$	Multiplying a number by 1 does not change the value of that number.
Inverse Property of Addition	For every a, there exists a number $-a$ such that $a + (-a) = (-a) + a = 0$	Adding a number and its opposite results in a sum equal to 0.
Inverse Property of Multiplication	For every a, there exists a number $\dfrac{1}{a}$ such that $a \cdot \dfrac{1}{a} = \dfrac{1}{a} \cdot a = \dfrac{a}{a} = 1$	Multiplying a number and its multiplicative inverse results in a product equal to 1.
Distributive Property of Multiplication over Addition	$a \cdot (b + c) = a \cdot b + a \cdot c$	Multiplying a sum is the same as multiplying each addend by that number, then adding their products.
Distributive Property of Multiplication over Subtraction	$a \cdot (b - c) = a \cdot b - a \cdot c$	Multiplying a difference is the same as multiplying the minuend and subtrahend by that number, then subtracting their products.

2. Demonstrate the ability to follow an arithmetic or algebraic procedure by carrying it out or analyzing it

Questions that fall in this category require an understanding of verbal/written steps for solving a problem. Because the steps are typically all written out, knowing how to work backwards from a solution is the key to being able to correctly answer these types of questions.

Example question

Kelvin told his friends that he is thinking of a perfect square, x. He states that following the steps below will help find the number.

- Double the sum of the number and 2.
- Subtract 6.
- Divide by 2.
- Add 4.

The result should be 28. What is the perfect square that Kelvin is thinking?

    A. 5

    B. 6

    C. 25

    D. 36

    E. 49

Correct answer: C

There are a couple of ways to find the number. Working backwards from 28 is the easiest way to arrive at the original number. To work backwards, perform the inverse operation on the final number for each step, starting from the bottom.

- Starting with 28,
- Subtract 4 to get 24.
- Multiply 24 by 2 to get 48.
- Add 6 to 48 to get 54.
- Divide 54 by 2 to undo the doubling to get 27.
- Subtract 2 from 27 to get the original number, 25.

Therefore, the correct answer is C, 25. Be careful not to take the square root of 25 because the problem mentions perfect square. The perfect square is 25, and its square root is 5.

MATH

3. Use properties of operations to identify or generate equivalent algebraic expressions

Applying properties of operations to expressions to generate other equivalent expressions and recognizing when two expressions are equivalent are foundational skills in mathematics. When generating equivalent expressions, the commutative, associative, and distributive properties are often used for operations. On the GACE Mathematics Subtest, be prepared to recognize equivalent expressions through the use of these properties.

Example question

Which property should be used first to rewrite the expression so that like terms can be combined? $3(x + 7) - 8x + 1$

    A. Associative Property of Multiplication

    B. Commutative Property of Multiplication

    C. Distributive Property

    D. Inverse Property of Addition

    E. Additive Identity Property

Correct answer: C

For this example, you need to distribute the 3 to both terms inside the parentheses in order to add the terms with like variables (the x terms) and the constants (numbers without a variable).

$3(x + 7) - 8x + 1$

$= 3x + 21 - 8x + 1$

$= 3x - 8x + 21 + 1$

$= -5x + 22$

BONUS: Can you identify the property that was used in the third line? If you said Commutative Property of Addition, you're right!

Example question

Which of the following is an equivalent expression to $(2x - 8 - 4x) - (3x + 2 - 5x)$?

    A. -10

    B. $-6x - 6$

    C. $-10x - 10$

    D. $14x - 10$

    E. $-10x - 6$

Correct answer: A

To simplify this expression, first "distribute" the minus sign to each of the terms in the second set of parentheses.

$(2x - 8 - 4x) - (3x + 2 - 5x)$

$= 2x - 8 - 4x - 3x - 2 + 5x$

Next, rearrange the expression, using the commutative property, to make it easy to combine like terms.

$2x - 8 - 4x - 3x - 2 + 5x$

$= 2x + 5x - 4x - 3x - 8 - 2$

Last, combine like terms to get -10. Therefore, the correct answer choice is A.

Example question

Which of the following is an equivalent expression, $3 - (5y + 9 - 8y) - 2(-2 - 3y) - 7$?

   A. $3y + 10$

   B. $9y - 9$

   C. $-16y + 7$

   D. $-3y - 2$

   E. $-16y$

Correct answer: B

Distribute, paying attention to negative signs, then rearrange to collect like terms, and last, simplify.

$3 - (5y + 9 - 8y) - 2(-2 - 3y) - 7$

$= 3 - 5y - 9 + 8y + 4 + 6y - 7$

$= -5y + 8y + 6y + 3 + 4 - 9 - 7$

$= 9y - 9$

The correct answer choice is B.

Note that for this answer choice, the 9 can be factored out creating another equivalent expression. This may happen on the exam, so don't get worried if you do not see your answer. It may be there but just in a different form.

$9y - 9 = 9(y - 1)$

4. Write an equation or expression that models a real-life or mathematical problem

Although there is an endless number of examples that represent questions requiring an expression or equation, a general pattern exists when writing them. Be prepared to write algebraic equations, inequalities, and expressions from a table, a description, and a word problem.

Writing Linear Equations Given Key Features

One of the more advanced skills on the GACE Mathematics Subtest is being able to identify, write, and manipulate linear equations in various forms. The following table lists the forms of a linear equation you'll need to know and what each form reveals about the graph of the equation.

Form of Equation	Equation	What the Equation Reveals
Slope-intercept form	$y = mx + b$	slope (m) and y-intercept (b)
Standard form	$Ax + By = C$	x-intercept ($Ax = C$) and y-intercept ($By = C$)
Point-slope form	$y - y_1 = m(x - x_1)$	slope (m) and a point on the graph (x_1, y_1)

Knowing the formal name for the form of the equation is not necessary, but you should be able to recognize what the equation reveals and also know how to get from one form to another to reveal a key feature or determine if an answer written in another form is correct.

Slope-Intercept Form

Equations in slope-intercept form always start with $y =$. The slope of the line (which identifies the **constant rate or rate of change** in a real-life scenario) is always the number with x. Be careful not to think that it is the first number because sometimes equations are switched around so that the term is second instead of first after the equal sign.

Example (Quick Check)

Identify the slope, m, and the y-intercept, b, for each of the equations below.

a) $y = -3x$

b) $y = 2 + 5x$

c) $y = x + \dfrac{1}{2}$

Solution:

a) $m = -3$, $b = 0$

b) $m = 5$, $b = 2$

c) $m = 1$, $b = \dfrac{1}{2}$

Point-Slope Form $y - y_1 = m(x - x^1)$

Equations in point-slope form will contain both a point and a slope. Most likely, this form will not appear very often on the test because it is used most often for writing equations from a graph when the y-intercept is not visible. If a question on the test is in this form, you may have to identify the slope or point, or you may have to rewrite the equation in another form.

The point-slope form of an equation is the formula for slope rearranged.

Slope: $m = \dfrac{y_2 - y_1}{x_2 - x_1}$

Point-slope form: $y - y_1 = m(x - x_1)$

Example question

Identify a point on the line and the slope for the equation, $y - 4 = -(x + 2)$.

Solution:

Point on the line: $(-2, 4)$; Slope: -1.

Standard Form $Ax + By = C$

Writing an equation in standard form is most likely to occur with word problems. More often than not, equations you write from word problems will be in slope-intercept form, but there is a chance they may be in standard form as well. You may also have to identify the x- or y-intercept of an equation in standard form. The x-intercept is the point where the line of the equation crosses the x-axis. The y-intercept is the point where the line of the equation crosses the y-axis.

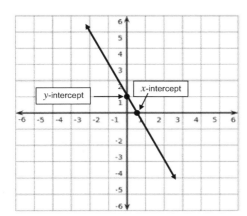

To find the x-intercept in standard form, remove the y term from the equation and solve for x. To find the y-intercept, remove the x term from the equation and solve for y. (This works because the terms we are removing have a value of 0 when they are part of an intercept.)

Example question

Find the x-intercept and the y-intercept for the equation of the line $5x + y = 10$.

Solution:

x-intercept: $5x = 10$, so $x = 2$; y-intercept: $y = 10$

Example question

What is the equation of a line with a slope of $\dfrac{2}{5}$ and a y-intercept of (0, 3)?

    A. $2x - 5y = -15$

    B. $2x - 5y = -3$

    C. $2x + 5y = 3$

    D. $5x + 2y = -3$

    E. $2x + 5y = 15$

Correct answer: A

When given the y-intercept and the slope, substitute into slope-intercept form, $y = mx + b$, to get the equation of the line. Doing so, we get $y = \dfrac{2}{5} + 3$. Looking at the answer choices, they are all in standard form, $Ax + By = C$, which requires converting $y = \dfrac{2}{5} + 3$ to standard form as well. Equations in standard form do not contain fractions, and usually the x-term is positive.

To convert,

    1. Get x and y terms on the same side of the equal sign.

    2. Multiply each term in the equation by the denominator of the fraction to eliminate the fraction.

    3. Multiply all terms by a –1 so the x term is positive.

$$y = \frac{2}{5}x + 3$$

$$-\frac{2}{5}x + y = 3$$

— Step 1

$$5\left(-\frac{2}{5}x + y = 3\right)$$

$$-\frac{10}{5}x + 5y = 15$$

— Step 2

$$-2x + 5y = 15$$

$$-1(-2x + 5y = 15)$$

— Step 3

$$2x - 5y = -15$$

The correct answer choice is A.

Example question

Which of the following equations could the slope of a line be found just upon inspection?

I. $y - 8 = 4(x + 6)$

II. $y = -\frac{2}{3}x$

III. $2x + 4y = 10$

A. I only

B. I and II

C. II and III

D. I and III

E. I, II, and III

Correct answer: B

Option I is in point-slope form, and 4 is the slope. Option II is in slope-intercept form, and $-\frac{2}{3}$ is the slope. Option III is in standard form, so some manipulation would need to occur before being able to identify the slope. Therefore, the correct answer choice is B.

Equation of a Line from a Word Problem

Equations you'll write from a word problem will either be in slope intercept form, $y = mx + b$, or standard form, $Ax + By = C$. The following examples are how these problems might be represented on the exam.

Slope-intercept form (y = mx + b) in a Word Problem

If the question gives one value that changes and one value that never changes, the equation will be in slope-intercept form. In this scenario, a total value is unknown and is represented by y. The value that changes based on another value is the slope, and the value that does not change is the y-intercept.

Example question

> As a car salesman, Henry earns \$300 each week plus a 3% commission on each car he sells. Write an equation to determine his salary for one week, S, if he sells c number of cars.
>
> **Solution:**
>
> Amount that does not change: \$300
>
> Amount that changes: 3% commission per car, $0.03c$
>
> Because his salary, S, is dependent on the number of cars he sells, c, S is the dependent variable, or is substituted for y, and c is the independent variable, substituted for x.
>
> Therefore, the equation is $S = 0.03c + 300$.
>
> Written in slope-intercept form, the equation is $y = 0.03x + 300$.

Example question

> Carlos has already read 72 pages in his required summer reading. He plans to read 20 pages a day until he has finished reading the book. Write an equation that represents the total number of pages, p, Carlos has read after any number of days.
>
> **Solution:**
>
> Amount that does not change: 72. Therefore, $72 = b$
>
> Amount that changes: total number of additional pages read at 20 pages per day, $20 = m$
>
> Equation: $p = 20d + 72$
>
> Written in slope-intercept form, the equation is $y = 20x + 72$.

Test Tip

It is not important that you know the math vocabulary associated with different forms of linear equations, such as slope-intercept form or standard form.

What you need to know is how to write equations when situations presented lend themselves to each form.

Standard Form (Ax + By = C) in a Word Problem

Usually equations for word problems will be in slope-intercept form, but sometimes a question will give two values that are unknown and a total value that is known. In this case, the equation will be in standard form with the first unknown as Ax and the second unknown as By. The total that is given will be substituted for C.

Example question

> Sarah sells two types of bracelets. One costs her \$4 to make and the other costs her \$5 to make. Write an equation that could be used to find how many of each bracelet she can make with \$50.
>
> **Solution:**
>
> Amount 1 that varies: \$4 bracelet, $Ax = 4x$
>
> Amount 2 that varies: \$5 bracelet, $By = 5y$
>
> Total amount: \$50, $C = 50$
>
> Equation: $4x + 5y = 50$

Preston wants to spend $30 on music downloads from two different websites. Site A charges $0.50 per song, and site B charges $1 per song. Write an equation to represent how many songs he can download.

Solution:

Amount 1 that varies: $0.50, $Ax = 0.50x$

Amount 2 that varies: $1, By = 1y = y$

Total amount: $30, C = 30$

Equation: $0.50x + y = 30$

Quick Tip

When an equation is in standard form, it does not matter which constant replaces A and which constant replaces B.

Equation of a Line from a Table

Use slope-intercept form, $y = mx + b$, to write an equation of a line from a table. When writing an equation of a line from a table, two different scenarios may occur, one where the y-intercept is part of the table, and one where it is not. In both cases, find the slope of the line, then determine the y-intercept based on the information given.

To find the equation of a line when the y-intercept is included:

Write the equation of a line for the table below.

x	y
−1	3
0	1
3	−5
8	−15

Slope:

To find the slope from a table, use any two points, stack them vertically, and subtract. This is a shortcut.

$(-1, 3)$
$- (\ 0, 1)$
_____
$\quad -1\ \ 2$

Last, use the two differences to write the slope, $\dfrac{\text{change in } y}{\text{change in } x} = \dfrac{2}{-1}$. Be careful to write the y value for the numerator of the fraction.

Before finding the y-intercept, look to see if one of the x values is 0. If so, its y value is the y-intercept, and no further solving is required.

From the table above, the y-intercept is part of the table and is 1.

The equation of the line for this table is

$y = \dfrac{2}{-1}\, x + 1$, or simplified, $y = -2x + 1$.

Quick Tip

For this type of problem, the proper way to solve is to use $\dfrac{y^2 - y^1}{x^2 - x^1}$. However, we like to use short cuts. Your math teacher may cringe at this method, but all you have to do is take two points, stack them, and subtract them. See the example to the left.

Caution

The y-intercept and the y coordinate are two different things. The y-intercept is represented as b in the slope intercept form equation $y = mx + b$. The y coordinate as in (x, y) is represented as y in $y = mx + b$.

To find the equation of a line when the y-intercept is NOT included:

Write an equation of the line for the table.

x	y
−3	−6
3	−2
6	0
18	8

First find the slope:

$$
\begin{array}{r}
(-3, \quad 6) \\
- (\quad 6, \quad 0) \\
\hline
-9 \quad -6
\end{array}
$$

Slope: $\dfrac{-6}{-9} = \dfrac{2}{3}$

Next, choose a point, and substitute the x and the y point and the slope into $y = mx + b$.

x	y
−3	−6
3	−2
6	0
18	8

Quick Tip

Note: Answer choices may be in standard form. You still need to find the equation of the line in slope-intercept form, then convert the equation you wrote into standard form.

Point: (3, −2)

Slope: $\dfrac{2}{3}$ (from above)

$y = mx + b$

$-2 = \dfrac{2}{3}(3) + b$

Solve the equation for b.

$-2 = \dfrac{2}{3}(3) + b$

$-2 = 2 + b$

$-4 = b$

Once b is found, substitute b and m, the slope, back into $y = mx + b$.

$y = \dfrac{2}{3}x - 4$

MATH

Which of the following is an equation of the line represented by the table?

x	y
−1	−3
0	−1
1	1
2	3
3	5

Quick Tip

When finding the y-intercept, or b, look to see if there is a zero anywhere in the table for x. If so, the y-intercept, or b, is the number in the y column for the same row where x is 0. You can only do this shortcut if there is a zero in one of the x columns.

A. $y = -2x - 1$

B. $y = x - 1$

C. $y = -2x - 3$

D. $y = 2x - 1$

E. $y = \dfrac{1}{2}x - 1$

Correct answer: D

We got lucky in this problem because we can easily find the y-intercept or b. Because there is a 0 for x in the table (second row), we can immediately determine that the y intercept or $b = -1$.

To find the slope, choose two points from the table, and find the difference of the y-coordinates and the difference of the x-coordinates. We like to take two points and stack them to subtract. Doing so avoids subtracting mistakes.

$$\begin{array}{r} (3, 5) \\ - \ (2, 3) \\ \hline 1 \ \ 2 \end{array}$$

Because slope is $\dfrac{\text{change in } y}{\text{change in } x}$ the slope for the equation of the line represented by the table is $\dfrac{2}{1}$.

Therefore, we have: $m = \dfrac{2}{1}$ and $b = -1$. Substituting into $y = mx + b$ we get,

$y = \dfrac{2}{1}x - 1$ or $y = 2x - 1$, which is answer choice D.

5. Solve word problems, including problems involving linear relationships and problems that can be represented by Venn diagrams

Venn diagrams are used to show the relationship between two or more sets of data. Each set of data is represented by a circle which may or may not overlap onto one another. The following diagram will be used to explain the concept of Venn diagram.

In the diagram, information is classified into sets. Each set has a title and includes the elements inside brackets { }.

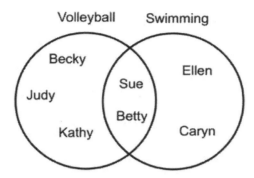

Volleyball: {Becky, Judy, Kathy, Sue, Betty}

Swimming: {Ellen, Caryn, Sue, Betty}

Set notation defines parameters about the information. The union (∪) symbol means to combine sets together.

Volleyball ∪ Swimming = {Becky, Judy, Kathy, Sue, Betty, Ellen, Caryn}

The intersection (∩) symbol means only the elements that are in both sets.

Volleyball ∩ Swimming = {Sue, Betty}

Example question

On a Friday night at the movie theater, movies A and B were both showing. If the movie theater sold a total of 53 movie tickets and 13 people watched both movies, how many people were at the movies on Friday night?

Solution:

Since 13 people saw both movies, 13 belongs in space where the circles overlap. The rest of the people saw either Movie A or B. Since there is not enough information to determine how many people were in A and in B, and the question only asks for total people, subtract 13 from 53 and you get 40.

The reasoning behind this is that a person can only be counted once. Even though they attended two movies, it was the same person.

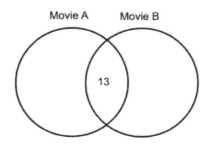

Test Tip

When finding the total number of elements from a Venn diagram, only include numbers that are part of an overlap ONE time.

6. Solve linear equations in one variable algebraically

Solving linear equations may include one-step equations, two-step equations, multi-step equations, and equations that include variables on both sides of the equal sign. Luckily, solving linear equations all have the same process, some just requiring an extra step or two.

To solve an equation, isolate the variable by using inverse operations. Remember that what you do to one side of the equation, you must do to the other side to keep the statement equal. Work using a reverse order of operations.

Linear Equation with Variables on Both Sides

Example: Solve $4x - 5 = x + 13$

STEP 1: Distribute and combine like terms on the same side of the equal sign if needed (not required for this problem)

STEP 2: Move all the variables to one side.

$4x - 5 = x + 13$

$-x \qquad -x \qquad$ *Subtract from both sides of the equation.*

STEP 3: Move all the constants (numbers) to the other side of equation (not with x).

$3x - 5 = 13$

$+5 \quad +5 \qquad$ *Add 5 to both sides (this is an application of the addition equality property).*

STEP 4: Divide by the number with the variable.

$3x = 18 \qquad$ *Divide both sides of the equation by 3.*

$x = 6$

Multistep Linear Equations

To solve multistep linear equations, isolate the variable using inverse operations, remembering what is done to one side has to be done to the other to keep the expressions equal. The steps below outline one way to approach multistep equations.

1. Distribute any numbers outside of parentheses on both sides of equation, if necessary.
2. Combine like terms **on the same side** of the equal sign.
3. Move variables to one side of the equation using inverse operations (add or subtract).
4. Isolate the variable term using inverse operations (add or subtract).
5. Divide both sides by the coefficient with the variable.
6. Look out for no solution or infinitely many solutions.

When an equation has **no solutions** or **infinitely many solutions**, the variable terms are eliminated when moved to one side. This leaves only numbers on both sides of the equation.

- No solutions: equation in the form
  Ex: $2 = 3$; There are no solutions because 2 does not equal 3.

- Infinitely many solutions: equation in the form
  Ex: $2 = 2$; There are infinitely many solutions because 2 equals 2; any solution will work for the equation.

Example question

Solve: $-2(2x + 3) - 5 = -(5 - x)$

Solution:

$-2(2x + 3) - 5 = -(5 - x)$

$-4x + (-6) - 5 = -5 + x$ 1. Distribute on both sides of the equation.

$-4x + (-11) = -5 + x$ 2. Combine like terms on the same side.
$-4x - 11 = -5 + x$ *Inverse operations not needed when combining on the same side.*

$-4x - 11 = -5 + x$ 3. Move variables to one side of the equation by adding or subtracting.
$+4x \qquad\quad +4x$ *It is always best to move smaller variables to avoid negative values.*

$-11 = -5 + 5x$ 4. Isolate the variable term by adding or subtracting.
$+5 \quad +5$

$\dfrac{-6}{5} = \dfrac{5x}{5}$ 5. Divide both sides by the coefficient with the variable.

$x = -\dfrac{6}{5}$

MATH

Example question

Solve: $2(x + 3) = 2x - 8$

Solution:

$2x + 6 = 2x - 8$
$-2x \qquad\ -2x$
$\overline{\qquad 6 = -8}$

Because 6 does not equal -8, **there are no solutions.**

Example question

Solve: $-2x + 3 - 6x = -8x + 3$

Solution:

$-8x + 3 = -8x + 3$
$+8x \qquad\ +8x$
$\overline{\qquad 3 = 3}$

Because 3 equals 3, any solution will work for x, so there are **infinitely many solutions.**

7. Solve simple quadratic equations

Although solving simple quadratic equations sounds like a complicated process, these equations require a lot fewer steps than solving larger linear equations. **The one BIG idea you need to know when solving a quadratic equation is that there are two solutions, not just one.**

When finding the square root of a number, for example $\sqrt{25}$, the answer is either 5 or –5 because $5 \cdot 5 = 25$ and $-5 \cdot (-5) = 25$. We typically only give the positive answer, but there is a negative answer as well, and when solving simple quadratic equations, both solutions are required.

Solving a simple quadratic equation

1. Take the square root of both sides.

2. Divide the equation into two equations, one that equals a positive number and one that equals a negative number.

3. Solve for the variable, if needed.

Example question

Ellie says the answer to the equation below is 6. Is Ellie correct?

$x^2 = 36$

    A. Yes, because $\sqrt{36} = 6$.

    B. Yes, because when you substitute 6 in for x, the equation is true.

    C. No, because $\sqrt{36} = 18$.

    D. No, because and $\sqrt{36} = 6$, so $\sqrt{36} = -6$, Ellie is missing part of the answer.

    E. No, because and $\sqrt{36} = 18$, so $\sqrt{36} = -18$, Ellie is missing part of the answer.

Correct answer: D

To solve the equation, $x^2 = 36$, remember to rewrite the equation into two equations after taking the square root of both sides.

$x^2 = 36$

$\sqrt{x^2} = \sqrt{36}$

$x = 6$ and $x = -6$

No more solving is required, so the answers are 6 and –6. Ellie is missing part of the solution.

Example question

Solve the equation.

$(x + 10)^2 = 81$

Solution:

Follow the steps listed above.

$(x + 10)^2 = 81$

$\sqrt{(x + 10)^2} = \sqrt{81}$

$x + 10 = 9$ and $x + 10 = -9$
$ -10 -10 \qquad -10 -10$
$\overline{}$
$ x = -1 \qquad\qquad x = -19$

Simplifying exponents

When simplifying expressions that contain rational exponents, follow the exponent rules outlined in the table that follows.

	Example	Explanation
Like Bases Multiplied	$5^3 \cdot 5^6 = 5^9$	Add exponents for like bases that are multiplied.
Like Bases Divided	$\dfrac{3^8}{3^2} = 3^6$	Subtract exponents for like bases that are divided.
Raising a Power to a Power	$(4^3)^2 = 4^6$	Multiply exponents for a power raised to another power.
Zero Exponent	$7^0 = 1$	Anything to the zero power equals 1.
Negative Exponent	$9^{-2} = \dfrac{9^{-2}}{1} = \dfrac{1}{9^2}$	A negative exponent indicates the base should be written as a fraction over 1; flip the fraction and make the exponent positive.

MATH

B. Geometry

1. Utilize basic properties of common two-dimensional shapes to solve problems

2. Utilize facts about angles to solve problems

3. Utilize facts about congruency and similarity of geometric figures to solve problems

4. Use the formulas for the area and circumference of a circle to solve problems

5. Use the formulas for the perimeter and area of a triangle and a rectangle and the formula for the volume of a rectangular prism (box) to solve problems

To be successful in the geometry section, it is important to be able to visualize each scenario. Geometry questions involve 2-dimensional shapes, 3-dimensional shapes, lines, points, and angles. Being able to visualize figures and having an understanding of the geometric properties of these figures and how they are related in a problem will increase your success in answering these types of questions.

1. Utilize basic properties of common two-dimensional shapes to solve problems

Triangles

Properties of triangles are useful when solving a variety of problems. On exam questions, characteristics of different triangles do NOT need to be stated in a problem if the type of triangle is named. The tables that follow provide definitions, characteristics, and examples of possible ways triangle types may be displayed in an exam question.

Triangle	Definition and Characteristics	Examples
Classification by Sides		
Scalene	A triangle with no congruent sides and no congruent angles.	
Isosceles	A triangle with two congruent sides. Angles opposite the congruent sides are also congruent.	
Equilateral	A triangle with all sides congruent. Angles in an equilateral triangle are all congruent, or equal to $60°$ (sometimes called equiangular).	

Triangle	Definition and Characteristics	Examples
Classification by Angles		
Acute	A triangle with all angle measures less than 90°	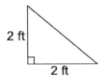
Right	A triangle with one angle equal to 90°	
Obtuse	A triangle with one angle greater than 90°	

Example question

What is the BEST way to classify the triangle below?

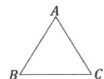

2 ft

2 ft

A. Right, scalene

B. Right, isosceles

C. Acute, scalene

D. Acute, equilateral

E. Obtuse, isosceles

Correct answer: B

Because the triangle has two congruent sides, it is isosceles, and because it contains a right angle, it is also a right triangle. The correct answer choice is B.

Triangle Inequality Theorem

The **Triangle Inequality Theorem** states that the sum of the lengths of any two sides of a triangle is always greater than the length of the third side.

$$AB + BC > AC$$

$$BC + AC > AB$$

$$AC + AB > BC$$

Quick Tip

To determine if 3 side lengths form a triangle, **check all three combinations of sides**. Two combinations may work, so it is always necessary to check them all.

Select all of the following that are a possible combination of side lengths for a triangle.

   A. 4 inches, 7 inches, 10 inches

   B. 2 inches, 3 inches, 5 inches

   C. 6 inches, 5 inches, 6 inches

   D. 4 inches, 4 inches, 4 inches

Correct answers: A, C and D

Use the Triangle Inequality Theorem to check all three combinations of sides for each answer choice.

$4 + 7 > 10, 11 > 10$ ✓ $2 + 3 > 5, 5 > 5$ ✗ $6 + 5 > 6, 11 > 6$ ✓ $4 + 4 > 4, 8 > 4$ ✓

$7 + 10 > 4, 17 > 4$ ✓ $6 + 6 > 5, 12 > 5$ ✓

$4 + 10 > 7, 14 > 7$ ✓

     YES   NO   YES   YES

Which of the following is NOT a possible third side of a triangle with lengths 8 centimeters and 7 centimeters?

   A. 1 centimeter

   B. 2 centimeters

   C. 3 centimeters

   D. 4 centimeters

   E. 10 centimeters

Correct answer: A

For option A, $1 + 7 > 8$ is not true, so 1 centimeter cannot be a possible side length. All the other side lengths work as possible sides because the sum of two sides is greater than the third side for all possible combinations.

Quadrilaterals

A quadrilateral is any polygon with four sides. There are special types of quadrilaterals because of unique properties describing their sides and angle measures. When a special quadrilateral is named, its unique properties are understood to be true. Each special quadrilateral and its properties are given in the tables that follow.

Note: Because special quadrilaterals can have up to 3 defining characteristics, common marks are used to show sides and angles that are congruent and sides that are parallel.

MATH

Congruent Sides	A single small slash on two or more sides means the sides are **congruent**, or the same measure.
	Double small slash marks on two sides means the sides are congruent to one another but not to the sides without the double slash marks.
Parallel Sides	A single arrowhead on two sides means those two sides are parallel.
	A double arrowhead on two sides means those two sides are parallel to one another but not to the sides without the double arrowheads.
Congruent Angles	A single arc in two or more angles means the angles are congruent.
	A double arc in two angles means the angles are congruent to one another but not to the angles without the double arcs.

Name	Figure	Definition
Parallelogram		A quadrilateral with • Opposite sides and opposite angles congruent • Opposite sides parallel
Rhombus		A parallelogram with • All sides congruent • Opposite angles congruent (1 pair obtuse, 1 pair acute)
Rectangle		A parallelogram with • Opposite sides congruent • All angles congruent
Square		A parallelogram with • All sides congruent and all angles congruent (90°)
Trapezoid		A quadrilateral with • One pair of parallel sides
Kite		A quadrilateral with • 2 pairs of adjacent sides congruent

Choose all of the following that are not a parallelogram.

    A. Rectangle

    B. Rhombus

    C. Kite

    D. Square

    E. Trapezoid

Correct answers: C and E

A kite and a trapezoid are not parallelograms because they do not have 2 pairs of parallel sides with opposite sides and opposite angles congruent.

Example question

If $\angle B$ in parallelogram $ABCD$ measures 65°, what are the measures of all the other angles?

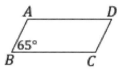

    A. $\angle A = 65°$, $\angle C = 115°$, $\angle D = 115°$

    B. $\angle A = 115°$, $\angle C = 65°$, $\angle D = 65°$

    C. $\angle A = 115°$, $\angle C = 115°$, $\angle D = 65°$

    D. $\angle A = 65°$, $\angle C = 65°$, $\angle D = 115°$

    E. $\angle A = 115°$, $\angle C = 115°$, $\angle D = 115°$

Correct answer: C

Opposite angles have the same measure in a parallelogram, so if $\angle B = 65$ then $\angle D = 65$. Because a parallelogram is a quadrilateral, all four angles add to 360°. Subtract the measures of angles B and D from 360 to get the sum of A and C.

$360 - 65 - 65 = 230$

Because A and C are congruent, divide their sum by 2 to get the measure of each angle.

$230 \div 2 = 115$

Therefore, the correct response is C.

Circles

The most important information to find when solving problems involving circles is the radius and diameter and where these values are in the circumference and area formulas for a circle.

- The diameter goes through the center of the circle to the edge of the circle.

- The radius starts at the center of the circle and ends on the edge of the circle.

- The radius is half the length of the diameter.

Remember that the radius of a circle can be drawn from the center of the circle to anywhere on the circle.

A **central angle** in a circle is an angle with its vertex at the center of the circle. The part of the circle intercepted by the angle is called an **arc**. If several central angles were drawn in a circle, like a pizza, the sum of these angle measures would be 360°.

Arcs are measured two different ways: in degrees based on the measure of the central angle and in a unit of length based on the circle's circumference.

- *Arc measure* is equal to the degree of the central angle.

- *Arc length* is equal to the fractional part of the circumference of the circle represented by the arc.

To find the arc length of an arc created by a central angle, set up a proportion using the two ways arcs can be measured:

$$\frac{\text{arc measure}}{\text{degrees in a circle}} = \frac{\text{arc length}}{\text{circumference of circle}}$$

OR

$$\frac{\text{arc measure}}{360°} = \frac{\text{arc length}}{2\pi r}$$

Example question

A circle with a radius of 3 inches has a central angle that measures 40°. What is the length of the intercepted arc?

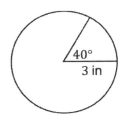

A. π

B. $\dfrac{2}{3}\pi$

C. 2π

D. 6π

E. 9π

Correct answer: B

To solve, use the proportion, $\dfrac{\text{arc measure}}{360°} = \dfrac{\text{arc length}}{2\pi r}$, filling in missing values to solve for arc length.

$$\frac{40}{360°} = \frac{\text{arc length}}{2\pi r}$$

Simplifying the fractions before cross-multiplying,

$$\frac{1}{9} = \frac{x}{6\pi}$$

$$9x = 6\pi$$

$$x = \frac{6}{9}\pi = \frac{2}{3}\pi$$

The correct answer choice is B.

Quick Tip

When solving formulas that include π, look at the answer choices BEFORE working out the problem. If the symbol is part of all the answers, you do not need to multiply by 3.14.

2. Utilize facts about angles to solve problems

Angles are two rays with a common endpoint, called the **vertex**. Angles may be named using only the vertex if there are no other angles. Otherwise, angles are named with a point from one ray, the vertex, then a point from the other ray. Below are examples of naming angles.

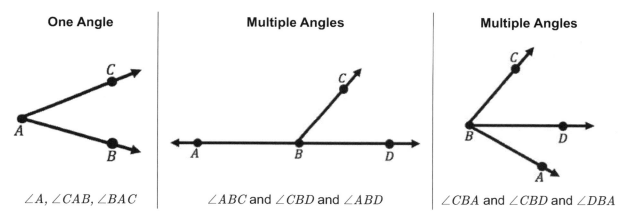

One Angle	**Multiple Angles**	**Multiple Angles**
$\angle A$, $\angle CAB$, $\angle BAC$	$\angle ABC$ and $\angle CBD$ and $\angle ABD$	$\angle CBA$ and $\angle CBD$ and $\angle DBA$

When lines intersect, the resulting angles have special names and properties that help to identify the measure of the angle(s). Angles formed by intersecting lines are defined in the following table.

Angle Name	Example	Definition
Complementary Angles		**Two angles that add to 90°** *Note:* The angles may share a side, as pictured, or may be two separate angles.
Supplementary Angles		**Two angles that add to 180°** *Note:* The angles may share a side, as pictured, or may be two separate angles.
Vertical Angles		Pairs of angles that are opposite or across from one another when two lines intersect **Vertical angles always have the SAME measure.**

Quick Tip

The terms complementary angles, supplementary angles, and vertical angles may appear in problems without an accompanying sketch, so knowing their names is important.

MATH

Corresponding Angles	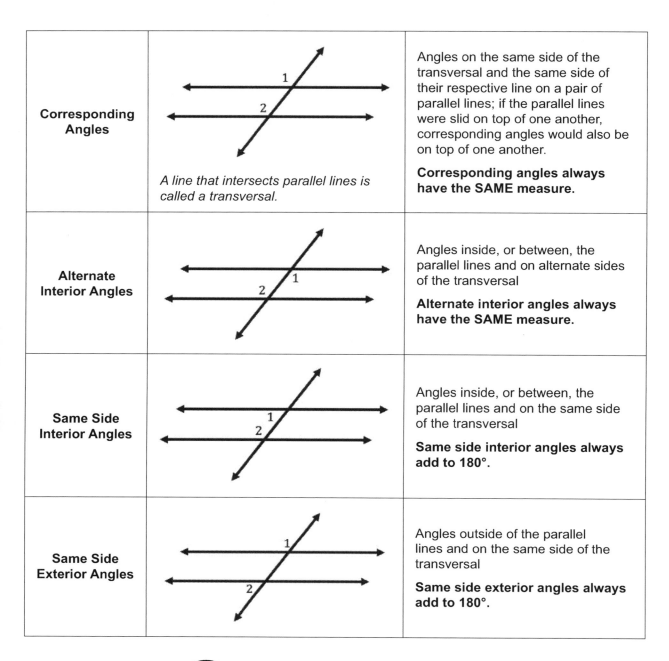*A line that intersects parallel lines is called a transversal.*	Angles on the same side of the transversal and the same side of their respective line on a pair of parallel lines; if the parallel lines were slid on top of one another, corresponding angles would also be on top of one another. **Corresponding angles always have the SAME measure.**
Alternate Interior Angles		Angles inside, or between, the parallel lines and on alternate sides of the transversal **Alternate interior angles always have the SAME measure.**
Same Side Interior Angles		Angles inside, or between, the parallel lines and on the same side of the transversal **Same side interior angles always add to 180°.**
Same Side Exterior Angles		Angles outside of the parallel lines and on the same side of the transversal **Same side exterior angles always add to 180°.**

Quick Tip

For angles formed by parallel lines and a transversal, it is not important to remember their names, only their angle measure properties.

Example question

The complement to angle A is 42°. What is the measure of angle A?

A. 42°

B. 48°

C. 58°

D. 138°

E. 180°

Correct answer: B

Complementary angles add to 90°. Therefore subtract 90 − 42 to find the measure of angle A. The measure of angle A, $m\angle A = 48$.

Example question

Which of the following angle pairs is NOT equivalent?

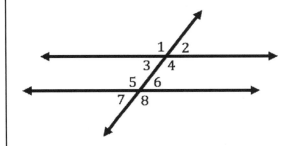

I. 1 and 2

II. 1 and 4

III. 3 and 6

IV. 1 and 5

    A. I

    B. II

    C. III

    D. IV

    E. III and IV

Correct answer: A

Angles 1 and 2 are supplementary and add to 180°. The only time two angles that are next to each other are equivalent is when both angles equal 90°. If angles are equal to 90°, they must be marked or must say so. Angles 1 and 4 are vertical, angles 3 and 6 are alternate interior, and angles 1 and 5 are corresponding, all of which have the same measure.

3. Utilize facts about congruence and similarity of geometric figures to solve problems

When two figures are congruent, all corresponding angle measures and all corresponding sides are congruent. Therefore, if a side measure or an angle measure is missing from a figure, the values from the congruent figure may be substituted. The images below are congruent, therefore, side a in the figure on the right is 5 cm.

Similar figures have corresponding sides that are proportional and corresponding angle measures that are equal. To find the missing length of a side when similar figures are given, use a proportion. (This skill was covered in the Number and Quantity section of the textbook.)

4. Use the formulas for area and circumference of a circle to solve problems

Circumference

The circumference of a circle is the measurement around the outside of a circle. To find the circumference of a circle use either formula, $C = \pi d$ or $C = 2\pi r$, depending on whether the diameter or radius is given (recall the radius is two times the diameter).

The area of a circle measures the amount of space inside a circle. To find the area of a circle, use the formula, $A = \pi r^2$. You may need to find the radius before finding the area if only the diameter of the circle is given.

Test questions about circles often expect that you can manipulate or extract information from one formula to use in another. These types of problems require less computational work but a better understanding of the formulas.

Example question

The area of a circle is 49π inches^2. What is the circumference of the circle?

A. 7π inches

B. 14π inches

C. 28π inches

D. 49π inches

E. 98π inches

Correct answer: B

If the area of the circle is 49π inches^2, then 49 represents r^2 in the formula for area. Therefore, $r = 7$ inches. Using this to find the circumference,

$C = 2\pi r$

$C = 2 \cdot \pi \cdot 7$

$C = 2 \cdot 7 \cdot \pi$

$C = 14\pi$

5. Use the formulas for the perimeter and area of a triangle and a rectangle and the formula for the volume of a rectangular prism (box) to solve problems

Solving real-life problems involving perimeter, circumference, area, and volume are also known as **geometry word problems.**

Geometry word problems often require more than one step to solve. It is important to organize the information you are given, determine the steps needed to find missing information, and answer what the question is asking.

Perimeter

To find the perimeter of any figure, add all the sides.

Formulas: Circumference, area, surface area, and volume

Concept	Formula	Description	Picture
Area Rectangle	$A = bh$	Multiply the length and width of a rectangle to find the area.	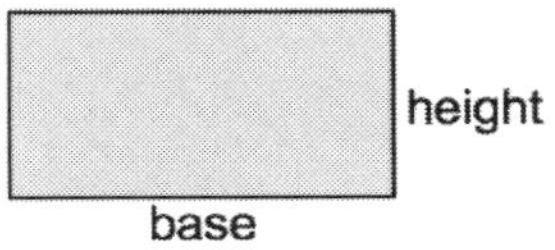
Area Parallelogram	$A = bh$	The base (b) and height (h) are always perpendicular to one another.	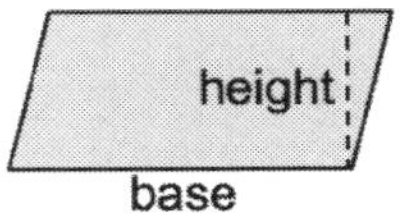
Area Triangle	$A = \dfrac{1}{2}bh$	The base and height are always perpendicular to one another, so a dotted line is added to show the height for different types of triangles.	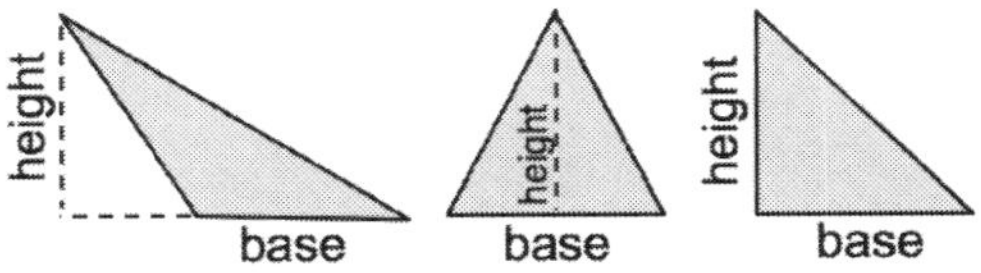
Area Trapezoid	$A = \dfrac{1}{2}h(b_1 + b_2)$	A trapezoid has two bases. The height is perpendicular to the bases.	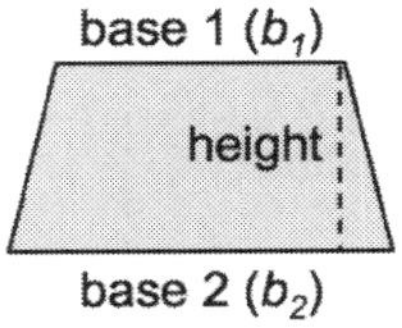
Area Circle	$A = \pi r^2$	The area of a circle uses the radius, which is the length from the center of the circle to a point on the circle.	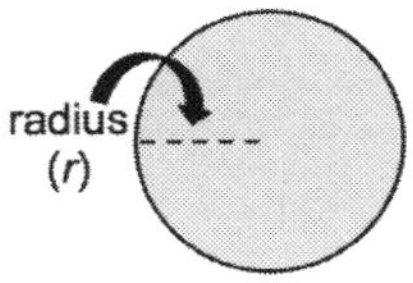

MATH

Concept	Formula	Description	Picture
Circumference Circle	$C = \pi d = 2\pi r$	The circumference measures the distance around the outside of a circle.	
Surface Area Prism	$SA = 2(lw + wh + hw)$	The surface area (SA) of a prism is found by finding the area of all 6 sides and adding these areas together.	
Surface Area Cylinder	$SA = 2\pi r^2 + 2\pi rh$	The surface area of a cylinder is found by finding the area of the top and bottom circles and adding these areas to the area of the rounded outside surface.	
Volume Prism	$V = l \cdot w \cdot h$	The volume of a rectangular prism is found by multiplying the length, width, and height together.	
Volume Sphere	$V = \dfrac{4}{3}\pi r^3$	To find the volume of a sphere, cube the radius, multiply by 4, then divide by 3. If necessary, multiply by 3.14.	

Test Tip

Questions involving a formula rarely state what formula to use. Instead they give clues as to a shape and the type of units being measured. Area is measured in square units, and volume is measured in cubic units. For example, if a problem states, "square tiles and square inches," you will use the area formula for a square.

Example question

The perimeter of a rectangle is 52 ft. If the length is 10 less than 2 times the width, what is the width?

Solution:

In this example, there are 3 clues: perimeter, length, and type of shape. Solve the problem using these three clues.

First, determine the expressions for each of the sides of the rectangle. The problem states that the length is 10 less than 2 times the width, which is written algebraically as $2w - 10$. Make sure when you see the words *less than,* you write -10 in the correct position in the equation. The shape of the object is a rectangle, which means the widths are the same measure and the lengths are the same measure.

$$2w - 10$$

w | $P = 52$ | w

$$2w - 10$$

Next, use the clue of perimeter to write an equation using the expressions for the sides.

$$2w - 10 + 2w - 10 + w + w = 52$$

Last, solve the equation for w.

$$2w - 10 + 2w - 10 + w + w = 52$$

$$6w - 20 = 52$$

$$6w = 72$$

$$w = 12 \text{ feet}$$

Example question

Stacey wants to plant one row of bushes along the length of her front yard. The length of Stacey's front yard is 6 less than three times the width. If the perimeter of her yard is 284 feet, what is the length of the yard where she is planting the bushes?

$$3w - 6$$

w | P=284 feet | w

$$3w - 6$$

A. 37 feet

B. 39 feet

C. 74 feet

D. 105 feet

E. 210 feet

Correct answer: D

To solve, draw a picture and label the sides. The length is given in terms of the width. Therefore, the width is w, and the length is $3w - 6$ (remember less than switches the order).

The question gave the perimeter, which is a BIG hint that the perimeter of a rectangle formula is needed to solve. Substitute the expressions for the length and width into the perimeter formula and solve.

$w + (3w - 6) + w + (3w - 6) = 284$

$8w - 12 = 284$

$8w = 296$

$w = 37$

$3(37) - 6 = 111 - 6 = 105$ feet. The correct answer choice is D.

Caution

Be careful because solving the equation finds the width and the question asks for the length. Substitute into the expression for length, $3w - 6$.

Area

The area of all polygons (figures with straight sides such as a rectangle or triangle), can be found by using some combination of base times height. The base and height are always at right angles. When a figure is slanted, the height is drawn, usually by a dotted line. Most test questions involving area are word problems, which means you will usually be required to use the area of a rectangle.

Example question

A rectangular playground is being refurbished and covered in rubber mulch. Each bag of rubber mulch covers 1,500 square inches. If the playground measures 30 feet by 10 feet, how many bags of rubber mulch are needed?

    A. 5 bags

    B. 28 bags

    C. 29 bags

    D. 50 bags

    E. 51 bags

Correct answer: C

To solve, find the area of the playground. Then, because the area the mulch covers is given in inches, the sides of the playground need to be converted to inches. Multiply each side by 12 to convert to inches. Last, find the area of the playground.

$30 \cdot 12 = 360$

$10 \cdot 12 = 120$

1,500 in²

Quick Tip

When converting feet to inches in geometry word problems, **always** convert **before** finding the area.

Playground area: $360 \cdot 120 = 43,200$

Each bag of mulch covers 1,500 square inches, therefore divide the total area by 1,500 to get the number of bags needed.

$43,200 \div 1,500 = 28.8$

Because bags of mulch cannot be split, 29 bags are needed to cover the playground, which is answer choice C.

Volume of a Prism (box)

The volume of box is the space inside the box. To find the volume, multiply the values for the length, width, and height together.

Example question

Sally bought a new box of almond milk. She estimates she will drink 500 cubic centimeters of the almond milk each day. How long will it take her to finish the almond milk?

    A. 9 days

    B. 10 days

    C. 11 days

    D. 12 days

    E. 15 days

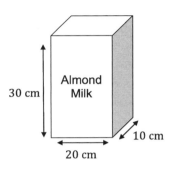

Correct answer: D

First find the volume of the carton.

$V = lwh$

$= 30 \text{ cm} \times 20 \text{ cm} \times 10 \text{ cm}$

$= 6{,}000 \text{ cm}^3$

Next, divide 6,000 cm³ by 500 cm³.

$6{,}000 \div 500 = 12$. The answer is answer choice D, 12 days.

Example question

Which of the following cereal boxes holds the most cereal?

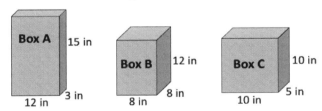

    A. Box A

    B. Box B

    C. Box C

    D. Both Boxes A and C

    E. Both Boxes A and B

Correct answer: B

Find the volume of each box (rectangular solid).

Box A: $V = lwh = 12 \cdot 3 \cdot 15 = 540 \text{ in}^3$

Box B: $V = lwh = 8 \cdot 8 \cdot 12 = 768 \text{ in}^3$

Box C: $V = lwh = 10 \cdot 5 \cdot 10 = 500 \text{ in}^3$

Box B will hold the most cereal, therefore the correct answer choice is B.

Pythagorean Theorem

The Pythagorean Theorem, $a^2 + b^2 = c^2$, is used to find a missing side of a right triangle when two of the sides are given. If the triangle is NOT a right triangle or only one side is given, the Pythagorean Theorem will not work. Pythagorean Theorem questions appear in many forms, including:

- finding one missing side of a right triangle.

- finding the shortest distance between two points.

- finding the perimeter or area of a right triangle that initially has one missing side.

- finding the length of a real-world object that makes a right angle, e.g., a ladder leaning against a building.

For the formula, a and b are called the **legs** of the right triangle. The legs are the two sides that make the right angle. Side c is called the **hypotenuse** and is always the longest leg and is always located across from the right angle.

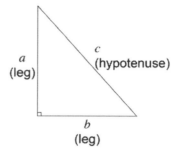

Test questions will often use sides of a right triangle that are known as Pythagorean triples. **Pythagorean triples** are positive whole numbers that satisfy the Pythagorean Theorem. The most used Pythagorean triples are 3-4-5, 6-8-10, and 5-12-13. The largest number in Pythagorean triples represents the length of the hypotenuse. An example of a 3-4-5 right triangle is shown at the right.

Example question

Sid and Keanan both leave school at the same time to go home. When Sid leaves, he drives west 3 miles to his house. When Keanan leaves, he drives 7 miles north to his house. What is the shortest distance between Sam's and Keanan's houses? Round to the nearest tenth of a mile.

A. 6.3 miles

B. 7.6 miles

C. 10.0 miles

D. 29.0 miles

Correct answer: B

The best way to determine what to do to answer this question is to draw a quick sketch of the scenario.

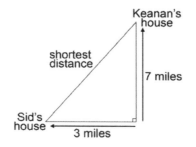

The scenario forms a right triangle with the shortest distance between Sid's and Keanan's houses being the hypotenuse of the right triangle. Using the Pythagorean theorem to solve you get:

$a^2 + b^2 = c^2$

$3^2 + 7^2 = c^2$

$9 + 49 = c^2$

$58 = c^2$

$\sqrt{58} = \sqrt{c^2}$

$7.6 \approx c$

Test Tip

If you know the common Pythagorean Triples, you don't have to waste time using the Pythagorean theorem to find the third side of a right triangle.

Common Pythagorean Triples are 3-4-5, 6-8-10, and 5-12-13. The largest number is always the hypotenuse.

This page intentionally left blank.

III – Algebra and Geometry Practice Problems

1. Which of the following is an equivalent expression to $(2x - 8 - 4x) - (3x + 2 - 5x)$?

   A. -10

   B. $-10x - 10$

   C. $14x - 10$

   D. $-10x - 6$

   E. $6x - 10$

2. Which of the following is an equivalent expression for $3 - (5y + 9 - 8y) - 2(-2 - 3y) - 7$?

   A. $3y + 10$

   B. $-16y + 7$

   C. $-9y - 9$

   D. $-16y$

   E. $-3y + 10$

3. Find an algebraic expression that is equivalent to the expression given.

   $$\frac{a}{2b} - \frac{5}{ab}$$

   A. $\dfrac{a - 5}{2a}$

   B. $\dfrac{a - 5}{2ab}$

   C. $\dfrac{a - 10}{2ab^2}$

   D. $\dfrac{a^2 - 10}{2ab}$

   E. $a - 5$

4. What is the exponent when the expression is simplified? $x^5 \cdot x^4$

   A. 1

   B. 9

   C. 20

   D. $\dfrac{5}{4}$

   E. 0

5. Choose the expression that is equivalent to $\dfrac{(3a^2bc^3)^2}{a^3b^4}$.

   A. $\dfrac{9ac^6}{b^2}$

   B. $6a^7b^5c^5$

   C. $\dfrac{9a^4c^6}{b^4}$

   D. $\dfrac{3ac^6}{b^2}$

   E. $9a^{-1}b^{-3}c^6$

6. Cecil is laying wood flooring in his living room. Each of the wood planks is 9 inches by 36 inches. If his living room measures 13 feet by 18 feet, how many boxes of wood flooring will he need if each box contains 10 planks?

   A. 9 boxes

   B. 10 boxes

   C. 11 boxes

   D. 12 boxes

   E. 13 boxes

7. A ladder is leaning on the side of a building and reaches up 24 feet on the side of the building. If the ladder is 5 feet from the base of the building, how tall is the ladder? Round to the nearest tenth of a foot.

   A. 24.5 feet

   B. 23.5 feet

   C. 29.0 feet

   D. 31.0 feet

   E. 33.3 feet

8. A model of a park bench measures $1\dfrac{3}{4}$ inch in height and 3.6 inches in length. If the actual park bench measures $4\dfrac{1}{2}$ feet in length, what is the height of the actual park bench? Round to the nearest tenth.

   A. 24.5 inches

   B. 26.3 inches

   C. 27.0 inches

   D. 111.1 inches

   E. 120.2 inches

9. Which of the following is the correct name for the triangle pictured?

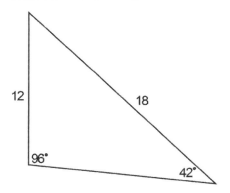

   A. Right scalene

   B. Obtuse scalene

   C. Acute isosceles

   D. Equilateral

   E. Obtuse isosceles

10. The image below is a scale drawing of a local lake. If each square on the grid represents $\frac{1}{2}$ mile, estimate the perimeter of the lake.

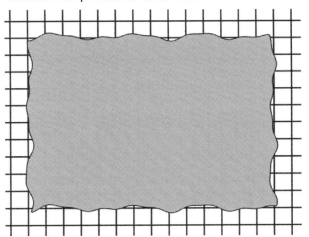

   A. 140 miles

   B. 70 miles

   C. 48 miles

   D. 24 miles

   E. 14 miles

This page intentionally left blank.

Practice Problems Answer Explanations

Number	Answer	Explanation
1	A	To simplify this expression, first distribute the minus sign to each of the terms in the second set of parentheses. (Although we say, *distribute the minus sign,* what is really happening is that we are changing the minus sign to an addition sign and then distributing a −1 to all the terms in the parentheses.) $(2x - 8 - 4x) - (3x + 2 - 5x)$ $= 2x - 8 - 4x - 3x - 2 + 5x$ Next, rearrange the expression, using the commutative property, to make it easy to combine like terms. $= 2x - 4x - 3x + 5x - 8 - 2$ Now combine like terms. $= -10$ The variable terms add to 0, so we are left with −10 for the solution.
2	C	Distribute, paying close attention to negative signs, rearrange to combine like terms, and simplify. $3 - (5y + 9 - 8y) - 2(-2 - 3y) - 7$ Remember to only distribute to the terms the parentheses. $= 3 - 5y - 9 + 8y + 4 + 6y - 7$ $= -5y + 8y + 6y + 3 - 9 + 4 - 7$ $= 9y - 9$ After combining like terms, the correct answer choice is C.

GACE   III – Algebra and Geometry Practice Problems | 223

Number	Answer	Explanation
3	D	Sometimes expressions are presented as math problems. When the question asks for an equivalent expression, what it is really asking is for you to solve. For this question, the fractions need a common denominator. Don't let the variables intimidate you. Just think, *what is in the denominator of the first fraction that is not in the second fraction, and what is in the denominator of the second fraction that is not in the first?* The denominator of the first fraction has a 2 that the second fraction does not have. Therefore, we need to multiply the top and bottom of the second fraction by 2. The denominator of the second fraction has an a that the first fraction does not. Therefore, we need to multiply the top and bottom of the first fraction by a. $$\frac{a}{2b} - \frac{5}{ab}$$ $$= \frac{a}{2b} \cdot \frac{a}{a} - \frac{5}{ab} \cdot \frac{2}{2}$$ $$= \frac{a^2}{2ab} - \frac{10}{2ab}$$ Last, rewrite as one fraction with the common denominator. $$\frac{a^2 - 10}{2ab}$$ The correct answer choice is D.
4	B	The number being raised to a power is called the base. When like bases are being multiplied, add the exponents to simplify. This is better seen if you write the powers out in expanded form. $x^5 = x \cdot x \cdot x \cdot x \cdot x$ $x^4 = x \cdot x \cdot x \cdot x$ $x^5 \cdot x^4 = x \cdot x \cdot x \cdot x \cdot x \cdot x \cdot x \cdot x \cdot x = x^9$ Therefore, the correct answer choice is B.

MATH

Number	Answer	Explanation
5	A	To find the equivalent expression, distribute the power of 2 to all bases in the parentheses, including the 3 and the b. These two terms have an exponent of 1 and are easy to skip when distributing a power, so be careful. Next, simplify variables in the numerator and denominator of the fraction. We've written the exponent form of each variable in expanded form to show why exponents are subtracted when in a fraction. You do not need to write out exponential expressions in expanded form unless you find it helpful; just keep in mind this is a timed test.

$$\frac{\left(3a^2bc^3\right)^2}{a^3b^4}$$

$$=\frac{3^2a^4b^2c^6}{a^3b^4}$$

$$=\frac{9\cdot a\cdot a\cdot a\cdot a\cdot b\cdot b\cdot c\cdot c\cdot c\cdot c\cdot c\cdot c}{a\cdot a\cdot a\cdot b\cdot b\cdot b\cdot b}$$

$$=\frac{9\cdot \cancel{a}\cdot \cancel{a}\cdot \cancel{a}\cdot a\cdot \cancel{b}\cdot \cancel{b}\cdot c\cdot c\cdot c\cdot c\cdot c\cdot c}{\cancel{a}\cdot \cancel{a}\cdot \cancel{a}\cdot \cancel{b}\cdot \cancel{b}\cdot b\cdot b}$$

$$=\frac{9\cdot a\cdot c\cdot c\cdot c\cdot c\cdot c\cdot c}{b\cdot b}$$

$$=\frac{9ac^6}{b^2}$$

Therefore, answer choice A is the correct answer choice. |

Number	Answer	Explanation
6	C	The first step to solving is to convert the dimensions all to feet or all to inches. We are converting all to feet because we typically relate to room dimensions in feet. After finding the new dimensions of a wood plank, find the area of the room and the area of a wood plank. **Conversion of wood plank dimensions:** $9 \div 12 = 0.75$ feet $36 \div 12 = 3$ feet New dimensions: 0.75 by 3 feet **Area of floor:** $13 \times 18 = 234$ ft^2 **Area of plank:** $0.75 \times 3 = 2.25$ ft^2 Divide the area of the floor by the area of the plank to find how many planks are needed. $234 \div 2.25 = 104$ planks needed Last, divide the number of planks by 10 to find the number of boxes needed. $104 \div 10 = 10.4$ Because you cannot purchase part of a box, 11 boxes are needed.
7	A	The ladder leaning against the building forms a right triangle with the ladder representing the hypotenuse, or c in the Pythagorean Theorem. Substitute the building height and ground length in for a and b in the Pythagorean Theorem. 24 ft. 5 ft. $$a^2 + b^2 = c^2$$ $$24^2 + 5^2 = c^2$$ $$576 + 25 = c^2$$ $$601 = c^2$$ $$c = \sqrt{601} \approx 24.5$$

Number	Answer	Explanation
8	B	To find the height of the actual park bench, set up a proportion. Before setting up the proportion, make sure to convert feet to inches so that all the measurements match. Once the proportion is created, simplify the fractions in the proportion, then cross-multiply to find the height. $4\frac{1}{2}$ feet = 4 feet 6 inches, or $48 + 6$ inches = 54 inches $$\frac{1\frac{3}{4}}{3.6} = \frac{x}{54}$$ $$\frac{1.75}{3.6} = \frac{x}{54}$$ $$3.6x = 1.75(54)$$ $$3.6x = 94.5$$ $$\frac{3.6x}{3.6} = \frac{94.5}{3.6}$$ $$x = 26.25 \text{ inches}$$
9	E	To determine the type of triangle, first find the measure of the missing angle by subtracting the angle measures provided from 180. $180 - 96 - 42 = 42$ Because two of the angles are congruent, two sides are also congruent, making the triangle an isosceles triangle. Also, because there is an angle greater than 90°, the triangle is obtuse. Classifying the triangle by both sides and angles, it is an obtuse isosceles triangle.
10	D	The wavy rectangle has dimensions that are approximately 14 squares by 10 squares. To find the perimeter, add all the sides. $10 + 10 + 14 + 14 = 48$ Because each square represents $\frac{1}{2}$ mile, multiply 48 by $\frac{1}{2}$ or 0.5, so $48 \times 0.5 = 24$ miles.

MATH

Math
Practice Tests

DIRECTIONS: Choose the answer choice that represents the best solution.

1. During the election, people in 10 major metropolitan areas had the opportunity to vote three different ways: mail-in ballot, early voting, and day of voting. For this election, 12 million people voted using a mail-in ballot, and 5 million people used early voting. On election day, 16 million people voted. What percent of the total votes were from people who voted on election day?

    A. 33%

    B. 35%

    C. 37%

    D. 44%

    E. 48%

2. If the number 23,489.6 is divided by 1,000, what digit would be in the tenths place?

    A. 3

    B. 4

    C. 8

    D. 9

    E. 6

3. If A is a point between –2 and –3 and B is a point between 0 and 1, which of the points on the number line could be the value of $A \cdot B$? Choose all that apply.

    A. c

    B. d

    C. x

    D. y

    E. g

4. A designer wallpapers $1\frac{3}{5}$ ft² of a room per hour. How many hours will it take her to wallpaper $4\frac{1}{2}$ ft² of the wall?

    A. 1.5

    B. 2.8

    C. 4.3

    D. 5.9

    E. 6.8

5. The price of oranges was originally $2.98 per pound but dropped to $1.99 per pound as part of a promotion. What was the percent of decrease in the price of the oranges to the nearest whole percent?

   A. 32%

   B. 33%

   C. 50%

   D. 68%

   E. 71%

6. At a batting cage, a pitching machine throws balls in a pattern of 2 sliders, then 3 curve balls, then 4 fast balls, in that order. The pattern repeats for 5 min. If Sam hit 75 balls in total, how many were curve balls?

   A. 8

   B. 9

   C. 11

   D. 12

   E. 25

7. A sequence of numbers occurs by subtracting three from the preceding number then multiplying by two. If the fifth number is 88, what is the fourth number?

   A. 41

   B. 42

   C. 44

   D. 47

   E. 170

8. A three-pack of paper towels costs $6.85. A 12-pack of paper towels costs $15.64. What is the price difference of one roll when buying a 12-pack vs the cost of one roll when buying a three-pack?

   A. $0.62

   B. $0.73

   C. $0.98

   D. $1.38

   E. $1.95

9. An online music streaming app charges $0.10 per downloaded. The app also charges a flat fee of $8 per month. If your monthly bill totaled $12.50, how many songs did you download this month?

   A. 34

   B. 35

   C. 45

   D. 125

   E. 205

10. A utilities employee earns $28 per hour for the first 8 hours worked in a day and h dollars for any hours over the regularly scheduled 8 hours. If the employee makes $260 in one 10-hour day, what is the hourly rate, h, in dollars, for working overtime?

    A. 8

    B. 18

    C. 19

    D. 36

    E. 64

11. The altitude of a sky diver during the freefall is recorded at two different times shown in the table. To the nearest tenth of a foot, how many feet per minute does the skydiver descend?

Time	Altitude (in feet)
2:16 P.M.	16,560
2:22 P.M.	5,980

    A. 1581.2

    B. 1763.3

    C. 2,645.0

    D. 2,697.2

    E. 2,759.1

12. Which of the following shows 0.148, 0.099, 0.2, and 0.21 in order from least to greatest?

    A. 0.099, 0.148, 0.2, 0.21

    B. 0.099, 0.2, 0.148, 0.21

    C. 0.21, 0.2, 0.148, 0.099

    D. 0.2, 0.099, 0.148, 0.21

    E. 0.148, 0.2, 0.21, 0.099

13. The cheerleading team is selling coupon cards for $20 each. For each card they sell, they make a $5 profit. Which answer choice represents how many cards they need to sell in order to raise at least $1,400?

    A. $5x \geq 1,400$

    B. $5x \leq 1,400$

    C. $5x > 1,400$

    D. $5x < 1,400$

    E. $20x \geq 1,400$

14. Solve for x. Write the solution as a fraction in the boxes provided.

$$\frac{5}{9} + x = 7$$

$$\boxed{} \atop \boxed{}$$

15. A snack mix has 2 cups of almonds, $\frac{3}{4}$ cup of raisins, and 1 cup of chocolate chips. Which of the following ratios represents a ratio of almonds to raisins to chocolate chips?

   A. 8:3:4

   B. 3:1:2

   C. 4:2:3

   D. 8:1:4

   E. 2:3:4

16. Stocking up on snacks for a team road trip, Miguel bought 16 bags of chips for $0.75 each, 28 pieces of candy for $.20 each, 12 bottles of water for $1.25 each, and 4 packs of gum for $1.99 each. How much did Miguel spend on snacks for the team's road trip?

   A. $40.50

   B. $40.56

   C. $41.56

   D. $41.78

   E. $41.98

17. The manager at an office supply store buys 3-gallon jugs of coffee for the annual office breakfast. During the breakfast, the staff drank $2\frac{1}{2}$ jugs of coffee. How many pints of coffee did they drink?

   1 gallon = 4 quarts

   1 quart = 2 pints

   A. 7.5

   B. 24

   C. 30

   D. 48

   E. 60

18. If there are 18 fiction books for every 3 autobiographies in the library. How many autobiographies are there in the library if there are 8,154 fiction books?

   A. 453

   B. 463

   C. 579

   D. 1,359

   E. 2,718

19. Which is the prime factorization of $25 \times 40 \times 48$?

    A. $2^2 \times 3^1 \times 5^3$

    B. $2^4 \times 3^2 \times 5^2$

    C. $2^7 \times 3^1 \times 5^3$

    D. $2^{12} \times 3^1 \times 5^2$

    E. $2^7 \times 3^2 \times 5^3$

20. Minerva and Estrella are making a string art project. Minerva has used 32 feet of string, which is 64% of the amount of string Estrella has used. How many feet of string did the girls use in all to create both art projects?

    A. 18

    B. 32

    C. 50

    D. 68

    E. 82

21. Kara's bake shop sells the most wedding cakes from May through September because that is wedding season in her town. The number of cakes she sold during each of these five months is shown below. How many more cakes did she sell in June than in August?

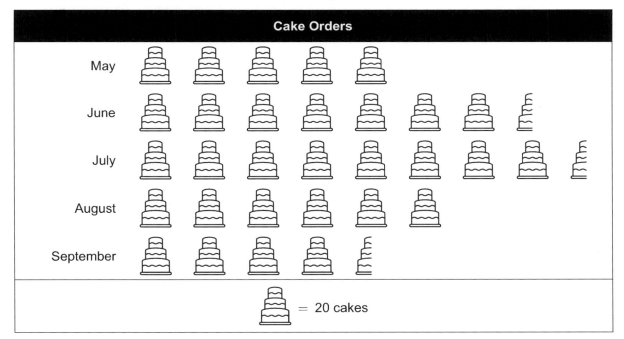

    A. 15

    B. 20

    C. 25

    D. 30

    E. 35

22. Which of the following models the line of best fit for the scatterplot?

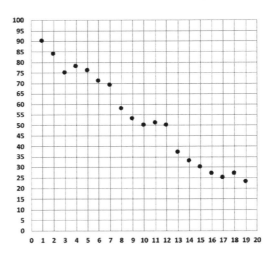

A. $y = \dfrac{1}{3}x + 100$

B. $y = -\dfrac{1}{3}x + 100$

C. $y = 3x + 100$

D. $y = -3x + 100$

E. $y = 3x$

23. The graph below gives the number of sales during the holiday season at a local department store. What is the range in the number of sales during the first 8-hour period?

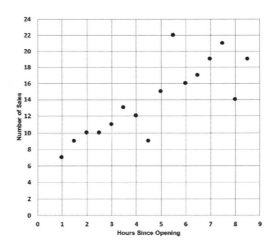

A. 7.5

B. 8.5

C. 12

D. 15

E. 16

24. Given the scatterplot, which statement can be concluded?

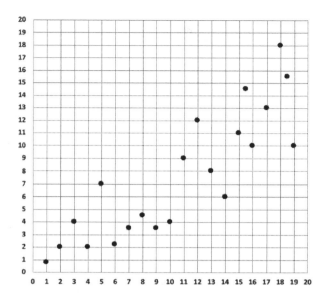

A. There is a strong positive correlation between x and y.

B. There is a weak positive correlation between x and y.

C. There is a negative correlation between x and y.

D. The number of x increases as the number of y decreases.

E. There is no correlation between the data sets.

25. Given the scatterplot, which statement can be concluded?

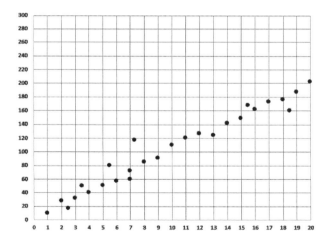

A. As x increases by 10, y increases by 10.

B. As x increases by 1, y increases by 10.

C. As x increases by 5, y increases by 10.

D. As x increases by 10, y increases by 1.

E. As x increases by 1, y increases by 1.

26. What can be concluded from the scatterplot? Choose all that apply.

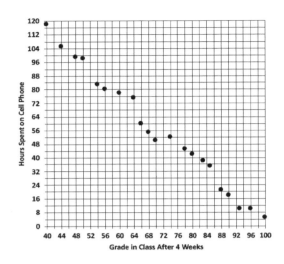

A. As time spent on a cell phone increases, a student's grade in the class increases.

B. As time spent on a cell phone increases, a student's grade in the class decreases.

C. There is a strong positive correlation between a student's time spent on their cell phone and their grade in the class.

D. There is a negative correlation between a student's time spent on a cell phone and their grade in the class.

E. There is no relationship between a student's time spent on a cell phone and their grade in the class.

27. The Smith's total monthly budget is $3600. How much do they allocate to groceries and eating out?

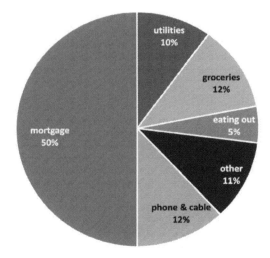

A. $180

B. $220

C. $360

D. $432

E. $612

28. The bar graph shows the number of pets each student in Mr. Rodríguez's class has. How many students have fewer than 3 pets?

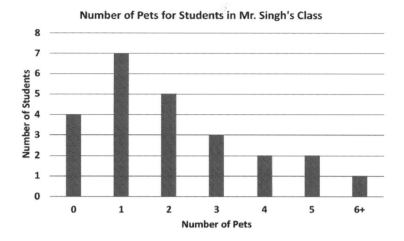

Number of Pets for Students in Mr. Singh's Class

A. 16

B. 11

C. 7

D. 4

E. 3

29. The following graph represents two cross country teams: Wildcats and Rebels. As the teams begin the race, the stopwatch is initiated, and splits are recorded every 5 seconds. Given the graph, what is ratio of Wildcats to Rebels at 20 seconds?

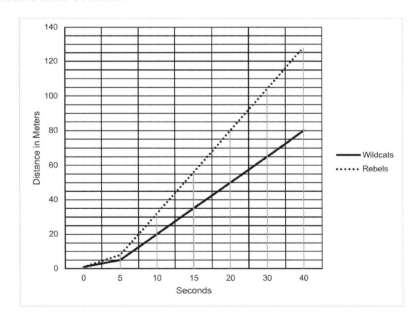

30. The timeline below shows major events that occurred during U.S. space exploration in the 20th century. How many years after the Russians launched Sputnik did it take for the U.S. to complete the moon mission?

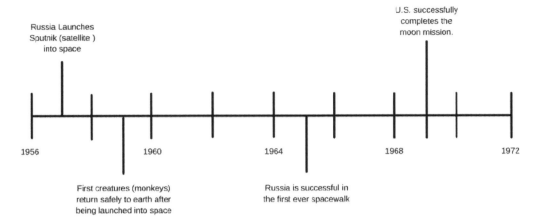

A. 12

B. 15

C. 18

D. 20

E. 22

31. The table below represents survey data from 8,000 people ages 22-50. The survey was used to measure how many people are dissatisfied with their jobs. If this is a representative sample of a population of 1.2 million people, predict how many people between the ages of 41 and 50 are currently unhappy with their employment.

Age Group	Percent
22-25	12%
26-30	24%
31-35	38%
36-40	10%
41-45	9%
46-50	7%

A. 1,280

B. 84,000

C. 108,000

D. 124,000

E. 192,000

32. A researcher conducted a survey to determine how many people watched T.V. and how many people exercised during a given week. Of those surveyed, 405 people said they watched T.V., and 522 said they exercised. Of those people, 368 said they both watched T.V. and exercised that week. How many people surveyed only watched T.V. and did not exercise during that week.

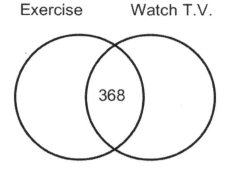

Exercise   Watch T.V.

368

A. 17

B. 37

C. 47

D. 117

E. 154

33. Given the information in the table below, what is the probability of selecting a student at random who is a female student attending the college part-time?

	Male	Female
Part-time	345	286
Full-time	590	872

34. Omar bought a computer system for $1500. If he doesn't put any money down and pays $75 per month, which of the following graphs represents how long it will take him to pay off the computer system?

A.

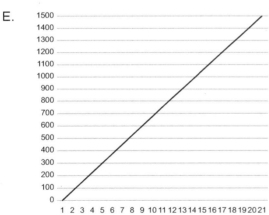

B.

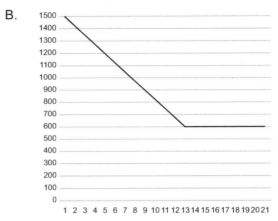

C.

D.

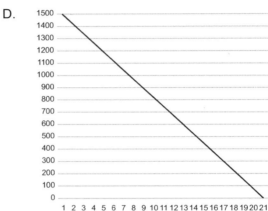

E.

35. Find the average (arithmetic mean) of the numbers, –5, 4, –2, 1, 0, 7, 4, –1.

A. –1

B. 1

C. 0

D. 1.1

E. 8

36. The set M is a set that contains whole numbers from 12 to 28 exclusively. What is the median of the set of values for M?

   A. 19

   B. 19.5

   C. 20

   D. 20.5

   E. 21

37. A jar contains blue, pink, and yellow gumballs. There are 10 blue gumballs and 8 pink gumballs. If the probability of picking a yellow gumball is $\frac{1}{4}$, how many yellow gumballs are in the jar?

   A. 3

   B. 4

   C. 5

   D. 6

   E. 7

38. There are 400 of both white and blue cards in a bag. If the probability of picking a white card is 0.64, how many more white cards than blue cards are in the bag?

   A. 101

   B. 102

   C. 110

   D. 112

   E. 256

39. How many solutions does the equation have?

   $4 + 5x = x - 7 + 4x$

   A. None

   B. One

   C. Two

   D. Three

   E. Infinitely many

40. One solution to the equation $(x - 4)^2 = 25$ is $x = 9$. What is another possible solution?

   A. −1

   B. 1

   C. 2

   D. 3

   E. 4

41. Which of the following is equivalent to $-4a + 3b - 8 + 9a + 7b - 11$?

    A. $5(a - 2b) - 19$

    B. $15ab - 19$

    C. $5(a + 2b) - 19$

    D. $19 + 5a + 10b$

    E. $-5a + 10b - 19$

42. The total profits for a large pest control company are $5 million dollars per year. The company services individual homes, housing communities, and businesses. If the profits were graphed in a circle graph, the profits from the company represented by housing communities would be represented by a central angle of 108°. How much does the company make in profits from housing communities?

    A. $15,000

    B. $150,000

    C. $500,000

    D. $1,500,000

    E. $2,500,000

43. Select all of the following that are equivalent to $10a^2$.

    ❑ $(2a)(5a)$

    ❑ $(4a)(6a)$

    ❑ $4a + 6a$

    ❑ $\dfrac{20a^3}{2a}$

    ❑ $10a(a)$

    ❑ $\dfrac{1}{2}a(20)^2$

44. Lines s and t are parallel, and line u is a transversal. Find the value of x.

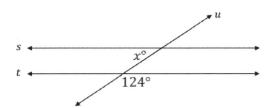

    A. 24

    B. 26

    C. 36

    D. 56

    E. 124

45. What is the value of x?

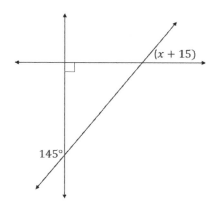

A. 50

B. 45

C. 40

D. 35

E. 30

46. A rectangular shipping box has a length of 12 inches and a width of 8 inches. If the volume of the box is 1,056 cubic inches, what is the height of the box in inches?

A. 11

B. 12

C. 13

D. 14

E. 15

47. A mirror has a diameter of 14 inches. What is the circumference of the mirror to the nearest hundredth of an inch?

A. 21.98 inches

B. 43.96 inches

C. 87.92 inches

D. 153.86 inches

E. 192.13 inches

48. The scale on a map is 2 centimeters for every 5 kilometers. If the actual distance between two locations is 12 kilometers 50 meters, what is the distance between the locations on the map?

A. 4.7 cm

B. 4.80 cm

C. 4.82 cm

D. 4.85 cm

E. 5.0 cm

49. Which of the following shapes has two sides that are parallel but not equal and two sides that are not parallel or equal?

A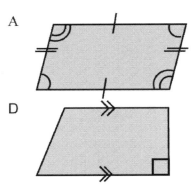

B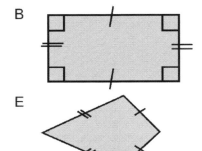

C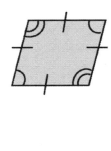

D

E

50. To find a number, you are given the following directions.

- Start with x
- Add 5
- Multiply by 2
- Subtract 4
- Divide by 10.

If the final number is 68, what is the value of x?

A. 7.8

B. 10.6

C. 337

D. 347

E. 680

51. Given the equation, $2x + 9y = 32$, what is y in terms of x?

A. $\dfrac{32 + 2x}{9}$

B. $\dfrac{-2x + 32}{9}$

C. $9(32 - 2x)$

D. $-2x + \dfrac{32}{9}$

E. $-\dfrac{30x}{9}$

52. If $\dfrac{w}{x} = \dfrac{5}{6}$ and $\dfrac{y}{x} = \dfrac{7}{12}$, what is $\dfrac{w}{y}$?

A. $\dfrac{72}{35}$

B. $\dfrac{7}{10}$

C. $\dfrac{7}{5}$

D. $\dfrac{5}{7}$

E. $\dfrac{10}{7}$

53. There are 1,240 people attending their company's annual Christmas party. Susie is tasked with figuring out seating arrangements and planning how many tables will need to be rented for the party. If 12 people can sit at a table in the banquet room, what is the minimum number of tables needed for the banquet?

A. 100

B. 101

C. 102

D. 103

E. 104

54. Read the scenario below and answer the question that follows.

Jose was the 80ᵗʰ person to get on the beach trolley from a community parking lot 2 miles from the beach. If the trolley picks up a new load of people every 5 minutes, and all the seats have been full for each trip, how many trips did the trolley make to the beach prior to Jose getting on the trolley?

What additional information is needed to answer the question?

A. The number of attendants on the trolley.

B. The number of people in line before Jenna.

C. How long Jenna waited in line.

D. The maximum number of people that can fit on the trolley at one time.

E. How long it takes the trolley to drive to the beach.

55. Using the rectangle, find the value of $a + b$.

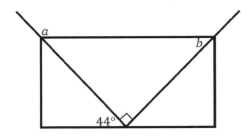

    A. 182

    B. 136

    C. 92

    D. 90

    E. 88

56. Olivia made a model of a statue that is in the courtyard of her school. What is the width of the model she made?

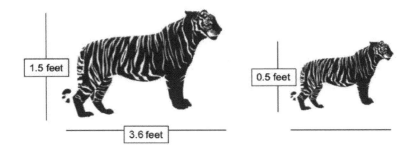

    A. 1.0

    B. 1.1

    C. 1.2

    D. 1.8

    E. 2.2

Practice Test 1 – Answer Explanations

Number	Answer	Content Category	Explanation
1	E	I	To find the percentage use the following formula $\dfrac{\text{election day votes}}{\text{total votes}}$. Note that even though the votes are tallied in millions, it is not necessary to input the values using all the zeros. Because all the values are in the millions, we can use 12, 5 and 16, making the problem more manageable. $\dfrac{16}{12 + 5 + 16} = 16/33 \approx .4848 \approx 48\%$.
2	B	I	Use your calculator and input $23{,}489.6 \div 1{,}000$. The result is 23.4896. The tenths place is the first number to the right of the decimal place, $23.\mathbf{4}896$, so 4 is in the tenths place. Another way to approach this problem is knowing that dividing by 1,000 moves the decimal point three places to the left. This eliminates the need to use the calculator and speeds up solving.
3	A & D	I	This problem is testing your knowledge of number sense and what happens to a number greater than 1 when it is multiplied by a decimal less than 1. Eliminate all answer choices greater than 0 because the result of multiplying a negative by a positive is negative. Find the range of possible numbers. Because the result is a negative number, the point must be greater than -3 and less than 0. Therefore, points c and y are the only possibilities.
4	B	I	Use your calculator to convert the fractions to decimals in order to make the problem more manageable ($1\frac{3}{5} = 1.6$, and $4\frac{1}{2} = 4.5$). Next, use a proportion to solve. Each ratio should be in the form $\dfrac{\text{ft}^2}{\text{hours}}$. Set up the proportion as follows: $\dfrac{1.6\text{in}^2}{1\text{ hour}} = \dfrac{4.5\text{in}^2}{x\text{ hour}}$. Solve using cross-multiplication $1.6x = 4.5$ Last, divide to get the variable by itself. $\dfrac{1.6x}{1.6} = \dfrac{4.5}{1.6} \rightarrow x = 2.8$.

Number	Answer	Content Category	Explanation
5	B	I	To find the percent decrease use the formula $\dfrac{\text{new price} - \text{old price}}{\text{old price}}$. Make sure to substitute the correct values: $$\frac{1.99 - 2.98}{2.98} = \frac{-0.99}{2.98} \approx -0.332 \approx -33\%.$$ The negative is only significant to show that it was a percent decrease and is not necessary to keep for the final answer.
6	E	I	The pattern of the pitching machine is S-S-C-C-C-F-F-F-F And the pattern continues to repeat itself. Since there were 75 pitches, it is important to find out how many times the pattern repeats itself within those 75 pitches. Because there are 9 pitches in each repeating pattern, divide 75 by 9. $75 \div 9 = 8.33$, This means the pattern will fully repeat itself 8 times and then continues 0.33 of the way. To fully understand this, multiply 8×9 to get 72. The last F (fastball) in the pattern will be pitch number 72. Continue to count from the beginning of the pattern with the first S (slider) as 73, then the next one as 74, and finally the 75th pitch will be the first C (curve ball). The pattern repeated itself 8 times plus the 75th pitch, which was a curve ball, so $8 \times 3 + 1 = 25$ curve balls.
7	D	I	This problem can be solved multiple ways. One way is to write an equation given the sequence. $(x - 3) \times 2 = 88$ $2x - 6 = 88$ $2x = 94 \rightarrow x = 47.$ The problem may also be worked backwards, but remember everything is opposite, divide instead of multiplying and add instead of subtracting. $88 \div 2 = 44 + 3 = 47.$
8	C	I	To solve this problem, first find the cost of a single roll for each pack. $\dfrac{\$6.85}{3} = \$2.28$ and $\dfrac{\$15.64}{12} = \$1.30$. Next, find the difference between the two single roll prices. $\$2.28 - \$1.30 = \$0.98.$

Number	Answer	Content Category	Explanation
9	C	I	To solve this problem, work backwards starting with the total of the monthly bill. Take away the $8 flat fee first and then divide by $0.10 to figure out how many were downloaded. $12.50 − $8.00 = $4.50 $$\$4.50 \div \$0.10 = 45$$
10	B	I	First, because a 10-hour day is made up of the regularly scheduled 8 hours plus another 2 hours, we need to figure out how much the worker makes for his daily rate of $28 for the first 8 hours. $28 × 8 = $224 Next, subtract that value from the $260 total for the day. $260 − $224 = $36 Finally, divide that total by the 2 remaining hours to determine the overtime hourly rate. $$\$36 \div 2 = \$18$$
11	B	I	Use the chart to determine the difference in time and the difference in altitude. Finally, divide the altitude by time. Difference in time: 2:22 − 2:16 = 6 minutes Difference in altitude: 16,560 − 5,980 = 10,580 feet $10,580 \div 6 \approx 1763.33 \approx 1763.3$
12	A	I	ANSWER: 0.099, 0.148, 0.2, 0.21 Since all of the values are decimals, start with the tenths place (first value to the right of the decimal). The 0 in 0.099 is lower than any other value in that place, therefore it is the smallest number in the sequence. Process of elimination will rule out the last three answer choices. Continuing on, the 1 in 0.148 is next smallest value which solidifies that the first answer choice is correct without having to compare any other values. Just to be sure, the 2 in the last two are the same so move to the next place value where nothing is a 0 and is smaller than 0.21.
13	A	I	One of the most important parts of this problem is the phrase, "at least." This means that the value has to be equal to or greater than 1,400 and the $\geq$ sign will be used in the expression. That eliminates answers B, C and D right away. If every card represents $5 in profit, then $5x$ represents the amount made from cards sold, resulting in the inequality $5x \geq 1,400.$

Number	Answer	Content Category	Explanation
14	$\dfrac{58}{9}$	I	Multiply everything by 9, which will remove the denominator. The resulting equation will be $5 + 9x = 63$. Continue to solve for x by subtracting 5 from both sides, getting $9x = 58$. Divide by 9 and keep the answer in fraction form. $x = \dfrac{58}{9}$
15	A	I	The key to this problem is noticing that there is a fraction in the original ratio. Ratios must be in whole numbers. Therefore, to eliminate the fraction, multiply the value of the denominator to all values in the ratio. $$2(4) : \frac{3}{4}(4) : 1(4) = 8 : 3 : 4$$
16	B	I	Use your calculator to compute the value of each item purchased and add them together for the total. $16 \times \$0.75 = \$12.00$ $28 \times \$0.20 = \$5.60$ $12 \times \$1.25 = \$15.00$ $4 \times \$1.99 = \$7.96$ $$\$12.00 + \$5.60 + \$15.00 + \$7.96 = \$40.56$$
17	E	I	To solve, first convert the 3-gallon jugs to pints. A good rule to remember is anytime a conversion is going from a larger unit to a smaller unit, the amount is always multiplied by the conversion number. If 1 gallon = 4 quarts and the jugs are 3 gallons each, multiply 3 gallons by 4 to get the number of quarts in 3 gallons. $3 \times 4 = 12$ quarts. The same reasoning applies for converting quarts to pints. Multiply the 12 quarts by 2 because for every 1 quart there are 2 pints. $12 \times 2 = 24$ pints. Therefore, every 3-gallon jug of coffee is equivalent to 24 pints. The problem states there are $2\frac{1}{2}$ jugs, so multiply 24 by $2\frac{1}{2}$ to get the total amount of pints. $$24 \times 2\frac{1}{2} = 24 \times 2.5 = 60$$

Number	Answer	Content Category	Explanation
18	D	I	To solve this problem setup a proportion using the following ratio: $$\frac{\text{Fiction}}{\text{Autobiographies}}$$ Using the numbers given in the problem, set up the proportion according to the ratio above. $$\frac{18}{3} = \frac{8{,}154}{x}$$ $18x = (3)(8{,}154)$ $18x = 24{,}462$ $$\frac{18x}{18} = \frac{24{,}462}{18}$$ $x = 1{,}359$
19	C	I	It is tempting to multiply all three numbers together and factor the total, 48,000. An easier method is to factor out each of the three factors given and combine them to find the answer. $25 \rightarrow 5 \cdot 5$ $40 \rightarrow 2 \cdot 20 \rightarrow 2 \cdot 2 \cdot 10 \rightarrow 2 \cdot 2 \cdot 2 \cdot 5$ $48 \rightarrow 2 \cdot 24 \rightarrow 2 \cdot 2 \cdot 12 \rightarrow 2 \cdot 2 \cdot 2 \cdot 6 \rightarrow 2 \cdot 2 \cdot 2 \cdot 2 \cdot 3$ Next, combine all the prime factors for the final answer. $2 \cdot 2 \cdot 2 \cdot 2 \cdot 2 \cdot 2 \cdot 2 \cdot 3 \cdot 5 \cdot 5 \cdot 5$ $$2^7 \times 3^1 \times 5^3$$
20	E	I	First, we need to find the amount of string Estrella used. The problem states that Minerva used 64% of the amount Estrella used, so the problem we are solving is, "64% of what number is 32?" 64% of $(x) = 32$ $0.64x = 32$ $$\frac{0.64x}{0.64} = \frac{32}{0.64}$$ $x = 50$ Now that we know Estrella used 50 feet of string, to find the amount both girls used, add 50 and 32. $50 + 32 = 82$ feet

Number	Answer	Content Category	Explanation
21	D	II	This is a pictograph. In this question, you have full cakes and half cakes. A full cake represents 20 cakes. That means a half cake represents 10. The question asks you to compare June with August. In June, she sold 150 cakes (7 full cakes = 140 and 1 half cake = 10). In August, she sold 120 cakes (6 full cakes = 120). $150 - 120 = 30$
22	D	II	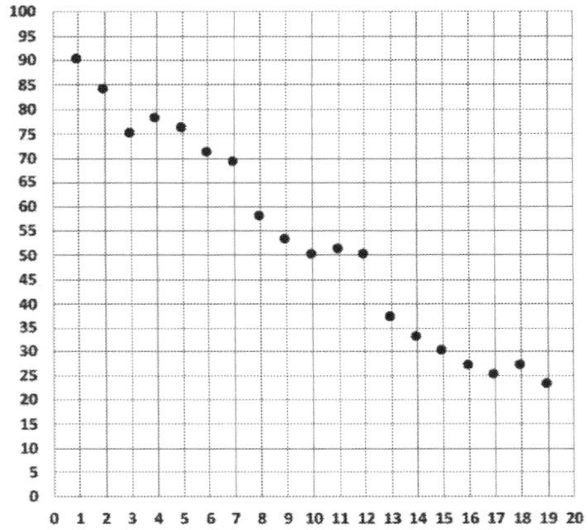 Process of elimination is going to help you tremendously here. Notice the slope of the line is going down; therefore, the slope is negative. In an equation, slope is the fraction or whole number attached to the x. Therefore, you can eliminate answers A, C, and E. ~~A. $y = \frac{1}{3}x + 100$~~ B. $y = -\frac{1}{3}x + 100$ ~~C. $y = 3x + 100$~~ D. $y = -3x + 100$ ~~E. $y = 3x$~~ Finally, it comes down to either a slope of $-\frac{1}{3}$ or -3. Slope is the change in y over the change in x, or rise over run, which means to go from one point to the next, the direction is up or down (number in numerator) and left or right (number in denominator). The scale on the y axis is in increments of 5, and the scale on the x axis is in increments of 1. Starting from 100 on the y axis, the slope of best fit is to go down 3 and right 1 (or $-\frac{3}{1}$ or -3) for every point on the line which yields a line of best fit for this graph of $y = -3x + 100$. If you went down 1 and over 3 ($-\frac{1}{3}$) the line would be much less steep and not fit the graph above.

Number	Answer	Content Category	Explanation
23	D	II	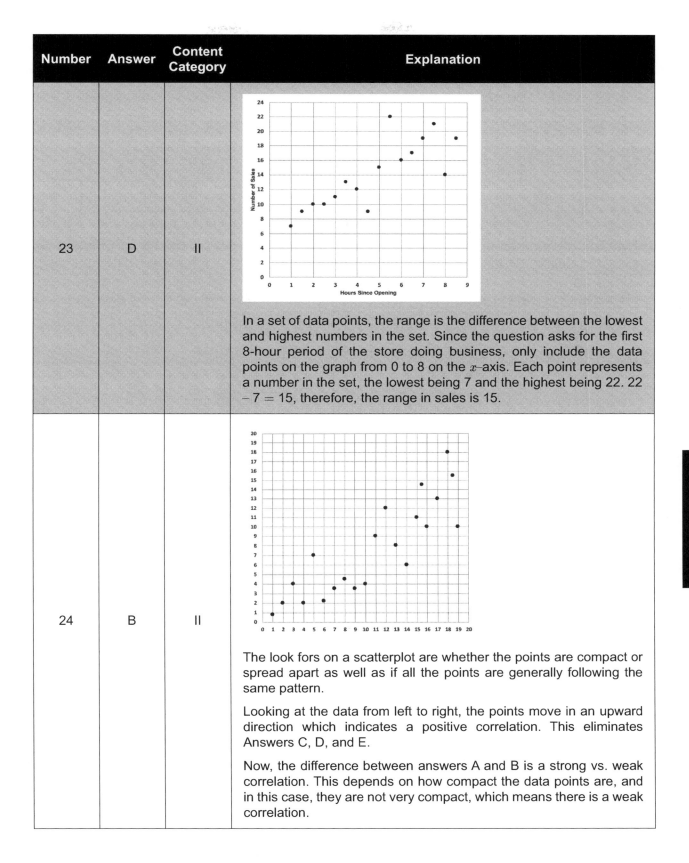 In a set of data points, the range is the difference between the lowest and highest numbers in the set. Since the question asks for the first 8-hour period of the store doing business, only include the data points on the graph from 0 to 8 on the x-axis. Each point represents a number in the set, the lowest being 7 and the highest being 22. $22 - 7 = 15$, therefore, the range in sales is 15.
24	B	II	The look fors on a scatterplot are whether the points are compact or spread apart as well as if all the points are generally following the same pattern. Looking at the data from left to right, the points move in an upward direction which indicates a positive correlation. This eliminates Answers C, D, and E. Now, the difference between answers A and B is a strong vs. weak correlation. This depends on how compact the data points are, and in this case, they are not very compact, which means there is a weak correlation.

Number	Answer	Content Category	Explanation
25	B	II	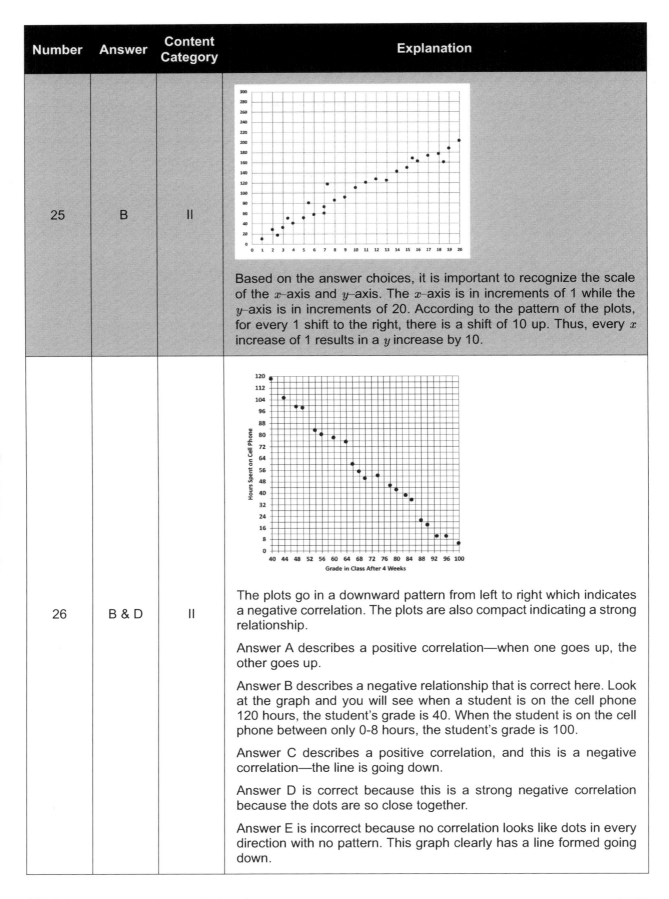 Based on the answer choices, it is important to recognize the scale of the x-axis and y-axis. The x-axis is in increments of 1 while the y-axis is in increments of 20. According to the pattern of the plots, for every 1 shift to the right, there is a shift of 10 up. Thus, every x increase of 1 results in a y increase by 10.
26	B & D	II	The plots go in a downward pattern from left to right which indicates a negative correlation. The plots are also compact indicating a strong relationship. Answer A describes a positive correlation—when one goes up, the other goes up. Answer B describes a negative relationship that is correct here. Look at the graph and you will see when a student is on the cell phone 120 hours, the student's grade is 40. When the student is on the cell phone between only 0-8 hours, the student's grade is 100. Answer C describes a positive correlation, and this is a negative correlation—the line is going down. Answer D is correct because this is a strong negative correlation because the dots are so close together. Answer E is incorrect because no correlation looks like dots in every direction with no pattern. This graph clearly has a line formed going down.

Number	Answer	Content Category	Explanation
27	E	II	Make sure to correctly identify which wedges of the pie chart are for "groceries" and "eating out." Combine both percents and multiply by the total monthly budget. $$(0.12 + 0.05) \times \$3,600$$ $$(0.17)\$3,600 = \$612$$
28	A	II	The bars on the graph that count in this scenario are students with 0, 1 and 2 pets. Since 4 students have zero pets, 7 students have one pet, and 5 students have 2 pets, the sum will be answer. $$4 + 7 + 5 = 16$$
29	$\dfrac{50}{80}$ or $\dfrac{5}{8}$	II	Make sure to understand the graph before beginning to solve this problem. The x-axis is time in seconds and the y-axis is speed. The y-axis increases by increments of 5 until the next major number. Next, find the values for Wildcats and Rebels at 20 seconds. According to the graph, at 20 seconds, Wildcats is at 50 meters and Rebels is at 80 meters. The problem asks for a ratio, so substitute the values in the order stated in the question. $$\text{Wildcats: Rebels} = \frac{50}{80} = \frac{5}{8}$$ (It is not necessary to reduce for fill in the blank types of questions. Either answer is correct.)
30	A	II	When reading a timeline, first determine what the unmarked scales represent. In this case, the timeline increases in increments of 4 for each major tick mark. The secondary tics are by 2s. Thus, the Russians launched Sputnik in 1957, and the U.S. completed the moon mission in 1969. Therefore, there is a 12-year difference between the two events.
31	E	III	Using the chart, notice that the values for people ages 41 to 50 are a combination of two age groups. The 41 – 45 age group is 9% and the 46 – 50 age group is 7%. Add these values and change to a decimal. $$9\% + 7\% = 16\% = 0.16$$ Next, multiply the decimal by the total population to predict the number of people expected. Note that 1.2 million written out is 1,200,000. $$0.16 \times 1,200,000 = 192,000$$
32	B	II	With the information given in the problem, fill out the remaining portions of the Venn diagram. To find out how many people only watched T.V. and didn't exercise, use the method below. Watched television only $\rightarrow 405 - 368 = 37$

Number	Answer	Content Category	Explanation
33	$\dfrac{286}{2,093}$	II	For this problem the desired outcome is the number of part-time female students, which is the upper-right value in the chart. To find the total sample size, add all the numbers in the chart because this represents all the students at the school. $$\dfrac{\text{part-time female}}{\text{all students}} = \dfrac{286}{2,093}$$
34	D	II	A quick way to start eliminating answer choices is to determine if the line is negative or positive. If Omar is paying down his debt from \$1500 to zero, the slope of the line is negative. Therefore, eliminate answers C and E right away. Next, we know that the payments are consistent (\$75 every month), and that means the line must start on the y–axis at 1500 and end on the x–axis at 20. The last month's payment is \$75. So at month 20 the line is at \$75 and at month 21, Omar is at 0. The only graph that matches these characteristics is answer D.
35	B	II	To find the mean or average, take the sum of all values in the set and divide by the number of values in the set. $$\dfrac{(-5) + 4 + (-2) + 1 + 0 + 7 + 4 + (-1)}{8} = \dfrac{8}{8} = 1$$
36	C	II	The median in a set of values is the exact middle value of the set. In this case the numbers 12 to 28 are the set. Be careful if you are trying to use a shortcut by subtracting, $28 - 12 = 16$ and determining that there are only 16 numbers in the set, making the 8th number the median – because it is not! It may take extra time, but in order to be safe quickly write the numbers $12 - 28$ out in ascending order. 12, 13, 14, 15, 16, 17, 18, 19, 20, 21, 22, 23, 24, 25, 26, 27, 28 Notice that there are actually 17 numbers in the set. In order to find the place of the median in an odd numbered set, divide the amount of values by two and round up to the nearest whole number. That number will be the median. $$\dfrac{17}{2} = 8.5 \approx 9$$ This means that the 9th value in the set is the median which is 20.

Number	Answer	Content Category	Explanation
37	D	II	It is important to have a good understanding of probability. Probability is found by taking the number of desired outcomes divided by the entire number of outcomes or $\dfrac{\text{number of desired outcomes}}{\text{total number of outcomes}}$. In this scenario, the total number of gumballs is not given, but the probability of choosing a yellow gumball is. The probability should be set up as $\dfrac{\text{yellow}}{\text{total}}$. The only way to solve for yellow is to make a proportion using the probability for yellow. $$\dfrac{Y}{10+8+Y} = \dfrac{1}{4}$$ $$\dfrac{Y}{(18+Y)} = \dfrac{1}{4}$$ $$4Y = 1(18+Y)$$ $$4Y = 18 + Y$$ $$3Y = 18$$ $$\dfrac{3Y}{3} = \dfrac{18}{3}$$ $$Y = 6$$
38	D	II	This is a multi-step problem involving probability given as a decimal. Usually, probability is written as a fraction or a percentage, so don't let the decimal confuse you. Since 100% includes the total of any sample size, its decimal equivalent is 1. This problem states that 0.64 represents the probability of getting a white card which means that $1 - 0.64$ must equal the probability of getting a blue card. Therefore, $1 - 0.64 = 0.36$ represents the probability of getting a blue card. To find the difference between the two colors, the amount of each color must be found first. White $400 \times .64 = 256$ Blue $400 \times .36 = 144$ White $-$ Blue $= 256 - 144 = 112$

Number	Answer	Content Category	Explanation
39	A	III	First simplify the equation by combining like terms on the right. $$4 + 5x = x - 7 + 4x$$ $$4 + 5x = -7 + 5x$$ Notice at this point the variables are going to be eliminated because the same term, $5x$, is on both sides. After eliminating the $5x$ from both sides, we are left with the statement $4 = -7$. When this happens, ask yourself, "Does 4 equal -7?" $$4 \neq -7$$ Since 4 will never equal -7, this equation has no solutions. No matter what is substituted for the x value, the equation will not be true.
40	A	III	Guess and check is a viable strategy for solving this problem. Just be careful with negative signs when evaluating. Start with the first answer choice by substituting it for x. $$(-1 - 4)^2 = 25$$ $$(-5)^2 = 25$$ $$25 = 25$$ Remember that when a negative number is squared it becomes positive. A second method is to take the square root of each side of the equation and then break the equation into two answers, one positive and one negative because the square root of a number always has a positive solution and a negative solution. $$(x - 4)^2 = 25$$ $$\sqrt{(x - 4)^2} = \sqrt{25}$$ $$x - 4 = 5 \text{ and } x - 4 = -5$$ $x = 9$ or $x = -1$, so -1 is the second solution.
41	C	III	First, simplify the expression by combining all like terms. Next, cross reference with the answer choices to see which one matches up. Be careful because the answer may not look exactly as the one that was simplified. $$-4a + 3b - 8 + 9a + 7b - 11$$ $$5a + 10b - 19$$ The third choice is the factored form of the simplified form above; the a and b terms were both divided by 5, and the 5 was placed outside the parentheses. This is an application of the distributive property. $$\frac{5a}{5} + \frac{10b}{5} - 19$$ $$= 5(a + 2b) - 19$$

Number	Answer	Content Category	Explanation
42	D	III	The key to this problem is that the information is being represented using a pie chart, which is a circle. Given the central angle measure of 108°, and knowing that a circle is 360°, the full amount of money allocated to housing developments is $\frac{108}{360}$ of the total value. $\$5,000,000 \times \frac{108}{360}$ $\$5,000,000 \times 0.3 = \$1,500,000$
43	Boxes 1, 4, & 5	III	Solve each answer choice accordingly using the proper multiplication and exponent rules $(2a)(5a) = 10a^2$ ✓ $(4a)(6a) = 24a^2$ $4a + 6a = 10a$ $\frac{20a^3}{2a} = 10a^2$ ✓ $10a(a) = 10a^2$ ✓ $\frac{1}{2}a(20)^2 = \frac{1}{2}a(400) = 200a$
44	D	III	It is important to note that if lines s and t are parallel and are intersected by line u, the angles created by line u are special angle pairs. At the intersection of line t and u, the 124° angle creates a linear pair with the angle to its left. Thus, 180° − 124° = 56°. The relationship with the newly found 56° angle and angle x is that they are corresponding angles, or equivalent to each other. Thus, $x = 56°$.
45	C	III	Use your knowledge of supplementary angles, vertical angles, and sum of the angles in a triangle to solve this problem. First, the angle 145° creates a supplementary pair (two angles that add up to 180°) with the angle to its right. Therefore, 180° − 145° = 35° for the bottom angle in the triangle. The triangle is a right triangle, denoted by the square, so find the last angle measure by subtracting the two known angles from 180°. 180° − 90° − 35° = 55°. The new 55° angle makes a vertical pair with the angle $(x + 15)$. To solve for x, set the two angles equal to each other. $x + 15 = 55$ $x = 40$

Number	Answer	Content Category	Explanation
46	A	III	The formula for volume of a rectangular prism is $V = l \times w \times h$. Input all the values available and solve for the missing variable, in this case height (h). $1{,}056 = (12)(8)(h)$ $1{,}056 = 96h$ $h = 11$
47	B	III	There are two formulas to find the circumference of a circle: $C = \text{Diameter}(\pi)$ or $C = 2(\pi)(\text{radius})$. Since the diameter is given in the problem, use the first formula. A quick look at the answer choices will let you know if you have to use a value for pi (π). In this case because the answer is being rounded to the nearest hundredth, use $\pi = 3.14$. $C = (14)(3.14) = 43.96$
48	C	III	The easiest way to solve a scale problem is to create a proportion. Since this problem is talking about the distance on a map in relation to actual distance, the key to the proportion is setting up the ratio as follows: $\dfrac{\text{map distance}}{\text{actual distance}}$. Using the units given, setup the proportion to solve. $\dfrac{2 \text{ cm}}{5 \text{ km}} = \dfrac{x}{12 \text{ km } 50 \text{ m}}$ Make sure to realize that the denominators are not in the same units and must be converted. Convert km values to meters by multiplying by 1000, rewrite the proportion, and solve. $\dfrac{2 \text{ cm}}{5{,}000 \text{ m}} = \dfrac{x}{12{,}050 \text{ m}}$ $5{,}000x = (2)(12{,}050)$ $5{,}000x = 24{,}100$ $\dfrac{5{,}000x}{5{,}000} = \dfrac{24{,}100}{5{,}000}$ $x = 4.82$ Alternatively, you could convert 12 km 50 meters to kilometers. 12 km 50 m = 12.05 km. Then the proportion would be, $\dfrac{2 \text{ cm}}{5 \text{ km}} = \dfrac{x \text{ cm}}{12.05 \text{ km}}$ Use the conversion you feel most comfortable with.

Number	Answer	Content Category	Explanation
49	D	III	The only figure with one pair of parallel sides is the trapezoid. The parallelogram, rectangle, and rhombus (first three choices) all have two pair of parallel sides. The kite (last choice) has no sides that are parallel.
50	C	III	Use the directions to set up an equation in order to solve for x $x + 5$ $(x + 5)(2)$ $(x + 5)(2) - 4$ $\dfrac{(x + 5)(2) - 4}{10} = 68.$ Once the equation is set up correctly, solve for x. Start by eliminating the 10 in the denominator by multiplying both sides by 10. $10\left(\dfrac{(x + 5)(2) - 4}{10}\right) = (10)(68)$ $(x + 5)(2) - 4 = 680$ $2x + 10 - 4 = 680$ $2x + 6 = 680$ $2x = 674$ $\dfrac{2x}{2} = \dfrac{674}{2}$ $x = 337$ Alternatively, you could work backwards using inverse operations for each step.
51	B	III	In this problem it is important to know that y in terms of x means that the equation needs to be solved for y, or be in the form $y =$. $2x + 9y = 32$ $9y = -2x + 32$ $\dfrac{9y}{9} = \dfrac{-2x + 32}{9}$ $y = \dfrac{-2x + 32}{9}$

Number	Answer	Content Category	Explanation
52	E	III	In the numerators, there are two different variables being used, each with a unique value. In the denominator there are two different values for the same variable. The easy answer would be to choose $\frac{5}{7}$ because that is how the variables match up with the values, but that is incorrect. The key to the answer is finding the common denominator for x. In this case 12 is the common denominator which means 2 must be multiplied to both the 5 and the 6 in $\frac{5}{6}$. $$\frac{5 \times 2}{6 \times 2} = \frac{10}{12}.$$ Once the denominators are the same, the corresponding variables in the numerators are now equivalent to each other. $$\frac{w}{x} = \frac{10}{12} \text{ and } \frac{y}{x} = \frac{7}{12}$$ $$\frac{w}{y} = \frac{10}{7}$$
53	E	III	In order to find how many tables are needed for the banquet, divide the numbers of attendees by the number of people per table. $$\frac{1,240}{12} = 103.33$$ This means that 1,240 people with 12 people per table will completely fill 103.33 tables. Because tables are whole objects and cannot be broken into fractional parts, the answer needs to be a whole number. Do not make the mistake of rounding the 0.33 down because 103 tables are not enough tables to seat all people. Whenever dealing with whole objects, such as people or tables, always round based on what is needed in the question. Therefore $103.33 \approx 104$ tables.
54	D	III	Because the question states that additional information is needed to solve the problem, focus on how you would write an equation to solve this problem. If Jose is the 80th person for the day, it is important to know the maximum number of people the trolley can hold during each trip. Therefore, the maximum number of people the trolley can hold is the missing information for this problem.

Number	Answer	Content Category	Explanation
55	A	III	To find the missing angles use your knowledge of angle pairs and properties of parallel lines to solve. Since the shape of the figure is a rectangle, the top and bottom lines are parallel to each other. The bottom line is cut into three angles: 44°, a right angle, and a missing angle. To find the value of the missing angle, set all three angles equal to 180° because they all lie on a straight line, or form a straight angle. $180° - 44° - 90° = 46°$ Using the 46° angle first, extend the top line of the rectangle to the left and the right and notice that angle b is the alternate interior angle to 46°. Therefore, angle $b = 46°$. Next, with the lines extended on the upper left side of the rectangle, notice that the 44° angle is supplementary to angle a. $180° - 44 = 136$ Therefore, angle $a = 136°$, and angle $b = 46°$. Last, take the sum of both values to solve the problem $a + b$. $$136 + 44 = 182$$
56	C	III	To solve this problem, use the information given to set up a proportion using the ratio $\dfrac{\text{height}}{\text{width}}$. $$\frac{1.5}{3.6} = \frac{0.5}{x}$$ $1.5x = (3.6)(0.5)$ $1.5x = 1.8$ $$\frac{1.5x}{1.5} = \frac{1.8}{1.5}$$ $x = 1.2$

This page intentionally left blank.

1. Rank the following numbers from least to greatest.

   $$\frac{1}{10}, -1, -\frac{1}{3}, \frac{1}{5}$$

   A. $-\frac{1}{3}, -1, \frac{1}{10}, \frac{1}{5}$

   B. $-1, -\frac{1}{3}, \frac{1}{5}, \frac{1}{10}$

   C. $\frac{1}{10}, -1, -\frac{1}{3}, \frac{1}{5}$

   D. $-\frac{1}{3}, -1, \frac{1}{5}, \frac{1}{10}$

   E. $-1, -\frac{1}{3}, \frac{1}{10}, \frac{1}{5}$

2. What percent of 190 is 57?

   A. 0.30%

   B. 33%

   C. 3%

   D. 30%

   E. 0.33%

3. Jocelyn and Ella both left their houses to go shopping. Jocelyn drove 18 miles to the store, which was 60% of the distance that Ella had to drive. How many more miles did Ella have to drive to get to the store?

   A. 12

   B. 18

   C. 22

   D. 28

   E. 30

4. An odometer on an old truck reads 194,682. What is the value of the 9 in this number?

   A. 9 tens

   B. 9 hundred

   C. 9 thousand

   D. 9 ten thousand

   E. 9 hundred thousand

5. A $6,500 donation was made to a local recreation center. With these funds, the center was able to purchase two basketball goals for $450 each, resurface the gym floor for $3,000, install a new volleyball net for $1,500, and purchase miscellaneous sporting goods for $775. If floor mats cost $25 each, how many mats will the recreation center be able to purchase with the remaining funds?

    A. 4

    B. 11

    C. 13

    D. 18

    E. 25

6. Each child at a Halloween party receives 2 bags of candy. In each bag, there are 3 lollipops, 5 chocolates, and 7 pieces of gum. Which of the following expressions shows the total amount of candy per child? Check all that apply.

    ❏ $3 + 3 + 5 + 5 + 7 + 7$

    ❏ $2 + 3 \times 2 + 5 \times 2 + 7$

    ❏ $2 + (3 + 5 + 7)$

    ❏ $2(3 + 5 + 7)$

    ❏ $3 \times 2 + 5 \times 2 + 7 \times 2$

7. Over the weekend, a shoe store is running a promotion. Every third person who walks through the door gets a 20% off coupon, every fourth person gets a 25% off coupon, and every tenth person gets a 50% off coupon. This continues until 150 people enter the store. How many people received a 25% off coupon?

    A. 36

    B. 37

    C. 38

    D. 40

    E. 50

8. A local ice cream cart offers vanilla, chocolate, strawberry, and coffee ice cream flavors. Along with the ice cream, the toppings they offer are whipped cream, hot fudge, caramel, sprinkles, nuts, and fruit. If ice cream comes in a waffle cone, regular cone, or cup, and customers are only allowed one ice cream flavor and one topping, how many different ice cream order combinations are available?

    A. 13

    B. 24

    C. 30

    D. 48

    E. 72

9. Three children received an inheritance in the ratio of 3:5:6. If the smallest share was $150,000, what was the total amount of the inheritance?

   A. $150,000

   B. $250,000

   C. $300,000

   D. $500,000

   E. $700,000

10. A researcher is studying snapping turtles. Over 3 months, the researcher captures, tags, and releases 200 turtles in a large lake. Two weeks later the researcher catches 100 turtles from the same lake. He notices that 20 turtles are tagged. Based on this information, how many turtles can the researcher assume are in the lake?

    A. 200

    B. 400

    C. 600

    D. 1,000

    E. 1,200

11. Which of the following is the correct action to take in order to convert 26 miles per hour to feet per minute?

    A. Multiply 26 by 5,280

    B. Divide 26 by 60

    C. Multiply 26 by 88

    D. Divide 26 by 88

    E. Multiply 26 by 176

12. In a sequence of numbers, the pattern from one number to the next is defined as three less than five times a number. If the fifth term is 187, what is the value of the fourth term?

    A. 37

    B. 38

    C. 39

    D. 42

    E. 45

13. A random number generator creates 2-digit integers and is set to produce odd numbers 0.4 of the time. The first four numbers created are 12, 59, 73, and 44. What is the percentage that the fifth number will be an even number?

    A. 0

    B. 0.2

    C. 0.4

    D. 0.8

    E. 1

14. A teacher purchases supplies for her classroom. She bought 75 pens at $0.25 each, 46 markers at $0.50 each, 22 erasers at $0.15 each, and 3 three-ring binders at $6.00 each. How much did all the school supplies cost?

    A. $63.05

    B. $65.15

    C. $67.45

    D. $68.00

    E. $69.30

15. Sam and Tom bought their first house for $125,500. Ten years later, they sold the house for $236,250. What was the percent increase in the sale price of the home?

    A. 26%

    B. 35%

    C. 53%

    D. 74%

    E. 88%

16. A recipe for a cake calls for 18 cups of flour to be split between a small bowl and a large bowl in a ratio of 1:3. Using the ratio, how much flour should be in the large bowl?

    A. 3 cups

    B. $4\frac{1}{2}$ cups

    C. 6 cups

    D. $13\frac{1}{2}$ cups

    E. 17 cups

17. Given the number below, which of the following operations would result in the 9 being in the hundredths place?

    23,897.04

    A. Multiply by 100

    B. Multiply by 0.001

    C. Divide by 100

    D. Divide by 10

    E. Multiply by $\frac{1}{100}$

18. A family's Labrador Retriever grows at the following rate:

Month	Weight (lbs.)
1	12
2	20
3	28

If the pattern continues for the next 6 months, how much will the dog weigh in month 6?

A. 36 lbs.

B. 44 lbs.

C. 52 lbs.

D. 60 lbs.

E. 68 lbs.

19. The area of a house floorplan can best be defined in which of the following units?

A. square centimeters

B. square inches

C. square yards

D. square feet

E. square kilometers

20. Which of the following could result in a number between 0 and 1? Choose all that apply.

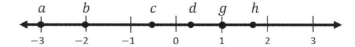

☐ $a + b$

☐ $\dfrac{c}{b}$

☐ $c + h$

☐ $a \times g$

☐ $d \times g$

21. The following chart represents peppers in Sam's garden.

	Green	Red
Bell Pepper	4	8
Hot Pepper	7	9

What is the probability that a pepper picked at random is a red pepper, a hot pepper, or a red, hot pepper?

A. $\dfrac{1}{7}$

B. $\dfrac{6}{7}$

C. $\dfrac{3}{7}$

D. $\dfrac{13}{28}$

E. $\dfrac{33}{28}$

22. For a local business, the yearly office budget, not including employee salaries, is represented in the pie chart below. If the total office budget is $50,000 per year, how much money was spent on printing materials?

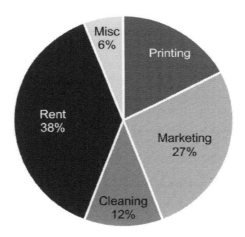

A. $8,500

B. $13,500

C. $17,000

D. $26,350

E. $31,300

23. What is the probability of rolling a pair of regular six-sided dice and having the numbers facing up total 7?

A. $\dfrac{7}{36}$

B. $\dfrac{1}{6}$

C. $\dfrac{1}{7}$

D. $\dfrac{7}{12}$

E. $\dfrac{7}{18}$

24. A bowl of candy contains 7 mints, 5 pieces of gum, and 10 caramels. What is the probability of picking a caramel, not putting it back, and then picking a mint?

A. $\dfrac{17}{462}$

B. $\dfrac{17}{22}$

C. $\dfrac{5}{33}$

D. $\dfrac{70}{484}$

E. $\dfrac{35}{242}$

25. The pictograph shows the number of cars parked on each floor of a parking garage. Each symbol represents the same number of cars. If the 1st and 5th floor have a combined total of 72 parked cars, how many cars are parked on the 2nd floor?

A. 4

B. 8

C. 32

D. 40

E. 48

26. The Venn diagram below represents three electives students can choose from during their course selection week. Registration for art and dance totaled 285 students, with 70 students registering for both art and dance. In addition, 135 students only signed up for gym. What is the total number of students who registered during course selection week?

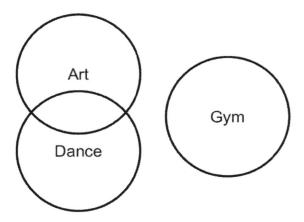

A. 350

B. 400

C. 425

D. 440

E. 465

27. The chart below represents the average rainfall in the southeast region of Central America. Which two-month period has the highest average increase in rainfall?

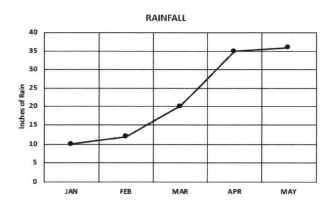

RAINFALL

A. March-May

B. February-March

C. April-May

D. January-April

E. February-April

28. Find the median of the following hourly wages. Write your answer in the box.

$11.85 $7.50 $8.65 $12.14

$7.85 $9.75 $10.34

29. The chart below shows sales for an electronics company for the first part of the year. What number most closely represents sales from January to May?

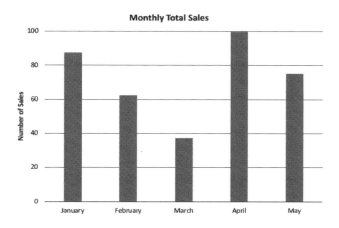

A. 290

B. 315

C. 320

D. 360

E. 445

30. Based on the scatterplot, what is the trend in the data points?

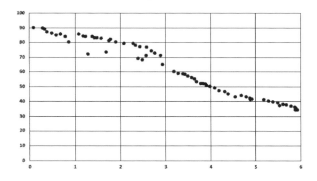

A. Negative linear correlation

B. Positive linear correlation

C. Neutral linear correlation

D. Inverse correlation

E. No correlation

31. The mean of 5 test scores is 60. Which of the following scenarios will increase the range of all five scores?

A. Add 10 points to the highest test score

B. Add 10 points to the highest and lowest test score

C. Subtract 10 points from the highest score

D. Subtract 10 points from the highest and lowest score

E. Add 10 to the lowest and subtract 10 from the highest

32. A recent study found that high school GPAs are positively correlated with university freshmen GPAs. Which of the following statements can be used to describe the findings from the study? Check all that apply.

❑ Students with high GPAs in high school tend to have high GPAs as freshmen in college.

❑ Achieving good grades in high school will cause students to have good grades in college.

❑ Students with high GPAs in high school tend to see decreases in their GPAs in college.

❑ Achieving bad grades in high school will cause students to have bad grades in college.

❑ Students with low GPAs in high school tend to have low GPAs as freshmen in college.

33. How many years from incorporation did it take the company to reach $2,000,000 in sales?

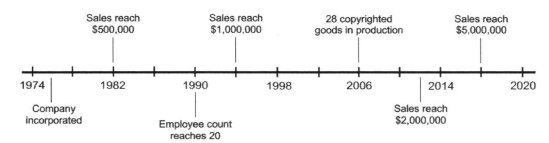

A. 24

B. 28

C. 30

D. 34

E. 36

34. Which of the following can be concluded from the scatterplot?

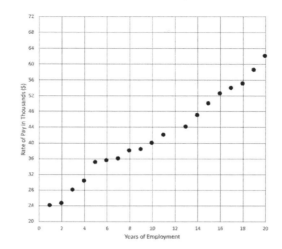

A. There is a strong negative correlation between rate of pay and years of employment.

B. There is a weak negative correlation between rate of pay and years of employment.

C. There is a weak positive correlation between rate of pay and years of employment.

D. There is a strong positive correlation between rate of pay and years of employment.

E. There is no correlation between rate of pay and years of employment.

35. The chart below represents a town divided into square mile blocks. The number inside each square indicates the number of drug stores within the square mile. What is the average number of drug stores per square mile in the town?

0	1	2
8	4	5
1	0	1
5	6	3

A. 3

B. 12

C. 16

D. 36

E. 42

36. At a sushi restaurant, patrons can choose their meal from a tank. There are 12 red fish, 5 white fish, and some blue fish. How many of the fish are blue if the probability of picking a white fish out of the tank is $\frac{1}{6}$?

A. 4

B. 13

C. 14

D. 24

E. 30

37. A student solves the following problem step-by-step. In which step did the student make the mistake?

$$4(x - 1) + 3x = 14 - x$$
$$\text{Step 1: } 4x - 4 + 3x = 14 - x$$
$$\text{Step 2: } 7x - 4 = 14 - x$$
$$\text{Step 3: } 6x - 4 = 14$$
$$\text{Step 4: } 6x = 18$$
$$\text{Step 5: } x = 3$$

A. Step 1

B. Step 2

C. Step 3

D. Step 4

E. Step 5

38. Solve for x:

$$\frac{x}{5} = \frac{2x - 1}{9}$$

A. $x = 5$

B. $x = 1$

C. $x = -1$

D. $x = -5$

E. $x = \dfrac{5}{19}$

39. How many solutions does the equation have?

$$3(x + 4) + 2x = x + 12 + 4x$$

A. None

B. One

C. Two

D. Three

E. Infinitely many

40. Which inequality is represented by the number line?

A. $x < 1$

B. $x \leq 1$

C. $x > 1$

D. $x \geq 1$

E. $x = 1$

41. How many non-congruent triangles can you make using the sides of the rectangle below?

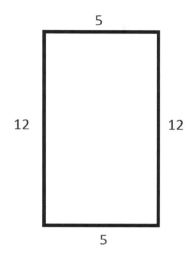

A. 0

B. 1

C. 2

D. 3

E. 4

42. Find the value of x.

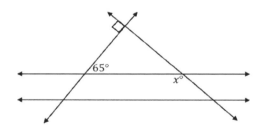

A. 155°

B. 115°

C. 85°

D. 75°

E. 65°

43. The area of a circle is 16π. What is the circumference of the circle?

A. 4π

B. 8π

C. 16π

D. 32π

E. 64π

44. Find the value of x.

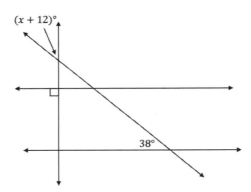

A. 26

B. 38

C. 40

D. 90

E. 116

45. A rectangular prism has base dimensions of 7 inches and 3 inches. If the volume of the prism is 420 in³, what is the height of the prism?

A. 14 in.

B. 20 in.

C. 21 in.

D. 28 in.

E. 42 in.

46. If $\dfrac{x}{8} = 0$ and $\dfrac{5}{y} = 5$, what is the value of $x + y$?

A. −1

B. 0

C. 1

D. 4

E. 7

47. Due to expansion in the neighborhood, High Street is being added to accommodate new construction. If High Street is parallel to Low Street, what are the angle measures of x and y?

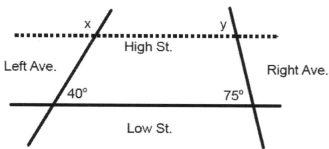

A. $x = 140°$, $y = 105°$

B. $x = 140°$, $y = 75°$

C. $x = 40°$, $y = 75°$

D. $x = 40°$, $y = 105°$

E. $x = 50°$, $y = 15°$

48. Select all the quadrilaterals that have at least one pair of opposite sides parallel.

❑ Square

❑ Rectangle

❑ Rhombus

❑ Parallelogram

❑ Trapezoid

❑ Kite

49. Given the following information, what is the equation of the line?

x	1	2	3	4	5
y	4	7	10	13	16

A. $y = x + 3$

B. $y = 3x + 1$

C. $y = 3x$

D. $y = 3x + 3$

E. $y = 4x + 1$

50. Select all of the options that are solutions to the equation.

$(x + 2)^2 = 16$

☐ 4

☐ –2

☐ 2

☐ 6

☐ –6

51. The product of 6 and a number is decreased by the quantity of 3 plus the same number can be written algebraically as which of the answer choices?

A. $6n - 3 + n$

B. $6 + n - (3 + n)$

C. $(3 + n) - 6n$

D. $(6n - 3) + n$

E. $6n - (3 + n)$

52. A line passes through the points (–4, 4) and (2, –3). What is the slope of the line?

A. $m = \dfrac{6}{7}$

B. $m = -\dfrac{7}{6}$

C. $m = -\dfrac{2}{7}$

D. $m = \dfrac{7}{6}$

E. $m = -\dfrac{2}{1}$

53. The three angles in a triangle are named a, b and c. What is the measure of angle a if $b + c = 85°$?

A. 5°

B. 30°

C. 85°

D. 95°

E. 100°

54. The base of a rectangular prism measures 2 inches by 3 inches, and it has a height of 6 inches. What is the volume of the prism?

A. 36 cubic inches

B. 30 cubic inches

C. 40 cubic inches

D. 28 cubic inches

E. 45 cubic inches

55. In an inventory report for a school supply manufacturer, crayons make up 5 million units. When shown on a pie chart, the central angle measure for crayons is 60°. What is the total amount of inventory the company has?

   A. 300,000

   B. 830,000

   C. 3,000,000

   D. 8,000,000

   E. 30,000,000

56. In a school play, male and female members are represented by the variables m and f respectively. If half the males and $\frac{1}{3}$ of the females are sophomores, what does the expression $\frac{3m + 2f}{6(m + f)}$ represent?

   A. Number of sophomores in the play

   B. Fraction of sophomores in the play

   C. Number of students in the play

   D. Fraction of males to females in the play

   E. Number of students who are not sophomores in the play

This page intentionally left blank.

Number	Answer	Content Category	Explanation
1	E	I	Ranking the numbers from least to greatest means to put them in order from the smallest to the largest. To make this easier, convert the fractions to decimals. $\frac{1}{10} = 0.1$ $-1 = -1$ $-\frac{1}{3} = -0.333$ $\frac{1}{5} = 0.2$ Finally, rank them accordingly. $-1, -\frac{1}{3}, \frac{1}{10}, \frac{1}{5}$ Use your answer choices. You can see that -1 is definitely going to be the lowest number, so right away you can eliminate choices A, C, and D. Then $\frac{1}{10}$ is less than $\frac{1}{5}$. Save time by being strategic.
2	D	I	The fraction that represents the percent is $\frac{57}{190}$ and this equals 0.30. When converted to a percent, the final answer is 30%. Understanding how to set this problem up is the key. When asking for the percent **of** a number, in this case 190, the "percent of" number is going to be the denominator (bottom number) of the fraction. The remaining number, 57, or the "**is**" value, will be the numerator of the fraction.

Number	Answer	Content Category	Explanation
3	A	I	The problem is asking how many <u>more</u> miles it was to the store, which means finding difference between the two distances. To do this, find the total distance each girl drove, and then subtract. We know Jocelyn drove 18 miles, which is 60% of what Ella had to drive. If 18 miles is 60% of Ella's distance, we need to find 60% of a number that equals 18. $60\% \cdot x = 18$ $0.6x = 18$ $\dfrac{0.6x}{0.6} = \dfrac{18}{0.6}$ $x = 30$ **Be careful; you're not done!** Ella drove 30 miles to get to the store and Jocelyn drove 18 miles. Thus, the difference in the number of miles they drove is $30 - 18 = 12$. Ella had to drive 12 more miles than Jocelyn to get to the store. Another way to approach the problem is to estimate. If you know that 18 miles is 60% of what Ella drove, then she drove a little more than half the distance. If you were to double 18, you get 36. Knowing this is too high, estimate the distance to be approximately 32. The difference of 32 and 18 is 14. Knowing that this is just an estimate, look at all possible answer choices and you will notice the only one that is at or below 14 is the first answer choice, which is the correct answer.
4	D	I	The fifth space to the left of the decimal is the ten thousand's place. Therefore, the 9 represents ninety thousand.
5	C	I	Subtract all of the purchases from 6,500. $6,500 - (450 \times 2) - 3,000 - 1,500 - 775 = 325$ If each mat costs \$25, divide this into 325 to find the answer. $$325 \div 25 = 13$$

Number	Answer	Content Category	Explanation
6	Statements 1, 4, & 5	I	We have added parentheses to the statements below to show that order of operations must be applied. ❑ $3 + 3 + 5 + 5 + 7 + 7 = 30$ ✓ ❑ $2 + (3 \times 2) + (5 \times 2) + 7 = 25$ ❑ $2 + (3 + 5 + 7) = 17$ ❑ $2(3 + 5 + 7) = 30$ ✓ ❑ $(3 \times 2) + (5 \times 2) + (7 \times 2) = 30$ ✓ When you total the number of pieces of candy, each kid gets 30 total pieces. Performing the order of operations in options 1, 4, and 5 yields the correct amount of candy per child. Options 2 and 3 have the multiplication and addition signs incorrectly placed, and when order of operations (PEMDAS) is applied, they do not equal 30.
7	B	I	This problem is an example of the application of multiples. If every fourth person gets a 25% off coupon for the first 150 people, divide 150 by 4, $150 \div 4 = 37.5$. Because we can't have half of a person, 37 people received the 25% off coupon.
8	E	I	Use the counting principle to find the answer to this problem, which means multiply the number of options for each type of choice together. Count carefully as the number of items is not given because they are listed out. There are 4 ice cream flavors, 6 toppings, and 3 container choices. Thus, the number of ways to pick one of each is found by multiplying each of these numbers together. $$4 \times 6 \times 3 = 72$$
9	E	I	To solve, set up a proportion using the smallest share and the total inheritance. Note that the ratio of 3:5:6 means that the sum of the parts of the inheritance is $3 + 5 + 6 = 14$. $$\frac{\text{smallest share}}{\text{total inheritance}} = \frac{3}{14} = \frac{150{,}000}{x}$$ Cross multiply and solve to find the total inheritance, x. $3x = 14(150{,}000)$ $3x = 2{,}100{,}000$ $$x = 700{,}000$$

Number	Answer	Content Category	Explanation
10	D	I	To solve, use a proportion. Make sure the top and bottom units for each fraction match. $$\frac{\text{tagged (1st sample)}}{\text{total (1st sample)}} = \frac{\text{tagged (2st sample)}}{\text{total (2st sample)}}$$ Notice, the proportion matches. **tagged over total = tagged over total**. Therefore: $$\frac{200x}{20,000} = \frac{20}{100}$$ $$20x = 20,000$$ $$\frac{20x}{20} = \frac{20,000}{20}$$ $$x = 1,000$$
11	C	I	To solve this problem, it is important to have an understanding of how to convert units using conversion factors. If converting miles to feet, for example, the conversion is 1 mile for every 5,280 feet. This can be written in fraction form as $\frac{1 \text{ mile}}{5,280 \text{ feet}}$. The following solution will show how to solve using this process. $$\frac{\text{miles}}{\text{hour}} \cdot \frac{5,280 \text{ feet}}{1 \text{ mile}} \cdot \frac{1 \text{ hour}}{60 \text{ minutes}}$$ As you can see, all of the ratios are multiplied together in order to cancel out miles per hour and leave only feet per minute. $$\frac{\cancel{\text{miles}}}{\cancel{\text{hour}}} \cdot \frac{5,280 \text{ feet}}{\cancel{1 \text{ mile}}} \cdot \frac{\cancel{1 \text{ hour}}}{60 \text{ minutes}} = \frac{5,280 \text{ feet}}{60 \text{ minutes}} = 88 \text{ ft/min}$$ Therefore, the conversion factor from miles per hour to feet per minute is to multiply by 88.
12	B	III	Since the pattern is given, work backwards to get the solution. The most important thing is to understand that three less than five times a number is $5n - 3$. Use this to solve. $$5n - 3 = 187$$ $$5n = 190$$ $$\frac{5n}{5} = \frac{190}{5}$$ $$n = 38$$

Number	Answer	Content Category	Explanation
13	E	II	Be careful on how you interpret this problem. It is important to know what 0.4 means (0.4 is the same as 40%). Therefore, this number generator will produce odd numbers 40% of the time. Since you know what four out of the five numbers are, you can determine what the fifth will be. 40% of five numbers is 2, which means two of the five numbers generated will be odd numbers. 59 and 73 have been created, and are odd, so the remaining three numbers have to be even. Since the fifth number has to be even, there is a 100% chance or 1 that this number is even.
14	A	I	Make sure to calculate all the values correctly. $75(0.25) + 46(0.50) + 22(0.15) + 3(6)$ $18.75 + 23 + 3.30 + 18 = 63.05$
15	E	I	To find percent increase use the formula: $$\frac{\text{new price} - \text{original price}}{\text{original price}} = \% \text{ increase}$$ $$\frac{236{,}250 - 125{,}500}{125{,}500} = \frac{110{,}750}{125{,}500} = 0.882 = 88\% \text{ increase.}$$
16	D	I	To solve this problem, set up a proportion. $$\frac{\text{large bowl}}{\text{total flour in both bowls}}$$ Note: Remember the total flour combines the ratio 1 and 3 to make 4. $\dfrac{3}{4} = \dfrac{x}{18}$ $4(x) = 3(18)$ $4x = 54$ $\dfrac{4x}{4} = \dfrac{54}{4}$ $x = 13\dfrac{1}{2}$
17	B	I	The hundredths place is two place values to the right of the decimal. In order for the 9 to be in the hundredths place, the decimal point would need to move 3 places to the left. This would happen if the number 23,897.04 were multiplied by 0.001.

Number	Answer	Content Category	Explanation
18	C	I	Given the information in the chart, the constant rate of change in weight is 8lbs. To get to the sixth month, add 8 to 28 three times.$$28 + 8 + 8 + 8 = 52$$
19	D	I	Area of a house floor plan, or living space, is commonly defined in square feet. Centimeters and inches are too small. Conversely, square kilometers are too big.
20	Boxes 2 and 5	I	For each of the answer choices, it is easiest to estimate the value of the point and substitute the estimated values in for the variables.$a = -3$ $b = -2$ $c = -0.5$ $d = 0.4$ $g = 1$ $h = 1.6$ ☐ $a + b = -3 + (-2) = -5$ ☐ $c/b = \dfrac{-0.5}{-2} = 0.25$ ✓ ☐ $c + h = -0.5 + 1.6 = 1.1$ ☐ $a \times g = -3(1) = -3$ ☐ $d \times g = 0.4(1) = 0.4$ ✓ The answer choices that fall between 0 and 1 are $\dfrac{c}{b}$ and $d \times g$.

MATH
PRACTICE TESTS

Number	Answer	Content Category	Explanation
21	B	II	This problem deals with the probability of picking any one of three specified objects. With probability, put the total number of possible outcomes on the bottom of the fraction. The total number of outcomes is 28 because all the values in the table add to 28.$$\frac{(4 + 8 + 7 + 9 = 28)}{28}$$In this case you can pick the red pepper, which is 17 possibilities because bell peppers and hot peppers can be red. In this case, there are 8 red bell peppers and 9 red, hot peppers. You can also pick hot peppers. There are 7 green hot peppers, and 9 red hot peppers. However, notice that the red, hot peppers overlap from the previous pick of red, hot peppers. You cannot count the option twice so leave that out. You cannot have a bigger number on top of the fraction in a probability problem. Therefore, immediately eliminate answer E. When considering the overlap in picks you can pick the shaded area below. $8 + 9 + 7 = 24$. The probability of picking a red pepper, a hot pepper, or a red, hot pepper is $\frac{24}{28} = \frac{6}{7}$. <table><tr><td></td><td>Green</td><td>Red</td></tr><tr><td>Bell Pepper</td><td>4</td><td>8</td></tr><tr><td>Hot Pepper</td><td>7</td><td>9</td></tr></table>
22	A	II	This is a two-step problem. First you have to figure out the percentage of the printing costs because it is missing from the graph. Therefore, add up all the other percents in the graph and you get 83%. Then subtract 83 from 100 and you get 17. The printing costs are 17% of the total $50,000 budget. Next, figure out how much money 17% of $50,000 is by simply multiplying $50,000 \times 0.17 = \$8500$
23	B	II	There are 6 possible ways for two dice to add to 7. 1-6, 2-5, 3-4, 6-1, 5-2, and 4-3 Since each die has 6 faces with one of the digits 1 through 6, there are 36 possible combinations ($6 \times 6 = 36$) when rolling two at the same time. Therefore, the probability of rolling a 7 is $\frac{6 \text{ desired outcomes}}{36 \text{ total outcomes}}$ or $\frac{1}{6}$.

Number	Answer	Content Category	Explanation
24	C	II	The important information in this problem is that the picks are consecutive without replacement, which means the total number of outcomes changes after the first pick. When finding the probability of multiple events, multiply the probability of the first pick by the probability of the second pick. Remember there is a total of 22 pieces of candy to choose from. After the first pick there will be only 21 pieces of candy left. Remember to always reduce when possible. $$\frac{10}{22} \times \frac{7}{21}$$ $$= \frac{5}{11} \times \frac{1}{3} = \frac{5}{33}$$
25	C	II	To solve you must determine how many cars the symbol represents. Since the 1st and 5th floors have a total of 9 symbols, which is 72 cars, divide 72 by 9 to get the value of each car symbol, which is 8. Because there are 4 car symbols for the 2nd floor, multiply 4 and 8 to get 32 cars.
26	A	II	To find the total number of students who registered during course selection week, you must identify how many students signed up for art and dance, not including the overlap. Simply take $285 - 70 = 215$. Next add the students who signed up for gym, which was 135. $215 + 135 = 350$
27	E	II	Do not overthink this question. Just because it uses the term *average*, doesn't mean you have to find an average. First, eliminate choices B, C, and D because they are not a 2-month span. Next, figure out the change in rainfall for the remaining 2-month periods: March – May: $20 \rightarrow 36 = 16$ February – April: $12 \rightarrow 32 = 20$ Therefore, the highest average increase occurred between February and April.
28	$9.75	II	To find the median, put the values in order from least to greatest. The median is the number in the exact middle. $7.50, $7.85, $8.65, **$9.75**, $10.34, $11.85, $12.14

MATH
PRACTICE TESTS

Number	Answer	Content Category	Explanation
29	D	II	This problem is designed to test your skills of estimation. Because the values are difficult to pinpoint, estimate as closely as possible. The following are estimated values: January: 90 February: 60 March: 40 April: 100 May: 70 The sum of all these values is closest to 360.
30	A	II	To determine if a relationship exists among a set of points, first draw a line so that it is as close as possible to all or most of the points. If most of the points are close to, or somewhat close to, the line, the relationship is said to be linear. For the scatterplot in this problem, the data is linear because the points are all relatively close to the line. Next, the slope of the line determines if the relationship is positive or negative. From left to right the line decreases, meaning it is negative. Therefore, this is an example of a negative linear correlation.
31	A	II	Range is the difference between the highest and lowest numbers. To help visualize the answer choices, substitute values in for the test scores. Let's use 50 and 70, this would make the range 20. Here are the scenarios: A. 70 + 10 = 80, 80 − 50 = 30, 30 is greater than 20; increase B. 50 + 10 = 60, 70 + 10 = 80, 80 − 60 = 20; no change C. 70 − 10 = 60, 60 − 50 = 10, 10 is less than 20; decrease D. 50 − 10 = 40, 70 − 10 = 60, 60 − 40 = 20; no change E. 50 + 10 = 60, 70 − 10 = 60, 60 − 60 = 0, 0 is less than 20; decrease

Number	Answer	Content Category	Explanation
32	Statements 1 and 5	II	The study uses correlation not causation. Therefore, you can eliminate any statements that use the word *cause*. It is also important to remember, positive correlation doesn't necessarily mean that everything is always going "up." Positive correlation means a relationship between two variables in which both variables move in tandem—when one goes up, the other goes up, and when one goes down, the other goes down also. Statements 1 and 5 are positive correlations. Statement 1 indicates when 1 goes up, the other also *tends* goes up. When one goes down, the other *tends* goes down.
33	E	II	The first step to solving this problem is figuring out the scale on the timeline (how far apart from one another each mark is). From 1974 to 1982 is 8 years, so the unlabeled tick marks are 4 years from the years on either side. Therefore, the company was incorporated between 1974 and 1978. Because this date appears to be in the middle of this time span, assume that they were incorporated in 1976. Following the same assumption for when they reached $2,000,000 in sales, this appears to have happened in 2012. Thus, it took from 1976 to 2012 to reach $2,000,000 in sales, which is 36 years.
34	D	II	Because the data is increasing from left to right and is very close to a line, there is a strong positive correlation between the data. Strong because the data points are close to forming a line, and positive because the data is increasing from left to right (the line is going up).
35	A	II	To calculate the number of drug stores per square mile, find the sum of all stores and divide by the total number of square miles. $0 + 1 + 2 + 8 + 4 + 5 + 1 + 0 + 1 + 5 + 6 + 3 = 36$ $\dfrac{36}{12} = 3$

Number	Answer	Content Category	Explanation
36	B	II	Use a proportion to solve this problem. $\dfrac{\text{white fish}}{\text{total fish}}$ $\dfrac{1}{6} = \dfrac{5}{12 + 5 + b}$ $\dfrac{1}{6} = \dfrac{5}{17 + b}$ Next, cross-multiply and solve for b. $(1)(17 + b) = (5)(6)$ $17 + b = 30$ $b = 13$ Another way to this problem is to use the ratio given and compare it to the number of fish given. A ratio of $\dfrac{1}{6}$ means 1 white fish to the total number of fish. Since there are more than 6 total fish, as stated in the problem $(12 + 5) = 17$. This must mean the fraction has been reduced. The opposite of reducing a fraction is multiplying both parts by a common factor. The numerator of the ratio means 1 white fish. The problem states there are 5 total white fish. This means to get from 1 to 5 you have to multiply by 5. Whatever you do to one part of a fraction has to be done to the other. Since you multiply the 1 by 5, you have to multiply the 6 by 5 to get 30. This means there are 30 total fish in the tank. If 12 are red and 5 are white, $30 - 12 - 5 = 13$ which is the number of blue fish in the tank.
37	C	III	The mistake occurs in the third step of the problem. The student incorrectly subtracts the x from the right side of the equation to the left. The correct operation would have been to add the x, which causes the error.

Number	Answer	Content Category	Explanation
38	A	III	To solve a proportion, cross-multiply and use algebra to solve for x. $$\frac{x}{5} = \frac{2x-1}{9}$$ $5(2x-1) = 9(x)$ distribute the 5 $10x - 5 = 9x$ subtract $10x$ from both sides $-5 = -1x$ $$\frac{-5}{-1} = \frac{-1x}{-1}$$ divide by -1 $5 = x$ Another method to use if the above method escapes you is to guess and check. To do this, substitute each answer in for x. The one that proves the equation true is the correct answer. The following example uses the first answer choice. $$\frac{(5)}{5} = \frac{2(5)-1}{9}$$ $$\frac{5}{5} = \frac{10-1}{9}$$ $$\frac{5}{5} = \frac{9}{9}$$ $1 = 1$
39	E	III	Linear equations can only have none, one, or infinitely many solutions. Therefore, the answer choices C and D can be eliminated. Determine the number of solutions by combining like terms and solving. First, distribute the 3, then combine like terms on each side of the equation. $3(x + 4) + 2x = x + 12 + 4x$ $3x + 12 + 2x = x + 12 + 4x$ $5x + 12 = 5x + 12$ If the expression on the left is exactly the same as the expression on the right, any value substituted for x will make the equation true, so no need to solve any further; there are infinitely many solutions.
40	B	III	Because the point is solid, or filled in, the symbol will include the "or equal to" line under the inequality. The correct symbol is the less than or equal to symbol, $\leq$. All answer choices contain 1, so the symbol is all that needs to be determined.

Number	Answer	Content Category	Explanation
41	C	III	Congruent means the sides, or angles are the same. Therefore, non-congruent means they are not the same. With four sides of the rectangle, there is a possibility of making four triangles. However, there are only 2 unique triangles out of the four. See below for the 4 different triangles that can be made. $\triangle\ 5-12-5$ $\triangle\ 12-5-12$ $\triangle\ 5-12-5$ $\triangle\ 12-5-12$ The stipulation given is that they must be **non-congruent** or not the same. Therefore, there are *only 2 non-congruent triangles*. $\triangle\ 5-12-5$ $\triangle\ 12-5-12$
42	A	III	To find the value of x for the figure, it is important to be able to recognize the supplementary angles and also recall that three angles in a triangle add to 180°. The angle next to the right angle and inside the triangle is also 90° because the two angles are supplementary angles (labeled 90° in the image below). Next, because three angles in a triangle add to 180°, angle a equals $180° - (65° + 90°)$ $180° - 155° = 25°$ Last, angle a and x are supplementary, which means they add to 180°, so $x = 180° - 25° = 155°$.
43	B	III	The formula for the area of a circle is $A = \pi r^2$. If the area of the circle is 16π, then $r^2 = 16$ and $r = 4$. If the radius of the circle is 4, use the equation, $C = 2\pi r$ to find the circumference. $C = 2\pi \cdot 4 = 8\pi$

Number	Answer	Content Category	Explanation
44	C	III	Vertical angles are angles formed by intersecting lines; they are the angles across from each other and are equal in measure. Both $(x + 12)$ and the 90° angle have a vertical angle pair inside the triangle that is formed. Thus, we have two of the three angles in the triangle. 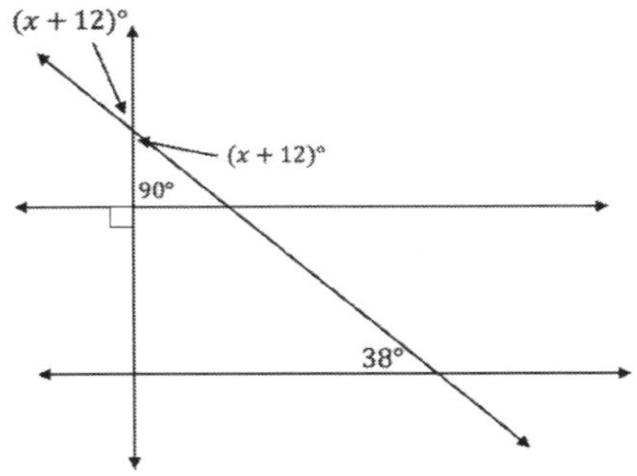 The third angle and the angle that is 38° are corresponding angles formed by parallel lines and a transversal, so they are congruent, or equal, to one another. In the diagram below, the third angle is marked a. 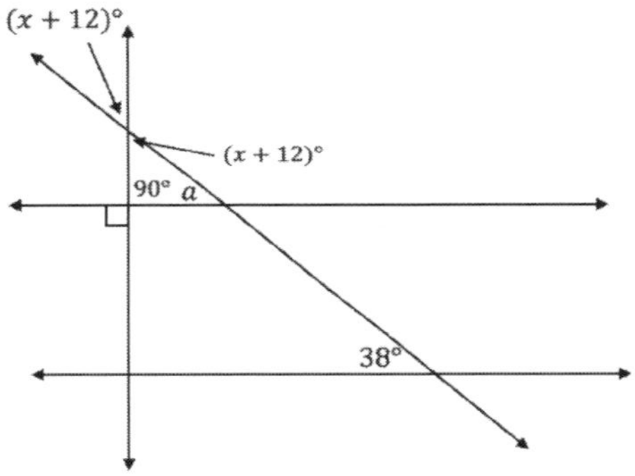 Now that we have the three angles in the triangle, we can add them together and set the sum equal to 180. $(x + 12) + 90 + x = 180$ $(x + 12) + 90 + 38 = 180$ $x + 12 + 128 = 180$ $x + 140 = 180$ $x = 40$

Number	Answer	Content Category	Explanation
45	B	III	A rectangular prism is a three-dimensional shape with a rectangle as its base. The formula for volume is $v = l \times w \times h$. Substitute all the values and solve for the missing variable, height. $420 = (7)(3)(h)$ $420 = 21h$ $\dfrac{420}{21} = \dfrac{21h}{21}$ $20 = h$
46	C	III	In order to solve this problem correctly you must first solve for x and y and then add them together. $\dfrac{x}{8} = 0$ $8\left(\dfrac{x}{8}\right) = (8)(0)$ $x = 0$ $\dfrac{5}{y} = 5$ $y\left(\dfrac{5}{y}\right) = (5)(y)$ $5 = 5y$ $\dfrac{5}{5} = \dfrac{5y}{5}$ $y = 1$ $0 + 1 = 1$
47	B	III	Any time a line intersects two parallel lines it is called a transversal, and special angle pairs are formed. Since Left Ave. is a transversal, the two given angles are supplementary or equal to 180°. 180° − 40° = 140°. Right Ave. is a transversal which means the given angles are corresponding or the same thus $y = 75°$.
48	square rectangle rhombus parallelo-gram trapezoid	III	The quadrilaterals that have at least one pair of parallel sides include a square, rectangle, rhombus, parallelogram, and trapezoid.

Number	Answer	Content Category	Explanation
49	B	III	There are a number of ways to find the equation of a line given the information in the chart. First, look at the answer choices to see what form they're in; in this case, they are in slope-intercept form or $y = mx + b$. Next, look at the y row; Notice the pattern that every number increases by 3. Therefore, the slope of this line is 3. We can eliminate the first and last choices. Next, the y-intercept is found when the x-coordinate equals 0. Even though there is no 0 in the x-coordinate row, use the pattern to work backwards. Since x increases by 1, subtract one from 1 to get 0. The same must be done with the y-coordinate. We added a column to the chart and provided it below for context. The new column is circled. $\begin{array}{\|c\|c\|c\|c\|c\|c\|c\|} \hline x & 0 & 1 & 2 & 3 & 4 & 5 \\ \hline y & 1 & 4 & 7 & 10 & 13 & 16 \\ \hline \end{array}$ If y increases by three, take 3 away to get 1. The new point is (0, 1), which is the y-intercept. The line in this set of points crosses the y-axis at 1 with a slope of 3, so the correct answer is $y = 3x + 1$. **Quick Tip** The slope is always the fraction or whole number attached to the x in the slope intercept form $y = mx + b$. Slope is m.

Number	Answer	Content Category	Explanation
50	Boxes 3 & 5	III	Quadratic equations, equations where the x term is squared, may have none, one, or two solutions. For testing purposes, it is likely the equations given will have two solutions (there will never be more than 2). Recall that when taking the square root of a number, for example $\sqrt{16}$, the resulting solution can be positive or negative because $4 \cdot 4 = 16$ and $-4 \cdot (-4) = 16$. So, when we take the square root in order to solve an equation, the equation gets broken up into two smaller equations. The simplest way to solve this problem is to substitute the answer choices in the equation to determine which value(s) equal 16. ❑ $(4 + 2)^2 = 36 \neq 16$ NO ❑ $(-2 + 2)^2 = 0 \neq 16$ NO ❑ $(2 + 2)^2 = 16 = 16$ YES ❑ $(6 + 2)^2 = 64 \neq 16$ NO ❑ $(-6 + 2)^2 = 16 \neq 16$ YES Alternately, if you understand solving using algebra, use the following method. First, take the square root of both sides. Because squaring and taking the square root are opposite actions, this removes the squared exponent. $$\sqrt{(x + 2)^2} = \sqrt{16}$$ $x + 2 = 4$ $x + 2 = -4$ $-2 - 2$ $-2 - 2$ ―――――― ―――――― $x = 2$ $x = -6$ Therefore, the solutions to the equation are 2 and −6.
51	E	III	Product means to multiply the 6 with the variable. To decrease is to subtract, and quantity means to use parentheses. Inside the parentheses is the addition of 3 and n.

Number	Answer	Content Category	Explanation
52	B	III	Slope is the fraction that represents the change in the y values over the change in x values. The formula for slope is $\frac{y_2 - y_1}{x_2 - x_1}$. $\frac{-3 - 4}{2 - (-4)}$ $= \frac{-7}{6} = -\frac{7}{6}$ We suggest a short cut for problems like these. We stack the coordinates and subtract them, keeping the x and y in mind and then using rise over run. This works every time and will save you valuable time. For $(-4, 4)$ and $(2, -3)$ $\begin{array}{ccc} & x & y \\ & -4 & 4 \\ - & 2 & -3 \\ \hline & -6 & 7 \end{array}$ $-4 - 2 = -6$ *(which is the x)* $4 - (-3) = 7$ *(which is the y)* $\frac{\text{rise}}{\text{run}}$ which is $\frac{y}{x}$ $= \frac{7}{-6} = -\frac{7}{6}$
53	D	III	The three angles in a triangle add to 180°. If angles $b + c = 85°$, then $a + 85 = 180$. Subtract 85 from 180 and angle $a = 95°$.
54	A	III	Volume of a prism is found by finding area of the base and multiplying by height or doing length × width × height. $2 \times 3 \times 6 = 36$.
55	E	III	To solve this problem correctly, it is important to have an understanding of central angle measures in circles. For this problem, 60° represents only crayons. Since there is 360° in every circle, the 5,000,000 units of crayons represents $\frac{60°}{360°}$ of the pie chart. If you multiply the total units of inventory by $\frac{60°}{360°}$, it should yield 5,000,000. The following equation shows the solution: $\frac{60°}{360°}(x) = 5,000,000$ $\frac{1}{6}(x) = 5,000,000$ $x = 5,000,000 \left(\frac{6}{1}\right)$ $x = 30,000,000$

Number	Answer	Content Category	Explanation
56	B	III	The quickest way to do this problem is evaluate the terms on the top of the fraction and on the bottom and see if the fractions match what is in the question. $$\frac{3m+2f}{6(m+f)} = \frac{3m+2f}{6m+6f} = \frac{1m+1f}{2m+3f} = \frac{2}{5}$$ Notice the $\frac{1}{2}m$ and $\frac{1}{3}f$, which matches the fractions in the question. Another method to use on this problem is guess and check. Based on the information given, it is important to choose numbers that are easy to work with. Since male sophomores represent $\frac{1}{2}$, pick a number that is divisible by 2. Female sophomores represent $\frac{1}{3}$ so pick a number that is divisible by 3. Since time is critical during the exam, choose numbers which are easily computed. For this problem let $m = 2$ and $f = 3$. Remember, use the smallest possible numbers you can because they are easiest to work with. When substituting the new values in the expression: $$\frac{3(2)+2(3)}{6(2+3)} = \frac{6+6}{6(5)} = \frac{12}{30} = \frac{2}{5}$$ It is important to understand what $\frac{2}{5}$ represents. Using 2 for males and 3 for females gives you a total of 5 students in the play. Since half of the males are sophomores, then $\frac{1}{2}$ of 2 is one. There is a total of one male sophomore. Since a third of the females are sophomores, then $\frac{1}{3}$ of 3 is one. This gives a total of 2 sophomores out of a combined 5 students which yields the fraction $\frac{2}{5}$. This expression represents the fraction of sophomores that are in the play.

This page intentionally left blank.

1. Choose the correct symbol to make the statement true.

   $-3\dfrac{2}{3}$ _____ -3.6

   A. $>$

   B. $<$

   C. $\cong$

   D. $\geq$

   E. $\leq$

2. Sam measured the length of the worms in his Earthworm farm and recorded their lengths in inches below.

   2.5

   2.27

   $2\dfrac{1}{5}$

   $2\dfrac{2}{8}$

   2.215

   Which of the following shows the length of the worms in order from greatest to least?

   A. $2\dfrac{1}{5}$, 2.215, $2\dfrac{2}{8}$, 2.27, 2.5

   B. 2.27, $2\dfrac{2}{8}$, $2\dfrac{1}{5}$, 2.5, 2.215

   C. 2.27, $2\dfrac{2}{8}$, 2.215, $2\dfrac{1}{5}$, 2.5

   D. 2.5, 2.215, 2.27, $2\dfrac{2}{8}$, $2\dfrac{1}{5}$

   E. 2.5, 2.27, $2\dfrac{2}{8}$, 2.215, $2\dfrac{1}{5}$

3. A customer service center earns a rating on an Internet site after they've received 40 reviews. The average of the reviews is weighted by the number of stars received, and those reviewing a company can rate the company from 0 to 4 stars. A new bicycle shop just received their 40th review. Based on the 40 reviews they received below, what will be the bicycle shop's overall rating on the Internet site?

Number of Stars	Number of Ratings
★	2
★★	3
★★★	20
★★★★	15

A. 2.5

B. 3.2

C. 3.5

D. 3.6

E. 4.2

4. Adelle's company allots $500 each month for office expenses. They lease two copy machines, a larger one that costs $0.05 per page to make copies and a smaller one that costs $0.03 per page to make copies. This month, the company made 500 copies on the large machine and 2,500 on the small machine. In addition, twice this month Adelle needed to buy six cases of paper for $9.95 per case. She also placed an order that totaled $85.50 for folders, envelopes, and labels and bought 200 stamps for $0.55 each. If Adelle spent $20 on miscellaneous items along with all the other office supplies, how much of the monthly office expenses budget is remaining?

A. $65.10

B. $85.10

C. $124.80

D. $174.55

E. $185.20

5. An exercise bike company charges $35 per month for an online subscription to their live classes. A local gym charges an application fee of $99 and a monthly fee of $18.50. After how many months will the gym be less expensive than the exercise bike company?

A. 5

B. 6

C. 7

D. 8

E. 9

6. Simplify the expression.

$8 + 2(-3 - 2)^2 \div 5 \times (-2)$

A. −25

B. −12

C. 3

D. 4

E. 5

7. Select an equivalent expression for the given expression.

$-2(-1)^3 - (-3) - 2^2(-1)^4$

A. −2

B. −1

C. 0

D. 1

E. 2

8. Driver A drives at a constant rate of 56 miles per hour for 6 hours. Leaving from the same location, driver B drives at a constant rate for 7 hours. If both drivers traveled the same distance, at what rate was driver B traveling?

A. 48 miles per hour

B. 52 miles per hour

C. 56 miles per hour

D. 58 miles per hour

E. 60 miles per hour

9. The scale on a map is $\frac{1}{4}$ inch for every 5 miles. If the actual distance between two cities is 88.6 miles, how far apart are the cities on the map?

A. 4.43 in.

B. 3.54 in.

C. 9.28 in.

D. 11.08 in.

E. 12.05 in.

10. If there are 6 people in a room, and they all shake hands once with one another, how many handshakes occurred?

A. 6

B. 12

C. 15

D. 30

E. 36

11. Of the following, which number is greatest?

$$-12, \quad -10, \quad -\frac{21}{2}, \quad -\sqrt{145}, \quad -21$$

    A. -12

    B. -10

    C. $-\dfrac{21}{2}$

    D. $-\sqrt{145}$

    E. -21

12. Which of the following statements below is true?

    A. $4^3 = 3^4$

    B. $5^0 \times 8^2 > 2^5$

    C. $7^4 + 7^3 = 7^7$

    D. $5^4 - 5^2 = 5^2$

    E. $5^0 = 0$

13. A newlywed couple each have annual salaries of \$52,000. While doing their taxes, they see that with their investments, they have a total gross income of \$156,000 Any monies collected after their salary is the result of a return on investments. What fraction of the year's total income is from investments?

    A. $\dfrac{1}{3}$

    B. $\dfrac{1}{2}$

    C. $\dfrac{2}{3}$

    D. $\dfrac{4}{9}$

    E. $\dfrac{3}{4}$

14. A preschool has 200 children who attend during the day. The caregiver to toddler ratio is currently 1:5. The law requires the ratio to be 1:3. How many more caregivers does the director need to hire to be in accordance with the law?

    A. 20

    B. 26

    C. 27

    D. 66

    E. 67

15. During a game of Frisbee. Person A starts by throwing the Frisbee 5 meters forward. Person B throws the Frisbee, and a gust of wind takes it 5 meters backward. Person C throws the Frisbee 2 meters forward. Finally, Person D throws the Frisbee up in the air, and it travels 1 meter forward. Where is the Frisbee in relation to the start?

    A. −3

    B. −1

    C. 0

    D. 1

    E. 3

16. Miss Williams is collecting water from her lab groups after a science lesson. She collected the following amount of water from the groups: 4 oz., 1c 3oz., 6 oz., 1c, 1oz., and 2oz. How many cups of water did Miss Williams collect?

    A. 2 cups

    B. 3.5 cups

    C. 4 cups

    D. 4.5 cups

    E. 5 cups

17. When buying a new brand of computer, consumers are able to choose from 3 screen sizes, 2 operating systems, and 4 different memory storage options. How many different computers could be built with the available options?

    A. 9

    B. 10

    C. 24

    D. 48

    E. 56

18. There are 8 teams in a basketball tournament. For round 1, each team has to play every other team once. How many games will be played during the first round?

    A. 8

    B. 16

    C. 28

    D. 56

    E. 106

19. Jake is putting random numbers into his calculator. When he puts an equation in the calculator, the result is 0.23452345. The calculator only displays 8 places after the decimal. He decides to challenge himself and determine what the 100th place after the decimal is. If he calculates correctly, what is the number 100 places after the decimal.

A. 1

B. 2

C. 3

D. 4

E. 5

20. Dominic and Erin are selling their larger house in a rural neighborhood to move to a smaller house in the city. In their current home, they use approximately 1200 kilowatts of energy per month. Their realtor has told them that their new home in the city will only use about 900 kilowatts of energy per month. The electric company currently charges them $0.15 per kilowatt in the rural neighborhood, but in the city, the electric company charges $0.11 per kilowatt. What will be the percent of decrease in the cost of their monthly energy bills when they move? Round to the nearest whole percent.

A. 2%

B. 33%

C. 45%

D. 67%

E. 75%

21. A class of 30 students recently took a test. Three students scored a 75%, five other students scored a 95%, and the rest of the students scored an 85%. Which of the following statistical measures results in the highest value?

A. Mean

B. Median

C. Mode

D. Range

E. Standard deviation

22. In a bag, there are 15 marbles: 4 red marbles, 6 yellow marbles, 3 blue marbles, 1 green marble, and 1 purple marble. After making a selection, the marble must stay out of the bag. On the first selection, you choose a red marble. What is the probability of choosing a red marble on the second selection?

A. $\dfrac{4}{15}$

B. $\dfrac{3}{15}$

C. $\dfrac{3}{14}$

D. $\dfrac{1}{3}$

E. $\dfrac{1}{3}$

23. A local newspaper reports that August tends to be the hottest month in the city of Chicago and provides the data below to show average temperatures in the month of August for the years 2010-2020. Describe the trend for the city of Chicago's high temperatures during the month of August from 2010 to 2020.

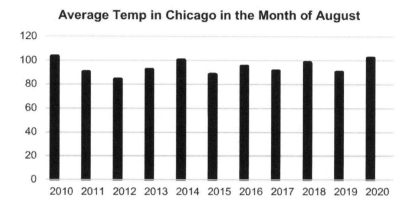

Average Temp in Chicago in the Month of August

A. There is a continual increase in the high temperature from 2010 to 2020.

B. There is a decrease in the high temperature from 2010 to 2020.

C. The hottest temperature in August from 2010 to 2020 is 100°.

D. The lowest temperature in August from 2010 to 2020 is 80°.

E. There is no apparent trend in the high temperatures from 2010 to 2020.

24. The graph below shows the average price for stock ABC per month. What can be inferred from the graph?

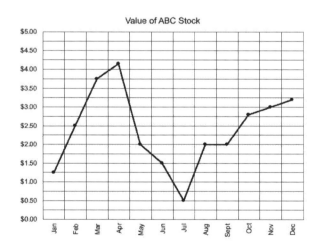

Value of ABC Stock

A. The average price for the stock never falls below $1.00.

B. The average price for the stock was higher in May than in February.

C. The average price for the stock declined near the end of the year.

D. January was the worst month overall in the stock market.

E. The average price for the stock for the year is above $1.50.

25. The frequency table shows the ranges for the ages of presidents at the time of their inauguration. What can be inferred from the frequency table?

Range	Frequency
41-45	2
46-50	8
51-55	16
56-60	9
61-65	7
66-70	3

A. The median age of a president at inauguration is 50.

B. There have been 10 presidents over the age of 60 at inauguration.

C. The same number of presidents have been inaugurated in their 40s as in their 60s.

D. At least one president was 70 at their inauguration.

E. The most common age for presidents at their inauguration is 53.

26. Mr. and Mrs. Jones have 7 children. Two of the children are 5 years old. The median age of the children is 9. The oldest child is 15. Finally, the range of the children's ages is 11. Which is a possible age of the second oldest Jones child? Choose all that apply.

A. 7

B. 8

C. 9

D. 12

E. 13

27. Company A is hiring for several positions with varying salaries as shown in the table.

Salary/Year	$25,000	$30,000	$35,000	$100,000	$150,000
Number of Positions available	1	5	8	1	1

Which statistical measure should Company A use when advertising to make their salary options look the most promising for potential applicants?

A. Mean

B. Median

C. Mode

D. Minimum

E. Standard deviation

28. At a marketing company, starting salaries range from $40,000 to $80,000, depending on experience. The company has agreed to a yearly Christmas bonus of $1000 for every employee. If that bonus is averaged into the salary for every employee, which of the following is true?

   A. The mean and median salaries stay the same; the standard deviation changes.

   B. The mean and median salaries increase; the standard deviation stays the same.

   C. The mean and median salaries decrease; the standard deviation changes.

   D. The mean and median salaries stay the same; the standard deviation stays the same.

   E. The mean and median salaries stay the decrease; the range increases.

29. A company that specializes in training people to type quickly for jobs like administrative assistant and court reporter advertised that their clients improve their typing speed to 65 words per minute (WPM) after using their program. The data from 8 clients who used the program is shown below. Which statistical measure did the company use to support their claim?

   65, 50, 65, 58, 60, 61, 70, 65

   A. Median

   B. Mode

   C. Mean

   D. Standard deviation

   E. Range

30. Ryan has an average of 89% in his math class after the first four tests. What does Ryan need to score on the 5th test to receive at least a 90% in the class?

   A. 92%

   B. 93%

   C. 94%

   D. 95%

   E. 96%

31. The two charts show two different countries' GDP over a period of time. Which of the following statements are true? Choose all that apply.

Country A GDP	
Year	$ (Billions)
1	3
3	7
5	11
7	15
9	19
11	23

Country B GDP	
Year	$ (Billions)
1	2
2	4
3	6
4	8
5	10
6	12

A. Country A increased GDP by $2 billion per year.

B. Country A's yearly GDP were greater than Country B's GDP earnings.

C. Both countries' yearly GDP increased at the same rate.

D. Country B's GDP increased at a greater rate than Country A's GDP.

E. The difference or similarities in GDP cannot be determined based on the charts.

32. A school is having a bake sale to raise money for new baseball equipment. Below is a chart of total sales per volunteer. Which number is closest to the mean?

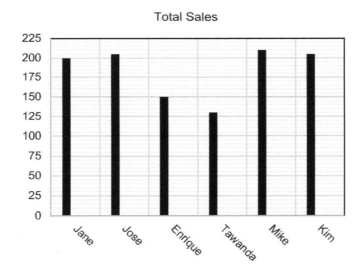

Total Sales

A. $130

B. $170

C. $183

D. $198

E. $200

33. The table below shows grade levels of students in sports. If one student is picked at random, what is the probability the student will be a sophomore and a tennis player or soccer player?

	Tennis	Soccer
Freshman	15	20
Sophomore	10	25

A. $\dfrac{2}{7}$

B. $\dfrac{1}{3}$

C. $\dfrac{2}{8}$

D. $\dfrac{1}{2}$

E. $\dfrac{3}{4}$

34. The chart below shows a family vacation budget. If airfare was $2700, what was the total budget for the trip?

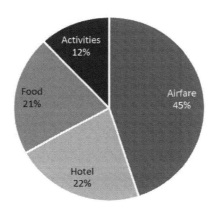

A. $5000

B. $6000

C. $7000

D. $8000

E. $9000

35. In the class treasure chest, there are erasers, stickers, and bouncy balls. The probability of picking an eraser is $\frac{1}{6}$. The probability of picking a sticker is $\frac{1}{2}$. What is the probability of picking a bouncy ball?

A. $\frac{1}{3}$

B. $\frac{1}{2}$

C. $\frac{2}{3}$

D. $\frac{5}{6}$

E. $\frac{6}{7}$

36. The chart below represents the relationship between the number of times people in an average sized town traveled in a year and the average rates of positive flu cases. What is the most reasonable generalization based on the data in the scatter plot below?

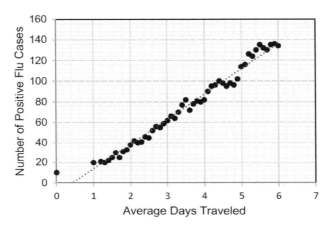

A. There is a weak positive correlation between number of days people traveled and number of positive flu cases.

B. There is a strong positive correlation between number of days people traveled and number of flu cases.

C. Traveling more than 3 days per year did not cause more than 60 people to contract the flu.

D. There is no correlation between number of days traveled and the number of positive flu cases.

E. There is a weak negative correlation between traveling and number of flu cases.

37. Cindy writes position papers for an online academic journal and charges based on the average number of pages she writes. This month she writes two 15-page papers, one 18-page paper, and two 20-page papers. If she adds an additional 18-page and 20-page paper, how does the mean amount change?

    A. The mean increases by 0.5.

    B. The mean decreases by 0.5.

    C. The mean increases by 0.4.

    D. The mean decreases by 0.4.

    E. The mean does not change.

38. The stem-and-leaf plot shows the average life span of various mammals. What are the median and range of the life span of the mammals in the plot?

Stem	Leaf
0	5 5 8
1	0 0 2 2 2 2 2 3 6
2	0 0 5
3	5
4	1
5	

key $1 \mid 2 = 12$

    A. Median: 2; Range: 4

    B. Median: 12; Range: 45

    C. Median: 2; Range: 36

    D. Median: 12; Range: 36

    E. Median 16; Range 45

39. Simplify

    $x^3 y^3 (xy)^{-2}$

    A. xy

    B. $x^2 y^3$

    C. $\dfrac{1}{xy}$

    D. x

    E. y

40. A car salesperson makes a base pay amount of $540 plus 20% commission from all sales during the week. Which of the following equations represents his pay at the end of the week so that he earns no less than $1200?

   A. $0.2x + 540 < 1200$

   B. $0.2x + 540 > 1200$

   C. $0.2x + 540 \leq 1200$

   D. $0.2x + 540 \geq 1200$

   E. $0.2x + 540 = 1200$

41. Solve.

   $$5x - 7 \leq 2x - 10$$

   A. $x \leq 1$

   B. $x \leq -1$

   C. $x \geq 1$

   D. $x \geq -1$

   E. $x \leq 0$

42. A family wants to install pavers in a 10 ft by 20 ft area in their backyard. The pavers are 4 in by 8 in. If the pavers are $500 per pallet and there are 200 pavers on a pallet, how much will the family spend on pavers?

   A. $900.00

   B. $1000.00

   C. $1500.00

   D. $2000.00

   E. $2500.00

43. Classify a triangle with interior angle measurements of 20°, 50°, and 110°.

   A. acute scalene

   B. isosceles

   C. obtuse scalene

   D. equilateral

   E. right triangle

44. What is the angle measure for x?

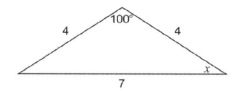

A. 20°

B. 30°

C. 40°

D. 50°

E. 60

45. The end of a 15-foot ladder rests on the top of a 12-foot wall. What is the distance between the bottom of the wall and the bottom of the ladder?

A. 7 feet

B. 9 feet

C. 13.5 feet

D. 15 feet

E. 19 feet

46. Jim is filling up his rectangular 8-foot by 10-foot pool for the summer. He will fill it all the way up, leaving only 6 inches from the top of the pool. If the pool is 6 feet deep, how many cubic feet of water will he use to fill his pool?

A. 540

B. 480

C. 440

D. 400

E. 340

47. Jose is shipping two boxes of shoes to his brother. The shoe boxes are 6 in by 4 in by 12 in. He puts both boxes into a third box, with dimensions of 12 in by 12 in by 12 in. How much empty space is in the third box?

A. 456 in³

B. 660 in³

C. 868 in³

D. 1048 in³

E. 1152 in³

48. A 6-inch by 4-inch by 5-inch box has a wrap that covers the outside of the box, but does not include the top and bottom. What is the area, in square inches, of the wrap?

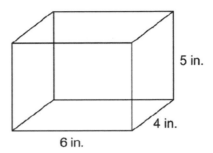

5 in.

4 in.

6 in.

A. 120

B. 100

C. 96

D. 80

E. 75

49. Solve for x.

$$\frac{5x - 3}{5} = 2x + 1$$

A. $-1\frac{3}{5}$

B. $1\frac{3}{4}$

C. $-\frac{4}{5}$

D. $\frac{4}{5}$

E. $1\frac{4}{5}$

50. The figure below is a rectangle. Which of the following is/are true? Choose all that apply.

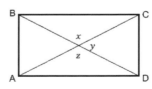

☐ $\overline{AB} \cong \overline{CD}$

☐ $x \cong y$

☐ $x \cong z$

☐ $x° + y° = 180°$

☐ $\angle A + \angle B + \angle C + \angle D = 360°$

51. The figure below is made of 5 squares. All of the squares are the same size. If the perimeter of the figure is 84 in, what is the area of the figure?

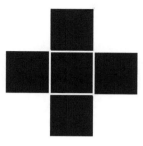

    A. 49 in²

    B. 98 in²

    C. 144 in²

    D. 235 in²

    E. 245 in²

52. The triangle below is a right triangle. If the total area of the triangle is 48. What is the length of side B?

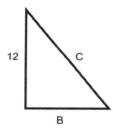

    A. 8

    B. 7

    C. 6

    D. 5

    E. 4

53. The courtyard of a high school is in a shape of a circle. A walkway forms a straight line through the center of the courtyard from point A to B. The area of the courtyard is 361π ft^2. What is the length of the walkway?

    A. 19

    B. 36

    C. 38

    D. 42

    E. 52

54. Read the scenario below and answer the question.

    Jan is dividing up her weekend into 3 activities: homework, video games, and playing outside. If she has 18 hours of her weekend for these activities, how many minutes does she spend playing video games?

    The question above is missing important information. Which of the following statements needs to be included in order to solve the problem?

    A. Jan spends 360 min playing video games.

    B. Jan spends 5 hours total playing outside.

    C. Jan has 1080 total min in her weekend to do homework, play video games, and play outside.

    D. Jan spent twice as much time playing video games than she did doing her homework.

    E. Jan spent equal amount of time playing video games and doing homework and half that time playing outside.

55. The graph below represents the number of miles driven over time. Which equation represents this scenario?

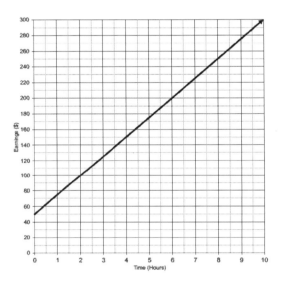

    A. $y = 50x$

    B. $y = 25x + 50$

    C. $y = 50x + 50$

    D. $y = 25x$

    E. $y = 25x - 50$

56. Which of the following statements is/are true? Choose all that apply

    A. $x(a + b) = x(b + a)$

    B. $x + (a + b) = (x + a) + b$

    C. $x - x = x + (-x)$

    D. $x + y = x - y$

    E. $2(x + y) = 2x + y$

Practice Test 3 – Answer Explanations

Number	Answer	Content Category	Explanation
1	B	I	Rewrite $-3\frac{2}{3}$ as a decimal, writing out the decimal to three places. Then, add additional zeros after -3.6 to compare the two values. $-3\frac{2}{3} \approx -3.667$ $-3.6 = -3.600$ Because -3.600 is closer to zero than -3.667, -3.6 is the larger value. **Quick Tip** Be careful with negatives because the smaller negative number is actually the larger number. Think of it in terms of money. Would you rather have $-\$10$ in your bank account or $-\$5$?
2	E	I	Convert each of the lengths to decimals, writing each decimal out three places after the decimal point. $2.5 = 2.500$ $2.27 = 2.270$ $2\frac{1}{5} = 2.200$ $2\frac{2}{8} = 2.250$ $2.215 = 2.215$ Looking at the numbers this way is easier to order them. $2.5, \quad 2.27, \quad 2\frac{2}{8} \quad 2.215, \quad 2\frac{1}{5}$

Number	Answer	Content Category	Explanation
3	B	I	To find the average of the ratings, we first have to multiply the ratings at each level by the number of stars in that level. 1 star: $1 \times 2 = 2$ 2 stars: $2 \times 3 = 6$ 3 stars: $3 \times 20 = 60$ 4 stars: $4 \times 15 = 60$ Next, find the average of the star ratings by adding the totals above and dividing by 40 (the number of ratings). $$\frac{2 + 6 + 60 + 60}{40} = \frac{2 + 6 + 60 + 60}{40} = 3.2$$
4	A	I	It is important to pay attention to the quantities of each item for this question. Find the amount spent per item, then find the total and subtract from the monthly allotment. Large copier: $\$0.05 \cdot 500 = \$25$ Small copier: $\$0.03 \cdot 2{,}500 = \$75$ Paper: $2 \cdot 6 \cdot \$9.95 = \$119.40$ Mailing supplies: $\$85.50$ Stamps: $\$0.55 \cdot 200 = \$110$ Miscellaneous: $\$20$ Total: $\$25 + \$75 + 119.40 + \$85.50 + \$110 + \$20 = \$434.90$ Remaining Budget: $\$500 - \$434.90 = \$65.10$
5	B	I	The equations below represent the total price per month for each membership. Exercise bike: $y = 35x$ Gym: $y = 99 + 18.50x$ To find when one membership is equal to the other, set the equations equal to one another and solve for x, which represents the number of months. $35x = 99 + 18.50x$ $-18.50x \qquad -18.50x$ $16.50x = 99$ $\dfrac{16.50x}{16.50} = \dfrac{99}{16.50}$ $x = 6$ After 6 months, the gym will cost less than the exercise bike company for a membership.

Number	Answer	Content Category	Explanation
6	B	I	$8 + 2(\underline{-3-2})^2 \div 5 \times (-2)$ $= 8 + 2\underline{(-5)^2} \div 5 \times (-2)$ $= 8 + \underline{2(25)} \div 5 \times (-2)$ $= 8 + \underline{50 \div 5} \times (-2)$ $= 8 + \underline{10 \times (-2)}$ $= \underline{8 + (-20)}$ $= -12$
7	D	I	$-2(-1)^3 - (-3) - 2^2(-1)^4$ $= -2(-1) - (-3) - \underline{2^2}(-1)^4$ $= -2(-1) - (-3) - 4\underline{(-1)^4}$ $= \underline{-2(-1)} - (-3) - 4(1)$ $= 2 - (-3) - \underline{4(1)}$ $= \underline{2 - (-3)} - 4$ $= \underline{5 - 4}$ $= 1$ **Caution** Order of operations states that you must do exponents before multiplication. Think of that negative sign in from of the 2 in the second step as a -1×2^2. Therefore, you must work the exponent first without the negative. If the -2 were in parentheses, then it would be included in the exponent operation.
8	A	I	This question requires the use of the distance formula, $d = rt$. The information given about driver B is that she drove for 7 hours, and she drove the same distance as driver A. Thus, we need to find the distance driver A drove. $d = rt$ $d = 56 \cdot 6$ $d = 336$ miles Now, substitute the distance and hours into the distance formula to find the rate at which driver B drove. $d = rt$ $336 = r \cdot 7$ $\dfrac{336}{7} = \dfrac{r \cdot \cancel{7}}{\cancel{7}}$ $48 = r$

Number	Answer	Content Category	Explanation
9	A	I	To answer this question, set up a proportion using the ratio. Then solve for x. $$\frac{\frac{1}{4}}{5} = \frac{x}{88.6}$$ $$5x = \frac{1}{4}(88.6)$$ $$5x = 0.25(88.6)$$ $$5x = 22.15$$ $$\frac{5x}{5} = \frac{22.15}{5}$$ $$x = 4.43$$
10	C	I	If everyone shakes hands with everyone else in the room, remember that everyone only needs to shake someone else's hand just once and no one shakes their own hand. For example, once person 1 shakes person 2's hand, person 2 does not need to shake person 1's hand. If we label the people 1 through 6, we get the following: Person 1 shakes hands with: 2, 3, 4, 5, 6 Person 2 shakes hands with: 3, 4, 5, 6 Person 3 shakes hands with: 4, 5, 6 Person 4 shakes hands with: 5, 6 Person 5 shakes hands with: 6 There is no one left for person 6 to shake hands with. Therefore, the number of handshakes is $5 + 4 + 3 + 2 + 1 = 15$.

Number	Answer	Content Category	Explanation
11	B	I	We need to find the greatest value in the list of numbers. For the first two values, −12 and −10, −10 is greater, so we can eliminate −12 from the list. We can also eliminate −21 from the list because it is much smaller than all the numbers. For the remaining numbers, you can either estimate the values and choose the largest number, or you can change the remaining values to decimals and compare. Both methods are shown. Choose which method works best for you. Estimating: Comparing −10 and $\frac{-21}{2}$, −10 is greater because −21 divided by 2 is −10.5. This means we can eliminate $\frac{-21}{2}$ from the list as well. Although we don't know we do know that it is very close to which equals . Because −10 is greater than −12 we can eliminate $-\sqrt{145}$. Converting: Change the remaining numbers to decimals so that it is easy to compare them. $-10 = -10$ $\frac{-21}{2} = -10.5$ $-\sqrt{145} = -12.04$ Based on the list, −10 is the greatest value.
12	B	I	To prove this, we can use our rules for exponents and work out each of the answer choices: $4^3 = 3^4 \rightarrow 64 = 81$ FALSE $5^0 \times 8^2 > 2^5 \rightarrow 1 \times 64 > 32$ TRUE $7^4 + 7^3 = 7^7 \rightarrow 2{,}401 + 343 = 823{,}543$ FALSE $5^4 - 5^2 = 5^2 \rightarrow 625 - 25 = 25$ FALSE $5^0 = 0 \rightarrow 1 = 0$ FALSE We could have stopped after answer choice B because it is correct. Remember to work efficiently through the answers.
13	A	I	First you have to figure out the total income. If each person makes $52,000 per year, their total gross is $104,000. However, they have a total income with investments of $156,000. To figure out how much of the income is just from investments, subtract 104 from 156 (you do not need to add the zeros here because the place value is the same (100,000). $156 - 104 = 52$ $\frac{52}{156} = \frac{1}{3}$

Number	Answer	Content Category	Explanation
14	C	I	Use a proportion to set up this problem. You will need to do this 2 times.

First you need to figure out how many teachers are currently at the school because that information is not given in the problems. However, we can figure this out with the ratio and a proportion. The ratio is 1 caregiver to every 5 students. Therefore, the fraction is $\frac{1}{5}$.

Next, we do not know how many caregivers there are total, but we do know the total number of students, which is 200. Therefore, that fraction is $\frac{x}{200}$.

Set up the proportion like this:

$$\frac{x}{200} = \frac{1}{5}$$
$$5x = 200$$
$$x = 40$$

Cross multiply and solve and you get 40 teachers. However, that is how many are currently at the school. Now we need to find out the desired amount to comply with the law. Do the same thing with the new proportion.

$$\frac{1}{3} = \frac{x}{200}$$
$$200 = 3x$$
$$x = 66.67$$

Cross multiply and solve, and you get 66.67. However, the principal cannot hire 0.67 of a teacher. Therefore, the school needs not 66 but 67 teachers to be in compliance with the law.

Be careful; you're not done.

Now subtract to figure out how many more teachers need to be hired.

$67 - 40 = 27$ more teachers. |
| 15 | E | I | Start at zero and use addition and subtraction to figure this out.

Person 1: $0 + 5 = 5$

Person 2: $5 - 5 = 0$

Person 3: $0 + 2 = 2$

Person 4: $2 + 1 = \mathbf{3}$ |

Number	Answer	Content Category	Explanation
16	C	I	To answer this question, it is easier and faster to convert all measurements to ounces. You need the convert cups to ounces. 1 cup = 8 ounces To solve, convert the two measurements that include cups to ounces. 1 cup 3 oz. = 8 + 3 oz. = 11 oz. 1 cup = 8 oz. Then add all the values in the list together. 4 + 11 + 6 + 8 +1+ 2 = 32 ounces Because the answer choices are in cups, convert 32 ounces to cups by dividing by 8 (because there are 8 ounces in 1 cup). 32 ÷ 8 = 4 cups
17	C	I	To find the total number of possible combinations, multiply the number of choices for each option. 3 × 2 × 4 = 24
18	C	I	There are 8 teams and each one has to play all the others. Make a list to find the total number of games played. Using letters for the teams we get the following: A plays: B, C, D, E, F, G, and H B plays: C, D, E, F, G, and H C plays: D, E, F, G, and H D plays: E, F, G, and H E plays: F, G, and H F plays: G and H G plays: H Adding the number of games each played we get: 7 + 6 + 5 + 4 + 3 + 2 +1= 28
19	E	I	The pattern is 4 numbers (2, 3, 4, 5). Even though the calculator shows 8 numbers, the pattern is still 4. If you are looking for the 100th number, simply divide 100 by 4 and you get 25. Since the pattern divides evenly into a whole number, the last number will be the 100th number, which is 5.

Number	Answer	Content Category	Explanation
20	C	I	Solve by using the percent decrease method: $$\frac{\text{new price} - \text{original price}}{\text{original price}}$$ Rural House: 1200 x 0.15 = $180 per month City House: 900 x 0.11 = $99 per month $$\frac{99 - 180}{180} - \frac{-81}{180} = -.45$$ Convert −.45 to a percent and drop the negative sign and you get a 45% decrease.
21	A	II	For this data set, we can determine the median and mode without having to write out all the numbers in a list. The mode and the median are both 85%. This eliminates answer choices B and C. The range, which is 20, will be significantly smaller than the mean, which will fall between 70 and 90. This eliminates answer choice D. Standard deviation is how spread out the numbers are. In this case the standard deviation is 10 because 75 to 85 is 10 and 85 to 95 is ten. Ten is too low, which leaves choice A, mean
22	C	II	For the first selection, the probability of choosing a red marble is $\frac{4}{15}$ because there are 15 total marbles. (denominator) and there are 4 possible red marbles to be picked (numerator). However, when selecting a red marble first, the total number drops to 14 (denominator) and the possibility of choosing a red marble also drops to 3 (numerator). Therefore, the probability of choosing a red marble as the second pick after a red marble is chosen is $\frac{3}{14}$.
23	E	II	The data varies without forming a pattern. Therefore, there is no trend in the data. In addition, if we look at all the other statements, they are false.
24	E	II	Just by estimating, you can see that there are more values over $1.50 than below, which makes answer E the best answer. None of the other assertions are true based on the data in the graph.
25	B	II	There is not enough information in the chart for answers A or E to be true, so eliminate those. Answer choice C can also be eliminated because the age ranges are not grouped by decades, such as 40s or 60s. Instead, the decades overlap in the ranges, e.g., 36-40. You may be tempted to choose D. However, we cannot tell from the information how many people were 70 because only a range is given. Answer B is correct because we can conclude from the data that 10 people were at least 60 years old or older at their inauguration.

Number	Answer	Content Category	Explanation
26	C, D, & E	II	From the clues in the question, you can figure out 5 out of the 7 children's ages. There are 7 kids, the median age is 9. 9 is the middle number with 3 kids on each side. According to the question, there are two 5-year-old children, but you cannot figure out where they go until you solve the range. Range is the biggest number minus the smallest number in the set. Therefore, if the oldest child is 15, according to the question, and the range is 11, the youngest child is 4 because $15 - 4 = 11$. Therefore the 5-year-olds go between the 4 and 9-year-old. That leaves two possible slots open. The children must be between 9 and 15, making answers C, D, and E all possible answer choices. 4, 5, 5, 9, __, __, 15 You may be hesitant to choose 9, or answer C. However, 9 is a possibility.
27	A	II	When having to find the mean, median, and mode, start with finding the median and mode because they are easiest. If they do not lead to the answer, then find the mean. We can eliminate D because the minimum is the lowest and not that attractive to potential employees. We can also eliminate E, standard deviation, because the distance between numbers is different and standard deviation does not apply. Notice that in the table there are 7 positions listed at $35,000, 5 positions listed below $30,000 and 2 listed above $35,000. Without listing out all these salaries, we can see that $35,000 will be the median and the mode. See example below. 25, 30, 30, 30, 30, 30, 35, <u>35</u>, 35, 35, 35, 35, 35, 100, 150 Because these values are the same, answer choices B and C can be eliminated because there can only be one correct answer. This leaves the mean, which is $46,000. The salary of $46,000 is above the mode and median and most attractive to potential employees.
28	B	II	To best understand this problem, assume there are 5 people with salaries of 40, 50, 60, 70, and 80 thousand. The median of this set is 60 thousand, and the mean is 60 thousand. The standard deviation is 10 thousand because there is a difference of 10 thousand between each salary. If each person gets a bonus of $1,000, the data changes to 41, 51, 61, 71, and 81 thousand. The mean and median now change to 61, but the standard deviation is still 10 because there is still a difference of 10 between each number. In addition, the range stays the same because $80 - 40 = 40$ and $81 - 41 = 40$, which makes answer E incorrect. Thus, when adding the same number to every number, the standard deviation and range remain the same, but the mean and median change.

Number	Answer	Content Category	Explanation
29	B	II	Because the company claims that their program yields a typing speed of 65 words per minute, the mode, which is 65, best supports their claim. Look at all the statistical measures to verify the mode is the best answer. 50, 58, 60, 61, 65, 65, 65, 70 Mean: $50 + (58 + 60 + 61 + 65 + 65 + 65 + 70) \div 8 = 494 \div 8 = 61.75$ Median: $\frac{61 + 65}{2} + \frac{126}{2} = 63$ Mode: 65 Range: $70 - 50 = 20$
30	C	II	The easiest way to solve these problems is to use the set up below. $\frac{4 \times 89 + x}{5} = 90$ $\frac{356 + x}{5} = 90$ Isolate the variable by multiplying both sides by 5. $356 + x = 450$ Solve for x. $x = 94$ **Quick Tip** $4 \times 89 + x$ is the sum of all 5 tests added together. The x is the fifth test. Don't forget to divide by 5 not 4 because there will be a total of 5 tests.
31	A & C	II	Be careful not to jump to a conclusion before thinking through this question. Any time you are comparing data from two tables, find the slope, or rate of change for each. The rate of change, which is $2 billion per year, is the same for both companies. You can also look at the graphs and see that Country A is reporting 4 billion in sales every 2 years, which is an average of 2 billion per year. Country B is reporting 2 billion in sales every year. Therefore, they are the same.

Number	Answer	Content Category	Explanation
32	C	II	You can calculate the mean by adding up all the values and dividing by 6, which will get you $183. However, you can also estimate by using your answer choices to save time. Answers A and B are too small to be the average. Answers D and E are too large.
33	D	II	Take the total number is 70 and the number of sophomore tennis and soccer players is 35. $\dfrac{35}{70} = \dfrac{1}{2}$
34	B	II	To solve this problem, simply take 2700 and divide by the percentage. $2700 \div 0.45 = 6000$ You can take 2700 and divide by the answer choices until you get 0.45. $2700 \div 6000 = 0.45$ or 45%
35	A	II	To solve this problem, you have to remember that these are parts of a whole. The whole is 1. Set it up as: $1 - \dfrac{1}{6} - \dfrac{1}{2}$ Find the common denominator. $\dfrac{6}{6} - \dfrac{1}{6} - \dfrac{3}{6} = \dfrac{2}{6} = \dfrac{1}{3}$ Another way is to add the probabilities you know and subtract them from 1. $\dfrac{1}{6} + \dfrac{1}{2}$ Find the common denominator $\dfrac{1}{6} + \dfrac{3}{6} = \dfrac{4}{6} = \dfrac{2}{3}$ $1 - \dfrac{2}{3}$ or $\dfrac{3}{3} - \dfrac{2}{3} = \dfrac{1}{3}$ Either way gets you the correct answer: $\dfrac{1}{3}$

Number	Answer	Content Category	Explanation
36	B	II	The line is moving up and all the dots are very close together. Therefore, the graph represents a strong positive correlation. **Test Tip** Stay away from answer choices that use the word cause. Scatter plots show correlation not causation.
37	C	II	First find the mean of the data set. $(15 + 15 + 18 + 20 + 20) \div 5 = 88 \div 5 = 17.6$ Because she is adding more papers, the mean will increase. Therefore, we can eliminate answer choices B and D. The new average or mean will be: $(88 + 18 + 20) \div 7 = 126 \div 7 = 18$ The difference between the two means is 0.4, so the correct answer choice is C.
38	D	II	There are 17 values in the data set, so the median for the data will be the 9th value, which is 12. Be careful not to choose 2 by misreading the plot. The range is found by subtracting 5 from 41. $41 - 5 = 36$
39	A	III	First distribute the –2 power to each variable in the parentheses. Next, add exponents with like bases. $x^3 y^3 (xy)^{-2}$ $= x^3 y^3 x^{-2} y^{-2}$ $= x^{(3-2)} y^{(3-2)}$ $= x^1 y^1$ $= xy$
40	D	III	The salesperson wants to make no less than $1200. This can be interpreted as the amount he earns should be $1200 or more than $1200. Thus, we are first looking for an inequality that is greater than or equal to, which is answer D.

Number	Answer	Content Category	Explanation
41	B	III	Solve just like you would an equation with an equal sign; isolate the variable. $5x - 7 \leq 2x - 10$ Add 7 to both sides $5x \leq 2x - 3$ Subtract $2x$ from both sides. This keeps the left side of the inequality positive. $3x \leq -3$ Divide both sides by 3. $x \leq -1$ By keeping the side with the variable positive, you avoid having to flip the sign. However, the inequality can also be solved this way: $5x - 7 \leq 2x - 10$ Add 10 to both sides $5x + 3 \leq 2x$ Subtract $5x$ from both sides. $3 \leq -3x$ Divide both sides by -3 and change the sign because you are dividing by a negative. $-1 \geq x$ This is the same as $x \leq -1$. Remember, if you divide by a negative in an inequality, you must change the sign.

Number	Answer	Content Category	Explanation
42	E	III	There are 6 steps to this problem: 1. Convert feet to inches for the backyard. Remember there are 12 in a foot, so you have to multiply by 12. 10 ft × 20 ft becomes 120 in × 240 in 2. Find the area of the backyard in inches 120 × 240 = 28800 in² 3. Find the area of the pavers. 8 × 4 = 32 in² 4. Divide the area of the yard by the area of the pavers to figure out how many pavers you need. 28800 in² ÷ 32 in² = 900 5. Divide 900 by 200 since each pallet holds 200 pavers. 900 ÷ 200 = 4.5 6. Pallets come in units of 1 at $500, so you will need 5 pallets. $500 × 5 = $2500.00
43	C	III	The 110° angle measure should lead you to obtuse. There is only one answer choice with the obtuse option. Also, all interior angles are different. Therefore, this is a scalene triangle.

Number	Answer	Content Category	Explanation
44	C	III	The question is asking for the value of an angle measure, but two angle measures are missing. This means there is other information in the drawing that can be used to help determine the third angle measure. For this triangle, there are two side lengths that are the same measure, which makes the triangle an isosceles triangle. It is important to know that when a triangle is isosceles, not only are two sides the same length, but the two base angles are the same measure. 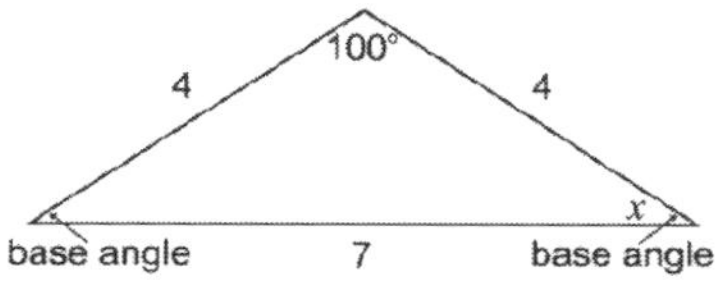 *Note: This is especially important to remember because you may have to classify an isosceles triangle with only angle measures given.* Because we know the two base angles are the same measure, they are both equal to x. Recalling that all three angles in a triangle add to 180°, we get the following: $x + x + 100 = 180$ $2x + 100 = 180$ $\underline{\quad -100 \ -100}$ $2x = 80$ $\dfrac{2x}{2} = \dfrac{80}{2}$ $x = 40$ *Remember, on the test nobody is checking your work. If you see that you can quickly subtract 100 from 180 and then divide by 2, you do NOT need to work out the formal equation. It is only shown here to help you understand how the problem works. This is a timed test, and every minute counts!*

Number	Answer	Content Category	Explanation
45	B	III	This is another real-world problem that is helpful to visualize with a quick sketch. The ladder forms a right triangle with the wall and the ground. Therefore, we can use the Pythagorean theorem to find the distance from the base of the wall to the base of the ladder. Pythagorean Theorem: $a^2 + b^2 = c^2$ Based on our sketch: $a = 12$ $b = ?$ $c = 15$ $a^2 + b^2 = c^2$ $12^2 + b^2 = 15^2$ $144 + b^2 = 225$ $\underline{-144 \qquad -144}$ $b^2 = 81$ $\sqrt{b^2} = \sqrt{81}$ $b = 9$

Number	Answer	Content Category	Explanation
46	C	III	Because the pool is rectangular and is also three-dimensional, the space taken up by the water is the volume of the pool. Leaving 6 inches at the top changes the height used for volume from 6 feet to 5.5 feet. To find the volume taken by the water, substitute values into the formula for the volume of a rectangular prism (box). $V = lwh$ $V = 10 \text{ feet} \cdot 8 \text{ feet} \cdot 5.5 \text{ feet}$ $= 440 \text{ feet}^3$
47	E	III	Find the total volume of both shoeboxes ($l \times w \times h$) $6 \times 4 \times 12 = 288$ $288 \times 2 = 576 \text{in}^3$ Then find the volume of the larger box Jose is using to ship the two shoeboxes. $12 \times 12 \times 12 = 1728 \text{in}^3$ Now subtract the total volume of the two shoeboxes from the volume of the big box to find how much room will be left over. $1728 \text{in}^3 - 576 \text{in}^3 = 1152 \text{in}^3$
48	B	III	Find the area of each of the sides of the box to find the area of the wrap. $2 \times (5 \times 4) = 40$ $2 \times (5 \times 6) = 60$ Total area of wrap: $40 + 60 = 100$ square inches

Number	Answer	Content Category	Explanation
49	A	III	To solve the equation, multiply both sides by 5 to eliminate the fraction, then continue to solve for the variable. $$\frac{5x-3}{5} = 2x+1$$ $$5 \cdot \frac{5x-3}{5} = 5 \cdot (2x+1)$$ $$5x - 3 = 10x + 5$$ $$\underline{-5x \qquad -5x}$$ $$-3 = 5x + 5$$ $$\underline{-5 \qquad -5}$$ $$-8 = 5x$$ $$\frac{-8}{5} = \frac{5x}{5}$$ $$\frac{-8}{5} = -1\frac{3}{5} = x$$
50	Boxes 1, 3, 4, & 5	III	Opposite sides in a rectangle are congruent (have the same length. ❏ $\overline{AB} \cong \overline{CD}$ ✓ Opposite angles are congruent. ❏ $x \cong z$ ✓ A straight line $=$ ❏ $x° + y° = 180°$ ✓ All interior angles of a rectangle $=$ ❏ $\angle A + \angle B + \angle C + \angle D = 360°$ ✓
51	E	III	If the perimeter is 84in² and the figure is made up of squares (all sides are equal), you can find the length of each side by taking 84 and dividing by 12 because there are 12 sides to the shape. 84 ÷ 12 = 7 Because each side is 7, to find the area of one square, multiple 7 times 7 ($a = b \cdot h$). 7in × 7in = 49in² The shape is made up of 5 squares, so multiply 49 (the area of one square) by 5. 49in² × 5 = 245in²

Number	Answer	Content Category	Explanation
52	A	III	The area of a triangle is $\frac{1}{2}(b \cdot h)$. $\frac{1}{2}(b \cdot h) = 48$ $\frac{1}{2}(b \cdot 12) = 48$ Rewrite the equation so it's easier to work with. Multiplying by $\frac{1}{2}$ is the same as dividing by 2. $\frac{(b \cdot 12)}{2} = 48$ Isolate the variable by multiplying both sides by 2. $(b \cdot 12) = 96$ $12b = 96$ $b = 8$
53	C	III	The question is asking you to find the diameter of the circle. The diameter of a circle is 2 times the radius. You do not have the length of the radius, but you do have the area of the courtyard. The area of a circle is $A = \pi r^2$ The area of the courtyard is $361\pi = \pi r^2$ In this case, cancels out from both sides because you can divide both sides by π. To find radius, take the square root of both sides and you get $\sqrt{361} = \sqrt{r^2}$ $19 = r$ Since it is asking for the diameter, which is $2r$ then the diameter is 38. $19 \times 2 = 38$

Number	Answer	Content Category	Explanation
54	E	III	To solve the problem, you'll need algebraic thinking and a ratio. First start by elimination. Answers A and B still do not give you enough information to form a ratio or an equation. Therefore, they can be eliminated. Next, answer C gives you the same information in the original question. However, it gives you the total time in minutes instead of hours. That still is not enough information to solve the problem. Answer D gives you a little more information but not enough to solve. Answer E gives you just enough to form a proportion and solve. The question asks for how many minutes, so change 18 hours to 1080 minutes. Use the ratio below to solve. The ratio is $1:1:\frac{1}{2}$, which is also equivalent to $2:2:1$ (these numbers are easier to work with). Since 1080 is the total number of minutes, then you can solve using the methods below. **Homework** $1080 \times \dfrac{2}{2+2+1} = 432$ min **Playing video games** $1080 \times \dfrac{2}{2+2+1} = 432$ min **Playing outside** $1080 \times \dfrac{1}{2+2+1} = 216$ min Another way to solve: Once you find the amount of time doing homework, you can solve without all the other equations. Since homework and video games are equal, they are both 432 $432 + 432 = 864$ $1080 - 864 = 216$ Both methods work.

MATH
PRACTICE TESTS

Number	Answer	Content Category	Explanation
55	B	III	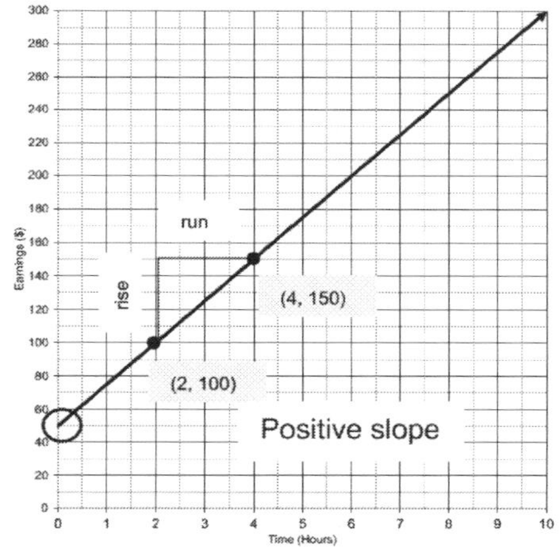 Use the formula $y = mx + b$ First, the line is moving in a positive direction. Therefore, you can eliminate answer E. Answer E has a negative sign next to the slope. Remember, the slope is attached to the x. It is the ^{m} in the equation. Recall b represents the y-intercept (or where y crosses the x-axis) The y crosses the x-axis at 50 (circled on the graph above). Therefore, b is 50. Eliminate answers A and D because in those equations, b is zero. To find the slope of this line, there are two methods you can use. Pick two points on the line and use our short cut for $\frac{y_2 - y_1}{x_2 - x_1}$, or eyeball it and use $\frac{rise}{sun}$. Shortcut for $\frac{y_2 - y_1}{x_2 - x_1}$ (Find two points, stack coordinates and subtract). $\begin{array}{r} 2 \quad 100 \\ -4 \quad 150 \\ \hline -2 - 50 \end{array}$ $\frac{rise}{run}$ or $\frac{x}{y}$ $\frac{-2}{-50} = 25$ Slope is 25 Therefore, $y = 25x + 50$
56	A, B, & C	III	A. $x(a + b) = x(b + a)$ YES because this is the communitive property B. $x + (a + b) = (x + a) + b$ YES because this is the associative property C. $x - x = x + (-x)$ YES because this is the invers property of addition. D. $x + y = x - y$ NO these do not equal each other. E. $2(x + y) = 2x + y$ NO this should be $2(x + y) = 2x + 2y$ in order for it to be the distributive property.

212 Writing

About the Test

The GACE Writing Test is a combine test of selected response questions and 2 essay tasks. The score for the writing is a combined score of your performance in those two areas. It is important to acquire points on the grammar selected response section because those points can help you compensate for any lost points on the essay tasks.

The two tasks you will perform on this exam assess your abilities in:

1. **Grammar and Mechanics** – This part of the exam will test all the basic grammar and mechanics rules. This includes usage, sentence correction, revision in context, and research skills.

2. **Writing** – This part of the exam requires you to write 2 separate essays that are well organized and display proper grammar usage

Test Tip

The essay and grammar are connected. Be sure to apply all the grammar and mechanics rules that are outlined in the grammar portion of this book to your essays. All of the tips and tricks in the grammar part of the book will help you during the essay task.

Test at a Glance	
Test Name	GACE Program Admission: Writing
Test Code	212
Time	100 minutes
Number of Questions	Approximately 40 selected-response questions and two essay questions
Format	Selected response questions involving usage, sentence correction, revision in context, and research skills
Test Delivery	Computer delivered

Content Category	Approx. Number of Questions	Approx. Percentage of Exam
I. Text Types, Purposes, and Production.	6-12 selected response and 2 essays	60%
II. Craft, Structure, and Language Skills	28-34 selected response	40%

II. 40%

I. 60%

I. Text Types, Purposes, and Production

Text Production: Writing Arguments

1. Produce an argumentative essay to support a claim using relevant and sufficient evidence.
2. Write clearly and coherently.
   - Address the assigned task appropriately for an audience of educated adults.
   - Organize and develop ideas logically, making coherent connections between them.
   - Provide and sustain a clear focus or thesis.
   - Use supporting reasons, examples, and details to develop clearly and logically the ideas presented.
   - Demonstrate facility in the use of language and the ability to use a variety of sentence structures.
   - Construct effective sentences that are generally free of errors in standard written English.

We have included the scoring rubric for the argumentative essay. Notice that a score of 4 shows **competence**. We recommend working towards a 4 or higher for the essay.

Score	Criteria
6 – Demonstrates a *high degree of competence* in response to the assignment but may have a few minor errors.	• Author provides a clear and declarative thesis statement • Organizes and develops ideas logically, providing cogent details and supporting examples that connect to the thesis • Clearly explains key details, supporting them with tangible examples • Demonstrates and successfully applies varied sentence structures • Clearly displays facility in the use of language • Displays a thorough command of grammar, usage, and mechanics
5 – Demonstrates *clear competence* in response to the assignment but may have minor errors.	• States or clearly implies the writer's position or thesis • Organizes and develops ideas clearly, making connections between them • Explains key ideas, supporting them with relevant reasons, concrete examples, and specific details • Displays some sentence variety • Displays facility in the use of language • Is virtually free from errors in grammar, usage, and mechanics
4 – Demonstrates *competence* in response to the assignment.	• States or implies the writer's position or thesis • Shows control in the organization and development of ideas • Offers some key ideas, details and examples, but lacks specificity • Displays adequate use of language • Shows control of grammar, usage, and mechanics, but may contain errors
3 – Demonstrates *some competence* in response to the assignment.	• Limited in stating or implying a position • Limited control in the organization and development of ideas • Inadequate reasons, example, or examples to explain key ideas • An accumulation of errors in the use of language • An accumulation of errors in the use of grammar, usage and mechanics.

WRITING

This page intentionally left blank.

Argumentative Essay

You will have a total of 30 minutes to plan and write an argumentative essay on the topic presented in the following section. The essay should be based on your own reading, experience, and observations.

Read the topic carefully. DO NOT WRITE ON A TOPIC OTHER THAN THE ONE SPECIFIED. Essays on topics of your own choice are not acceptable. In order for your test to be scored, your response must be in English.

The essay questions are included in this test to give you an opportunity to demonstrate how well you can write. You should consider the topic, organize your thoughts, and take care to write clearly and effectively, using specific examples where appropriate. How well you write is much more important than how much you write; however, to cover the topic adequately, it is suggested that you write more than one paragraph.

Read the opinion stated below.

> *The only important criterion by which to judge a prospective teacher is his or her ability to get along with students.*

Discuss the extent to which you agree or disagree with this point of view. Support your position with specific reasons and examples from your own experience, observations, or reading.

Sample Response of a 4 or Higher

I disagree with the idea that prospective teachers should be judged solely on his or her ability to get along with students. I do not feel that popularity is an accurate way to determine how effective an educator is. Prospective teachers should be judged on more important and substantial factors, such as being able to deliver information clearly and preparing students for the next step in their academic career. There are a variety of important factors involved in judging prospective teachers.

It is more important for teachers to be experts in their content areas than it is for them to be popular among students. For example, a biology teacher must have a detailed understanding of topics like cell division, osmosis, and photosynthesis. Similarly, English teachers must have a thorough academic understanding of grammar, usage, structure, composition, and literature. It takes an immense amount of knowledge to disseminate information and develop skills students will need to be successful in education and beyond.

In high school, I had an English teacher who was notorious for being difficult to deal with. I, along with others, found him abrasive and stuffy; he certainly wasn't getting along with most of his students at the time. We found his teaching style to be outdated and boring; he demanded us to diagram sentences, rewrite paragraphs over and over, and proofread constantly. However, during my freshman year of college I quickly realized that, because of my English teacher's approach, my knowledge of grammar, punctuation, and structure was far beyond my classmates' skills and understanding. It turns out, my English teacher had prepared me to be a successful college writer, even though he was easily the least popular teacher I'd ever had.

Being an effective teacher is not a popularity contest. Teachers must be experts in their fields to be able to give students the information they need to be successful. Although it is helpful for a teacher to be well-liked, that is not the only quality that makes a teacher effective.

Essay Breakdown

The essay example used here would be scored as a 4 or higher because of several reasons:

1. The writer made the position clear: *I disagree with the idea that prospective teachers should be judged solely on his or her ability to get along with the widest possible variety of students.*

    -   Be sure to pick one side or the other. The argumentative prompt is usually a strong statement like the one above, so agreeing or disagreeing is usually easy.

    -   Be sure you EITHER agree OR disagree. This is not the time to be in the middle on a topic. Both agreeing and disagreeing in your writing can lead to disorganization and incohesive writing. We recommend picking a position and sticking with it throughout your essay.

2. The essay is organized and easy to ready.

   - Notice the essay starts with the position clearly stated in the first paragraph.

   - The writer takes a *definitive* position.

   - There is a clear thesis statement in the last sentence of the first paragraph: *There are a variety of important factors involved in judging prospective teachers.*

   - The entire essay goes on to support the thesis and position of the writer.

   - The second paragraph is devoted to why the writer disagrees.

   - The third paragraph uses a personal example.

3. There are specific details referenced throughout the essay.

   - Specific examples in the second paragraph include biology and English teacher examples.

   - The third paragraph includes a personal experience with specific examples: an English teacher who was not likeable who made the class diagram sentences and other seemingly tedious tasks.

4. The writer uses proper grammar and mechanics.

   - The essay is free from major errors.

   - Punctuation is used properly.

   - Spelling is correct.

   - Varied sentence structure is used.

IMPORTANT: The example essay is a 4-paragraph essay. However, you could drop the last paragraph and still get a 4 or above on this task. The conclusion paragraph certainly rounds out the essay. However, for the sake of time, you could drop that last paragraph and still do very well.

Test Tip

The most important thing you can do while writing this essay is to use specific details and examples. Notice in the rubric, the biggest difference between a score of a 3 and a score of a 4 is the use of reasons and examples to support your position. Get specific in your essay. For example, in the sample essay, the writer describes biology and English. The writer even uses words like *photosynthesis* and *osmosis*. When the writer explains the personal experience, the writer uses specifics like diagraming sentences and constant proofreading. The reader can visualize this with detail.

Things to Avoid

While proofreading your essay, you will want to look for a variety of things in your writing:

   - Clichés

   - Awkward wording

   - Poor parallel structure

   - Misplaced/dangling modifiers

   - Slang or informal language

   - Improper grammar—see the English grammar section of this book for more details

Your turn.
You try to write an argumentative essay using the prompt below.

You will have a total of 30 minutes to plan and write an argumentative essay on the topic presented in the following section. The essay should be based on your own reading, experience, and observations.

Read the topic carefully. DO NOT WRITE ON A TOPIC OTHER THAN THE ONE SPECIFIED. Essays on topics of your own choice are not acceptable. In order for your test to be scored, your response must be in English.

The essay questions are included in this test to give you an opportunity to demonstrate how well you can write. You should consider the topic, organize your thoughts, and take care to write clearly and effectively, using specific examples where appropriate. How well you write is much more important than how much you write; however, to cover the topic adequately, it is suggested that you write more than one paragraph.

Read the opinion stated below.

> *Advanced degrees have limited usefulness in the job market and are not worth the expense. It is best for people to work towards experience on the job rather than to seek advanced degrees.*

Discuss the extent to which you agree or disagree with this point of view. Support your position with specific reasons and examples from your own experience, observations, or reading.

Sample Response Score of 4 or higher

I disagree with the statement "Advanced degrees have limited usefulness in the job market." In today's job market there are many careers in which an advance degree would be useful or necessary. An advanced degree is almost always seen as a positive addition to one's resume; having an advanced degree can mean increased yearly earnings.

There are a variety of advantages to earning an advanced degree. A master's degree provides graduate students with the opportunity to work in specialized fields. For instance, having an MBA would make someone qualified for a variety of business and management positions, which means an increase in pay. Research shows, those who obtain advanced degrees earn, on average, $25,000-$50,000 more per year than those who do not obtain advanced degrees.

In my experience, having an advanced degree has been extremely useful throughout my career. I was able to be part of several exciting research teams because of my advanced degree. I also had the opportunity to be part of an interdisciplinary team that studied connections between my two passions: astrophysics and Science Fiction. Finally, because I earned an advanced degree, I am currently making $10,000 more per year than I would if I did not have an advanced degree, and I have the opportunity to make even more.

This essay would receive a score of 4 or higher because:

- States or implies the writer's position or thesis.

- Shows control in the organization and development of ideas.

- Offers key ideas, details and examples: MBA, earnings statistics, astrophysics and Science Fiction.

- Displays adequate use of language.

- Shows control of grammar, usage, and mechanics

Quick Tip

Notice in paragraph 3, the writer gives a personal example. You may say to yourself, what if I do not have a personal example? Simple, *make one up*. No one is fact checking your essay. Therefore, if you make up a statistic or an experience, who cares? You're being assessed on your writing skills, not the how true your essay is.

Sometimes it is helpful to see a non-example so you know what to avoid. Below is a sample response that would receive a 3 or less.

Non-example: Score of 3 or less

In today's job market there are many careers in which an advance degree would be useful or necessary. Due to their specialized nature, jobs that require an advanced degree are often extremely competitive. Having an advanced degree is beneficial to one's career.

Though the job market can be competitive, there are a variety of advantages to earning an advanced degree. A master's degree provides students with the opportunity to work in more specialized fields. In my experience having an advanced degree has been extremely useful throughout my career. Thanks to my degree I will be exploring my newly discovered passion for teaching. Though my degree has obvious limitations, there is flexibility within my chosen specialty. I feel that most people who have chosen to pursue an advanced degree have some level of passion for the field and can find a job they enjoy within that field.

There are some clear advantages to having an advanced degree. Holding an advanced degree can provide a variety of opportunities for a fulfilling career.

What makes this essay a 3 instead of a 4?

You can see the author committed the following errors that contributed to a failing score of 3:

- The writer does not clearly and immediately state his/her opinion on the topic.

- There is a lack of fully formed ideas.

- The essay does not have specific examples to sufficiently support the argument.

- Ideas are started but never finished.

Think about it.

In this example, there is virtually no specificity or examples used to show why an advanced degree is important. To improve this essay, the writer could reference a statistic. For example, simply adding the sentence:

Research shows that those who earn advanced degrees make $25,000 more per year on average than those who do not ear an advanced degree.

That one detail sentence would do a lot to increase the score. Fake stats are a great way to enhance your writing for this task.

10 Additional Argumentative Writing Prompts

Here are 10 more prompts you can use to practice your argumentative writing. Remember, you can write to these prompts more than once. The first time, take one position, and the next time, take the opposite position.

1. Since schools have reopened, Covid-19 positive rates have increased exponentially. It is clear that the spread is due to millions of students returning to school. The only way to stop the spread of Covid-19 is to shut down face-to-face instruction in schools completely until the virus is gone.

2. All over the country, businesses have closed, and people have lost their jobs because of the shutdown brought about by Covid-19. It is clear that for the American economy to survive the country needs to reopen completely and stop all of the restrictions on businesses.

3. The only types of assessments teachers should use in the classroom are those that yield scores teachers can use to assign grades. All other assessments are a waste of time.

4. Because of the decline in American education, all students entering college should be required to take remedial reading and math as part of their courses their freshman year.

5. Because of the childhood obesity epidemic in this country, foods containing over a certain amount of sugar should be taxed.

6. There is a teacher shortage across the country and students are suffering due to lack of experienced teachers. The only way to reduce the teacher shortage is to pay teachers significantly more money than is currently offered.

7. Immigration is a huge problem in the United States. Because people come to the United States illegally for a free education, America should charge non-citizens for public education.

8. Vending machines should be banned from all public-school campuses.

9. Teacher certification exams are keeping good teachers out of the classroom. Therefore, teacher certification exams should be eliminated entirely.

10. Colleges and universities should do away with the ACT and SAT and admit students based on GPA only.

Test Tip

Practice your essay using these 11 steps:

1. Turn off spell check and grammar check in WORD. You do not have these luxuries on test day.

2. Set your timer for 30 min. and start.

3. Read the opinion only. (You will not have to read the instructions above the opinion because they're always says the same).

4. Use your scratch paper to plan and map your essay.

5. Jot down the specific details you will use.

6. Write the details paragraph first. It is often easier to start in the middle than it is to start with the intro.

7. Write the intro making sure you have a definitive thesis (last sentence in the first paragraph).

8. Proof and fix errors. Finish up.

9. Look at the time. Did you make it?

10. Read your essay back to yourself and use the rubric to score your essay.

11. Analyze what you could have done differently to make your essay better and repeat the process again.

This page intentionally left blank.

Text Production: Writing Informative/Explanatory Text

1. Produce an informative/explanatory essay to examine and convey complex ideas and information clearly and accurately through the effective selection, organization, and analysis of content.

2. Write clearly and coherently.

   - Address the assigned task appropriately for educated audiences
   - Draw evidence from informational texts to support analysis
   - Organize and develop ideas logically, making coherent connections between them
   - Synthesize information from multiple sources on the subject
   - Integrate and attribute information from multiple sources on the subject, avoiding plagiarism
   - Provide and sustain a clear focus or thesis
   - Demonstrate facility in the use of language and the ability to use a variety of sentence structures
   - Construct effective sentences that are generally free of errors in standard written English

This essay is often referred to as the source-based essay. In this task, you will be given two pieces of writing from two different authors. These are the sources. You must then summarize each author's position and use specific details from each source. You must also cite the authors when you paraphrase or quote their positions.

This task is easier than it looks. You do not have to come up with any new ideas. Everything is in the sources, which means all you have to do is locate information and then convey that in your writing.

Test Tip

The very best formula for this task is a 4-paragraph essay:

1. Intro: Summary of the issue or topic
2. Detail Paragraph: Summary of point of view of author one.
3. Detail Paragraph: Summary of point of view of author two.
4. Conclusion

WRITING

We have included the scoring rubric for the essay. Notice that a score of 4 shows *competence*. A score of 4 is the minimum score you want to achieve on this exam. Therefore, we recommend working towards a 4 or higher on this part of the exam.

Score	Criteria
6 – Demonstrates a **high degree of competence** in response to the assignment but may have a few minor errors.	• Insightfully explains why the concerns are important, supporting the explanation with effective links between the two sources and well-chosen reasons, examples, or details • Incorporates relevant information from both sources to identify and elaborate on important concerns discussed in the sources • Organizes and develops ideas logically • Displays effective sentence variety • Clearly displays facility in the use of language • Is free from errors in grammar, usage, and mechanics • Cites both sources when paraphrasing or quoting
5 – Demonstrates **clear competence** in response to the assignment but may have minor errors.	• Clearly explains why the concerns are important, supporting the explanation with clear links between the two sources and relevant reasons, examples, or details • Incorporates information from both sources to identify and explain important concerns regarding the issue discussed in the sources • Organizes and develops ideas clearly • Displays some sentence variety • Displays facility in the use of language • Is generally free from errors in grammar, usage, and mechanics • Cites both sources when paraphrasing or quoting
4 – Demonstrates **competence** in response to the assignment.	• Adequately explains why the concerns are important, supporting the explanation with some links between the two sources and adequate reasons, examples or details • Incorporates information from both sources to identify and explain important concerns regarding the issue discussed in the sources • Shows control in the organization and development of ideas • Displays adequate use of language • Shows control of grammar, usage, and mechanics, but may display errors • Cites both sources when paraphrasing or quoting
3 – Demonstrates **some competence** in response to the assignment nut is obviously flawed.	• Limited in explaining why the concerns are important • Incorporates only one source to identify and explain concerns regarding the issue discussed • Limited in supporting the explanation (establishes a weak link between the source and examples) • Limited control over organization and development of ideas • An accumulation of errors in use and language • An accumulation of errors in grammar, usage, and mechanics • Cites sources when paraphrasing or quoting

Source-Based Essay

Follow these steps when writing your source-based essay.

1. Read the **Assignment** because it gives you a general overview about the issue; you can reword the assignment portion and use it as your intro paragraph. You do not have to read the directions on test day. They will always be the same.

2. Next, summarize each source. You do NOT have to read these two sources in their entirety. In fact, we recommend that you do not read them fully. All you have to do is figure out which side of the argument each author is on. Reading both of these positions from top to bottom is unnecessary and wastes valuable time. Simply identify each person's position and jot them down on your scratch paper.

3. Then identify a few specific details in each source to support the authors' positions. Decide which specific detail(s) you will use for each author. Paraphrase those on your scratch paper.

4. Write the detail paragraphs first. Do NOT start with the intro. The intro can be difficult to write immediately. Starting with the summary of each author's point of view will be easier and save time.

5. Be sure to cite each author using APA format (Last Name, Date). Here are two ways to cite. Don't make this more complicated than it is. Just be sure to cite the authors when you use their ideas or language.

   - According to Yaffe (2016), voting it is a symbol with great psychological power.
   - Voting it is a symbol with great psychological power (Yaffe, 2016).

6. Write your intro and conclusion last. The bulk of the essay grade is coming from the detail paragraphs or the summary of each author's position. Therefore, you should write those first and if you have time, write the intro and conclusion paragraphs.

7. Proof. Be sure you have a couple of minutes left to read your essay back to yourself. Correct any grammatical or spelling errors.

Example Source-Based Essay Task

Directions: In the following section you will have 30 minutes to read two short passages on a topic and then plan and write an essay on that topic. The essay will be an informative essay based on the two sources that are provided.

Read the topic and the sources carefully. You will probably find it best to spend a little time considering the topic and organizing your thoughts before you begin writing. DO NOT WRITE ON A TOPIC OTHER THAN THE ONE SPECIFIED. Essays on topics of your own choice will not be acceptable. In order for your test to be scored, your response must be in English.

The essay questions are included in this test to demonstrate how well you can write. You should, therefore, write clearly and effectively, using specific examples where appropriate. Remember, that how well you write is more important than how much you write, but to cover topics adequately, you will probably have to write more than one paragraph.

Assignment: In recent years, the push to revise laws pertaining to a felon's right to vote has grown substantially. Many Americans feel that convicted felons should be able to regain their right to vote after they are released from prison. However, others feel that voting is a privilege, and once people are convicted of a serious crime, they should lose that privilege. Both of the following sources address whether or not these felons deserve to have their voting rights re-established and the positive or negative effect the revised law could have on the country.

Read the two passages carefully and write an essay in which you identify the most important concerns regarding the issue and explain why they are important. Your essay must draw on information from BOTH of the sources. In addition, you may draw on your own experiences, observations or reading. Be sure to CITE the sources whether you are paraphrasing or directly quoting.

Source 1

Adapted from: Yaffe, Gideon. "Give Felons and Prisoners the Right to Vote." *The Washington Post*. July 26, 2016. https://www.washingtonpost.com/opinions/let-felons-and- prisoners-vote/2016/07/26.

Most felons—whether in prison, on probation or parole, or entirely free of state supervision—are citizens. They should be afforded the right to decide who represents them and the laws by which they will be governed. By taking away their right to vote, you risk further alienating these individuals; in some cases that alienated feeling was the catalyst for their crimes in the first place.

The vast majority of felons are American citizens; therefore, they have no other geographic home. Taking away their right to vote removes any sense of citizenship they may still have after incarceration.

Even if one considers voting to be purely symbolic, it is a symbol with great psychological power. An increasing body of research in social psychology shows that those who feel a sense of ownership in their government are less likely to commit crimes. Re-establishing felons' voting rights is a potential source of criminal control—granting the vote to felons can discourage recidivism. Furthermore, research has proven that with this sense of ownership, ex-felons enjoy a quality of life that would be impossible without the freedoms that are re-established after their release.

In democracy, felon voting rights should not be a partisan issue. Both political parties must see the importance of reestablishing felon's voting right as a way to not only positively influence the ex-prisoners, but also as a way to protect their citizens by reducing crime. We should give the vote to citizens, in or out of prison, whom we wish to hold responsible for violating laws that are not just ours but also theirs.

Source 2

Adapted from: von Spakovsky, Hans A. "Ex-cons Should Prove They Deserve the Right to Vote." *The Heritage Foundation*. March 15th, 2013. www.heritage.org/election-integrity/commentary/ex-cons-should-prove-they-deserve- the-right-to-vote.

The proposal to automatically restore felons' right to vote as soon as they have completed their sentence is shortsighted and bad public policy. When presented as a measure of compassion and justice, it is also hypocritical, as automatic restoration is not in the best interest of felons or the general public.

An April 2012, a report from the Florida Department of Corrections showed that the recidivism rate of felons ranged from 31% to 34% on average over a five-year period. Recidivism among those convicted of robbery, burglary and sex offenses reached or exceeded 50%, while the overall recidivism rate of felons committing nonviolent offenses also approached 50%. Therefore, to restore voting rights to felons as soon as they leave prison is irresponsible.

Advocates of automatic restoration also seem reluctant to mention that voting rights aren't the only rights people lose when convicted of a felony. In most states, felons also lose their right to own a gun, hold public office, sit on a jury, and obtain certain types of professional and occupational licenses. Many such rights can never be restored without a full pardon.

Felons have, by definition, knowingly and intentionally violated the laws of society. A five-or-seven-year waiting period before restoring their voting rights is appropriate.

Sample Essay – Score of 4

The immediate reinstatement of felons voting rights continues to be a point of contention among American citizens and politicians. Some people feel that if one has committed a major crime, that individual has given- up the right to decide representation and policy changes. However, others feel that all American citizens-- regardless of whether they have committed been convicted of a felony or not—have the right to choose who represents them and can vote on local and national policy. Reestablishing felon's voting rights is an important topic of national concern.

In his piece "Give Felons and Prisoners the Right to Vote," published in *The Washington Post*, Yaffe (2016) suggests that giving felons and prisoners the right to vote has a positive impact on the lives of the offenders and a positive impact on the community. In passage one, Yaffe (2016) writes "An increasing body of research in social psychology shows that those who feel a sense of ownership in their government are less likely to commit crimes." This sense of ownership allows convicts and ex-convicts to feel that they have some control over the laws that they are breaking and the punishments they could receive for breaking those laws. The passage suggests that when these basic rights are stripped of them, criminals feel alienated and disenfranchised; once this mentality is instilled in the criminal, they are far more likely to commit further crimes (Yaffe, 2016).

However, as outlined by von Spakovsky (2013), the immediate reinstatement of felons' voting rights poses issues for both the offender and the general public. Studies have shown that, in more than 50 percent of cases, criminals who commit violent crimes will end up back in prison for similar crimes. In the same way a felon loses the right to own a gun, sit on a jury, run for public office, or obtain certain licenses, a felon losing his or her voting rights is simply another way for the government to protect its citizens (von Spakovsky, 2013).

The decision whether to give felons the right to vote or continue to take away that right as a form of punishment, will continue to be debated. The importance of every American citizens feeling as though they are being represented in government cannot be overstated. Yet, it is the government's responsibility to protect its citizens. Both sides will have to make some concessions if a definitive solution is to be reached.

This essay would receive a score of 4 or higher because the writer:

- Adequately explains why the concerns are important, supporting the explanation with some links between the two sources and adequate reasons, examples, or details.

- Immediately states the issue presented in the assignment. There is no doubt what the issue is and that it is an important topic that should be discussed.

- Presents the source authors' arguments and their supporting examples.

- Incorporates information from both sources to identify and explain important concerns regarding the issue discussed in the sources.

- Effectively summarizes the original sources.

- Shows control in the organization and development of ideas.

- Is well developed and organized. The summaries effectively explain each authors opinion, arguments, and examples.

- Displays adequate use of language, grammar vocabulary, and sentence variety.

- Correctly cites both authors when using ideas from the sources.

Quick Tip

We recommend APA for citing the authors because we feel it is the easiest. However, you can use MLA if you are more comfortable with that type of citation. Just be sure to cite when appropriate.

Sample Essay – Score of 3 or Lower

Some people feel that if one has committed a major crime, that individual has given-up the right to decide representation and policy changes. Others feel that all American citizens have the right to choose who represents them and can vote on local and national policy.

In source one the author suggests that giving felons and prisoners the right to vote has a positive impact on the lives of the offenders, and a positive impact on the community. In passage one, the author says, "An increasing body of research in social psychology shows that those who feel a sense of ownership in their government are less likely to commit crimes." This sense of ownership allows convicts and ex-convicts to feel that they have some control over the laws that they are breaking and the punishments they could receive for breaking those laws. The passage suggests that, when these basic rights are stripped of them, criminals feel alienated and disenfranchised, once this mentality is instilled in the criminal, they are far more likely to commit further crimes.

The decision whether to give felons the right to vote or continue to take away that right as a form of punishment, will continue to be debated. The importance of every American citizen feeling as though he or she is being represented in government cannot be overstated. Yet, it is the government's responsibility to protect its citizens. Both sides will have to will have to make some concessions if a definitive solution is to be reached.

This essay fails to meet the score of 4 because the writer:

- Fails to summarize both sources; only source one is referenced

- Fails to use specific details to support the positions

- Fails to cite when paraphrasing from the sources

Now you try with the following prompt.

Assignment: In many states, third grade students are required to achieve a "passing" score on statewide standardized tests in order to advance to the next grade. Because of these tests, student retention has grown significantly. Many parents and teachers feel that the mandated retention has a profoundly negative effect on these students. However, others feel that students who are retained show improved academic performance. The following sources address whether or not the mandated retention of third graders has a positive or negative effect on the students.

Read the two passages carefully and then write an essay in which you identify the most important concerns regarding the issue and explain why they are important. Your essay must draw on information from BOTH sources. In addition, you may draw on your own experiences, observations, and reading. Be sure to CITE the sources whether you are paraphrasing or directly quoting the author.

Quick Tip

Read the Assignment carefully. It summarizes the issue and will help you write your intro paragraph.

Source 1:

Jasper, Kathleen (2016). *The effects of mandated third grade retention on graduation rates and student outcomes: A policy analysis of Florida's a+ plan.*

Mandated retention of third graders who do not meet standardized testing requirements, creates enormous and unnecessary stress on children. In a study of first, third, and sixth graders, researchers asked students to rate a list of 20 stressful life events based on level. Researchers found students, across grade levels, rated the top three stressful life events in this order: losing a parent, going blind, and being retained in school. Sixth grade students rated grade retention as the most stressful life event, rating retention more stressful than losing a parent or going blind. Students who were retained faced difficulty in catching up to their peers, achieving academically, and obtaining a high school diploma. However, hundreds of thousands of students are retained in America each year.

The decision to retain so many students is not only costly, 589 million in FL alone over the last 10 years, but it is also detrimental to students' success. In recent studies, 17% of students who were retained did not graduate high school. In addition, many students who were retained never increased their reading levels. Despite all the retentions, reading and math scores have not improved significantly over the last 10 years.

Source 2:

Millbarge, Sharon L., Fitz-Hume, Claudia L. (2013) *Retention: Historical perspectives and new research.* Journal of School Psychology, 51*(3)* 229-232

Retention in third grade had large positive effects on reading and math achievement in the short run. Although these initial benefits faded over time, students who had been held back entered high school performing at a higher level relative to their grade level than similar students who'd been promoted. They needed less remediation, and they earned higher grades while enrolled. Being retained had no effect on students' chances of graduating.

In addition, test-based retention in third grade improved student performance. Students retained in third grade under Florida's test-based promotion policy experienced substantial short-term gains in both math and reading achievement. They were less likely to be retained in a later grade and better prepared when they entered high school. Being retained in third grade led students to take fewer remedial courses in high school and improved their grade point averages. There was no negative impact on graduation. Being held back did delay students' graduation from high school by 0.63 years but being older for their grade did not reduce their probability of graduating or receiving a regular diploma.

Sample Essay Score of 4

There is significant debate on the effect mandated retention has on students. Some believe the mandate hurts students academically and psychologically. While others argue that retaining students while they're young has a positive academic effect. The use of mandatory retention based on test scores is an important, publicly debated issue.

In her piece, *The effect of mandated third grade retention on graduation rates and student outcomes: A policy analysis of Florida's a+ plan,* Jasper (2016) argues that mandated third grade retention has a negative psychological impact on students, and provides little academic improvement. Students feel an incredible amount of stress when faced with the possibility of being held back from their classmates. According to Jasper (2016), a recent study showed that many students considered retention to be their most stress-inducing fear, "…students rated grade retention as the most stressful life event, rating retention more stressful than losing a parent or going blind." The traumatic experience of student retention has proven to have little positive academic impact on the students affected. Jasper (2016) claims, "Despite all the retentions, reading and math scores have not improved significantly over the last 10 years." It appears that there are some significant flaws in mandated standardized-test-based third grade retention.

However, in their work *Retention: Historical perspectives and new research,* Millbarge and Fitz-Hume (2013), outline the positive academic effects of test-based retention. The authors claim that students who were held back at a young age performed "at a higher level relative to their grade level than similar students who'd been promoted." The authors' research showed that students who were held back in third grade showed improved academic performance and were less likely to be held back in the future. Retained students took an extra 0.63 years to graduate from high school; however, the author states that "…being older for their grade did not reduce their probability of graduating or receiving a regular diploma" (Millbarge & Fitz-Hume, 2013).

The effect of test-based retention on third graders is an important issue that is subject to public debate. Many parents and teachers feel that the threat of retention places unnecessary stress on students. However, others feel that the positive academic outcome is worth holding students back a year. Until there is a resolution that benefits kids academically and reduces harmful stress, student retention will continue to be a highly debated issue.

This would receive a score of 4 or higher because the writer:

- Adequately explains why the concerns are important, supporting the explanation with some links between the two sources and adequate reasons, examples, or details.

- Immediately states the issue presented in the assignment. There is no doubt what the issue is and that it is an important topic that should be discussed.

- Presents the source authors' arguments and their supporting examples.

- Incorporates information from both sources to identify and explain important concerns regarding the issue discussed in the sources.

- Effectively summarizes the original sources.

- Shows control in the organization and development of ideas

- Has organized and developed the essay.

- Displays adequate use of language.

- Shows control of grammar, usage, and mechanics, but may display errors.

- Correctly uses APA format to cite both source passages.

Sample Essay - Score of 3

Some believe the mandate hurts students. While others argue that retaining students while they're young has a positive academic effect. The effect of the third grade retention mandate is an important, publicly debated issue.

Author one argues that mandated third grade retention has a negative psychological impact on students, while providing little academic improvement. Students feel an incredible amount of stress when faced with the possibility of being held back from their classmates. A recent study showed that many students considered retention to be their most stress-inducing fear. Students rated grade retention as the most stressful life event, rating retention more stressful than losing a parent or going blind. The traumatic experience of student retention has proven to have little positive academic impact on the students effected. There are some significant flaws in mandated standardized-test-based third grade retention.

The effect of test-based retention on third graders is an important issue that is subject to public debate. Until there is a resolution that benefits kids academically and reduces harmful stress, student retention will continue to be a highly debated issue.

This essay fails to meet the score of 4 because the writer:

- Fails to summarize both sources; only source one is referenced

- Fails to use specific details to support the positions

- Fails to cite when paraphrasing from the sources

WRITING

Additional Source-Based Prompt for Practice

Assignment: In recent months, the push to require face masks in public has been the topic of much debate. While many experts say that face masks prevent the spread of Covid-19, others believe masks do little to suppress the spread of the pandemic. Both of the following sources address whether or not face masks are effective.

Read the two passages carefully and then write an essay in which you identify the most important concerns regarding the issue and explain why they are important. Your essay must draw on information from BOTH of the sources. In addition, you may draw on your own experiences, observations, or reading. Be sure to CITE the sources whether you are paraphrasing or directly quoting.

Source 1:

Drake, John (2020). *The Case for Universal Face Masks to Curb the Spread of Covid-19*

A report in the Journal of the American Medical Association described what happened when Mass General Brigham—the largest healthcare system in Massachusetts and the parent organization of both Massachusetts General Hospital and Brigham and Women's Hospital—started to require face masks for all employees and patients. Note, these were not the most effective N95 masks, but ordinary surgical masks.

Key facts include:

- Overall, 1,271 healthcare workers tested positive for SARS-CoV-2.

- Before a system-wide policy of universal masking was adopted in late March 2020, new infections among healthcare workers were increasing at an average rate of 1.16% per day, which translates to a doubling time of 3.6 days.

- After implementation, cases went down at an average rate of 0.49% per day.

It appears that universal masking was the key intervention that turned around transmission in this setting. Of course, there are confounders. Other interventions were taken both in hospitals and in the community at the same time—things like canceling elective procedures, restricting visitors, and canceling non-essential business travel. But, most of these interventions were put in place before the universal masking policy. Indeed, cases continued to go up for about two weeks after these early interventions were put in place. Finally, the decline in cases in the healthcare system preceded the decrease in the general public, so it doesn't seem that community interventions like closing schools and reducing public transportation explain the epidemic pattern among healthcare workers.

It is telling that transmission among healthcare workers could be so effectively limited by the use of surgical masks, particularly because healthcare workers experience relatively high exposure (compared with the general public) as an occupational hazard. If face masks can reduce transmission to below the critical threshold in this population, they should be able to do it anywhere.

Source 2

Durden, Tyler (2020). *World's Top Epidemiologists - Masks Don't Work!*

Denmark boasts one of the lowest COVID-19 death rates in the world. As of August 4, the Danes have suffered 616 COVID-19 deaths, according to figures from Johns Hopkins University.

That's less than one-third of the number of Danes who die from pneumonia or influenza in a given year.

"All these countries recommending face masks haven't made their decisions based on new studies," said Henning Bundgaard, chief physician at Denmark's Rigshospitale, according to Bloomberg News.

Denmark is not alone.

Despite a global stampede of mask-wearing, data show that 80–90 percent of people in Finland and Holland say they "never" wear masks when they go out, a sharp contrast to the 80–90 percent of people in Spain and Italy who say they "always" wear masks when they go out.

Dutch public health officials recently explained why they're not recommending masks.

"From a medical point of view, there is no evidence of a medical effect of wearing face masks, so we decided not to impose a national obligation," said Medical Care Minister Tamara van Ark.

Others, echoing statements similar to the US Surgeon General from early March, said masks could make individuals sicker and exacerbate the spread of the virus.

"Face masks in public places are not necessary, based on all the current evidence," said Coen Berends, spokesman for the National Institute for Public Health and the Environment.

"There is no benefit and there may even be negative impact."

In Sweden, where COVID-19 deaths have slowed to a crawl, public health officials say they see "no point" in requiring individuals to wear masks.

"With numbers diminishing very quickly in Sweden, we see no point in wearing a face mask in Sweden, not even on public transport," said Anders Tegnell, Sweden's top infectious disease expert.

WRITING

II. Language and Research Skills for Writing

Grammatical Relationships

Recognize and correct:

- Errors in the use of adjectives and adverbs
- Errors in noun-noun agreement
- Errors in pronoun antecedent agreement
- Errors in pronoun case
- Errors in interrogative and relative pronouns
- Errors in the use of intensive pronouns
- Errors in pronoun number and person
- Vague pronouns
- Errors in subject-verb agreement
- Inappropriate shifts in verb tense

Adjectives and Adverbs

Adjectives modify or describe nouns or pronouns. They are either attributive adjectives (before the noun) or predicate adjectives (after a verb of being):

EXAMPLE: The <u>brave</u> girl rescued her mom from the burning home. She is a hero.

In this case, the adjective—brave—is describing the noun—girl.

EXAMPLE: The girl is so <u>brave</u>. She looks <u>brave</u>, too.

In both cases, the adjective—brave—is describing the noun—girl.

Adverbs modify or describe **verbs, adverbs or adjectives**.

EXAMPLE: The girl <u>bravely</u> rescued her mom from the burning home. She acted heroically.

Many times, adding an *ly*, *ally* or *i + ly to* an adjective, forms an adverb:

- brave + ly = bravely

  She **bravely walked** into battle.
- beautiful + ly = beautifully

  She **wrote** her name **beautifully** on the paper.
- gentle + ly = gently (drop the e)

  She **pets** the sick dog **gently** on the head.
- easy + i + ly = easily (drop the y and add the i to words that end in y)

  She **worked** through the math problems **easily**.

WRITING

Of course, there are exceptions to the **ly** rule. Some adjectives and adverbs cannot be adapted by adding or taking away endings. The following table is a common list of adjectives and adverbs.

Adjectives	Adverbs
good	well
fast, quick	fast, quickly
slow, deliberate, lethargic	slowly, deliberately, lethargically
tired	tiredly
needless	needlessly
sick, sickly	(sickly can be a verb or adj.; never an adverb)
super, superb	superbly
responsible	responsibly
near, far	nearly, far

Example question

She was moving along slow because she had not driven down that road before.

    A. slow because

    B. slow, because

    C. slowly because

    D. slowly, because

    E. very slow, because

Correct answer: C

In this case, the adverb, slowly, is needed because it is describing the verb *moving*. Also, there is no comma needed between *slowly* and *because*.

Noun-Noun Agreement

When looking through answer choices on the grammar of the exam, pay attention to noun-noun agreement. In other words, the number of nouns in the sentence should match throughout the sentence. The following are examples.

Incorrect

*The school counselors are looking over their students' academic **history** while making decisions on class placement.*

In this case, there are several school counselors for several students. Those students do not share just one academic history. They each have their own academic history.

Correct

*The school counselors are looking over their students' academic **histories** while making decisions on class placement.*

Incorrect

Every cat in the kennel had missing tails.

Correct

Every cat in the kennel had a missing tail.

Incorrect

It seemed like every girl at the party had ponytails.

Correct

It seemed like every girl at the party had a ponytail.

Quick Tip

Noun-noun agreement can be tricky because these errors are difficult to spot. For example, the following cat and ponytail examples seem correct; however, they both contains noun-noun agreement errors. Slow down when you see the word ***every***. *Every* is an adjective that indicates being one of a group or singular (we go over this in more detail later in the book).

Example question

Dentists should look over their patients' dental history before making suggestions for braces.

   A. Dentists should look over their patients' dental history before making suggestions for braces.

   B. Dentists should look over their patients dental history before making suggestions for braces

   C. Dentists should look over there patients' dental history before making suggestions for braces.

   D. Dentists should look over their patients dental histories before making suggestions for braces.

   E. Dentists should look over their patients' dental histories before making suggestions for braces.

Correct Answer E

The correct answer is **E** for two reasons. First, there are multiple dentists with multiple patients. Therefore, the plural possessive noun—patients'—should be used. Second, the multiple patients have multiple dental histories—plural. Also, the word *there* in answer choice C is incorrect.

Remember, it always helps to look over your answer choices. When you do, you will see that the choice **histories** is an option. That will help you remember to think about your noun-noun agreement.

Pronoun Antecedent Agreement/Pronoun Number and Person

We combined these two skills because they are essentially the same.

Pronoun antecedent agreement

Simply put, the pronoun used in the sentence should agree with the antecedent in the sentence.

First let's distinguish between a pronoun and an antecedent by looking at the sentence below.

My ***teacher*** was excited to learn that three of ***her*** students were accepted to Ivy League colleges.

Antecedent   Pronoun

In the case above, the pronoun, ***her***, matches the antecedent, ***teacher***.

Pronoun Number and Person

Things get complicated when the test makers present pronouns *they*, *them*, or *their* in a sentence. On the test, you will be required to identify and correct pronoun shifts. These are not easy to spot because most people use them incorrectly in their everyday language, so be on the lookout for these pronouns.

For example, the sentence below is ***incorrect*** because the plural pronoun, *they,* does not agree with the singular noun in the subject, *student*.

One person (singular)

When a student comes to see me, <u>they</u> usually want to discuss extra credit.

Plural pronoun

Correction

Change the subject to a plural noun.

When students come to see me, <u>they</u> usually want to discuss extra credit.

Now the plural pronoun matches the antecedent.

Caution

Whenever you see any one of the pronouns their, them or they, slow down and check the subject of the sentence. This is a classic grammar assessment trick where the test makers check your ability to maintain pronoun antecedent agreement and pronoun number case. If your subject is singular, you should change the subject to a plural noun. If that is not an option you should change the pronoun.

The board of directors had <u>their</u> <u>meeting and</u> decided to postpone the <u>event until</u> after the <u>holidays</u>. <u>No error</u>.

    A. its

    B. meeting, and

    C. event, until

    D. Holidays

    E. No error

Correct answer: A

In this case, there is a sneaky prepositional phrase and collective noun to navigate. *The board* is a collective noun and therefore singular. To have pronoun antecedent agreement, the pronoun *its* is appropriate for the singular *board*. The phrase *of directors* is a prepositional phrase and can be taken out. Then the sentence would read: *The board had its meeting*. This is correct.

In answer B, there is no need for the comma + conjunction because the *and* is only separating a dependent and independent clause, so the conjunction *and* by itself is correct. Finally, the term *holidays* is not a proper noun and does not need to be capitalized.

<u>A student should only go to their locker</u> before school, during lunch, or after school.

    A. A student should only go to their locker

    B. Students should only go their locker

    C. A student should go to their lockers

    D. Students should only go to their lockers

    E. Students should only go to his or her lockers

Correct answer: D

The way the sentence is written, the subject is singular—*a student*, and the pronoun is plural—*their*. Therefore, the best thing to do is change the subject to a plural noun—*students*. Also, because we have multiple students, there are multiple lockers. Therefore, *locker* should be changed to a plural noun as well. Otherwise, it reads as though there are multiple students using one locker.

WRITING

Pronoun Case

Just like verbs, pronouns have cases. Pronouns can be either subjective (occurring in the subject of the sentence), objective (occurring as the direct object in the predicate of the sentence), or possessive (showing ownership).

The following are examples of each pronoun case.

Subjective pronoun case happens in the subject of the sentence.

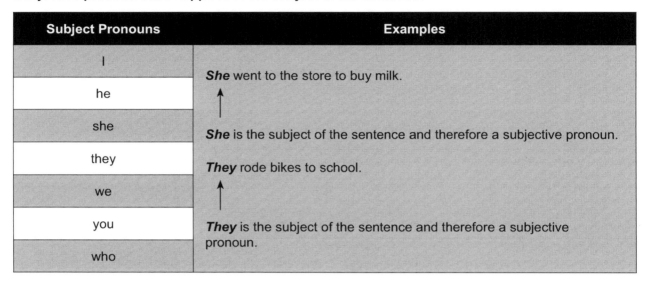

Subject Pronouns	Examples
I	*She* went to the store to buy milk.
he	
she	*She* is the subject of the sentence and therefore a subjective pronoun.
they	*They* rode bikes to school.
we	
you	*They* is the subject of the sentence and therefore a subjective pronoun.
who	

Objective pronoun case happens in the predicate as the direct object.

Object Pronouns	Examples
me	Jane went to the store to buy *him* some clothes.
him	
her	The pronoun *him* is the direct object of the sentence and therefore the objective pronoun.
them	
us	Sally came over to the house to see *me*.
you	
whom	The pronoun *me* is the direct object of the sentence and therefore the objective pronoun.

WRITING

Possessive pronoun case shows ownership.

Possessive Pronouns	Examples
my	She went to get *her* clothes from the house.
his	
her	The pronoun *her* is the possessive pronoun.
their	
our	We realized it was *their* car in the parking lot.
your	
whose	The pronoun *their* is the possessive pronoun.

On the exam, pronoun case can be tricky because the test makers will often intermingle subject and object pronouns.

The following test questions is how you will see this concept presented on the exam.

Example question

I was excited when the <u>university</u> professor <u>came</u> over to speak <u>with my</u> son <u>and I</u>. <u>No error</u>

    A. University

    B. come

    C. with, my

    D. and me.

    E. No error.

Correct answer: D

A lot of people have difficulty spotting this error. In fact, many people think, erroneously, that using the pronoun *I* in this way is grammatically correct. However, *I* is a subject pronoun. In the case above, *I* is used incorrectly as a direct object pronoun. The appropriate pronoun should be *me*.

Quick Tip

If you are ever confused as to which pronoun to use, take the other person out. If you did that with the example question above, the sentence as is would read:

*I was excited when the university professor came over to see **I**.*

However, the sentence should read:

*I was excited when the university professor came over to see **me**.*

WRITING

Another way you may see this presented on the exam is by switching the subject pronouns with object pronouns as shown in the following example.

Example question.

Her and I were very close when we were younger, but we grew apart when I moved away. No error

    A. She

    B. and me

    C. younger but

    D. apart, when

    E. No error.

Correct answer: A

In this case, *her*, an object pronoun is used, erroneously, as a subject pronoun. If you take out the *I* in the sentence, it reads:

Her was very close…

It should be:

She was very close…

Interrogative and Relative Pronouns

These are called interrogative pronouns because they are used to ask questions—an interrogative sentence asks a question.

- Who is going to the dance?
- With whom is she going to the dance?
- Whoever thought the dance would be this exciting?

You will see questions on the exam that require you to determine the correct pronoun who vs. whom. Most people just use who and never even think about using whom. We have some quick tricks for you to use, so you will never mess up who vs whom again.

Just like with regular pronouns—he/him/his, she/her/hers, we/us/ours, etc.—who, whom, and whose belong in certain parts of the sentence.

Subject Pronouns - They occur in the subject part of the sentence.	Object Pronouns – They are occur in the prepositional phrase or in the predicate part of a sentence.	Possessive Pronouns – show possession in the sentence.
who/whoever	whom/whomever	whose
Who went to the store? **Who** won the game? **Whoever** thought this would happen? **Whoever** decided to do that was wrong.	To **whom** are you speaking? He had a date with **whom**? That is the man with **whom** my father used to live. You can go with **whomever** you want.	**Whose** car is this? This is the lady **whose** generous funding created this scholarship.

The quick and easy way to distinguish between who/whoever and whom/whoever is to answer the question and decide whether you are answering with a subject pronoun—he/she—or an objective pronoun—him/her.

Correct

- Question: **Who** went to the store?
- Answer: **He** went to the store.
- Both he and who are subject pronouns. Therefore, *who* is used correctly here.

Incorrect

- Question: **Whom** went to the store?
- Answer: **Him** went to the store.
- Obviously, *him* is used incorrectly, so you would not use *whom* in this situation.

Correct

- Question: **Whoever** thought this would happen?
- Answer: **She** thought this would happen.
- Both *she* and *whoever* are subject pronouns. Therefore, *whoever* is used correctly here.

Incorrect

- Question: **Whomever** thought this would happen?
- Answer: **Him** thought this would happen or her thought this would happen.
- Obviously, *him* is used incorrectly, so you would not use *whom* in this situation.

Correct

- Question: He went to the dance with **whom**?
- Answer: He went with **her**.
- Both *whom* and *her* are direct object pronouns and are used correctly here.

Example question

My mother said I can go to the play <u>with whomever</u> I want.

 A. with whomever

 B. with whatsoever

 C. with whoever

 D. with whosever

 E. with who

Correct answer: A

Remember, *who* is a subject pronoun and *whom* is an object pronoun. In this case, the subject is *I*, as in "I can go with…" Therefore, an object pronoun (*whomever*) is needed.

Another trick is to answer the question. In the case above, the speaker can go with whomever because she can go with *him, her* or *them*. These are all direct object pronouns and match *whom*.

Test Tip

If you are stuck on *who* vs. *whom*, remember the pronoun *whom* follows the prepositions *with* and *of*. Therefore, if you see *with* or *of*, whom is the correct pronoun.

Intensive Pronouns

Intensive pronouns are pronouns ending in *self* or *selves* and are used to add emphasis to the subject or antecedent of the sentence. You'll often find the intensive pronoun right after the noun or pronoun it's modifying, but not all the time. Remember this is English, and English doesn't always follow the rules.

Intensive pronouns *intensify* the noun in the sentence.

Example

- The CEO <u>herself</u> came down to work on the factory floor.
- The purpose of this sentence is to emphasize the CEO came down to work on the factory floor. The word *herself* intensifies the **CEO**.

Example

- The teachers <u>themselves</u> were overwhelmed with the education changes.
- The term *themselves* intensifies the word *teachers*.

Reflexive pronouns are pronouns ending in *self* or *selves* and reflect back upon the subject of the sentence. Reflexive pronouns are not used to intensive anything. They just refer back to the antecedent of the sentence.

Example

- The CEO believed in <u>herself</u> to make the right decision about the merger.
- The purpose of the pronoun is just to refer back to who the sentence is about.
- The term *herself* is used to describe the **CEO** not to intensify.

Example

- The teachers needed to prepare <u>themselves</u> for a challenging year ahead.
- The purpose of the reflexive pronoun here is to refer back to the teachers.
- The term *themselves* is just to describe the *teachers* not to intensify.

Test Tip

To figure out if the pronoun is intensive or reflexive, remove it from the sentence. If it still makes sense without it, it is an intensive pronoun.

- The CEO ~~herself~~ came down to work on the factory floor.
- The CEO believed in ~~herself~~ to make the right decision about the merger.

Example question

If you have any questions, please do not hesitate to <u>contact my colleague or myself</u>.

    A. contact my colleague or myself.

    B. contact my colleague or I.

    C. contact my colleague or my.

    D. contact my colleague or me.

    E. contact my colleague and myself.

Correct answer: D

Avoid improper use of intensive and reflexive pronouns. When faced with this kind of question, take out the other person and see if the sentence works. You would not say, *please do not hesitate to contact myself*. You would say, *please don't hesitate to contact **me***. Therefore, answer D is the correct answer.

Vague Pronouns

Vague pronouns do not clearly identify a specific subject or antecedent. Usually this happens when the sentence contains more than one person or more than one object and only one pronoun.

For example, read the sentence below.

- My aunt and her sister took our dog to the beach, and on the way, **she** chewed the car seats.

- In this case, **she** is the pronoun. Most would assume the dog chewed the seats. However, the way it is written, the pronoun **she** can refer to the aunt, the sister or the dog.

Vague pronouns are a common mistake in writing. Look at the paragraph below and determine which sentences—numbered below—contain vague pronouns.

> (1) Online courses provide students with a variety of ways to access knowledge. Students like online courses because *they* provide flexibility in learning. (3) For example, students can access online courses from the comfort of their own home, at a coffee shop, or at the university library. (4) Students and teachers can use online courses to increase engagement in *their* lessons.

In the paragraph above, vague pronouns are present in sentence 2 because the pronoun **they** can be referring to the online classes or the students—both plural nouns. A vague pronoun is also present in sentence 4—**their** lessons. It is not clear if the pronoun is referring to the students or teachers.

Subject Verb Agreement

Subject verb agreement simply means the subject and verb must agree in number. This means both need to be singular or both need to be plural.

For example, the sentences below have subject verb agreement.

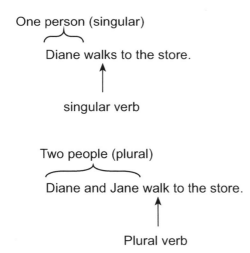

One person (singular)

Diane walks to the store.

singular verb

Two people (plural)

Diane and Jane walk to the store.

Plural verb

This is easy enough. However, test makers will often test this skill by using a sneaky prepositional phrase so that the subject's form, either singular or plural, may be difficult to determine. Look at the following examples to see how this will look on the exam.

WRITING

The use of cellphones and other recording devices are banned from the museum. No error

   A. The uses

   B. cellphones, and

   C. is

   D. for

   E. No error

Correct answer: C

In this case, the subject is *The use* (singular). The phrase *of cellphones and other recording devices* is also plural, but it is not your subject. Instead, it is a prepositional phrase. You can essentially remove the prepositional phrase and the sentence would read:

The use ***is*** prohibited.

Watch out for those sneaky prepositional phrases.

Neither/Either and Subject Verb Agreement

Another way this is presented is when using neither and nor, and either and or. These words make the subject of the sentence singular, as in the following example.

Example

• Neither Jane nor Diane walks to the store.

• In this case, ***neither*** separates each subject as one.

Example question

Either the dog or the cat have to be boarded while we are on vacation; we cannot take both. No error

   A. Neither

   B. nor

   C. has

   D. vacation, we

   E. No error

Correct answer: C

Because it is clear from the sentence that one or the other has to be boarded, we can eliminate neither and we can eliminate nor because nor goes with neither. The word *either* in this case makes each subject its own singular noun. Therefore, what we are saying here is the dog *has* to be boarded or the cat *has* to be boarded. We cannot take both.

Inappropriate Shifts in Verb Tense

Writing should maintain verb tense throughout a sentence or paragraph. For example, if a sentence is present tense, it should not suddenly shift to past tense. Similarly, if a sentence or paragraph begins in past tense, it should remain in past tense throughout the entire work.

Typically, verb form is assessed on the exam as questions that test your ability to spot and correct errors in maintaining consistent verb tense throughout the sentence or paragraph.

The following question is how shift in verb tense might be presented on the exam.

Example question

She drove <u>quickly</u> and still <u>didn't</u> make it. The professor <u>locks</u> her <u>out because</u> she was five minutes late. <u>No error.</u>

    A. quick

    B. did

    C. locked

    D. out, because

    E. No error

Correct answer: C

In this case, the verb *locks* does not match the verb tense of the rest of the sentence. This sentence is past tense. Therefore, *locks* should be changed to *locked*. The adverb *quickly* is used correctly. The word *didn't* is correct in the sentence. Finally, for answer choice D, do not use a comma before the word *because*.

This page intentionally left blank.

Grammatical Relationships – Practice Problems

1. Jose loved to play baseball so much that <u>he drives</u> 5 hours to see almost every game.

    A. he drives

    B. he drive

    C. he drived

    D. he drove

    E. he was driving

2. <u>Neither</u> the team <u>nor</u> the coach <u>has</u> any idea how <u>to get</u> to the away game. <u>No error</u>

    A. Either

    B. or

    C. have

    D. getting

    E. No error

3. Sally <u>was</u> <u>excited</u> to see her <u>sister, Diane</u>, as <u>she</u> was leaving town. <u>No error</u>

    A. Were

    B. excites

    C. sister Diane

    D. Sally

    E. No error

4. <u>The team decided they</u> would help out during the fundraiser and wash cars.

    A. The team decided they

    B. The team decided it

    C. The team decided he or she

    D. The team decided them

    E. The team decided we

5. Aunt Judy <u>was</u> happy to see that <u>my mom was</u> sitting with my sister and <u>me</u>. <u>No error</u>

    A. were

    B. mom

    C. were

    D. I

    E. No error

6. I wasn't sure <u>who</u> to ask about the <u>accident because</u> it was a <u>sensitive and</u> scary <u>subject</u>. <u>No error</u>

   A. whom

   B. accident, because

   C. sensitive, and

   D. subject

   E. No error

Instructions: Choose the underlined portion of the sentence that contains an error. If no error occurs, choose no error.

7. While my <u>sister and</u> cousin <u>were</u> out at a <u>party,</u> <u>she</u> got a flat tire. <u>No error.</u>

8. Everyone on the <u>crowded plane</u> <u>were</u> happy <u>that</u> flight attendants <u>began</u> to serve refreshments. <u>No error</u>

9. She <u>hasn't</u> chosen <u>her</u> major <u>yet because</u> she is not sure what she <u>wants</u> to do. <u>No error.</u>

10. No one <u>was</u> happy about the <u>situation because</u> <u>they</u> were trying to get <u>home, and</u> the flight was canceled. No error

Question	Answer	Explanation
1.	D	In this case, the tenses in the sentence should match. The sentence starts in past tense and then jumps to the present. Therefore, *drives* should be changed to *drove*.
2.	E	There is no error in the sentence because *neither* in this sentence makes the team (a collective singular noun) and the coach (singular noun) separate subjects. Therefore, the team *has* no idea, and the coach *has* no idea.
3.	D	The sentence contains a vague pronoun—*she*. The way the sentence is written, it could be *Sally* or *Diane* who is leaving town. To make that clear, the correction would be to replace *she* with *Sally*, so we know Sally is leaving town.
4.	B	*The team* is a collective singular noun. Therefore, *it* is the appropriate pronoun.
5.	E	All of the underlined portions are correct. The verb *was* is used correctly with *Judy*. The underlined phrase, *my mom,* is correct because without the possessive pronoun *my*, *Mom* becomes a proper noun and needs to be capitalized. Probably the most difficult part of the sentence is determining if the objective pronoun *me* is the correct pronoun to use at the end of the sentence. It is correct. If you were to take *my sister* out of the sentence, it would read: Aunt Judy was happy to see that my mom was sitting with ~~my sister and~~ *me.*
6.	A	*Who* is a subjective pronoun, but in this case, it is being used as the objective pronoun. The subject of the sentence is *I*. Therefore, *who* should be replaced with *whom*. In addition, if you were to answer the question *whom I should ask*, you would answer with *I should ask **him***, or ***her***, or ***them***—all direct objects.
7.	she	This error occurs because it is a vague pronoun. Did the cousin or sister get the flat tire? It is not clear.
8.	were	Everyone is a singular noun and therefore needs to agree with the proper verb. The sentence should read *Everyone **was** happy...*
9.	No error	Everything in this sentence is correct.
10.	they	The subject of the sentence is *no one*, which is singular. Therefore, the pronoun *they* is an error.

WRITING

This page intentionally left blank.

Structural Relationships

Recognize and correct:

- Errors in the placement of phrases and clauses within a sentence
- Misplaced and dangling modifiers
- Errors in the use of coordinating and subordinating conjunctions
- Fragments and run-ons
- Errors in the use of correlative conjunctions
- Errors in parallel structure

Errors in the placement of phrases and clauses within a sentence

Errors occur when clauses and phrases are awkwardly placed in a sentence. While not grammatically incorrect, these are errors of usage in modern English that should be avoided.

Incorrect

- He while doing his laundry missing sock he noticed.

Correct

- While doing his laundry, he noticed the missing sock.
- He noticed the missing sock while doing his laundry.

Incorrect

- The man because he couldn't hear did not notice the oncoming bus.

Correct

- Because the man couldn't hear, he did not notice the oncoming bus.

Incorrect

- The team in order to win had to score the next touchdown.

Correct

- In order to win, the team had to score the next touchdown.
- The team had to score the next touchdown in order to win.

Think about it.

Yes, you can start a sentence with **because**, as long as it is part of the introductory phrase.

- **Because** she was exhausted, she went home early from work.

- She went home early from work **because** she was exhausted.

Misplaced and dangling modifiers

A misplaced modifier is a word, phrase, or clause that is improperly separated from the word it modifies or describes. The separation causes an error that makes the sentence confusing.

For example, in the sentence below, the modifier is misplaced.

Yolanda realized too late that it was a mistake to walk the neighbor's dog in high heels.

In this sentence, the phrase *in high heels* modifies *the neighbor's dog*. The dog is not in high heels; Yolanda is.

WRITING

To correct the error, rearrange the sentence so the modifying clause is close to the word it should modify.

Yolanda realized too late that she shouldn't have worn high heels while walking the neighbor's dog.

The following is how misplaced modifiers might be presented on the exam.

Example question

> <u>While attending the political town hall, new laws were opposed by demonstrators that would negatively impact the city.</u>
>
> A. While attending the political town hall, new laws were opposed by demonstrators that would negatively impact the city.
>
> B. New laws were opposed by demonstrators while attending a town hall that would negatively impact the city.
>
> C. While attending the political town hall, demonstrators staged a sit-in to oppose a new law that would negatively impact the city.
>
> D. New laws that would negatively impact the city were opposed while attending a political town hall by demonstrators.
>
> E. While attending a political town hall, a sit in was staged by demonstrators to oppose new laws that would negatively impact the city.
>
> **Correct Answer: C**
>
> In this test item, the modifier is _while attending the political town hall_. Notice that in choice C, the modifier _while attending the political town tall_ is modifying the demonstrators.
>
> In choice A, _while attending the town hall_ is modifying _new laws_. That makes it sound like the new laws are attending the town hall.
>
> In choice B, _while attending the town hall_ is modifying _negatively impact the city_, making it sound like the town hall would negatively impact the city.
>
> In choice D, _while attending the town hall_ is modifying _new laws_, making it sound like the new laws are attending the town hall.
>
> In choice E, _while attending the town hall_ is modifying _a sit in_, making it sound like the sit in is attending the town hall.

Test Tip

Place the modifier next to the portion of the sentence it is modifying.

The demonstrators are attending the town hall.

While attending the political town hall, demonstrators staged a sit-in to oppose a new law that would negatively impact the city.

Errors in the use of coordinating and subordinating conjunctions

Coordinating Conjunctions

Coordinating conjunctions are the seven words that combine two sentences (independent clauses that can stand alone as a complete thought) with the addition of a comma. These are the ONLY seven words used to combine two sentences using a comma.

The 7 coordinating conjunctions **(FANBOYS):**

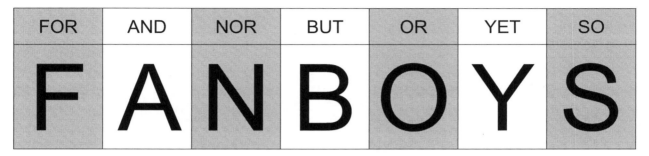

FOR	AND	NOR	BUT	OR	YET	SO

IMPORTANT

- A conjunction alone can separate an independent clause and a dependent clause.
- A comma + a conjunction must be used when separating two independent clauses.

Example - Independent Clause with a Dependent Clause

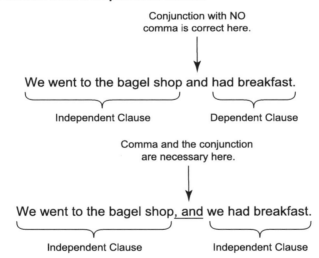

Conjunction with NO comma is correct here.

We went to the bagel shop and had breakfast.

Independent Clause   Dependent Clause

Comma and the conjunction are necessary here.

We went to the bagel shop, and we had breakfast.

Independent Clause   Independent Clause

Quick Tip

You **cannot** start a sentence with a coordinating conjunction.

Incorrect: I was very tired. <u>But</u> I went to the party anyway.

Correct: I was very <u>tired, but</u> I went to the party anyway.

Subordinating Conjunctions

Subordinating conjunctions are all the other conjunctions used to combine clauses.

Common subordinating conjunctions include:

- Since
- Because
- Although
- While
- Due
- Though
- Whenever
- When
- If
- Therefore

Grammatically, there are two patterns for these subordinating conjunctions.

Pattern 1

Independent Clause + Subordinating Conjunction + Clause (independent, dependent, or prepositional)

Example:

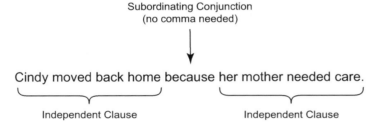

Pattern 2

Subordinating Conjunction + Clause (independent, dependent, or prepositional) + Comma + Independent Clause

Example:

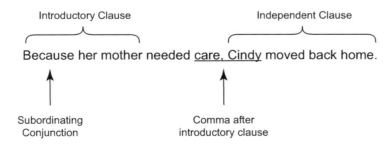

Quick Tip

YES, you can start sentences with subordinating conjunctions.

- **While** I was watching TV, I did my homework.

- **Since** it was cold, I wore a jacket.

- **Whenever** I go to Canada, I stop in Seattle.

- **Because** I was on the committee, I voted on the issue.

*When a subordinating conjunction starts a sentence, a comma will always follow.

While he worked all over the <u>world,</u> he <u>rarely</u> <u>slept because</u> he was always traveling <u>through</u> different time zones. <u>No error</u>

    A. world;

    B. rare

    C. slept, because

    D. threw

    E. No error

Correct Answer: E

The sentence starts off with a dependent clause with subordinating conjunction, *while*, and ending in a comma, which is correct. A semicolon in answer choice A is incorrect (we will go over punctuation in a following section of the book). *Because* is a subordinating conjunction and does not need a comma before it, eliminating choice C. The adverb *rarely* and preposition *through* are used correctly, eliminating choices B and D. The way the sentence is presented originally is correct. Therefore, there is no error.

Example question

In his <u>writing, he</u> claims to be an <u>environmentalist yet</u> that contradicts how he <u>lives in</u> <u>real life</u>. No error

    A. writing he

    B. environmentalist, yet

    C. lived in

    D. real-life

    E. No error

Correct Answer: B

The clause *In his writing* is an introductory clause, and a comma is needed after the word *writing*, eliminating answer A.

Notice the fanboy, *yet*, after the word *environmentalist* connects two independent clauses.

Remember, a fanboy alone cannot connect two independent clauses. The fanboy needs a comma. Therefore, select answer B for the correction.

Answer choice C, *lived in*, shifts tense from present to past, so eliminate that.

The phrase *real life* does not need a hyphen because it is not being used as an adjective You would use a hyphen in a case like this: He was a *real-life* hero. Notice real-life is describing hero. However, that is not how it is being used in the sentence. That eliminates answer D.

WRITING

Fragments and run-ons

FRAGMENTS

Dependent clauses, without the independent clause in a sentence, are fragments. Fragments are not sentences.

For example, in the sentences below, the bolded portions are fragments and are not correct.

Correction:

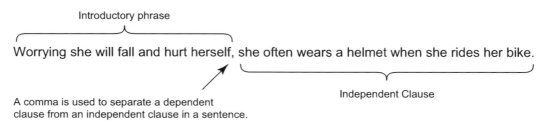

Notice that you can take the fragment and add it to the independent clause as long as you place a comma or a conjunction, separating them appropriately.

Example question

She is constantly checking her <u>work. Ensuring</u> sure she doesn't make any errors.

    A. work. Ensuring

    B. work, ensuring

    C. work; ensuring

    D. work ensuring

    E. work yet ensuring

Correct answer: B

The sentence should be written like this:

She is constantly checking her <u>work, ensuring</u> she doesn't make any errors.

In this case, *Ensuring she doesn't make any errors* is a fragment; it is just the verb phrase. Therefore, it cannot be a sentence on its own as it is originally presented. Therefore, eliminate A.

The semicolon in answer C is incorrect because semicolons separate two independent clauses (this will be covered in the punctuation section of the book). The clause *ensuring she didn't make any mistakes* is not an independent clause.

Having no punctuation between the two clauses makes the sentence a run-on, making answer D incorrect.

Finally, answer choice E is not correct because the coordinating conjunction does not fit.

WRITING

RUN-ONS

A run-on sentence occurs when two or more independent clauses are not joined correctly. There are several ways to punctuate two or more independent clauses in a sentence.

For example, the sentences below are run-on sentences, and in all cases, they are punctuated incorrectly.

Incorrect

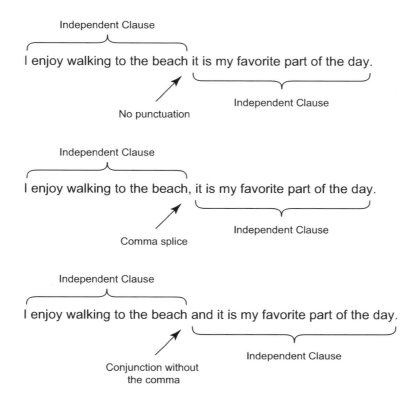

The run-on sentences above can be corrected with simple punctuation. The following are all acceptable corrections.

Correct:

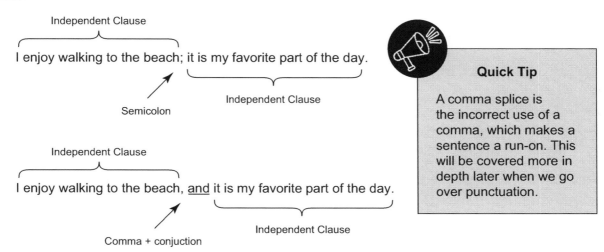

Quick Tip

A comma splice is the incorrect use of a comma, which makes a sentence a run-on. This will be covered more in depth later when we go over punctuation.

Example question

The <u>book, *To Kill a Mockingbird,*</u> <u>is</u> part of the high school <u>English</u> <u>curriculum but</u> many schools have banned the book. <u>No error</u>

    A. The book: *To*

    B. *Mockingbird* is

    C. english

    D. curriculum, but

    E. No error

Correct Answer: D

This sentence, as it is presented, is a run-on sentence because there is no comma before the conjunction, *but*. This sentence contains two independent clauses:

    1. The book, *To Kill a Mockingbird*, is part of the high school English curriculum.

    2. Many schools have banned the book.

Notice how both clauses can stand on their own as sentences. They are independent clauses; therefore, the conjunction by itself is incorrect. There needs to be a comma + conjunction as indicated in choice D.

Correlative Conjunctions

Correlative conjunctions are multi-word phrases that relate two terms, usually in a parallel fashion. These terms are often nouns, but they can also be verbs, modifiers and even clauses.

Correlative conjunctions	Examples in context
neither/nor	**Neither** the waiter **nor** the customer knew how to open the wine bottle.
either/or	**Either** he leaves, **or** I do.
not only/but also	**Not only** did Jane pass the GACE, **but** she **also** got the job.
rather/than	I would **rather** run **than** get caught.
more/than	Mom gave sis **more** dessert **than** me.
as/as	The giant spider was **as** big **as** a house.
whether/or	**Whether** you like it **or** not, we must go to see your parents.
such/that	She was **such** a success **that** they made her supervisor.
both/and	**Both** the father **and** the son are left-handed.

IMPORTANT: Correlative conjunctions must be used with their counterparts. If there is one, there has to be the other.

- **neither** has to go with **nor**
- **either** has to go with **or**
- **not only** has to go with **but also**
- **rather** has to go with **than**
- **more** has to go with **than**

- **as** has to have another **as**
- **whether** has to go with **or**
- **such** has to go with **that**
- **both** has to go with **and**

Example question

John was not only out of shape. He was weak and undernourished.

    A. John was not only out of shape. He was weak and undernourished.

    B. Out of shape, John was not only weak and also undernourished.

    C. Out of shape, John was weak but also undernourished.

    D. Not only was John out of shape, but he was also weak and undernourished.

    E. Out of shape, John was either weak or but also undernourished.

Correct Answer: D

This is the only correlative combination that is fully intact (not only…but also).

Test Tip

Test makers usually test correlative conjunction recognition by simply leaving out some or all of the second part. They just want to see if you can recognize the pair in the context of a sentence.

For example, if you see the phrase *not only*, you must have a *but also* in the sentence.

Comparatives and Superlatives

Comparatives and superlatives compare things. Comparatives compare two things while superlatives compare three or more things.

For example, the word <u>better</u> is a comparative. It compares only two things.

Steve is *better* than Joe at baseball.

The word *tallest* is a superlative. It compares three or more things.

Out of everyone in the class, Jody is the *tallest*.

When answering these questions, pay attention to words like *more* and *most* and *better* and *best*. People often use these incorrectly in everyday speech.

WRITING

The following example is how comparatives and superlatives will be presented on the test.

Example question

Out of all the hundreds of dresses in the store, Kelly liked the red dress <u>more</u>.

    A. more

    B. most

    C. better

    D. more better

    E. most better

Correct Answer: B

Because there are more than two dresses being compared, the comparative *more* is incorrect and should be replaced with the superlative *most*.

Never use answers D and E. Those choices will always be incorrect.

Common Comparative Errors

On the test, you may be faced with correlative conjunction errors. Most people have a hard time finding these errors because throughout language evolution, people have started to use these incorrectly.

For example, many people may think the sentences below are correct. However, they are incorrect.

Incorrect

- My sister is bigger <u>than me</u>.

- She is not as tall <u>as me</u>.

- Not only is she taller <u>than me</u>, but she is also younger <u>than me</u>.

Correct

- My sister is bigger <u>than I</u>.

- My sister is bigger <u>than I am</u>.

- She is not as tall as <u>I</u>.

- She is not as tall as <u>I am</u>.

- Not only is she taller <u>than I</u>, but she is also younger <u>than I</u>.

- Not only is she taller <u>than I am</u>, but she is also younger <u>than I am</u>.

Quick Tip

When trying to determine what pronouns to use, look at the surrounding words.

Ask yourself:

Is this a comparison? Do I see the word ***than***? If so, use the subject pronoun.

- She is taller ***than*** I.

- She is taller ***than I am***.

Parallel Structure

Parallel structure refers to the same pattern of words or repetition of a chosen grammatical form within a sentence. Parallel structure is when a sentence follows the same grammatical pattern.

For example, read the sentences below and notice the difference in the pattern in the lists.

Incorrect

The superintendent on the job was delighted to see that the crew had finished the job, cleaned up the site, and some were organizing the tools.

Correct

The superintendent on the job was delighted to see that the crew had finished the job, cleaned up the site, and organized the tools.

Notice the list in the second sentence is parallel; the verbs are all past tense and followed by nouns.

The following is how parallel structure might be presented on the exam.

Example question

After the party, we cleaned the patio, swept the stairs, washed the dishes, and <u>were finally able to go</u> to bed.

    A. were finally able to go

    B. after went

    C. was going

    D. will go

    E. went

In grammatical terms, parallel structure is used to organize a series or a list in a sentence. This type of organization is used with nearly all parts of speech, phrases, and clauses. The key to parallel structures is that all the things in the series must be the same part of speech.

Correct Answer: E

The correct answer is *went*. In the list in the sentence, there are past tense verbs followed by noun(s). *All* of the other answer choices break the parallel structure in the sentence. The word *went* is most appropriate because all the verbs are past tense: cleaned, swept, washed.

Parallel structure can be presented in different ways. The following is how you may see it in sentences.

Nouns and pronouns in a series.

- The good one, the bad one, and the skinny one are all in the last scene.
- The last scene contains the good one, the bad one, and the skinny one.

Adjectives in a series.

- The big, red, round beach ball is the one that I want.
- The beach ball that I want is big, red, and round.

Adverbs in a series

- I agree with you completely and wholeheartedly.

Predicates in a series

- They danced, laughed, and told stories all night.

Prepositional phrases in a series.

- We looked for your socks <u>in the living room</u>, <u>in the dining room</u>, and <u>in your bedroom</u>.

Participles in a series

- In the evening, she loves <u>jogging on the nature paths</u>, <u>drinking hot chocolate</u>, and <u>warming herself by the fire.</u>

Infinitives in a series

- Yes, I like to <u>jog</u> on nature paths, <u>drink</u> hot chocolate, and <u>warm</u> myself by the fire as well.

*Notice that the infinites to jog, to drink, and to warm all share the same "to" in the sentence.

Clauses in a series

- The person <u>who has the best resume</u> and <u>who has the best interview</u> will get the job.

Sentences in a series

- Go to your room, turn off the light, and go to sleep.

Quick Tip

When faced with a test question with a list of nouns, verbs, or phrases, think ***MATCHY MATCHY***. Everything in the list must match.

Example

While on vacation we **rode** bikes, **swam** in the ocean, and **visited** with friends.

Here you can see that all the verb tenses match; they are all past-tense verbs.

Also, the past tense verbs are all followed nouns: bikes, ocean, friends.

Example question

After reaching level three, you have three chances to defeat the dragon, finding the treasure chest, and collect the magic sword.

- A. After reaching level three, you have three chances to defeat the dragon, finding the treasure chest, and collecting the magic sword.
- B. After reaching level three, you have three chances to defeat the dragon, to find the treasure chest, and collect the magic sword.
- C. After reaching level three, you have three chances to defeat the dragon, find the treasure chest, and collect the magic sword.
- D. After reaching level three, you have three chances to defeating the dragon, finding the treasure chest, and collecting the magic sword.
- E. After reaching level three, you have three chances to defeat the dragon, to finding the treasure chest, and collect the magic sword.

Correct Answer: C

The correct answer is **C**. Here, the phrase, ***you have three chances to***, connects each of the parallel form items: ***defeat***, ***find***, and ***collect***.

Structural Relationships - Practice Problems

1. While away on vacation, Jill's neighbors helped her by collecting her mail.

    A. While away on vacation, Jill's neighbors helped her by collecting her mail.

    B. Jill's neighbors collected her mail while she was away on vacation.

    C. While away on vacation, Jill's mail was collected by her neighbors.

    D. Jill's neighbors, while away on vacation, collected her mail.

    E. Jill's mail was collected by her neighbors while away on vacation.

2. Before we were able to leave for the amusement park, we had to be sure we cleaned the house, boarded the dog, and got gas for the car.

    A. got gas for the car

    B. went to the gas station

    C. fueled the car

    D. put gas in the car

    E. got gas

3. We couldn't understand why she was upset. She had everything she wanted: a beautiful home, an exciting job, and a family that loved her. No error

    A. was upset, she

    B. anything

    C. wanted. A

    D. and a loving family

    E. No error

4. During the celebration, the teacher allowed her students to eat candy, this was a treat for all their hard work.

    A. candy, this

    B. candy; this

    C. candy: this

    D. candy and

    E. candy this

5. She couldn't understand what he was saying, she pretended to follow along.

    A. saying, she

    B. saying and she

    C. saying, but she

    D. saying; and

    E. saying yet she

6. He didn't understand the impact of his <u>work, he</u> was so immersed in the daily operations.

    A. work, he

    B. work; he

    C. work but he

    D. work and he

    E. work he

7. She is working towards a sustainable plan <u>for her business, and she</u> is trying to utilize resources effectively.

    A. for her business, and she

    B. for her business and she

    C. for her business but she

    D. for her business; and she

    E. for her business; yet she

8. <u>The team members</u> wanted to do something nice for <u>their</u> <u>coach so</u> they got <u>him</u> a gift certificate to his favorite restaurant. <u>No error</u>

    A. The team

    B. its

    C. coach, so

    D. them

    E. No error

9. Out of all the teachers in the <u>school, students loved Ms. Jackson more</u>.

    A. school, students loved Ms. Jackson more.

    B. school, students loved Ms. Jackson better.

    C. school students loved Ms. Jackson better.

    D. school, students loved Ms. Jackson better.

    E. school, students loved Ms. Jackson most.

10. I always wondered why she did so much better in school <u>than me.</u>

    A. than me.

    B. then me.

    C. then I.

    D. than I.

    E. than myself

WRITING

Number	Answer	Explanation
1.	B	This is a misplaced modifier question, so be sure the modifier is connected to the appropriate person or thing it is modifying. In this case, *while away on vacation* should be modifying Jill. In answer choices A and D, the phrase *while away on vacation* is modifying neighbors. In answer choices C and E, the phrase *while away on vacation* is modifying the mail.
2.	C	For the sentence to be parallel, the verbs and the nouns in the list should match. In this case, we have *cleaned* (past tense) and *boarded* (past tense). Also, in this case, a noun follows the past tense verb. The only answer that fits is fueled (past tense verb) the car (noun). All the other choices are unparallel.
3.	D	This question is testing parallel structure. The last item in the list at the end of the sentence is not parallel to the rest of the list. In this case we have *a beautiful home* (adjective and noun), *an exciting job* (adjective and noun), and *a family that loved her* (noun, verb and pronoun). The correction to this would be to switch out the last portion of the list to match the adjective and noun progression in the sentence. In this case, *loving* (adjective) and *family* (noun) are parallel. The period is used correctly in answer choice A, and the colon is also used correctly in answer choice B.
4.	B	This item presents a comma splice—there are two independent clauses incorrectly separated by a comma. The correct ways to separate two independent clauses is by using **A semicolon:** The teacher allowed her students to eat <u>candy; this</u> was a treat for all their hard work. **A period followed by a capital letter:** The teacher allowed her students to eat <u>candy. This</u> was a treat for all their hard work. **A comma plus a coordinating conjunction:** The teacher allowed her students to eat <u>candy</u>, <u>and this</u> was a treat for all their hard work.
5.	C	The way this is presented is a comma splice—two independent clauses incorrectly separated by a comma. Therefore, answer choice A is incorrect. The correct answer is C because the comma plus the conjunction is required here. Answer choice D has a semicolon with the conjunction. Semicolons should never be followed by coordinating conjunctions—for, and, nor, but, or, yet, so (FANBOYS). Answer choices B and E have the conjunction only, which is not enough to separate two independent clauses; they need a comma.
6.	B	This is a comma splice question. The comma is incorrectly separating two independent clauses. A semicolon is needed.

Number	Answer	Explanation
7.	A	The sentence is correct as it is. The comma + conjunction is correctly separating two independent clauses.
8.	C	In this case, there are two independent clauses. Therefore, the comma + conjunction (comma + so) is needed here.
9.	E	Because there are more than two teachers being compared, the comparative *more* is incorrect and should be replaced with the superlative *most*. Also, C is incorrect because there needs to be a comma after the introductory clause.
10.	D	In this case, there is a comparison. So, the sentence is really saying, ...she did so much better *than I did*. Watch out for words *then* and *than*. Test makers will often use them in questions to confuse you. *Then* indicates time; *than* indicates a comparison.

Word Choice

Recognize and correct:

- Errors in the use of idiomatic expressions
- Errors in the use of frequently confused words
- Wrong word use
- Redundancy

Idiomatic Expressions

Idiomatic expressions exist throughout the English language, but for the purpose of standardized testing, usually the idiomatic usage problem centers on verb + phrase usage. These idiomatic questions can be especially difficult for students whose first language is not English. There is no hard fast rule for idiomatic phrases. Here, if it sounds familiar, then usually it is correct.

Usually, the errors in idiomatic phrases happen in the verb + preposition part of a sentence. See the examples that follow.

Incorrect

- Let's plan <u>with</u> it.

Correct

- Let's plan <u>on</u> it.

Incorrect

- I'll meet you <u>at</u> the corner of the room.
- I'll meet you <u>in</u> the corner of Washington and Vine.

Correct

- I'll meet you <u>in</u> the corner of the room.
- I'll meet you <u>at</u> the corner of Washington and Vine.

Incorrect

- Please write this in accordance <u>to</u> the rules.
- According <u>with</u> her, the driver ran the stop sign.

Correct

- Please write this in accordance <u>with</u> the rules.
- According <u>to</u> her, the driver ran the stop sign.

Quick Tip

Because there is no rule for idiomatic phrases, it is best to go with the answer choice that sounds the best. A sentence with idiomatic errors in it will often sound awkward. We always say, if it sounds awkward, don't choose it.

Frequently Confused Words

Most standardized English exams will test your ability to distinguish among commonly confused words. These are usually homophones—words that sound the same but that are spelled differently and that have different meanings. The following table contains many of the commonly confused words used on English language skills assessments.

Commonly Confused Words	
accept - to agree to receive or do **except** - not including	**coarse** - rough **course** - a direction; a school subject; part of a meal
adverse - unfavorable, harmful **averse** - strongly disliking; opposed	**complement** - an addition that improves **compliment** - to praise or express approval; an admiring remark
advice - recommendations about what to do **advise** - to recommend something	**council** - a group of people who manage or advise **counsel** - advice; to advise
affect - to change or make a difference to **effect** - a result; to bring about a result	**elicit** - to draw out a reply or reaction **illicit** - not allowed by law or rules
aisle - a passage between rows of seats **isle** - an island	**ensure** - to make certain that something will happen **insure** - to provide compensation
all together - all in one place, all at once **altogether** - completely; on the whole	**foreword** - an introduction to a book **forward** - onwards, ahead
along - moving or extending horizontally on **a long** - referring to something of great length	**principal** - most important; the head of a school **principle** - a fundamental rule or belief
aloud - out loud **allowed** - permitted	**sight** - the ability to see **site** - a location
altar - a sacred table in a church **alter** - to change	**stationary** - not moving **stationery** - writing materials
amoral - not concerned with right or wrong **immoral** - not following accepted moral standards	**allusion** - indirect reference **illusion** - false idea
assent - agreement, approval **ascent** - the action of rising or climbing up	**allude** - to make indirect reference to **elude** - to avoid
bare - naked; to uncover **bear** - to carry; to put up with	**capital** - major city, wealth, assets **capitol** - government building
bated - in phrase *with bated breath*; in great suspense **baited** - with bait attached or inserted	**conscience** - sense of morality **conscious** - awake, aware
censure - to criticize strongly **censor** - to ban parts of a book or film	**eminent** - prominent, important **imminent** - about to happen
cereal - a breakfast food **serial** - happening in a series	**everyday** - routine, common **every day** - each day, all the day

Example question

He wasn't sure <u>how</u> the drug would <u>effect</u> his <u>patient, but</u> he went through with the <u>trial anyway</u>. <u>No error</u>

  A. what

  B. affect

  C. patient but

  D. trial: anyway

  E. No error

Correct Answer: B

Affect and *effect* are commonly confused words. *Affect* is the verb, and *effect* is the noun. In this case, the drug may affect (v) the patient. In the underlined portion for B, the comma is used correctly. The underlined portion for C is correct as well.

Caution

When you see the word *affect* or *effect*, slow down and determine if the sentence calls for a noun or a verb. Then make your choice.

Remember, *effect* is a noun, so it will be proceeded by *the* or *an*.

Example: *The effect* of the drug made me sleepy.

Example: *An effect* of the drug is drowsiness.

Example question

The storm was <u>eminent</u>. All we could do was head to the basement and wait until it was over.

  A. eminent

  B. imminent

  C. prominent

  D. blatant

  E. flagrant

Correct Answer: B

Eminent and *imminent* are commonly confused words. *Imminent* is the correct choice because it means looming or about to happen. *Eminent* means well-known, which is the same as prominent, blatant, and flagrant, so answer choices A, C, D, and E should be eliminated.

WRITING

Wrong Word Use

Common words are often misused in speech and text. In this case, one usually is misused for the other. The following are some that usually appear on the test.

Word usage	Examples in context
then/than • Then is used to mark time. • Than is used for comparisons.	**Error**: This is farther **then** I thought. **Correct**: This is farther **than** I thought.
between/among • Between involves two things • Among involves three or more things.	**Error**: That matter must be discussed **between** Jeff and his brothers. **Correct**: That matter must be discussed **among** Jeff and his brothers.
number/amount • Number is used for quantifiable nouns (things you can count). • Amount is used for non-quantifiable nouns (things you don't count).	**Error**: There was a large **amount** of people there. **Correct**: There was a large **number** of people there. **Error**: The **amount** of dollars she made was staggering. **Correct**: The **amount** of money she made was staggering. **Correct**: The **number** of dollars she made was staggering.
many/much • Many is used for count nouns. • Much is used for non-count nouns.	**Error**: **Much** of the people had left. **Correct**: **Many** of the people had left. **Correct**: **Much** of the cake was left over after the party.
less/fewer • Fewer is used for count nouns. • Less is used for non-counts.	**Error**: There are even **less** people here now. **Correct**: There are even **fewer** people here now. **Correct**: The population is **less** this year than last year.
imply/infer • The speaker implies. • The listener infers.	**Error**: The author **inferred** that Ned was the killer. **Correct**: The author **implied** that Ned was the killer.

WRITING

Redundancy

Some words and expressions are commonly used in the vernacular that needlessly relate the meaning. These redundancies should be correct in proper English practice.

Reason why, and also, every single, not hardly, double negatives

Word usage	Examples in context
reason why Both are reasons.	**Error**: That is the **reason why** I did it. **Correct**: That is **why** I did it. That is the **reason** I did it.
double negatives Negatives do not repeat in English lest they cancel out the original meaning.	**Error**: We <u>can't never</u> win against them. **Correct**: We <u>can never</u> win against them.
not hardly, hardly never **Hardly** is a negative word, so using it with another negative produces a double negative effect.	**Error**: I <u>can't hardly</u> wait. **Correct**: I <u>can hardly</u> wait.
and also Both mean additionally.	**Error**: She lacked the stamina to finish <u>and also</u> the will. **Correct**: She lacked the stamina to finish, <u>also</u> the will.

Here are some other examples of redundancy that may not be as obvious.

Incorrect

- He sat **alone** in **solitude**.

Correct

- He sat **alone**.
- He sat in **solitude**.

Incorrect

- She **quickly sped** up to catch the light.

Correct

- She **sped** up to catch the light.
- She drove **quickly** to catch the light.

Incorrect

- He **scrupulously** wrote **carful** notes.

Correct

- He wrote **careful** notes.
- He wrote **scrupulously**.

WRITING

This page intentionally left blank.

Word Choice – Practice Problems

Instructions: Choose the underlined portion of the sentence that contains an error. If no error occurs, choose no error.

1. Jane has been <u>positively</u> <u>affected</u> by the surge in <u>tourism, and</u> her business <u>is booming</u>. <u>No error</u>.

2. The <u>students</u> were not <u>aloud</u> to play on the <u>playground because</u> <u>there</u> was no supervision. No error.

3. The police <u>were</u> trying to <u>illicit</u> information from the <u>suspect, but</u> he wasn't <u>giving up</u> a thing. <u>No error</u>

4. The scientists <u>attribute</u> the surge in illness <u>to a</u> bacterium <u>found</u> in the water in the <u>southeast</u> area of the Philippines. No error

5. This <u>time, she</u> bought <u>less</u> avocados <u>than</u> she did the last time she <u>shopped</u>. <u>No error</u>

6. When the school year was about to <u>end, the</u> teacher <u>wrote</u> <u>thank-you</u> notes on her good <u>stationary</u>. <u>No error</u>

7. While she was fighting her case in <u>court, she</u> was unable to <u>except</u> that she <u>was</u> responsible for the damages of the car <u>accident</u>. <u>No error</u>

8. <u>There</u> were so many different opinions <u>between</u> team <u>members; getting</u> all fifteen of <u>them</u> to agree was impossible. <u>No error</u>

9. When she went out on the <u>town, she</u> wore her <u>everyday</u> <u>clothes, but</u> she always <u>wore</u> her diamond earrings for some flare. <u>No error</u>

10. All of the designers <u>were</u> to create <u>masterpieces</u> in accordance <u>to</u> the rules set <u>by</u> the judges. <u>No error</u>

Question	Answer	Explanation
1.	No error	This example assesses your knowledge of commonly confused words *affect* and *effect*. Remember, *affect* is the verb, and *effect* is the noun. The -ed ending belongs with verbs as in *walked, talked, stopped*. Therefore, *affected* is used correctly in this sentence as it is. When checking the other underlinedportions, positively is the correct use of the adverb for the verb *affected*. In addition, the comma + conjunction is used correctly in sentence. No error is the correct answer.
2.	aloud	This example assesses your knowledge of commonly confused words *aloud* and *allowed*. *Aloud* means out loud, and *allowed* means permitted. In this case, *aloud* is used incorrectly and should be changed to *allowed*.
3.	illicit	This example assesses your knowledge of commonly confused words *elicit* and *illicit*. *Elicit* means to draw out, and that is what the police were trying to do. *Illicit* means illegal. While the suspect may have done something illegal or illicit, it is the wrong choice for the underlined portion of the sentence.
4.	No error	The correct word to use is attribute or characterize. Bacterium is singular so using *to a* in front of bacterium is correct. The word found in the correct tense. Finally, *southeast* is a region and not a proper noun, so leaving it lowercased is correct. The sentence is correct the way it is written. No error has occurred.
5.	less	When describing things you can count, like avocados, use *fewer*. When describing things you cannot count, like food, use *less*. For example: She bought *fewer* avocados. She bought *less* food.
6.	stationary	Stationery and stationary commonly confused words. Stationary means immobile or motionless. Stationery is the fancy paper you write notes on.
7.	except	The words accept and except are commonly confused words. **Accept** - to agree to receive or do **Except** - not including The underlined word except should be changed to accept.
8.	between	The word *between* is used for two people; *among* is used for more than two. Since there are 15 people on the team, *between* should be replaced with *among*.
9.	No error	You may be tempted to choose *everyday*. However, *everyday* (one word) is the adjective and is used correctly here. It is describing the clothes. *Every day* (two words) means each and every day.

WRITING

Question	Answer	Explanation
10.	to	This is an idiomatic error. The correct way would be to say: …in *accordance with* the rules set by the judges.

This page intentionally left blank.

Mechanics

Recognize and correct:

- Errors in capitalization
- Errors in punctuation
  - o commas
  - o semicolons
  - o apostrophes

Capitalization

Capitalization for standard English follows a few basic rules.

1. **Always capitalize the first word of a sentence.**

The key here is to recognize where the sentences start and stop. For example, semicolons connect two sentences together as one; therefore, they do not need capitalization except at the beginning (unless the second sentence starts with a proper noun).

Example:

- Capitalization can be tricky; there are several rules.

Notice that the **C** in *capitalization* is capitalized, but the **t** in there is not.

2. **Always capitalize proper nouns and their titles as well as their abbreviations.**

Names of specific people and places are capitalized.

Examples:

- During the Civil War, President Abraham Lincoln was president of the United States.

Civil War is a specific name of a war. *President* is the title of *Abraham Lincoln* in the subject. However, *president* is a common noun in the predicate.

- Today, Congress passed a law banning congressional pay raises even though the Senate had to vote on it three times.

Congress and the *Senate* are, in this case, proper nouns.

3. **Capitalize the main words in a multiword title.**

Here, the emphasis is also on what **not** to capitalize: articles (other than the first word), conjunctions, and prepositions.

Examples:

- He works at the Federal Bureau of Investigation in Washington, DC.
- Poe's *Tales of Mystery and Imagination* is one of my favorite collections.

Notice that the articles and prepositions—is, in, of, and—are not capitalized in the title.

On the test, you will often be assessed on your ability to identify when NOT to capitalize, like in the example question below.

I wait every year for the <u>Fall; it's</u> my favorite holiday.

    A. Fall; it's

    B. fall; it's

    C. Fall, its

    D. fall, its

    E. Fall; my

Correct Answer: B

The seasons are not capitalized unless they are attached to a proper noun as in Fall Festival or Winter Dance.

Also, in this question, *it's* is the proper conjunction for *it is*. Finally, the semicolon is used correctly, separating an independent clause and dependent clause.

Punctuation

Standard punctuation is assessed many ways on the exam. It is best to understand commas, semicolons, apostrophes, and colons.

Commas (,)

No other punctuation mark is misused as often as the comma. Its use in items in a series is also hotly debated. The traditional Oxford comma separates items in a series of three items or more, including the item before the coordinating conjunction.

Example:

- I went to the store to buy milk, eggs, cheese**,** and bread.
- I went to the store to buy milk, eggs, cheese and bread.

Test Tip

The Oxford comma is used before *and* in a sentence. You will NOT be asked on a grammar test to choose between using the Oxford comma and not using the Oxford comma because both are considered correct. The choice is a stylistic one.

Comma Usage Rules

Usage	Example
After an introductory word, phrase, or clause	However, he did not follow the rules.
To separate a dependent clause from an independent clause when the dependent clause comes first	When he turned in his homework a day late, the teacher tossed it in the garbage.
Before a coordinating conjunction to separate two independent clauses	I went to my interview today, and I think it went really well.
To separate items in a series of three items or more	The girl went shopping for school supplies: notebooks, pens, pencils, highlighters, and more.
To separate two consecutive adjectives	The tall, muscular girl was the star of the basketball team.
On both sides of nonessential words, phrases, or clauses	The teacher, who had little experience, assigned reading from a banned book.
To set off someone's name or title	Excuse me, Alyssa, but I need to take this call.
To separate the day, month, and year in a date (and after the year if it is part of a sentence)	June 14, 1969, is my birthdate.
To separate a city from a state	I am from Baltimore, Maryland.
To introduce or separate a quote	She screamed, "I hate you!" "Why," I asked, "do you hate me?"
Before the end quotation mark if the quote is followed by an attribution such as he said	"I can't stand it anymore," he said.
To separate contrasting parts of a sentence	That is my drink, not yours.

COMMA SPLICE

When commas are incorrectly used to separate two independent clauses, it is called a comma splice. On the exam, you will be required to identify and correct comma splices.

Commas are used to separate an independent from a dependent clause. Commas are NOT used to separate two independent clauses.

The sentence below is an example of a comma splice.

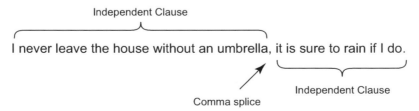

Example question

The teacher stood confidently to accept her <u>award, among</u> those in the audience were some of her former students.

   A. award, among

   B. award. Among

   C. but among

   D. and among

   E. award yet among

Correct answer: B

The sentence as is contains a comma splice, making answer choice A incorrect.

Removing the comma and inserting any of the conjunctions *but*, *and, yet* causes the sentence to be a run-on.

Example question

<u>After the movie,</u> she <u>said "I don't</u> understand why <u>there</u> is always so much violence in <u>film."</u> <u>No error</u>

   A. After the movie

   B. said, "I don't

   C. their

   D. film".

   E. No error

Correct Answer: B

A comma is needed to separate a quote in a sentence. Therefore, the comma must be added here. Notice in the intro clause, *After the movie*, the comma is used correctly, eliminating answer choice A.

Semicolons (;)

Semicolons join two independent clauses that are related. Semicolons are alternatives to a period or comma conjunction.

Examples:

- I needed to go to the store; I was almost out of milk, egg, cheese, and bread.
- He knew he would be punished for skipping school; he did it anyway.

In both examples above, there are two independent clauses joined by the semicolon. This is the only way to use a semicolon.

Example question

<u>Last year,</u> we tried to <u>build</u> the house on our <u>own; but</u> we soon realized we <u>needed</u> help. <u>No error</u>

   A. Last year

   B. built

   C. own, but

   D. need

   E. No error

Correct Answer: C

You do not use a semicolon and a coordinating conjuction together. Never use a semicolon before fanboys in a sentence. This part of the sentence needs a comma.

Also, the intro clause, *Last year*, is punctauted correctly with a comma.

Colons (:)

Colons are used to separate an independent clause and a list. Colons can also be used to separate an independent clause and an independent clause or dependent clause that elaborates, restates, explains, or defines.

As a List Example:

- I brought all the necessities to the campsite: tent, food, fishing pole, and lighter.

  o Notice that the clause, *I brought all the necessities to the campsite*, is a sentence—an independent clause. Therefore, the colon is used correctly.

As a Definition Example:

- We decided to focus on the most important thing: increasing student achievement.

  o Notice that the independent clause is *We decided to focus on the most important thing.* The dependent clause, which is *increasing student achievement*, defines what the most important thing is.

- I had lunch with the president of the university: Dr. Cunningham.

  o Here you have an independent clause followed by the name of the person mentioned in the first clause. Therefore, the colon is appropriate.

Example question

We were waiting on several of our <u>items such as: books, scissors, and pencils</u>.

    A. items such as: books, scissors, and pencils.

    B. items: books, scissors, and pencils.

    C. Items like our: books, scissors, and pencils.

    D. items, books, scissors, and pencils.

    E. items for example: books scissors, and pencils

Correct Answer: B

Correct use of a colon requires an independent clause before the colon and a list or definition after the colon. The phrase *such as* should be removed from the sentence. Doing so creates an independent clause before the colon. This is the same reason answers C and E are incorrect.

Apostrophes (')

There are two main reasons to use apostrophes:

1. To form a contraction such as do + not = don't. In this case, the apostrophe replaces or stands in for the letter that is taken out when the words are combined.

2. To show possession. When the noun is singular or plural but does not end in **s**, add **'s** to show possession. When the noun is singular or plural but does end in **s**, add the apostrophe **after the s** to show possession—**s'**.

Below are some examples for using the apostrophe to show possession.

Correct Apostrophe Usage Examples:

- Please bring **Lisa's** book when you come to class tomorrow.
  - o **Lisa** is a singular proper noun (there is only one Lisa here); therefore, the **s'** is appropriate.
- We will be going to the **women's** soccer tournament on Wednesday.
  - o **Women** is a plural noun that does NOT end in s; therefore, the **s'** is appropriate.
- Please bring all the **girls'** books when you come to class tomorrow.
  - o **Girls** is a plural noun that ends in s; therefore, the **s'** is appropriate.
- We will be going to the **ladies'** luncheon on Friday.
  - o **Ladies** is plural and ends in -s, and the ladies own the luncheon. Therefore, the **s'** is appropriate.

On the exam, apostrophes can be tricky because they are assessed in ways with which you may not be familiar.

Example question

I am not excited about <u>tomorrows</u> meeting.

- A. tomorrows
- B. tomorrow
- C. tomorrow's
- D. tomorrows'
- E. tomorrowes

Correct Answer: C

In cases like this, the meeting belongs to tomorrow. Therefore, it should be ***tomorrow's meeting.***

Quick Tip

Be able to distinguish among the following possessive pronouns and contractions.

its - ownership
The team had its game yesterday.

it's - contraction
It's a beautiful day.

whose - ownership
We weren't sure whose book it was.

who's - contraction
Who's coming to the game tonight.

Mechanics – Practice Problems

1. I <u>haven't</u> <u>seen</u> <u>uncle Dave</u> in fourteen years. I wondered if he <u>has</u> changed. No error

   A. hasn't

   B. saw

   C. Uncle Dave

   D. have

   E. No error

2. <u>She forgot her list when she went to the grocery store;</u> this oversight caused her to forget many of the items she needed.

   A. She forgot her list when she went to the grocery store;

   B. Her list was forgotten at home when she went to the grocery store;

   C. Forgetting her list when she went to the grocery store,

   D. Because she forgot her list when she went to the grocery store,

   E. She forgot her list when she went to the grocery store

3. <u>The little girls' dresses were of her mothers' favorite colors.</u>

   A. The little girls' dresses were of her mothers' favorite colors.

   B. The little girls' dresses were of their mothers' favorite colors.

   C. The little girls dresses were of her mothers' favorite colors.

   D. The little girls' dresses were of their mother's favorite colors.

   E. The little girls's dresses were of her mothers favorite colors.

4. <u>At 3:05 p.m., on January 5, 2017, a huge crowd gathered outside the building.</u>

   A. At 3:05 p.m., on January 5, 2017, a huge crowd gathered outside the building.

   B. At 3:05 p.m. on January 5 2017, a huge crowd gathered outside the building.

   C. At 3:05 p.m. on January 5, 2017 a huge crowd gathered outside the building.

   D. At 3:05 p.m. on January 5, 2017, a huge crowd gathered outside the building.

   E. At 3:05 p.m., on January 5, 2017; a huge crowd gathered outside the building.

WRITING

5. The teacher asked the students, who were finished with their tests, to choose one of these options, read a book, write a story, or draw a picture.

    A. The teacher asked the students, who were finished with their tests, to choose one of these options, read a book, write a story, or draw a picture.

    B. The teacher asked the students, whom were finished with their tests, to choose one of these options; read a book, write a story, or draw a picture.

    C. The teacher asked the students, whom were finished with their tests, to choose one of these options: read a book, write a story, or draw a picture.

    D. The teacher asked the students, who were finished with their tests, to choose one of these options: read a book, write a story, or draw a picture.

    E. The teacher asked the students, whom were finished with their tests, to choose one of these options, read a book, write a story, or draw a picture.

6. He knew he would get in trouble for skipping school but he did it anyway.

    A. school but he did it anyway.

    B. school, he did it anyway.

    C. school and he did it anyway.

    D. school yet he did it anyway.

    E. school; he did it anyway.

7. The doctor's assistant mistakenly overbooked the schedule, and causing frustration on the part of the doctor and the patients.

    A. schedule, and causing frustration on the part of the doctor and the patients.

    B. schedule, causing frustration on the part of the doctor and the patients.

    C. schedule therefore causing frustration on the part of the doctor and the patients.

    D. schedule and causing the effect of frustration for the doctor and the patients.

    E. schedule, but causing frustration on the part of the doctor and the patients.

8. Without making a sound Geoffrey crept down the stairs.

    A. sound Geoffrey crept

    B. sound; Geoffrey crept

    C. sound, Geoffrey crept

    D. sound, crept Geoffrey

    E. sound and Geoffrey crept

9. At 15-years-old, he shipped as a cabin boy, bound for Ireland.

    A. a cabin boy, bound for

    B. a cabin boy; bound for

    C. a cabin boy: bound for

    D. a cabin boy and he was bound for

    E. a cabin boy. Bound for

10. She <u>came</u> to visit me last <u>Spring</u> and during the <u>Fall Festival</u> held in the <u>north</u> part of the town. <u>No error.</u>

    A. comes

    B. spring

    C. Fall festival

    D. North

    E. No error

WRITING

Number	Answer	Explanation
1.	C	In this case, *Uncle Dave* is a proper noun. If the sentence said, *I haven't seen my uncle Dave*, uncle would be lowercase.
2.	A	The semicolon is used correctly in this sentence. It connects two related independent clauses. Therefore, no change is necessary
3.	D	Choice D has the correct punctuation for *girls'* (plural possessive). Also, the pronoun *their* is used property because there is more than one girl. Finally, mother is singular and should have the singular possessive—*mother's*.
4.	A	This sentence has a number of introductory clauses that must be separated using commas. *At 3:05 p.m.* is an introductory clause and must have a comma after it. The same is true for *on January 5, 2017.* There is always a comma separating the month and day from the year, eliminating choice B. Choice C is incorrect because a comma is missing after the introductory clause *At 3:05 p.m. on January 5, 2017.* Choice D is incorrect because it is missing the comma after *At 3:05 p.m.* Choice E is incorrect because the semicolon is used improperly.
5.	D	First, we can eliminate any option with whom because it is used improperly here. Ask yourself, "*who* finished the tests?" Then answer, "*He* finished, *she* finished, or *they* finished." Therefore, *who* is the correct pronoun. This eliminates answers B, C, and E. The next part is the punctuation. The proper punctuation is the colon because it separates the independent clause and the list.
6.	E	You either need a comma plus a conjunction, which eliminates answers A, C, and D, or you need a semicolon. That makes answer choice E correct. The comma only in answer B is a comma splice and is incorrect because it makes the sentence a run-on.
7.	B	The verb phrase *causing frustration on the part of the doctor and patients* should be separated from the independent clause before it with a comma. All of the other answer choices are either missing the comma, or they erroneously add a conjunction (and/but) that is unnecessary.
8.	C	Introductory clauses should be followed by a comma. *Without making a sound* is an introductory clause. Therefore, the correct answer is C.
9.	A	The sentence is correct the way it is, making A the correct choice. The semicolon in answer B is used incorrectly. A semicolon is used when connecting two independent clauses, and *bound for Ireland* is not an independent clause; it's a participle phrase. The colon is also used incorrectly, eliminating answer C. Answer D is a run-on, and answer E is a fragment.
10.	B	Seasons are not capitalized unless they are part of a proper noun as shown in *Fall Festival*. Only capitalize directions (north, south, east, west) when they are definite regions or part of a proper name.

Research Skills

- Assess the credibility and relevance of sources.
- Recognize the different elements of a citation.
- Recognize effective research strategies.
- Recognize information relevant to a particular research task.

Assess the credibility and relevance of sources

It is important to evaluate source information for relevancy, validity, and reliability. This is especially important with internet sources. Understanding credibility in resources is essential for scoring well on the GACE exam.

Questions to ask when evaluating sources:

1. **Is the research reliable and valid?**

   - **Validity** refers to how sound the research is in both the design and methods. Validity is the extent to which the findings in the study represent the phenomenon measured in the study.

   - **Internal Validity** refers to how well a study conducted.

   - **External Validity** refers to how applicable the findings are to the real world.

   - **Reliability** refers to the degree of consistency in the measure. A study is considered reliable when it yields similar results under similar conditions after being conducted repeatedly.

2. **Are the authors authorities or experts in their fields?** Authors who are prolific in their space tend to produce reliable and valid research. Be sure to check the author(s).

3. **Is the research current?** Using research conducted in the last 3 years is more effective than using research from the last 20 years. That doesn't mean that past studies are not important. Plenty of the early research in reading is considered seminal. But when looking for trends in reading and new ways to teach, using current research is best.

4. **Is the research scholarly?** Teachers should consider research that comes from peer-reviewed academic journals. Websites and blogs often contain valid and reliable research. However, to be sure that the research is legitimate, go straight to the academic journal where it was published. Be sure to check the bibliography in the study.

5. **Is the research objective?** Research should be unbiased and objective; it should address questions without opinions or agenda. Often, private companies that sell reading programs will publish research. It is important that teachers differentiate between objective research and research that is skewed one way. You can do this by looking at several studies about a topic. Look for trends and consistencies between and among the studies.

6. **Is the research relevant to the profession?** There are a lot of studies out there with important information. You should be seeking out research in the areas that fit your particular job. For example, if you are a reading teacher in a school with a large population of English language learners, you should seek out research relevant to that area.

WRITING

Types of Sources

- **Peer-reviewed journals/articles.** These academic sources of materials are found on a database and can be considered credible. These are effective to use when you need very specific research information on a topic but are not very helpful for general background information.

- **Websites.** Websites are helpful for background information, to evaluate different perspectives on a topic, and for current news evets. **This cannot be emphasized enough: Anyone can post information on a website, so it is very important to evaluate the site carefully.** Things like ads and heavy political or controversial opinion statements are red flags that the site is biased and unreliable.

- **Print sources (books, newspapers, magazines).** Books can be a good place to start for historical information or context, and magazines and newspapers will be useful for current events in an easy-to-understand format.

	Humanities	Sciences
Primary Sources	• Diaries, journals, and letters • Interviews with people who lived during a particular time (e.g., survivors of genocide in Rwanda or the Holocaust) • Songs, plays, novels, stories • Paintings, drawings, and sculptures • Autobiographies	• Published results of research studies • Published results of scientific experiments • Published results of clinical trials • Proceedings of conferences and meetings
Secondary Sources	• Biographies • Histories • Literary criticism • Book, art, and theater reviews • Newspaper articles that interpret	• Publications about the significance of research or experiments • Analysis of a clinical trial • Review of the results of several experiments or trials

Be on the lookout for questions that assess your critical thinking skills relating to sources of information. Credibility relates to the ability of the source to honestly provide information that is authoritative and objective. Relevance means the data relates directly to the question of the research.

Example question

A car commercial boasts that its brand is the most reliable of all brands based upon research. Which of the following types of information collection would be the most relevant and credible when assessing this claim?

   A. Survey of Chevrolet owners.

   B. Survey of car dealership mechanics from 2002 to 2012.

   C. Report of mechanical repairs by all Chevrolet dealerships.

   D. Report of mechanical repairs by Toyota, Honda, and Chevrolet dealerships.

   E. Report of mechanical repairs made on all types of cars by independent repair shops over the last five years.

WRITING

Correct Answer: E

There are bias and relevance issues with all answers except **E**. Answer choice A relates only one brand, not all. Owners of a product are likely to be biased as well. Answers C and D have similar issues. Choice B looks somewhat credible because it lists general car dealerships and has a data range date. However, car dealership mechanics could have bias, and they mostly see their brand of cars. The key concepts that make E valid are a report of statistics (instead of a survey, which could be opinion), the independence of the source (with no obvious bias towards one brand) and a time period for data collection.

Recognize the different elements of a citation.

On the GACE, you will be asked to distinguish between Modern Language Association (MLA) citations and the American Psychological Association (APA) citations. These are the main associations that govern the way we cite relevant research. It seems complicated at first glance; however, the two have distinct elements that make it easy to answer these questions correctly.

Where should citations occur?

Citations should occur in 2 places:

1. Within the body of the document. These are called in-text citations or parenthetical citations. See the example paragraphs below.

2. On a works cited page (MLA) or reference page (APA) at the end of the document.

Think about it.

Citations should always occur in the document (in-text) AND at the end of the document in a list. They should be in BOTH places.

Works Cited MLA

- In MLA, citations are organized on a **works cited** page that is placed at the end of the document. This lists all the references used in the paper. They are in alphabetical order according to author last name.

Example – Book (MLA)

- Last Name, First Name. *Title of Book*. Additional Contributors. City of Publication, Publisher, Publication Date.

*Notice the punctuation. Periods and commas matter in a citation.

Tolstoy, Leo. *War and Peace*. Translated by Anthony Briggs, Moscow, Viking, 1968

| Author's name. Last, First | Title | Other authors or contributors | Location | Publisher | Date |

WRITING

Example – Book (APA)

Author, (Year of publication). *Title of work: Capital letter also for subtitle*. Location: Publisher.

*Notice the punctuation. Periods and commas matter in a citation. Also, in APA, only the first letter of the title is capitalized. The rest of the title, unless it is a proper noun or occurs after a colon, is lowercased.

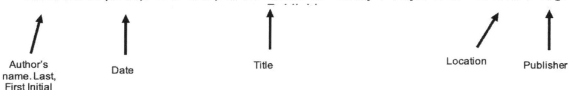

Jackson, L. (2010). *War and peace: A look at Tolstoy's major work*. Boston: Penguin

| Author's name.Last, First Initial | Date | Title | Location | Publisher |

Example – Journal Article (MLA)

Author(s). "Title." *Container.* Version (edition), Number (vol. and/or no.), Publisher, Publisher Date, Page Number(s) (pp.).

Burgess, Anthony. "Politics in the Novels of Graham Greene." *Literature and Society,* special issue of *Journal of Contemporary History,* vol. 2, no. 2, 1967, pp. 93-99.

Example – Journal Article (APA)

Author(s). (Date). Title. *Journal Name, Volume,* Page number(s).

Wegener, D. T., & Petty, R. E. (1994). Mood management across affective states: The hedonic contingency hypothesis. *Journal of Personality and Social Psychology, 66,* 1034-1048.

Quick Tip

Not every citation will have every element of the citation. For example, some publications do not have an edition number or volume number. The main thing to look for when determining whether the citation is MLA or APA is where the date is located in the citation.

- **MLA** – The date is located towards the end of the citation.
- **APA** – The date is located at the front of the citation.

In-Text Citations

Citations should also occur in the body of the research paper. As the writer is communicating information and supporting that information with research, the writer must cite as he or she writes the paper.

In-Text Example (MLA)

Smith asserted that third-grade students, who used technology in math class, increased their math learning gains by 72% **(223)**. In addition, students who were given time to use that technology at home also increased their math gains. Teachers also saw an increase in student engagement when technology was used **(Smith 223).**

*IMPORTANT: You will **not** bold the in-text citation in your own writing. We do here because we want it to stand out.

In the above example, there are two correct MLA citations.

1. The author's last name in the beginning of the first sentence, and the page of publication in parentheses at the end of the sentence.

2. The author's last name and page number at the end of the sentence. Notice the period comes **AFTER** the citation. The citation is part of the sentence.

In-Text Example (APA)

According to **Smith (2018)**, third-grade students, who used technology in math class, increased their math learning gains by 72%. In addition, students who were given time to use that technology at home also increased their math gains. Teachers also saw an increase in student engagement when technology was used **(Smith, 2018)**.

*IMPORTANT: You will **not** bold the in-text citation in your own writing. We do here because we want it to stand out.

In the above example, there are two correct APA citations.

1. In the beginning of the paragraph with the author's last name followed by the date of publication in parentheses.

2. At the end of the sentence with the author's last name, a comma, and date. Notice the period comes **AFTER** the citation. The citation is part of the sentence.

Example question

Which of the following citations is in APA format? Check all that apply.

☐ Romantic poetry is characterized by the "spontaneous overflow of powerful feelings" (Wordsworth 263).

☐ Wordsworth stated that Romantic poetry was marked by a "spontaneous overflow of powerful feelings" (263).

☐ Wordsworth extensively explored the role of emotion in the creative process (263).

☐ According to Wordsworth (2012), extensively explored the role of emotion in the creative process.

☐ Romantic poetry is characterized by the spontaneous overflow of powerful feelings (Wordsworth, 2012).

Correct Answer: Boxes 4 & 5

The last two options are the APA options. These are the only options containing a date. The other three have page numbers, which is indicative of MLA

Test Tip

To quickly determine if the citation is MLA or APA, look for whether or not the in-text citation has a date or a page number.

- **APA** is author and date.

- **MLA** is author and page number.

You don't even have to get bogged down with all the information in the citations. Just look for page numbers or dates to determine the type of citation.

Recognize Effective Research Strategies

Certain research strategies, especially related to texts, are tested on the GACE in the research section of the exam. The emphasis will be on recognizing common best practices in conducting research.

Example question

You just completed multiple database searches for an education research topic and found three academic references from peer reviewed journals. Your assignment requires a fourth peer reviewed article. What would be an effective strategy to find additional source? Choose all that apply.

☐ Expand your search with a search engine like Google.

☐ Contact the reference librarian at the local university for research assistance.

☐ Do searches on the authors of the articles that you already have since scholars are known to do multiple studies on related topics.

☐ Look through the reference list of the articles that you found for related studies.

☐ Use a database to search through newspaper archives on your topic.

Correct Answer: Box 2, 3 & 4.

Anything that mentions a non-academic source like Google or Wiki would not be satisfactory for academic purposes. While newspapers can be good secondary sources, they do not fulfill the peer reviewed requirement. Although most people do not use this resource, the reference librarian, box 2, is an asset when trying to find peer-reviewed relevant research. He or she is an expert in this area. Box 3 is also a good choice because researchers often write multiple papers and studies on one topic. Box 4 is probably the easiest way because reference lists have relevant authors and works related to the topic you are studying. Boxes 2, 3, and 4 are all strategies that researchers use for gathering their literature review.

Recognize Information Relevant to a Particular Research Task

Evaluating research sources requires an understanding of the purpose of the research, the relevance of the sources to the purpose of the research, and the credibility of those sources. The ability to distinguish primary from secondary sources can be a key to the credibility questions. The questions are usually written with multiple acceptable answers and one that is not acceptable.

Example question

You are researching the hardships endured by the people, both combatants and civilians, during the battle for Okinawa in WWII. Which of the following would NOT be a good source for the study?

A. A memoir of a Japanese soldier who fought in the battle.

B. Photographs of devastated villages made by a US Army journalist stationed with a fighting unit.

C. A biography of an Okinawan citizen who endured the battle.

D. Declassified field reports of the US military campaign of Okinawa.

E. Army intelligence reports of troop strengths and locations in the planning of the invasion.

Correct Answer: E

While all of these pertain to Okinawa and the battle, E does not relate to the purpose of the study because it is only about the US troops. Everything else could show the hardships endured by the people.

Which of the following would be the best primary source for understanding how Japanese soldiers felt about the battle?

    A. An autobiography of a Japanese soldier who fought in the battle.

    B. Japanese newspaper accounts written in Tokyo.

    C. A Stars and Stripes article written during the Korean conflict.

    D. A 1953 aerial photograph of the island.

    E. A biography of the Japanese fleet commander.

Correct Answer: A

The key phrase here is *primary source*. Therefore, A is the best answer because B, C, and E are secondary sources. While a photograph is a primary source, it does little to show how a Japanese soldier felt about the war.

WRITING

Research Skills – Practice Problems

1. Which of the following resources would be most appropriate for finding information on a social science topic for a research paper?

    A. The internet

    B. A blog

    C. A peer-reviewed journal

    D. Newspaper

    E. Television broadcast

2. Which of the following parenthetical citations is in proper APA formatting? Choose all that apply.

    ☐ (Williams, 2018)

    ☐ (293)

    ☐ (Jennifer Williams page 3)

    ☐ According to Williams (2018)

    ☐ (Jennifer 2018)

3. Which of the following requires a citation? Choose all that apply.

    ☐ When you use a direct quote from another author

    ☐ When you summarize another author's opinion

    ☐ When you use your original idea

    ☐ When you paraphrase a something from another author's work

    ☐ When you write your thesis statement

4. Which of the following would be considered a primary source?

    A. A letter from a president to a foreign leader

    B. A summary of WWII in a textbook

    C. A biography about a famous commander in WWII

    D. An editorial in the local newspaper about construction of a WWII memorial

    E. An analysis of letters written between presidents and world leaders

5. When using citations in a research paper, where should the works used be credited? Choose all that apply

    ☐ In the body of the paper in parenthetical citations

    ☐ In the works cited or reference page at the end of the paper.

    ☐ Only in the body of the paper

    ☐ Only in the works cited or reference page at the end of the paper

    ☐ In the index

Number	Answer	Explanation
1.	C	When looking for scholarly research for a formal paper, a peer-reviewed academic journal is the most appropriate because it is free from bias.
2.	Boxes 1 & 4	Proper APA formatting includes the authors last name and date.
3.	Boxes 1, 2 & 4	The only time you do not need a citation is when you are using your original ideas. Everything else should be cited. The last box is a nonsense answer. Your thesis statement may or may not need a citation depending on the information in it.
4.	A	A primary source is an original source. Answer choice A is the only original source coming straight from a president to a foreign leader. All the other answer choices are secondary sources.
5.	Boxes 1 & 2	Sources used in a research paper should be cited parenthetically in the body. They should also be listed alphabetically in the works cited or reference page at the end of the paper.

Writing
Practice Tests

Sentence Correction

Directions: In each of the following sentences, some part of the sentence or the entire sentence is underlined. Beneath each sentence, you will find five ways of writing the underlined part. The first answer choice (A) repeats the original, but the other four choices are different. If you think the original sentence is better than any of the suggested changes, you should select the first answer choice (A); otherwise, you should select one of the other answer choices.

This is a test of correctness and effectiveness of expression. In choosing answers, follow the requirement of standard written English; i.e. pay attention to acceptable usage and grammar, diction (choice of words), sentence construction and punctuation. Choose the answer that expresses most effectively what is presented in the original sentence; this answer should be clear and exact, without awkwardness, ambiguity, or redundancy.

1. For people escaping war, the most difficult part of leaving home is not leaving behind sacred possessions, but rather, lost memories of a life long ago.

    A. but rather, lost memories of a life long ago.

    B. but rather, losing memories of a life long ago.

    C. but rather also losing memories of a life long ago.

    D. but additionally, losing memories of a life long ago.

    E. however, losing memories of a life long ago.

2. His name is synonymously aligned to that of a warrior, so much so that his name has been appropriated for a wide range of military.

    A. synonymously aligned to that of a warrior

    B. synonymously and continuously aligned to that of a warrior

    C. synonymous to that of a warrior

    D. synonymous as warrior

    E. synonymous with warrior

3. She didn't know which was worst: traveling without credentials or sleeping in the subway.

    A. which was worst: traveling

    B. which was worst; traveling

    C. which was worse: traveling

    D. which was worse; traveling

    E. which was worst, traveling

WRITING

4. The university decided to reduce the number of academic <u>programs because they could no longer monitor them.</u>

   A. programs, because they could no longer monitor them.

   B. programs because it could no longer monitor them.

   C. programs because they essentially could no longer monitor them.

   D. programs, because they could no longer monitor and observer them.

   E. programs because they could essentially no longer monitor them.

5. <u>As a student at this university, one can accept</u> the status quo, or we can reject it, but we cannot pretend it is not happening.

   A. As a student at this university, one can accept

   B. As a student at this university, we can accept

   C. Either the students accept

   D. Either us students accept

   E. As students at this university, we can accept

6. <u>The actress, using a disguise, passing through the market without being detected by no one.</u>

   A. The actress, using a disguise, passing through the market without being detected by no one.

   B. The actress, who used a disguise, passed through the market without being detected by no one.

   C. The actress, who used a disguise, is passing through the market without being detected by no one.

   D. The actress, using a disguise, passed through the market without being detected by anyone.

   E. The actress, who using a disguise, passed through the market without being detected by anyone.

7. Even though she seemed unaffected, <u>the senator spoke passionately about the tragedy.</u>

   A. the senator spoke passionately about the tragedy.

   B. the senator did spoke passionately about the tragedy.

   C. the senator did actually speak passionate about the tragedy.

   D. the senator spoke passionate about the tragedy.

   E. The senator had spoken passionately about the tragedy.

8. <u>In the voting area, the use of cellphones and computers are prohibited.</u>

   A. In the voting area, the use of cellphones and computers are prohibited.

   B. In the voting area the use of cellphones and computers are prohibited.

   C. In the voting area; the use of cellphones and computers are prohibited.

   D. In the voting area, the use of cellphones and computers is prohibited.

   E. In the voting area where voting will take place, the use of cellphones and computers is prohibited.

9. When asked about the accident, <u>the witness was confused as to whom the driver was.</u>

    A. the witness was confused as to whom the driver was.

    B. the witness was confused as to who the driver was.

    C. the witness was confused as to whom the driver is.

    D. the witness was confused as to whomever the driver was.

    E. the witness was confused as to whoever the driver was.

10. Why is it that <u>every time a student comes to my office</u>, they want something?

    A. every time a student comes to my office,

    B. every time a student coming to my office,

    C. when a student comes to my office,

    D. every time each student comes to my office,

    E. every time students come to my office,

Usage

Directions: Each question consists if a sentence that contains four underlined portions. Read each sentence and decide whether any of the underlined portions contains a grammatical construction, a word use, or an instance of incorrect or omitted punctuation or capitalization that would be inappropriate in carefully written English. If so, select the underlined portion that must be revised to produce a correct sentence. If there are no errors in the sentence as written, select **no error** (E). No sentence has more than one error.

11. She was frustrated when she <u>walked</u> up to the front door of the <u>store; she</u> <u>had</u> just <u>realized</u> she forgot her wallet. <u>No error</u>

12. The <u>store owner's</u> employee <u>mistakenly</u> gave the customer back <u>too</u> much <u>change, which</u> caused the store owner to become frustrated. <u>No error.</u>

13. For <u>this weeks</u> <u>meeting, I</u> would like to <u>not only focus</u> on attendance, <u>but also</u> on academic engagement. <u>No error.</u>

14. When the university went through <u>its</u> academic programs, <u>they</u> saw students, who were never on campus, were more likely to drop out during <u>their</u> second year <u>than</u> those who were on campus all the time. <u>No error.</u>

15. <u>Everyone was</u> excited to get <u>started</u> on their projects that they trampled over <u>each other</u> as they dashed over to the <u>supplies</u> table. <u>No error.</u>

16. As scientists discover galaxies far <u>away,</u> <u>one has</u> to decide if they are going to publish every idea <u>or only</u> expand on theories that have been <u>substantiated.</u> <u>No error.</u>

17. Every <u>Fall,</u> tourists come from far and wide to <u>bear</u> witness to the leaves <u>changing</u> colors as the season <u>progresses.</u> <u>No error.</u>

18. As we move forward with <u>new employees, we</u> must be sure to train them <u>properly,</u> inspire them regularly, <u>and ask them appropriate questions.</u> <u>No error.</u>

19. <u>I not</u> only want you to succeed, <u>and I also want</u> you <u>to be happy.</u> <u>No error.</u>

20. She only <u>understood</u> three <u>things about that</u> time <u>period:</u> <u>being hungry,</u> <u>grace,</u> and acceptance. <u>No error.</u>

Revision

Directions: The following passage is a draft of an essay. Some parts of the passage need to be strengthened through editing and revision. Read the passage and choose the best answers for the questions that follow. Some questions ask you to improve particular sentences or portions of sentences. In some cases, the indicated portion of the passage will be most effective as it is already expressed and thus will require no changes. In choosing answers, consider development, organization, word choice, style and ton, and follow the requirements of standard written English.

Adapted from *Geronimo: The Warrior* by Edward Rielly. Retrieved from the Public Domain[1].

(1) Most people do not know who Geronimo really is, other than the famous phrase yelled out when jumping off of a high place. (2) But he is one of the most famous figures in the history of the American Indian resistance effort.

(3) His name is synonymous to warrior, so much so that his name has been appropriated for a wide range of military (or simply adventuresome) endeavors. (4) Geronimo's reputation is well deserved, for his very name excited fear in settlers both North and South of the U.S. – Mexican border.

(5) Geronimo lacked the social and political leadership skills to propel a movement forward with the U.S. Government. (6) Geronimo's fighting skills set him apart from all others. (7) His lasting led American paratroopers in World War II to call out the name "Geronimo" before plunging from their planes. (8) Schoolchildren, for decades after Geronimo's death, would similarly yell his name before undertaking a real or imagined feat of bravery, such as leaping from a swing into a river. (9) A much more recent, and highly controversial, use of Geronimo's name was its employment by the U.S. military as a code name linked to the 2011 operation that resulted in the death of Osama bin Laden.

21. Which of the following would be the most effective way to combine the two sentences below?

    Most people do not know who Geronimo really is, other than the famous phrase yelled out when jumping off of a high place. But he is one of the most famous figures in the history of the American Indian resistance effort.

    A. (As it is now)

    B. Even though most people today only know Geronimo as the word people yell when jumping off of something high in the air, Geronimo was one of the most famous figures during the American Indian resistance effort.

    C. Even though most people today do not know who Geronimo really is, he is essentially one of the most famously well-known figures in the history of the American Indian resistance effort.

    D. The fact that most people today do not know who Geronimo is, he is one of the most famous figures in the history of the American Indian resistance effort.

    E. Can you believe people today do not know who Geronimo is, even though he is one of the most famous figures in the history of the American Indian resistance effort?

22. The word employment, as highlighted below, means:

    A much more recent, and highly controversial, use of Geronimo's name was its employment by the U.S. military as a code name linked to the 2011 operation that resulted in the death of Osama bin Laden.

    A. service

    B. salary

    C. occupation

    D. work

    E. application

23. What revision would be the most appropriate for sentenced 4 (reproduced below)?

Geronimo's reputation is well-deserved, for his very name excited fear in settlers both North and South of the U.S-Mexican border.

A. Take the apostrophe off "Geronimo's"

B. Change the *N* in "North" and the *S* in "South" to lowercase letters.

C. Change the comma before "for" to a period, and capitalize the *f* in "for"

D. Change the hyphen in "U.S. – Mexican border" to a slash (/).

E. Change the comma to a semicolon.

24. The word *feat*, as highlighted below, means:

Schoolchildren, for decades after Geronimo's death, would similarly yell his name before undertaking a real or imagined feat of bravery, such as leaping from a swing into a river.

A. fear

B. excitement

C. enthusiasm

D. act

E. spare

25. Which of the following sentences can be eliminated from the passage without sacrificing meaning or detail?

A. 1

B. 3

C. 5

D. 7

E. 8

Test Tip

Notice that you can answer many of these questions without reading the entire passage above. In fact, many of the questions recreate the portion of the passage you need to evaluate, so you do not have to find it in the passage. Save yourself some time and read the questions first and determine which ones you can answer without actually reading the passage.

Directions: The following passage is a draft of an essay. Some parts of the passage need to be strengthened through editing and revision. Read the passage and choose the best answers for the questions that follow. Some questions ask you to improve particular sentences or portions of sentences. In some cases, the indicated portion of the passage will be most effective as it is already expressed and thus will require no changes. In choosing answers, consider development, organization, word choice, style and ton, and follow the requirements of standard written English.

(1) In today's modern world of technology people prefer to get information from the Internet instead of books. (2) Now, the creation of internet and other devices helped people to find information very easy and quick. (3) Everyday people rely on the internet for their routines.

(4) The internet is so responsive that in just a few seconds people can find the most recent information about current events and politics, latest products and services, and to get updates from all around the world. (5) Too often however, the internet provides unreliable information, and we fail to notice. (6) People have to research beyond one or two websites to find trustworthy websites.

(7) Modern technology has many positive uses. (8) Nowadays, people are using technology in their daily lives. (9) Internet users need to learn how to find and use reliable sources of information.

26. In context, which revision of sentence 3 (reproduced below) is most appropriate?

Every day people rely on the internet for their routines.

    A. Every-day people rely on the internet for their routines.

    B. Every day, people rely on the internet for their routines.

    C. Everyday people rely on the internet for their routines.

    D. Everyday people rely on the internet for their routines.

    E. Every day people rely on the internet for one's routines.

27. If the author wanted to draw attention to specific ways in which people use the internet in their daily lives, what sentence can be added to the first paragraph to support that idea?

    A. (As it is now)

    B. People wake up every morning, and the first thing they do is look at their phones.

    C. People going for a morning jog might search the web for upbeat music while people headed to work might use an app to check the weather.

    D. In other words, the internet is everywhere and used for so many things.

    E. People are so addicted to the internet, they can't stop looking at their phones.

28. Which revision uses parallel structure to revise sentence 4 (reproduced below)?

The internet is so responsive that in just a few seconds people can find the most up-to-date information about current events and politics, latest products and services, and to get updates from all around the world.

A. (As it is now)

B. The internet is so responsive that in just a few seconds people can find the most up-to-date information about current events and politics, latest products and services, and updates from all around the world.

C. The internet is so responsive that in just a few seconds people can find the most up-to-date information about current events and politics, latest products and services, and real-time updates from around the world.

D. The internet is so responsive that in just a few seconds people can find the most up-to-date information about current events and politics and latest products and services, and to get updates from all around the world.

E. The internet is so responsive that in just a few seconds people can find the most up-to-date information from around the world on current events, politics, products, and services.

29. In context, what would be the best way to combine and revise sentences 7 & 8 (reproduced below) so the author can introduce the conclusion and support the main idea of the essay?

Modern technology has many positive uses. Nowadays, people are using technology in their daily lives.

A. (As it is now)

B. Today, the internet has had a positive impact on people's daily lives.

C. Too many people use the internet without understanding how to get reliable information.

D. In conclusion, people must understand the internet can only produce what a person is searching for.

E. Even though the internet is convenient, it has a long way to go before it is truly reliable.

30. What error did the author make in sentence 5 (reproduced below)?

Too often, however, the internet provides unreliable information, and we fail to notice.

A. The author shifts from 3rd person to 1st person.

B. The author uses too many commas in the sentence.

C. The author uses the transitional word "however" incorrectly.

D. The author should put the word *unreliable* in quotations because it's the author's opinion.

E. There are no errors in sentence 5.

Directions: The following passage is a draft of an essay. Some parts of the passage need to be strengthened through editing and revision. Read the passage and choose the best answers for the questions that follow. Some questions ask you to improve particular sentences or portions of sentences. In some cases, the indicated portion of the passage will be most effective as it is already expressed and thus will require no changes. In choosing answers, consider development, organization, word choice, style and ton, and follow the requirements of standard written English.

(1) The subject of whether or not Shakespeare should be studied in high school English classes has caused much debate. (2) On the one side, you have the diehard traditionalists who insist that learning to appreciate Shakespearean language is the crux of a well-rounded education. (3) However, others will argue that the archaic language used in Shakespeare's works is a source of confusion for students. (4) They also argue that todays students need more practice reading and interpreting the type of text they will be exposed to in a professional setting. (5) With valid arguments on both sides, this debate will most likely not be settled any time soon.

31. What is the best placement for the sentence below?

They also point out that because many modern-day sayings have roots in his works, studying Shakespeare will help students grasp the history of our language.

A. after sentence 1

B. after sentence 2

C. after sentence 3

D. after sentence 4

E. after sentence 5

32. In sentence 2 (reproduced below) what is the most appropriate definition of the word *crux* as it pertains to the meaning in this passage?

On the one side, you have the diehard traditionalists who insist that learning to appreciate Shakespearean language is the crux of a well-rounded education.

A. intersection

B. piece

C. effect

D. foundation

E. portion

33. Which of the following statements would best enhance the author's position that Shakespeare's work can often be confusing to students?

A. Most universities want to see that students took at least some Shakespeare in high school.

B. Students can strengthen their reading skills by reading Shakespeare.

C. Shakespeare often used a language and dialect in his plays that many students have not been exposed to.

D. Watching movies based on Shakespearean plays can help students relate to the scenes in Shakespearean plays.

E. Traditionalists will always want students to stretch beyond their comfort zones and read Shakespeare.

34. How should sentence 4 (reproduced below) be revised so it is grammatically correct.

They also argue that todays students need more practice reading and interpreting the type of text they will be exposed to in a professional setting.

A. (As it is now)

B. They also argue that today's students need more practice reading and interpreting the type of text they will be exposed to in a professional setting.

C. They also argue that todays students needed more practice reading and interpreting the type of text one will be exposed to in a professional setting.

D. They also argue, that todays students actually need more practice reading and interpreting the type of text students will be exposed to in a professional setting.

E. They also argue that todays students need more practice by reading and interpreting the type of text they will be exposed to in a professional setting.

Research

35. What is the main purpose of reviewing the references in a research article in an academic paper?

    A. To check that the authors only used primary source documents

    B. To identify additional relevant resources on the topic

    C. To observe how to write citations correctly

    D. To verify the authors did not cite themselves

    E. To avoid plagiarism of the research article

36. What is the main purpose of a style guide?

    A. To find multiple meanings of words.

    B. To find synonyms of words.

    C. To research formatting guidelines and citation requirements in a document.

    D. To identify databases where academic articles can be found.

    E. To reference grammar and mechanics best practices.

37. Which of the following citations is written in correct APA formatting?

    A. Wordsworth, W. *Lyrical Ballads*. Oxford UP, 1967.

    B. William Wordsworth. *Lyrical Ballads*. Oxford UP, 1967.

    C. Wordsworth, W (1967). *Lyrical Ballads*. Oxford UP.

    D. *Lyrical Ballads* by Wordsworth, William. Oxford UP, 1967.

    E. *Lyrical Ballads* (1967) by Wordsworth, William. Oxford UP.

38. Which of the following is NOT included in the citation below?

    Whitehurst, G., & Lonigan, C. (1998). Child Development and Emergent Literacy. *Child Development, 69*(3)

    A. authors

    B. date

    C. name of publication

    D. volume number

    E. publishing location

39. A student is using a direct quote from a paper on student behavior. What would be the correct way to cite the direct quote (reproduced below) using MLA formatting?

James Rodriguez says, students are social beings, and teachers must encourage students to engage in cooperative learning activities.

A. According Rodriguez, "students are social beings, and teachers must encourage students to engage in cooperative learning activities."

B. According Rodriguez (1979), "students are social beings, and teachers must encourage students to engage in cooperative learning activities."

C. According the author James Rodriguez, "students are social beings, and teachers must encourage students to engage in cooperative learning activities" (direct quote).

D. Direct quote from Rodriguez: Students are social beings, and teachers must encourage students to engage in cooperative learning activities.

E. "Students are social beings, and teachers must encourage students to engage in cooperative learning activities" (Rodriguez 45).

40. Where is the best place for students to find scholarly information when writing a research paper?

A. database for academic journals

B. government website

C. Internet search engine

D. school website

E. blog

Number	Answer	Category	Explanation
1	B	Language Skills	By changing the word *lost* to *losing* the sentence maintains parallel structure between the two clauses. Both *leaving* and "losing" end in *-ing*.
2	E	Word Choice	The word *synonymous* means the *same* as *aligned*. Therefore, as is, the sentence is redundant. Answer E contains the most succinct version of the sentence. When in doubt, always go for the shortest answer on a grammar test. The shortest answer is usually the correct answer.
3	C	Structural Relationships	In this case, two items are compared. Therefore, *worst* should be replaced with *worse*. The colon is used correctly—to separate an independent clause and a definition or explanation.
4	B	Grammatical Relationships	This is a pronoun and number issue. While the university is a place where many people attend classes and work, it is still a collective singular noun. Therefore, *they* should be replaced with *it*.
5	E	Grammatical Relationships	In order to maintain pronoun antecedent agreement throughout the sentence, the word *student* becomes *students,* and the word *one* becomes *we*.
6	D	Structural Relationships	This sentence fragment contains 3 problems. First, it is a fragment as it is lacking a complete thought. Second, *no one* should be changed to *anyone* to avoid a double negative. Finally, *passing* should be changed to *passed* to avoid a shift in verb tense.
7	A	Grammatical Relationships	No change is needed. The word *passionately* is an adverb and should modify the verb spoke.
8	D	Grammatical Relationships	Often subject verb agreement becomes a problem when a prepositional phrase such as *of cellphones and computers* is placed between the subject and verb. By reading the sentence without the phrase, the subject *use* and the verb *are* clearly do not agree. The verb should be *is*. Finally, the comma is the correct punctuation here because it separates the dependent clause from the independent clause. The semicolon in answer choice C is incorrect because a semicolon is used to separate 2 independent clauses. Choice E is incorrect because it is redundant.
9	B	Grammatical Relationships	When determining whether to use *who* or *whom,* remember *who* is the subject of the sentence or phrase, while *whom* is the object of the verb or preposition. In this case, if I asked, "Who was the driver?" You would respond, "He is the driver," or "She is the driver." You would not say, "Him is the driver," or "Her is the driver." **He** and **she** are subject pronouns. **Who** is also a subject pronoun.

Number	Answer	Category	Explanation
10	E	Grammatical Relationships	The plural pronoun *they* is used to rename student, which is a singular noun. In order to maintain pronoun antecedent agreement, change student to students.
11	No error	Mechanics	No error. The semicolon is used correctly here in that it is used to separate two independent clauses.
12	No error	Mechanics	No error. The possessive form of the word *store owner* is correct. Also correct is the comma before *which*.
13	weeks	Mechanics	An apostrophe is needed in the word *week's*. The meeting referred to in the sentence is exclusive to that particular week, allowing for the word *week's* to show possession. Other examples of this would be *last night's class* or *tomorrow's conference call*.
14	they	Grammatical Relationships	The pronoun *they* should be changed to the impersonal pronoun *its* to maintain pronoun antecedent agreement. In addition, the university may have many people who attend and work there; however, the university is a collective singular noun and should have a singular pronoun—it.
15	everyone	Grammatical Relationships	The pronoun *everyone* is a singular indefinite pronoun which means its antecedent, the word *their*, needs to be singular as well. Because you do not have the option to correct *their*, you must change the subject *everyone* to something plural like *the students*. This will make the subject plural, and it will match the pronoun *their* and *they*.
16	one has	Grammatical Relationships	Change the words *one has* to *they have* to maintain pronoun antecedent agreement.
17	Fall	Mechanics	The word *Fall* in the sentence should be lowercase. The names of the season are not capitalized unless referring to a proper noun, such as the Fall Festival. Remember, summer, fall, winter, and spring are all lowercase in a sentence, unless they are part of a proper noun.
18	and ask them appropriate questions	Structural Relationships	Items or action in a list should have parallel structure. By changing *ask them appropriate questions* to *question them appropriately*, all items follow the same parallel structure.
19	and	Word Choice	The word *and* is used incorrectly here. Remember, if you have a *not only* in the intro clause, you must have a *but also* in the proceeding clause. The correct revision would be *I not only want you to succeed, **but I also** want you to be happy*
20	being hungry	Structural Relationships	Change *being hungry* to *hunger* to maintain parallel structure in the list of items.

Number	Answer	Category	Explanation
21	B	Structural Relationships	Using an introductory dependent clause followed by an independent clause is an effective way to not only join two statements without losing meaning, but also to create sentence variety within a passage. Answer C is incorrect because it contains redundancy—*the most famously well- known.* Answer D contains an error—*the fact that*—In the intro clause. Answer E is not the best choice because it begins by asking the reader a question. Answer B is the most effective choice here.
22	E	Word Choice	The U.S. military used Geronimo's name as stated in the line above the word employment. To employ can mean to hire, but here employ means to apply the name to a military operation. Also, if you substituted all the words in for employment, application makes the most sense.
23	B	Mechanics	Compass directional words (north, south, east, west) are never capitalized when offering directions. However, the directional words are capitalized when referring to a definite geographical region. (Example: *She goes to* **South** *Florida for the winter*).
24	D	Word Choice	The word ***feat*** means *an achievement that requires great courage, skill, or strength* making it the best choice. Also, if *feat* is replaced with the words in the answer choices, *act* makes the most sense.
25	C	Structural Relationships	Sentence 5 could be removed without changing the main idea of the passage. The article is primarily focusing on Geronimo's physical skills. Sentence 5 refers to mental skills that he was lacking.
26	B	Word Choice	First, there needs to be a comma after every day because that is the intro clause. Second, the word *everyday* should be changed to *every day*. As is, the word *everyday* is acting as an adjective describing the type of people (everyday people). However, the author is intending for it to mean that people use the internet every single day; therefore, it should be changed to *every day*.
27	C	Word Choice	The question stem is asking what could make the statement more specific than it is now. Answer C provides the most specific examples—morning jog, upbeat music, weather app— to back up the author's claim.
28	E	Structural Relationships	By creating a list of all nouns, the author is able to maintain parallel structure when describing the type of information found on the internet.
29	E	Structural Relationships & Word Choice	This sentence combines the two statements effectively while restating the main idea: the internet is convenient, but the internet can be unreliable. By recapping these two concepts addressed in the passage, the author is recapping the main idea.

WRITING

Number	Answer	Category	Explanation
30	A	Grammatical Relationships	Throughout the passage the author is using 3rd person by using words such as *people* and *they*. In sentence 5, the author switches to the 1st person by using the pronoun *we*.
31	B	Structural Relationships	This sentence would best fit after sentence 2 in the paragraph as it supports the use of Shakespearean works in schools. In addition, this sentence starts with "They also..." This makes it easy to place the sentence appropriately.
32	D	Word Choice	The word *crux* means the decisive or most important point at issue. In this case, the author is stating that Shakespearean language is the foundation of a well-rounded education. Also, out of all the answer choices, *foundation* makes the most sense when it is substituted for the word *crux*.
33	C	Structural Relationships	Choices A, B, D, E all argue the case to keep Shakespearean works in the high school curriculum. Choice C argues against it by stating that students are not familiar with the language. Thus, they will be confused.
34	B	Mechanics	The sentence contains an apostrophe error. Change *todays* to *today's* because the author is referring to students that belong to today.
35	B	Research Skills	Reviewing the reference page provides a wealth of additional and creditable sources on the same topic.
36	C	Research Skills	Style guides provide information on formatting and citing requirements.
37	C	Research Skills	For APA reference page citations, information is listed in the order of author last name, author's first initial, year, title, publication, publisher, volume, issue, page number(s).
38	E	Research Skills	The publication location is missing from this publication. Usually, the location of the publishing company is listed for books. This is from an academic journal.
39	E	Research Skills	For MLA, a direct quote will include quotation marks around quoted material followed by author and page number in parentheses.
40	A	Research Skills	Databases for academic journals are created to house scholarly, academic information for research purposes.

Sentence Correction

Directions: In each of the following sentences, some part of the sentence or the entire sentence is underlined. Beneath each sentence, you will find five ways of writing the underlined part. The first answer choice (A) repeats the original, but the other four choices are different. If you think the original sentence is better than any of the suggested changes, you should select the first answer choice (A); otherwise, you should select one of the other answer choices.

This is a test of correctness and effectiveness of expression. In choosing answers, follow the requirement of standard written English; i.e. pay attention to acceptable usage and grammar, diction (choice of words), sentence construction and punctuation. Choose the answer that expresses most effectively what is presented in the original sentence; this answer should be clear and exact, without awkwardness, ambiguity, or redundancy.

1. Last Saturday evening, we arrived early for the <u>movie, yet we were able to choose the best seats in the theater</u>.

   A. movie, yet we were able to choose the best seats in the theater.

   B. movie, we were able to choose the best seats in the theater.

   C. movie, so we were able to choose the best seats in the theater.

   D. movie and, yet, we choose the best seats in the theater.

   E. movie yet we had chosen the best seats in the theater.

2. <u>When the computer store checked their records,</u> it realized the company was improving in product sales, customer service, and customer satisfaction.

   A. When the computer store checked their records,

   B. When the computer store checked on their records,

   C. When the computer store, checking on their records,

   D. When the computer store looked at it's records,

   E. When the computer store checked its records,

3. After driving all over the neighborhood, <u>my cat was found casually wandering around a vacant lot</u>.

   A. my cat was found casually wandering around a vacant lot.

   B. casually wandering around the vacant lot, my cat was found.

   C. I found my cat casually wondering around a vacant lot.

   D. in a vacant lot my cat was found by me casually walking around.

   E. my cat was found by me casually walking around a vacant lot.

4. I was not sure <u>who I should ask for help with the calculus problem</u>, so I called my third-grade teacher.

   A. who I should ask for help with the calculus problem

   B. whom I should ask for help with the calculus problem

   C. whoever I should ask for help with the calculus problem

   D. as to who I should ask for help with the calculus problem

   E. as to whoever I should ask to help me with the calculus problem

WRITING

5. Although the new café is located in a neglected section of town, <u>it is nicely decorated, has great lighting, and comfortably arranged.</u>

    A. it is nicely decorated, has great lighting, and comfortably arranged.

    B. it is nicely decorated, lit well, and comfortably arranged.

    C. it is nicely decorated, well lit, and comfortably arranged.

    D. it is nicely decorated, lit with bright lights, and comfortably arranged.

    E. it is nicely decorated, has been well lit, and comfortably arranged.

6. <u>Before doctors make a diagnosis, they should review their patients' medical history.</u>

    A. Before doctors make a diagnosis, they should review their patients' medical history.

    B. Before doctors make a diagnosis they should review their patients' medical history.

    C. Before doctors make a diagnosis, he should review their patients' medical history.

    D. Before doctors make a diagnosis, they should review their patients' medical histories.

    E. Before doctors make a diagnosis they should review their patients' medical histories.

7. <u>Its mandatory at the university for every student to attend orientation before scheduling their classes.</u>

    A. Its mandatory at the university for every student to attend orientation before scheduling their classes.

    B. It's mandatory at the university for students to attend orientation before scheduling their classes.

    C. For every student at the university its mandatory to attend orientation before scheduling their classes.

    D. It's mandatory for every university student to attend orientation before scheduling their classes.

    E. As a student at the university, its mandatory to attend orientation before scheduling their classes.

8. <u>If every student could write as neat as Jamie,</u> I would not have to spend so much time grading papers.

    A. If every student could write as neat as Jamie,

    B. If every student could write neat like Jamie,

    C. If every student could write as neatly as Jamie,

    D. If every student could neatly write as Jamie,

    E. If every student could write neat like Jamie,

9. Although often thought to be shy animals, <u>the elephants in the large enclosure seems to show off for the crowds</u> visiting at the zoo.

    A. the elephants in the large enclosure seems to show off for the crowds

    B. the elephants in the large enclosure shows off seemingly for the crowds

    C. the elephants in the large enclosure seemingly shows off for the crowds

    D. the elephants in the large enclosure seem to show off for the crowds

    E. in the large enclosure, the elephants seems to show off the crowds

WRITING

10. <u>My dad, who loves westerns,</u> has always wanted to travel to a ghost town near the Grand Canyon.

   A. My dad, who loves westerns,

   B. My dad who loves westerns

   C. My dad a western lover

   D. My dad, whom loves westerns,

   E. My dad always loving westerns,

11. After visiting Disneyland and Disneyworld last year, both <u>parks seem to be one in the same to me.</u>

   A. parks seem to be one in the same to me.

   B. parks seem to be all in the same to me.

   C. parks seem to be one and the same to me.

   D. parks are basically one in the same to me.

   E. parks are one in the same to me.

12. After years of searching, <u>the money was found casually walking in the woods</u> on a long winter's hike.

   A. the money was found casually walking in the woods

   B. casually walking in the woods the money was found

   C. the money in the woods was found casually walking in the woods

   D. I found the money as I was casually walking in the woods

   E. I found the money casually walking in the woods

13. Each day, after a cruise ship docks nearby, <u>a busload of tourists arrives</u> to visit the ancient city of Tulum and admire the Caribbean ocean views.

   A. a busload of tourists arrives

   B. the tourists arrives by the busload

   C. a busload of tourists arrive

   D. a busload with tourists arrive

   E. tourists by the busload arrives

14. Jessica, realizing something was amiss, <u>entered the dark room then she screamed at the top of her lungs</u> when she saw a figure appear from the shadows.

   A. entered the dark room then she screamed at the top of her lungs

   B. then entered the dark room and she screamed at the top of her lungs

   C. entered the dark room then screaming at the top of her lungs

   D. entering the dark room, then screaming at the top of her lungs

   E. entered the dark room, and then she screamed at the top of her lungs

Usage

Directions: Each question consists if a sentence that contains four underlined portions. Read each sentence and decide whether any of the underlined portions contains a grammatical construction, a word use, or an instance of incorrect or omitted punctuation or capitalization that would be inappropriate in carefully written English. If so, select the underlined portion that must be revised to produce a correct sentence. If there are no errors in the sentence as written, select **no error** (E). No sentence has more than one error.

15. Each female participant in the <u>race</u> received <u>their</u> own t-shirt with the company <u>emblem</u> on the <u>back</u>. <u>No error.</u>

16. The mall was crowded with holiday <u>shoppers, therefore,</u> we decided to <u>shop</u> online this year. <u>No error.</u>

17. After the waiter <u>made</u> a mistake on the <u>bill,</u> the angry customer <u>refused</u> to <u>except</u> an apology from the manager. <u>No error.</u>

18. Each of <u>these</u> books <u>are</u> meant to help young people deal with difficult situations and to encourage <u>them</u> to seek additional help <u>when</u> necessary. <u>No error.</u>

19. Greg <u>enjoys</u> several outdoor <u>activities:</u> hiking in the woods, <u>swimming</u> in the lake, and <u>to camp</u> out overnight. <u>No error.</u>

20. <u>Due</u> to the heavy <u>rainfall,</u> the river was higher <u>than</u> usual and <u>floods</u> the roadway. <u>No error.</u>

21. My favorite season <u>used</u> to be <u>summer, but</u> now I <u>prefer</u> the cooler temperatures of the <u>other</u> seasons. <u>No error.</u>

22. Although he is <u>older,</u> my brother is <u>shorter</u> <u>than</u> <u>me</u>. <u>No error.</u>

23. <u>Because</u> last <u>months</u> schedule <u>was</u> filled with meetings and presentations, I <u>was</u> constantly working late. <u>No error.</u>

24. <u>Irregardless</u> of the <u>winter</u> storm, <u>several</u> people attended the high school <u>play and</u> stayed for the reception last night. <u>No error.</u>

Revision

Directions: The following passage is a draft of an essay. Some parts of the passage need to be strengthened through editing and revision. Read the passage and choose the best answers for the questions that follow. Some questions ask you to improve particular sentences or portions of sentences. In some cases, the indicated portion of the passage will be most effective as it is already expressed and thus will require no changes. In choosing answers, consider development, organization, word choice, style and ton, and follow the requirements of standard written English.

Adapted from *Kittens and Cats: A First Reader (1911)- Cats and Captions before the Internet Age*, Retrieved from the Public Domain.

(1) Before LOLCat, Grumpy Cat, Longcat, Nyan Cat and all the other famed kitties of the internet age, there were the felines featured in *Kittens and Cats: A First Reader* (1911). (2) If this delightful yet also slightly creepy book is anything to go by, then taking photos of cats and brandishing them with an amusing caption was far from being a phenomenon born with the internet. (3) Within its pages we meet "Queen Cat", "Dunce Cat", "Party Cat", and perhaps our favorite "Hero Cat", amongst others. (4) The book is attributed to the American children's author Eulalie Osgood Grover, who uses the pictures to tell the tale of the Queen's party and all the kitty characters attending.

(5) As for the photographs themselves, the book credits them courtesy of the Rotograph Company, a popular postcard manufacturer, which implies they are almost certainly an early example of the work of Harry Whittier Frees, their staff animal photographer. (6) A few years later Frees would become associated with a whole host of similar pictures under his own name such as The Little Folks of Animal Land. (7) Several other publications of photograph collections followed until he ended his own life in 1953. (8) How did Frees get his cats to pose for such photographs?

(9) Even before the days of super quick shutter speeds? (10) Although he denied the use of dead, taxidermized animals and asserted only humane methods were used, you can't help but wonder if this is really true, especially in the case of his later work which involved more elaborate scenes than displayed in this book.

25. What would be the best way to combine and rewrite sentences 8 and 9 (reproduced below)?

    How did Frees get his cats to pose for such photographs? Even before the days of super quick shutter speeds?

    A. (As it is now)

    B. Even before the days of super quick shutter speeds, so how did Frees get his cats to pose for such photographs?

    C. How did Frees get his cats to pose for such photographs even before the days of super quick shutter speeds?

    D. How did Frees get his cats to pose for such photographs, yet even before the days of super quick shutter speeds.

    E. Although without super quick shutter speeds available back then, how did Frees get his cats to pose for such photographs?

26. Which of the following sentences can be eliminated from the passage without sacrificing meaning?

    A. 1
    B. 2
    C. 3
    D. 5
    E. 10

27. What revision would be most appropriate for sentence 2 (reproduced below)?

    If this delightful yet also slightly creepy book is anything to go by, then taking photos of cats and brandishing them with an amusing caption was far from being a phenomenon born with the internet.

    A. Add commas before and after the phrase *yet also slightly creepy*.
    B. Add an apostrophe to the word *cats*.
    C. Capitalize the word *internet*.
    D. Add a comma after *delightful*.
    E. Add a comma after the word *caption*.

28. The word *brandishing* as highlighted below, means:

    If this delightful yet also slightly creepy book is anything to go by, then taking photos of cats and brandishing them with an amusing caption was far from being a phenomenon born with the internet.

    A. beating
    B. shaming
    C. alarming
    D. displaying
    E. correcting

29. What error did the author make in sentence 10 (reproduced below)? Choose all that apply.

    Although he denied the use of dead, taxidermized animals and asserted only humane methods were used, you can't help but wonder if this is really true, especially in the case of his later work which involved more elaborate scenes than displayed in this book.

    ☐ The author used too many commas in the sentence.
    ☐ The author switched from 3rd person to 2nd person.
    ☐ The author should delete the word *dead* as it means the same as the word taxidermized.
    ☐ The author used the subordinating conjunction *although* incorrectly.
    ☐ The author should use a question mark at the end because he is questioning the situation.

WRITING

30. Which of the following statements would be an appropriate conclusion for this passage?

   A. Clearly, the photographer was photographing deceased cats.

   B. In conclusion, by looking closely at photographs from the early 1900's, we can see that the cats were posed in comical positions.

   C. All in all, the art of cat photography has been around a long time.

   D. In the end, however, the photographer committed suicide before he could answer more questions about his work.

   E. Either way, Americans were amused with humorously captioned cat photographs long before silly cat memes posted online.

Directions: The following passage is a draft of an essay. Some parts of the passage need to be strengthened through editing and revision. Read the passage and choose the best answers for the questions that follow. Some questions ask you to improve particular sentences or portions of sentences. In some cases, the indicated portion of the passage will be most effective as it is already expressed and thus will require no changes. In choosing answers, consider development, organization, word choice, style and ton, and follow the requirements of standard written English.

Adapted from *The Dancing Plague of 1518*, Retrieved from the Public Domain Review.

(1) On a hastily built stage before the busy horse market of Strasbourg, scores of people dance to pipes, drums, and horns. (2) The July sun beats down upon them as they hop from leg to leg, spin in circles and whooped loudly into the crowd. (3) From a distance they might be carnival celebrators. (4) But closer inspection reveals a more disquieting scene. (5) Their arms are flailing and their bodies are convulsing spasmodically.

(6) Ragged clothes and pinched faces are saturated in sweat. (7) Their eyes are glassy, distant. (8) Blood seeps from swollen feet into leather boots and wooden clogs. (9) These are not revelers but "choreomaniacs", entirely possessed by the mania of the dance.

(10) In full view of the public, this is the summit of the choreomania that tormented Strasbourg for a midsummer month in 1518. (11) Also known as the "dancing plague", it was the most fatal and best documented of the more than ten such contagions which had broken out along the Rhine and Moselle rivers since 1374. (12) Once thought to be caused from a mold that grew on cornstalks and even believed to be caused by demonic possessions. (13) Numerous accounts of the bizarre events that unfolded that summer can be found scattered across various contemporary documents and chronicles compiled in the subsequent decades and centuries.

31. Which revision uses parallel structure to revise Sentence 2 (reproduced below)?

   The July sun beats down upon them as they hop from leg to leg, spin in circles and whooped loudly into the crowd.

   A. (As is now)

   B. The July sun beats down upon them as they hop from leg to leg, spin wildly, and whooped loudly into the crowd.

   C. The July sun beats down upon them as they hop around, spin in circles and whooped loudly into the crowd.

   D. The July sun beats down upon them as they hop from leg to leg, spin in circles and whoop into the crowd.

   E. The July sun beats down upon them as they hop crazily from leg to leg, spin wildly in circles and whooped loudly into the crowd.

32. What is the best placement for the sentence below?

Even though they are obviously suffering physically, they continued this trance-like dance for hours with no apparent intention of pausing anytime soon.

A. After sentence 3

B. After sentence 8

C. After sentence 9

D. After sentence 10

E. After sentence 12

33. How should sentence 12 (reproduced below) be revised so it is grammatically correct?

Once thought to be caused from a mold that grew on cornstalks and even believed to be caused by demonic possessions.

A. (As is now)

B. Once thought to be caused from a mold that grew on cornstalks, and even believed to be caused by demonic possessions.

C. Even once thought to be caused from a mold that grew on cornstalks and even believed to be caused by demonic possession

D. The dancing plague was once thought to be caused from a mold that grew on cornstalks and even believed to be caused by demonic possessions.

E. Once, the dancing plague, thought to be caused from a mold that grew on cornstalks and even believed to be caused by demonic possession.

34. In sentence 4 (reproduced below) what is the most appropriate definition of the word **disquieting** as it pertains to the passage?

But closer inspection reveals a more disquieting scene.

A. disturbing

B. loud

C. messy

D. sorrowful

E. annoying

Research Skills

35. Which of the following is not considered a credible source?

   A. The Journal of Infectious Diseases

   B. a peer reviewed academic paper

   C. www.science.gov

   D. America Cancer Society Newsletter

   E. social media outlet

36. Which of the following is a primary source?

   A. The Biography of John Smith

   B. The Autobiography of John Smith

   C. An article titled *How John Smith Lived his Life*

   D. An unauthorized book written by John Smith's brother.

   E. None of the above.

37. Which of the following citations is written in correct APA formatting?

   A. Smith, Sarah. Journal of Medicine. "A Cure on the Horizon" 2018. New York, New York.

   B. Smith, S. "A Cure on the Horizon" Retrieved from the Journal of Medicine, Issue 6. PG 10-12. (2018)

   C. Smith, Sarah. (2018). A Cure on the Horizon. *Journal of Medicine*, 6, 10-12.

   D. Journal of Medicine, "A Cure on the Horizon by Sarah Smith" 6, 10-12. 2018.

   E. A Cure on the Horizon. Smith, Sarah. *Journal of Medicine.6,10-12. 2018*

38. In both MLA and APA formatting styles, citations must be:

   A. Cited only on the reference page.

   B. Cited only after a direct quotation in the body of the paper.

   C. Cited only if the information is from a journal article.

   D. Cited within the paper and the reference or works cited page.

   E. As long as a citation is included, it does not matter where it is cited in either style.

39. Which of the following cited from pg. 5 of *The Success Principles* by Jack Canfield written in 2015 is in correct MLA style when using a direct quote.

   A. In his book, author Jack Canfield states that "you are the one person responsible for the quality of life that you live."

   B. In his book, the author suggests "you are the one person responsible for the quality of life that you live."

   C. In his book, author Jack Canfield states that "you are the one person responsible for the quality of life that you live." (2015).

   D. In his book, author Jack Canfield (5) states that "you are the one person responsible for the quality of life that you live."

   E. In his book, author Jack Canfield states that, "you are the one person responsible for the quality of life that you live" (5).

40. It is important to cite references within a research paper to

A. Credit the author(s) of the original material.

B. Avoid plagiarism,

C. To add creditability to the points made within the paper.

D. To offer additional resources for interested readers.

E. All the above.

Number	Answer	Category	Explanation
1	C	Grammatical Relationships	In the original sentence, the coordinating conjunction *yet* does not show the correct relationship between the two events. A better conjunction choice would be the word *so*, meaning as a result of arriving early. Also, a comma is needed before a conjunction when the conjunction is separating two independent clauses.
2	E	Grammatical Relationships	The possessive pronoun *their,* is referring to the company. However, the correct pronoun for an impersonal, non-gender specific item is the possessive pronoun *it.*
3	C	Structural Relationships	This is a misplaced modifier problem. When using a modifying phrase such as *After driving all over the neighborhood,* the next noun after the phrase should always be the noun that the phrase is describing. In the case above, if left as is, the next noun after the phrase is *cat.* Therefore, the phrase is suggesting that the cat was driving all over the neighborhood. This is known as a misplaced modifier. By placing the correct noun right after the modifying phrase, it is clear that the phrase is describing *I* instead of the *cat.*
4	B	Grammatical Relationships	When deciding to use *who* or *whom,* determine if it is being used in the phrase or sentence as a subject (who) or an object of the verb (whom). In this case, *whom* should be used because it is not the subject, but rather the object or person receiving the action. Another way to determine which to use is by replacing *who* with *he* or *whom* with *him.* In this case you would say, *I wasn't sure if I should ask **him**…*
5	C	Structural Relationships	Items in a list should have parallel structure. By changing *has good lighting* to *well lit,* all items used to describe the restaurant have the same parallel structure of adverb followed by an adjective.
6	D	Grammatical Relationships	First, the intro clause in the beginning—*Before making a diagnosis*—should be followed by a comma because it is a dependent clause followed by an independent clause. Because the word *doctors* is plural, all pronouns related to doctors should be plural as well. Therefore, the pronoun *they* is correct. Also, the word patients should be plural possessive—*patients'.* If there are multiple doctors, there are multiple patients. If those patients own the records, it should be *patients'.* Finally, for noun noun agreement and noun and number agreement, *history* should be plural—*histories*—because there are multiple patients with multiple *histories.*
7	B	Mechanics	The word *its* is used as a contraction to mean *it is* in this sentence. Therefore, an apostrophe is needed to form the contraction word, *it's. Its* without an apostrophe is used as a possessive pronoun. Also, every student is singular; therefore, the plural pronoun *their* is incorrect. The words *every student* should be changed to *students.* That way, the pronoun—*their*—and the antecedent—*students*—agree.

WRITING

Number	Answer	Category	Explanation
8	C	Grammatical Relationships	Because the word *neat* is used to describe how Jamie writes, it should be changed to the adverb form, *neatly*. Adverbs are used to modify verbs, adjectives, and other adverbs. While answer D does have the adverb *neatly*, it is placed before the verb. This this is often referred to as a split infinitive and makes the sentence read awkwardly. It is best to put the adverb *neatly* after the verb *write*.
9	D	Grammatical Relationships	Subject verb agreement can become tricky when a prepositional phrase such as *"in the large enclosure"* comes between the subject and verb. By reading the sentence without the prepositional phrase, the subject, *elephants* and verb, *seems* do not agree. Thus, change *seems* to *seem* to maintain subject verb agreement.
10	A	Structural Relationships	This sentence is correct as is. The commas around the phrase are used to set off nonessential information. In other words, the phrase could be removed without changing the meaning of the sentence.
11	C	Word Choice	The idiomatic phrase *"one in the same"* is often used instead of the correct phrase *"one and the same"* to describe two similar items. However, the phrase "one in the same" or "all in the same" would mean that one item is actually inside of a nearly identical item.
12	D	Structural Relationships	This sentence contains a misplaced modifier, or a modifying phrase without a nearby noun to modify. In this case, it is not apparent who was searching for years, who found the money, or who was walking in the woods. Without correction, it appears that after years of searching, the money itself was walking in the woods. Answer D correctly places the modifier in the sentence, so it is clear who is walking through the woods and who found the money.
13	A	Grammatical Relationships	The subject and verb agree in this sentence. The prepositional phrase *of tourists* may cause some confusion in this case. However, the word *busload* is the subject and is actually a singular noun which would require a singular verb.
14	E	Structural Relationships	Left as is, this sentence is a run-on because two independent clauses are inappropriately joined by the word *then*. To correct, a comma and a conjunction can be added to join the clauses. Choice B is wrong because there is not a comma before the conjunction, and choice D is wrong because there is not a conjunction after the comma.

WRITING

Number	Answer	Category	Explanation
15	their	Grammatical Relationships	The plural pronoun *their* is used incorrectly to refer to each singular female participant. To maintain pronoun number agreement, the word "her" should be used as each individual female received a t-shirt.
16	shoppers, therefore	Structural Relationships	A semi-colon is needed before the adverbial conjunction, therefore. In this case two independent clauses are combined with a semi-colon and conjunction. The correct punctuation is independent clause; adverbial conjunction, independent clause.
17	except	Word Choice	The word *except* means "not including," and it is commonly confused with the word *accept*. The word accept means "to receive" and should be used in this sentence as the man refused to receive an apology.
18	are	Grammatical Relationships	The verb *are* should be changed to the verb *is* to maintain subject verb agreement. The word *each* is a collective pronoun that requires a singular verb. Also, notice the prepositional phrase (of these books) in between the subject *each* and the verb. Try reading the sentence without the phrase "of these books" to check for subject verb agreement, and it reads *Each is meant...*
19	to camp	Structural Relationships	Change the word phrase *to camp* to *camping* in order to continue parallel structure throughout the sentence. Notice that *hiking* and *swimming* both end in *ing* as should the word camp. Also, the colon is used correctly here because it separates an independent clause and a list.
20	floods	Grammatical Relationships	To avoid a shift in verb tense, the verb *floods* needs to be changed to *was flooded* because both events occurred in the past; the water became high and the roadway was flooded.
21	No error	Mechanics	No error. The word *summer*, as with all seasons, should not be capitalized, unless referring to a specific time such as the *Summer of 2000* or part of a proper noun such as *Ohio's Summer Festival*. In addition, *used to* is correct because the sentence is referring to something in the past that no longer happens.
22	me	Grammatical Relationships	Choosing the correct pronoun in a comparison can be determined by finishing the sentence with an understood verb. For example, the sentence could read "Although he is younger, my brother is two inches taller than I *am*." The word *me* could not be interchanged with *I* when the understood verb is added making it clear as to which pronoun to choose.

WRITING

GACE

Writing Practice Tests | 457

Number	Answer	Category	Explanation
23	months	Mechanics	The word *months* requires an apostrophe. The schedule referred to is exclusive to a particular month, allowing the word *month's* to show possession of that schedule. Other example of this would be *yesterday's meeting* or *last year's concert*.
24	irregardless	Word Choice	The word *irregardless* is often mistakenly used in place of *regardless*, meaning in spite of. The word *irregardless* is not an actual word and should never be used.
25	C	Structural Relationships	Left as is, sentence 9 is considered a fragment as it is a dependent clause without a complete thought. Joining a dependent clause such as *How did Frees get his cats to pose for such photographs* with the depended clause *even before the days of super quick shutter speeds* is an effective way two join two clauses with losing meaning as well as correcting a fragment.
26	C	Structural Relationships	Although the information in sentence 3 adds interesting information to the passage, it can be removed with changing the main idea. Sentence 1 and 2 contain pertinent information, creating the main idea of the passage. Sentence 10 may seem like extra information as well; however, it cannot be removed as it answers the question before it.
27	A	Structural Relationships	The phrase *yet also slightly creepy* is a nonessential information, or information that can be removed without changing the meaning of a sentence. Nonessential information is set off with a comma before and after.
28	D	Word Choice	To *brandish* means to show or to make a display of. The author of the book *displayed* a caption with each picture. Also, out of all the other choices *displaying* makes the most sense when it is substituted for *brandishing*.
29	Boxes 2 & 3	Grammatical Relationships & Word Choice	**Box 2 & 3.** In sentence 10, the author mistakenly switches from the 3rd person point of view used throughout the passage, by using the word *you* which is in the 2nd. A better choice would be to use the word *one* or *people* here to avoid a shift a person. Also, an animal cannot be taxidermized if it is not already dead. Therefore, the author should eliminate either the word **dead** or **taxidermized** to avoid redundancy.
30	E	Structural Relationships	This statement is the best choice as it sums up the overall main idea of the passage. Choice A, B, C, D all mention just one of the supporting details in the text without mention of the main idea which is that cats' pictures with funny captions were around before the internet age.

Number	Answer	Category	Explanation
31	D	Structural Relationships	To maintain parallel structure in this sentence the three actions mentioned must be grammatically the same. Thus, the first two actions are written with a present tense verb followed by a preposition. Thus, the third action, *whooped into the crowd*, must follow the same pattern, by changing *whooped* to its present tense, *whoop*.
32	B	Structural Relationships	The best place for this additional sentence would be after sentence 8 as sentences 5-8 mention the dancers' apparent physical exhaustion. It would not follow sentence 9 as it is a concluding sentence for the first paragraph. Likewise, it would not fit anywhere in the second paragraph because it is discussing the general history of the disease.
33	D	Structural Relationships	If left as is, sentence 12 is a fragment. It is lacking a subject and complete thought. Therefore, the subject, The Dancing Plague, should be added. All other choices presented are fragments as well.
34	A	Word Choice	The word *disquieting* means disturbing or alarming. In this case, the author is describing something that is *disturbing*, as the crowd described is in a trance-like state. Also, out of all the other choices, the word *disturbing* makes the most sense when substituted for the word *disquieting*.
35	E	Research Skills	Social media sites are not considered credible sources as participants are able to post any information without documented research. All the other
36	B	Research Skills	A primary source is a document that provides firsthand information from the subject. An autobiography is written about the author by the author—a firsthand account. A biography, an article, and a study are all written about John Smith by other people—secondhand accounts.
37	C	Research Skills	APA citations use the following format for journal articles: Last, first initial. Year published. Article Title. *Journal Title*, Volume/Issue, Page numbers.
38	D	Research Skills	In both APA and MLA citations must be provided within the text as in-text citations and on the final page of the document.
39	E	Research Skills	When using a direct quote in MLA formatting both the authors name and page number(s) must be presented. All the other choices are missing at least one of those elements. Also, the page number comes before the period in the sentence.
40	E	Research Skills	Citing material is mandatory to avoid cases of plagiarism and to give the author credit. Offering additional resources and credibility are important in producing an effective research paper as well.

Made in United States
Orlando, FL
02 May 2022

17439507R00252